NOT

IN

OUR

BACKYARD

MARC MOWREY and **TIM REDMOND**

NOT

IN

OUR

BACKYARD

THE PEOPLE AND EVENTS THAT

SHAPED AMERICA'S MODERN

ENVIRONMENTAL MOVEMENT

WILLIAM MORROW AND COMPANY, INC.
NEW YORK

It is the policy of William Morrow and Company, Inc., and its imprints and affiliates, recognizing the importance of preserving what has been written, to print the books we publish on acid-free paper, and we exert our best efforts to that end.

Library of Congress Cataloging-in-Publication Data

Mowrey, Marc.
    Not in our backyard : the people and events that shaped America's modern environmental movement / Marc Mowrey and Tim Redmond.
        p.   cm.
    Includes index.
    ISBN 0-688-10644-7
    1. Environmental policy—United States.   2. Earth Day—United States.   I. Redmond, Tim.
GE180.M68   1993
363.7'0525'0973—dc20   93-24393
                                                                                                                  CIP

Printed in the United States of America

First Edition

1   2   3   4   5   6   7   8   9   10

BOOK DESIGN BY PATRICE FODERO

To Jean and Katharine, who kept the faith,

and

To Tennessee and Katie:

"Come, my friends,
'Tis not too late to seek a newer world..."

CONTENTS

ACKNOWLEDGMENTS

We never could have done this alone. Hundreds of people gave freely of their time (and in a few cases, their money) to help us with our research and writing. It would be impossible to list them all here. A few standouts:

David Israels and Randy Shilts told us how to find our agent. Bonnie Nadell believed enough in an unsolicited three-page proposal to sign on for the duration of the project; she sold our ideas, edited our copy, bought us lunch when we ran out of money, and ran interference for us when we missed our deadlines. Jim Landis, who was editor-in-chief at William Morrow in 1990, offered two first-time authors a major book contract; Bob Shuman, who became our book editor, helped rescue the manuscript (and the authors) two years later from the depths of delay and despair, always with a positive attitude and a great sense of humor.

John and Maria Weiser were always there when we needed them. Axil Comras was a source of endless ideas and inspiration. Raleigh Levine showed us how to stop worrying and love the library. Kilian Kerwin hooked us up with the RoboCar. Polly and Bill McKeon, John Barrat, Paul O'Connell, Carol Moldaw and Marty Edmunds, Lola Chester and Nick Riley, Karan Pond, Phil Helfer, Mike Tritico, and the kind folks at Rocky Mountain Institute (especially Stephanie Sack) gave us lodging and entertainment on the road.

Tom Turner, Art Kleiner, Denzel Ferguson, and especially Willie Fontenot took the time to answer more questions than we had the right to ask. Don Ray guided us down half a dozen twisted paper trails. Rich Schlackman helped us make a few key political connections. Joe Conason let us copy his Westway files.

Michael and Sharon Redmond, Eileen Ecklund, Laura Fraser, Jay Napolitan,

John Barrat, Frank Bolton, and John Weber read versions of our manuscript and told us—honestly—what we were doing wrong. Nic Sammond spent a very long weekend copyediting our first final draft. Mark Kempson transcribed the last bunch of interviews, when we were too tired to type.

Bruce Brugmann gave us considerable moral support (and considerable use of the Bay Guardian files, phones, and copy machine). Peter Franck gave us sound legal advice, and waited patiently while we didn't pay his bills. David Etayo tracked down countless arcane but crucial bits of information, and compiled it all neatly in plastic binders.

Dozens of activists, government staffers, librarians, public officials, and community organizers in big cities and small towns all over the country spent hours answering our questions and sharing their stories; more than anyone else, they made this book possible.

Special appreciation to Jim Balderston, Lavinia Currier, Jean Tepperman, Alice Weiser, the Very Reverend James Park Morton, Father Thomas Berry, Vawter "Buck" Parker, John Seed . . . and to Jack Loeffler, for being the first.

And to Andrea, Jane, Ellen, Ralph, Lee, Susan, Buck, jasin, Craig, Johnnie and Karen, Mary and Bruce, Jane and John, Steve and Honest, Alexandra, Leigh, Mr. Dave, Dr. Dan . . . and all our other wonderful friends who never let us down, what can we say? Thanks, folks, again and always.

—MARC MOWREY AND TIM REDMOND
San Francisco, August 1993

PART 1

EARTH DAY:
TAKING IT TO THE STREETS

I suspect that politicians and businessmen who are jumping on the environmental bandwagon don't have the slightest idea what they are getting into.

—*Denis Hayes, Washington, D.C., April 22, 1970*

By most historical accounts, the environmental movement in the United States came to life rather suddenly, on a bright, sunny April morning in 1970, when more than twenty million people took to the streets to celebrate something called Earth Day.

Earth Day was a stunning event, the largest demonstration in the nation's history. Its size and scope dwarfed the biggest Vietnam War protests; it was far bigger than Martin Luther King, Jr.'s famous "March on Washington." It caught the political establishment largely by surprise: with the nation in such turmoil, and so much energy going into the civil rights and antiwar movements, environmental issues seemed to be relatively low on the activist agenda. It was hard to believe an environmental rally would strike such a resounding chord.

But in retrospect, Earth Day wasn't such a big surprise. The potential energy had been building up for years. All it needed was an outlet—and a spark to set it on fire.

The concept of environmental preservation was nothing new to the United States. For almost a century, people like John Muir, John J. Audubon, and Henry David Thoreau had fought to save the vanishing American wilderness. Their efforts helped establish the national park system, protecting places like California's Yosemite Valley from the ravages of development. By the 1950s, groups like the Wilderness Society and Muir's Sierra Club were mounting successful campaigns to save natural treasures like the Grand Canyon, which federal officials wanted to flood for a water and power project. Their crusades helped ensure the passage of the Wilderness Act, which set aside nine million acres of federal land as protected wilderness preserve.

In 1962, a soft-spoken biologist named Rachel Carson sounded a new alarm. The book she called *Silent Spring* warned the nation about the deadly effects of chemical pollution. Pesticides sprayed on a field or dumped in a stream could turn up in fish and livestock hundreds of miles away; poisons that killed microscopic bugs could work their way up an entire food chain. The toxic refuse of human industry, Carson explained, was becoming a serious threat to human life.

Carson brought the message home, right into everyone's backyard. Slowly, people who had never questioned the value of the "Chemical Revolution" began to realize that the poisons they sprayed into the air and dumped into the water never really went away. And they began to ask whether some of those miracle products might be doing more harm than good.

Silent Spring created enough of a public stir that politicians began to pay attention. Laws banning DDT were introduced and enacted in statehouses and, eventually, in Congress. But it took a dramatic leap in environmental awareness and political interest to bring the nation to the point where an event like Earth Day was possible.

In fact, when veteran environmental activists look back at that period and consider how the uprising started, they often end up at Santa Barbara, California, the last Tuesday in January 1969. The day the tide turned black.

1

BLACK TIDE

January 28, 1969
Santa Barbara, California

It was about half past three on a clear, sunny Tuesday afternoon when Bud Bottoms learned that the peaceful paradise that had been his world was gone forever.

The forty-two-year-old graphic artist was sitting in his office at General Electric's Center for Advanced Studies, finishing up a mechanical drawing and thinking about fishing. Like a lot of Santa Barbara's 75,000 residents, Bottoms loved the outdoors—he spent most of his free hours on the ocean, teaching his sons how to fish for lobster and dive for abalone, and often took long hikes into the hills just outside of town.

Nature was Santa Barbara's biggest asset: the economy thrived on the money that flowed from the four million tourists who came each year from all over the country to soak up the warm sun on the endless acres of clean, white beaches, and swim in the cool waters of the Pacific. Over the past year, however, a stark new presence had invaded the Pacific scenery. Just off the Santa Barbara coast, several tall metal towers were rising out of the water. From platforms atop the structures, giant drills were probing for oil deposits beneath the ocean floor.

Like a lot of his neighbors, Bottoms had always been unhappy about the idea of oil drilling in the Santa Barbara Channel. The channel, a stretch of ocean between the mainland and several large islands twenty-five miles offshore, teemed with one of the richest collections of marine life anywhere in the world—swordfish, scallops, tuna, sea bass, migrating salmon and whales, and hundreds of other types of fish, along with thousands of sea birds and untold species of underwater plants. Bottoms feared that oil rigs would ruin the fishing; he worried that the drilling crews would disturb the small-town peace. Sometimes, in his worst nightmares, he imagined what would happen if one of the pipes suddenly sprang a leak. But like most people in the pleasant, prosperous town, he tried not to dwell on that sort of thing.

Dick Smith, a photographer for the *Santa Barbara News-Press,* was among the first to hear the bad news. He walked across the street to pass the word to his old friend Bud Bottoms. Something had gone terribly wrong with one of the offshore wells, some kind of a blowout. Oil—lots of oil—was spilling into the water. The Coast Guard said it was heading for shore.

The sticky black mess that was spreading across the Santa Barbara Channel was the product of millions of years of natural geologic activity, a century of industrial development, and a few short moments of normal human error. In retrospect, the accident was bound to happen.

Oil is just the remains of ancient plants and animals, buried deep beneath the Earth's surface. It takes a vast amount of pressure—the weight of millions of tons of water, rock, and sand, over tens of thousands of years—to transform those remains into petroleum, and when a drill bit punctures the subterranean reservoir, that pressure gets released. Sometimes, the oil bursts to the surface like a heavy black geyser. In Texas, oilmen used to call it a "gusher"; drilling crews would be forced to contain their excitement at hitting a rich strike while they struggled to cap the well and bring the flow under control.

In the empty West Texas plains, the damage from a gusher was fairly easy to contain—the oil would collect in ponds around the well, and most of it could eventually be recovered. In the open ocean, the story was very different. Strong currents could quickly spread loose oil over a wide area; wind and waves could make containment tricky. So the legal requirements for ocean drilling were much tougher: offshore oil rigs had to drill with a "casing," a thick steel pipe that surrounded the drill bit, forming a firm retaining wall around the edge of the well and serving as a conduit to bring the oil safely to the surface.

The geology of the Santa Barbara Channel made the process especially tricky. In most other places where offshore drilling was carried out, a thick layer of solid granite—known as "cap rock"—lay between the sea bottom and the oil deposits. When a drill cut a hole through the cap, oil would have only one way out, and the casing could contain it. But below the channel, the ocean floor consisted almost entirely of loose sand and silt, with no cap rock at all. To make matters worse, the subterranean region was laced with earthquake faults, providing hundreds of cracks and fissures that could let oil escape.

But oil company geologists insisted that the hazards were overstated and that the modern oil rigs could drill safely. Besides, they said, if a spill did occur, they could easily contain it. In February 1968, the Interior Department sold offshore drilling rights on seventy-one tracts in the Santa Barbara Channel for $603 million. To make the sales more palatable to environmentalists,

Congress earmarked a portion of the money for the Land and Water Conservation Fund, a pool of money the Interior Department used to buy up endangered wilderness and recreation areas.

By January 1969, Union Oil had authorization to drill five wells from Platform A, twenty-three miles due west of the Santa Barbara coast. The company had asked the U.S. Geological Survey, which oversaw drilling operations, for a waiver of the strict regulations on the size of the well casings that were to be sunk into the ocean floor to guard against oil seepage. The law said primary casings had to extend 500 feet below the surface, with smaller, secondary casings extending down to 861 feet. Union asked permission to end its primary casings at 15 feet, its secondary at 238. Geological Survey officials, who rarely challenged the oil companies, readily agreed.

The operation started off smoothly. The first three wells were drilled, tapped, and sealed without incident, and on January 28, the crew began work on number four. The drill struck a major oil deposit at 3,479 feet.

But this time, something went wrong. When the crew tried to draw the drill bit back to the surface, it hit a snag and stuck. When it finally broke free, oil and natural gas exploded up the well. The noise from the explosion was deafening; the gas pouring out of the well made it almost impossible to breathe, and the combination of gas and sea water enveloped the platform in a mist so thick that the workers could barely see. Still, over the next thirteen minutes, the crew managed to force the drill bit back into the well and close the blowout prevention valves. For the moment, everything seemed to be under control.

But pressure kept building up inside—and with the top sealed off, oil soon began to escape from the sides of the hole, below the shortened protective casings. The sticky black liquid oozed out, riding the fault lines upward, and within a few hours, the sea around Platform A had become a huge bubbling cauldron of California crude.

Early news reports were sketchy. Union Oil officials insisted that the spill was relatively minor, and largely under control. It would be almost twenty-four hours before company officials formally confirmed that a disaster of major proportions was under way. But by the time Bottoms returned home Tuesday night, he was sure something was very wrong. He stayed awake until dawn, listening to the waves breaking on the shore and scribbling notes on a pad of paper, not quite knowing what else to do.

When he got to work the next morning, Bottoms showed his notes to Marvin Stuart, a friend and colleague who did promotional work for GE's think tank. With the mind of a public relations expert, Stuart picked out a single phrase that kept appearing again and again in Bottoms's hand-written screed: Get Oil Out!

*   *   *

Five days later, with the Union well still out of control and Santa Barbara officials screaming for action, the Interior Department asked for a halt to all drilling in the area. On February 7, drilling temporarily stopped. By then, close to three million gallons of oil had poured into the channel.

Union Oil took responsibility for containing the spill and cleaning up any damage. But containment technology was primitive, and steady offshore winds and high tides rendered the floating plastic booms and chemical dispersants largely ineffective. Within days, the oil was washing onto the beaches in dark, gooey waves. The cleanup technology was primitive, too: the company simply dispatched crews of workers to spread straw and cat litter onto the sand to absorb the oil, then rake it up and cart it away. The dirty absorbent was dumped into a nearby canyon, and the next major rainstorm washed most of it back into the sea.

Two months after the blowout at Platform A, oil was everywhere on the Santa Barbara coast. It sat on the surface of the water, a dirty sheen that clung to skin and hair and left eyes red and sore for days. It floated below the tide in clumps that stuck to feet and turned toenails black. It covered the surf in a thick black blanket, so heavy that when Bottoms lay awake at night, he couldn't hear the waves anymore.

The beaches were almost deserted, save for curious visitors and a few groups of hard-core surfers, who showed up each day armed with gallons of turpentine. A turpentine bath wasn't pleasant—it stung like hell, and it smelled terrible—but it was the only way to wash off the oil. Santa Barbara was a town transformed: angry residents were packing into city council meetings and demanding action. The county supervisors were preparing to file suit against the federal government. Oil was making Santa Barbara a household word across the country. The spill had turned the comfortable, low-key town into a dirty, sticky symbol of America's hottest new villain: pollution.

By March 22, Bottoms and his neighbors had turned the spill into such a pressing public issue that President Nixon had decided to take a personal tour of the site. Bottoms had been frustrated by the way the government had responded to the spill, but as he walked toward the presidential helicopter, he was feeling optimistic. After all, Nixon had flown to Santa Barbara to see firsthand what had happened to the coastline of his home state. Bottoms was sure that once the president saw the stained beach and blackened water, the hundreds of dead birds and fish washing ashore, and the oily residue that the high tides left on the windows and walls of the expensive beachfront houses, he'd have to close down the wells.

Bottoms watched the big Marine helicopter cruise in low over the water and touch down gently onto the parking lot. Nixon emerged, smiling and waving, looking relaxed in a dark blue suit. He shook hands with the mayor of Santa Barbara, and, with about 150 reporters in tow, made his way toward the shore, where crews of workers in yellow rain gear and blue coveralls were busy raking piles of gooey straw and oily cat litter off one of the world's most spectacular beaches.

Bottoms started toward the helicopter, moving through the crowd of some five thousand people, clutching the box of petitions he was going to give to the president. The box was heavy; in the past few weeks, as news of the tragedy had made its way around the world, the signatures had been pouring in so fast Bottoms could barely keep count. At this point, he figured, there had to be at least fifty thousand.

As he approached the police barricades at the front of the crowd, Bottoms could hear Mayor Gerald S. Firestone telling the president that "the people of this community want the drilling stopped and the platforms removed." And he could see Mr. Nixon smiling and could hear him responding, "Mr. Mayor, I think you've made your point."

Bottoms watched from the edge of the security corridor as the president approached a group of three cleanup workers. He stopped for a brief chat, smiling and shaking hands while the television cameras rolled. As they talked, an oily wave rolled onto the beach and soaked the president's shoes.

And then, before Bottoms could get close enough to hand over his petitions, Nixon was gone, retreating to his helicopter and taking off into the bright afternoon sunshine of a perfect spring day on the southern California coast.

The crowd wandered off, but Bottoms stayed behind, watching the endless waves of oil wash ashore. He noticed the three workers who had talked with the president still hanging around, and wondered what the conversation had been like. It struck him as funny that none of the three was raking anymore. In fact, he noticed, they had begun to walk away from the shore, toward the parking lot.

As Bottoms watched, the three workers dropped their rakes and began removing their blue coveralls. Underneath, they wore dark suits and ties. They tossed the coveralls and rakes into the trunk of a black limousine, climbed in, and drove away.

2

THE NIGHT
OF THE FOX

March 1969
Montgomery, Illinois

In Montgomery, Illinois, fifty miles west of Chicago on the edge of the Great Plains, it was easy to miss the first day of spring. In late March, temperatures still dipped into the teens. The wind whipped off Lake Michigan, cutting through gloves, hats, and coats with bone-chilling force. The calendar said spring, but ice still covered the Fox River, the town's main waterway.

In Montgomery, there was only one sure sign that spring was on its way: around the middle of March, the warblers started to return.

Montgomery sat beneath a bird migration path known as the Mississippi Flyway. Millions of songbirds, cranes, ducks, geese, and other birds passed through the region twice a year as they traveled north and south along the vast watershed that fed the Mississippi River. All along the way, streams, rivers, and marshes provided food and shelter. It was the greatest flyway in the world.

By 1969, however, even the sharpest-eyed birds were having trouble finding clear, fresh water. The stretch of land between Montgomery and Chicago was rapidly becoming a single urban sprawl. The prairies and forests had given way to farms, highways, and developments. Marshes had been filled and streams rerouted. The rivers that still flowed into the Mississippi carried the waste products of industry.

The birds kept coming back to Montgomery, up and down the flyway, year after year, like clockwork: the black-and-white warblers in the last part of March, the yellow warblers a week or two later, and the black-throated warblers by early May. But the old-timers claimed that they saw fewer warblers every spring, and by 1969, biologists who studied the migration patterns had confirmed that observation. Over the past forty years, the data showed, the Mississippi Flyway had lost, at least in Illinois, 95 percent of its song-birds.

Montgomery, a town of 2,500, had only one high school, and the high school had only one science teacher. Earl Ray taught his students the basics of biology, chemistry, physics, and, recently, an old but neglected area of science called ecology.

Even in a town the size of Montgomery, the environment was becoming a popular issue. Only last month, Lake Erie had been closed to fishing for a week to assess lead levels in the striped bass. A week before that, the state issued a warning to people who ate fish from Lake Saint Clair and Lake Michigan—dangerous levels of mercury and other toxic chemicals were turning up in the pike and perch. The newspapers and television issued dire warnings, and Ray's students wanted to know what was happening. As the questions got tougher, Ray began to feel dissatisfied with his answers. Science, Ray had been taught, was about describing things, not changing them; for his students, that wasn't enough.

One spring day, in the midst of a lengthy class discussion about the impacts of the smog belched from the giant V-8 engines that rolled incessantly out of the factories in Detroit, Ray offered his students a chance to turn their lessons into action. Using water-soluble paint, he let them decorate his truck with messages about the environmental effects of driving. The kids went to work: in brightly colored tempera, they wrote "GM POLLUTES THE AIR" and "THIS CAR RUINS THE ATMOSPHERE." Before the first spring rain had washed the paint away, Ray got some strong reactions from passersby. From some came a victory sign, or a thumbs-up salute. Once, a car full of well-dressed men in a Cadillac flashed him the middle finger.

Ray's paint job had touched a nerve. He'd taken action, direct, visible action, and it was making the people in his community think, if just for a few minutes, about something they generally ignored. He liked the feeling.

There were still bits of paint on his truck when Ray received a phone call from an old friend named Dick Norman, a botanist who worked for the county. Norman had called to ask Ray for advice. There weren't many professional biologists or chemists in Montgomery, so when county officials needed a scientific opinion, they often turned to the best authority they knew—the high school science teacher.

Norman told Ray that he was concerned about the Fox River, which wandered through the county forest preserve. Ever since the arrival of the Armour-Dial soap factory, with its sewage line draining into a Fox tributary, the water in the river hadn't looked or smelled right. And the mortality rate among the animals living in the preserve, all of whom depended on the Fox for their water, was definitely on the rise. Norman asked Ray if he would mind going down to the river to take a look.

Ray hiked into the preserve that afternoon, passing under the bare branches of native red oak and silver maple trees. His gaze suddenly locked with that of a startled fox just six feet away. Frightened by the intruder, the fox dropped its supper and scurried away.

Ray hadn't seen the river in at least a year, but he remembered it well. As a boy, he'd spent endless summer days along its banks, fishing and swimming in the clear water. Even a quick glance told him something was very wrong. As he leaned over the bank, he was shocked that he couldn't see his reflection in the water below. The surface of the river was covered with a thick, brown scum. Methane gas bubbled up from the bottom. There were no spring frogs, and no sign of the once-numerous bass fingerlings. Stepping quickly over the cold mud, Ray headed upstream, tracing the brown crud to its source. He didn't have to look far.

The Armour-Dial sewer line was at least four feet wide. Foamy wastewater poured out of the pipe—as much as 700,000 gallons a day, he would later learn. The whole area reeked of chemicals. A quick inspection confirmed Ray's worst suspicions: above the sewer line, the stream thrived. Below it, nothing much seemed to live. Ecologically, Ray realized, the river of his childhood was dead.

Ray returned home, called Armour-Dial, described the pollution problem and asked what the company was planning to do about it. The response wasn't encouraging. An Armour-Dial official told him not to worry, that the foul discharge was just the result of a small, in-house problem. "We'll put our engineers on it right away," the official said, "and see what they come up with."

Several days later, Ray returned to the creek. On the shore, a mallard hen circled nervously among her dying chicks. Soap from the plant, Ray figured, had broken down the protective oils in their feathers. They were dying of exposure in the cold, polluted water. As he stood among the lifeless birds, Ray made a decision that would forever change his life. The Fox River, he vowed, would flow clean again. Armour-Dial's poisonous discharge would be shut off, if only for a day.

Several weeks later, in a deserted field not far from Armour's discharge location, Ray hopped from his pickup and unloaded its cargo. He'd spent weeks picking up garbage bags, old cans, rusted car parts, and anything else he encountered on the way to work; by now, he had five or six tons. Load by load, Ray hauled the trash across the moonlit field, dumping it all into the catch basin that fed the Armour-Dial sewage line. He rushed back to the creek, and saw in an instant that his experiment had worked. The sewage line was blocked. He had stopped the discharge. The Fox was running free.

Ray returned to the catch basin and wrote out a simple note. "Put your engineers on this problem," it said, "and see what they come up with." As he started to put away his pen, he remembered the frightened fox he'd seen on the riverbank a few weeks before. He took the cap back off the pen, and at the bottom of the note, he sketched a simple fox head. It wasn't great art, but the image was clear enough. It would become the trademark signature of a mysterious ecological saboteur who came to be known as the Fox.

3

CIVIL WAR

May 3, 1969
San Francisco

David Ross Brower was never a good loser. He had the sort of passion that made for great crusaders and lousy politicians—he took all his battles personally. He annoyed his friends, frustrated his allies and drove his associates crazy. But nobody ever questioned his basic motivation: David Brower was a true believer.

At fifty-seven, the white-haired, ruddy-faced Brower was developing a cult following in the world of conservationists and nature lovers. His supporters called him a modern John Muir, an inspirational and fearless leader who never gave up the good fight. His résumé read like a checklist of the most important conservation struggles of the mid–twentieth century. His achievements were the stuff of legend: Brower the war hero, who entered the service as a buck private in 1942 and left three years later as a decorated captain. Brower the mountain-climber, who racked up an astonishing seventy first ascents, in summer and winter, from Yosemite to the Himalayas. Brower the philosopher, whose speeches could bring an audience from laughter to tears and back again in a few short minutes. Brower the activist, who had joined the Sierra Club in the 1930s, become executive director in 1952, and turned the little-known organization of seven thousand people into a political power-house with more than seventy thousand members and a string of impressive victories.

It was hard to imagine Brower ever throwing in the towel. It was even harder to imagine him walking away from the top job at the Sierra Club. But on this Saturday, at the regular meeting of the Sierra Club board of directors, David Brower was about to do something very unlike David Brower: calmly admit defeat, abandon a major organizational crusade, and politely resign from the job that had been the center of his life for more than a decade.

From the outside, it looked like a typical organizational power struggle, but deep down, Brower knew, it had been a battle for the soul of the nation's best-known environmental group. The outcome would change environmental politics forever.

Brower was born and raised in Berkeley, California. His mother was blind, and he often described her sensitivity to the natural world as his first source of inspiration. In 1933, Brower met the photographer Ansel Adams on a hike in Yosemite; the two became close friends, and Adams sponsored him for membership in the Sierra Club.

Founded at the turn of the century by the great conservationist hero John Muir, the Sierra Club was part social club, part wilderness-exploration society, and part conservationist-action group. It had chapters all over the country, but its biggest area of influence was California. The leaders of the Sierra Club were a fairly respectable, even conservative, bunch—they made a point of acknowledging the need for growth and economic development, but urged government and industry to set aside space for nature.

In 1952, Brower became the Sierra Club's executive director, and quickly took the conservationist movement by storm. Unlike the club's past leaders, his tactics were risky, unorthodox, expensive—and brilliant. He poured Sierra Club resources into publishing a series of conservationist books. He became famous for his rabble-rousing full-page newspaper ads. And the more victories he won, the more he made some of his old colleagues nervous.

In the late 1950s, Brower made what he considered his one major personal and political mistake. The Bureau of Reclamation had proposed building a pair of huge dams to control flooding on the Colorado River, harness its energy for electric power, and provide reliable water supplies to the growing Southwest. One of the dams was slated for a remote site in northern Arizona known as Glen Canyon. The other, at Colorado's Echo Park, would have flooded part of Dinosaur National Monument.

The Sierra Club fought the Echo Park dam bitterly; Dinosaur Monument was part of the national park system, and conservationists recoiled at the notion of building a dam in a national park. Brower organized letter-writing campaigns, pressured congressmen and senators, and testified eloquently against the dam. Along with the Wilderness Society and other conservation groups, the Sierra Club offered an alternative proposal: expand and enlarge the Glen Canyon Dam, and leave Dinosaur Monument alone.

The crusade was a tremendous success. In 1956, congressional leaders agreed to scrap the Echo Park dam; in exchange, the conservationists, led by Brower and Wilderness Society director Howard Zahniser, agreed to support a bill authorizing the construction of a dam at Glen Canyon.

Brower had never seen Glen Canyon when he agreed to trade it away, and when he finally visited the site, in 1957, with dam construction well under way, he was stunned by its beauty. Years later, he remained convinced that the entire project could have been stopped, that the compromise deal was a terrible mistake. He never forgave himself; from that point on, he vowed he'd never accept "reasonable" concessions in the defense of the Earth. He'd never deal away the wilderness again.

His vow began to clash with Sierra Club policy in 1963, when Pacific Gas and Electric Company announced plans to build a nuclear power plant on the Nipomo Dunes, an isolated stretch of sand and grass halfway between Los Angeles and San Francisco. Local conservationists sounded the alarm: the dunes were a rare piece of undisturbed natural coastline, a small refuge for wildlife and wilderness lovers that somehow survived just a few miles away from civilization.

At the urging of the Santa Lucia Sierra Club chapter, Will Siri, a respected mountaineer who had just become the club's president, began to meet with PG&E to discuss alternatives to the Nipomo Dunes project. PG&E already had a team of public relations people working on the nuclear power plant proposal, and they were happy to work with the Sierra Club. In fact, the company was more than willing to consider alternative sites, as long as they were near the ocean (and thus a limitless water supply) and could be made accessible to heavy construction equipment. In 1965, the company quietly purchased a plot of coastal land a few miles north of the dunes, at a place called Diablo Canyon, and began preparing the site for construction.

Early in 1966, the utility announced its decision to relocate the nuclear plant to Diablo Canyon. Although PG&E never actually gave up the right to develop the dunes, the Sierra Club board of directors hailed the decision as a victory. The dunes had been saved; the new site had no particular environmental value. On May 7, the board voted to endorse the Diablo Canyon project and to thank PG&E for its good-faith efforts to preserve a scenic area.

David Brower was furious. From the start, he had refused to work with PG&E; he insisted that the club should oppose any power plants along the coast and reject any compromise over the specifics of the site. He launched a full-scale campaign to reverse the club's policy on Diablo Canyon, but made little progress. After a series of meetings and several lengthy debates, the board rejected its executive director's arguments and stuck to its position: opposing Diablo Canyon meant threatening the Nipomo Dunes, and reversing the endorsement would undermine the organization's credibility. Unable to make headway with the board, Brower insisted that the issue be put before the entire club membership, in a referendum. In February, the members voted overwhelmingly to back the board.

But Brower wasn't ready to give up. In May, the membership elected a new board, and some of Brower's opponents were replaced with potential allies. As the September board meeting approached, he began lining up support for a resolution rescinding the earlier stance, overruling the referendum, and announcing the club's total opposition to the construction of any nuclear power plant on the California coast. The lobbying on both sides was intense—at one point, PG&E officials flew some sympathetic Sierra Club directors over the Nipomo Dunes in a private plane owned by Frank Sinatra and piloted by Danny Kaye.

The board meeting was long and heated. Ultimately, the resolution narrowly lost, but a watered-down version was finally adopted. Brower seized it as an indication that the club had changed its position; opponents of the change insisted that the new resolution did not supersede the membership vote, and that the club's official position was still in support of Diablo Canyon.

In the spring of 1969, Brower took a leave of absence from his job as executive director, announced his candidacy for the board, and organized a slate to run beside him. The directors who had backed Diablo Canyon organized a competing slate, and for months, the two campaigned for the votes of the seventy thousand members. Brower and his supporters complained that the board had sold out to PG&E; the incumbent slate denounced Brower's recklessness and refusal to compromise, and charged that his wild tactics would break the organization financially. A victory for his slate, they insisted, would lead to years of bickering and divisiveness that could tear the organization apart.

The turnout was unprecedented—almost fifty thousand people cast ballots. When the votes were counted, Brower and his slate had been defeated by a margin of 3–2. The new board was openly hostile to his tenure, and long before the May 3 meeting, a majority of the directors had made clear they intended to fire him. Brower hung on until the last possible moment, but by the time he rose to address the board, he knew the battle was over.

His resignation speech was eloquent, graceful, and not at all bitter. He bid "good luck to the survivors of an unhappy war, and change of heart, too," and vowed to remain a Sierra Club member for life.

Outside the hotel, the morning edition of the *San Francisco Chronicle* was sitting in a newsrack, the big front-page headline visible to anyone who gave it a casual glance. A famous, ancient redwood tree, so big that cars could drive through a tunnel in its trunk, had fallen in a storm the night before. "A FALLEN GIANT," the headline screamed; below it, a photo taken several years earlier showed the tree in its prime, the trunk and tunnel dwarfing the lone figure standing at the base of the behemoth. The caption on the photo was tiny, but a close inspection showed the picture was taken by Ansel Adams, the legendary nature photographer who sat on the Sierra Club board. He had just voted with the majority—and, as it turned out, against the person in his classic photo. The man standing under the redwood tree on the front page of the *Chronicle* was David Ross Brower.

But Brower didn't even notice the picture or the newspaper headline. By the time he walked out the door, he was already at work on his next project:

he was forming a new organization, one that, he was determined, would never get bogged down in caution and compromise, that wouldn't try to reason with PG&E and the Bureau of Reclamation. He'd call it Friends of the Earth.

The soul of the environmental movement was up for grabs. And David Brower wasn't about to let it get away.

4

THE SENATOR
AND THE TEACH-IN

August 1969
Santa Barbara, California

Senator Gaylord Nelson looked around for something to read. The flight from Santa Barbara to Berkeley would take about an hour—enough time to relax before the last lecture of the day. There was no need to worry about preparing his remarks: Nelson could deliver a lecture on America's environmental crisis in his sleep. The August edition of *Ramparts* magazine was lying on the seat next to him; he picked it up and started flipping through the pages.

Ramparts was not part of Nelson's regular reading list—the magazine was decidedly antiestablishment, a loud mouthpiece of the radical left. But an article about the Vietnam War "teach-ins" caught his eye. The teach-ins were a series of day-long educational events, combining rallies, speeches, lectures, and other programs—and they were galvanizing political sentiment on college campuses. In fact, the article suggested, the teach-ins might have played an important role in turning the war into a major national issue.

Fascinating, Nelson thought. The radical magazine was onto something.

Nelson was not the sort of person you normally saw on the college lecture circuit. He was fifty-three years old, soft-spoken, balding, a World War Two veteran from a small town in Wisconsin who had survived Okinawa, returned home to practice law, and wound up in politics. In a state that spawned the likes of both Joe McCarthy and William Proxmire, Nelson cut an odd profile: he had nice things to say about almost everyone. Though his congressional votes were usually cast with the liberals, he somehow got along fine with the most die-hard conservatives. When his colleagues fought for the media spotlight, Nelson was happy to work backstage.

If Nelson was a reluctant politician, though, he was not a foolish one. Through ten years in the state senate and four as governor, he had built a reputation as a sharp campaigner, with a keen eye for a popular trend. He was also a moderate and a pragmatist: although he was strongly against the Vietnam War, he didn't think people should be blowing up buildings to stop it.

Nelson's real passion was the environment. Since the day he'd entered politics, he had been a tireless fighter for wilderness preservation and had attacked littering, industrial pollution, reckless development, overpopulation, and everything else he saw that threatened the natural resources—and natural beauty—of his state, his nation, and his world.

As governor of Wisconsin, he'd developed a program to purchase a million acres of wilderness and recreation areas, financed through a tax on cigarettes. In 1963, a year after Rachel Carson published *Silent Spring,* freshman senator Nelson became the first person in Congress to introduce a bill banning DDT. He championed the 1964 Wilderness Act, developed a program to employ the elderly in conservation projects, and sponsored bills to preserve the Appalachian Trail, the Apostle Islands, and numerous other wild and scenic areas.

It had been a lonely crusade. In fact, during the 1968 presidential campaign, none of the major candidates made a single speech about the environment. It wasn't even a minor issue. So Nelson had taken it upon himself to educate the nation. By August 1969, he had visited thirty-six states, preaching his environmental gospel at college campuses, town halls, and civic clubs.

His Santa Barbara talk had been especially successful. Nelson shuddered to think about it, but the oil spill had done wonders for the conservation cause. The disaster had awakened a community, and with pictures of dead birds and oily beaches making the evening news all over the country, the anger of the Santa Barbara citizens was spreading. Still, there was something missing. The conservationists might be growing in number, but the Washington establishment wasn't showing much interest—environmental issues didn't attract anywhere near as much attention as, say, the Vietnam War.

What the conservationists really needed, Nelson decided, was one of those teach-ins that *Ramparts* had talked about—a program that would get thousands of college students on dozens of campuses to devote a full day to speeches, seminars, and projects on natural resources and the environment. It might even reach a few high schools. Citizen groups and local governments could be asked to participate.

A national "Earth day": even in Washington, Nelson thought, that might turn a few heads.

5

THE SIEGE
OF BLACK MESA

April 1, 1970
Black Mesa, Arizona

Jack Loeffler and Bill Brown loaded a couple of cases of beer into Loeffler's aging Ford pickup and drove west out of Santa Fe, New Mexico. They were headed for a lonely stretch of high desert in northeastern Arizona known as Black Mesa. A few years ago, the trip would have been Loeffler's idea of a great time—Black Mesa was one of his favorite places, and Brown was one of his best friends. But this time, neither man was thinking about fun. As they drove and drank and talked, a sense of urgency filled the rattling old cab.

The way Brown explained it to Loeffler, their destination—an ancient rock formation that was home to thousands of Native Americans—was about to be carved up by a massive coal-mining operation. Giant bulldozers, heavy trucks, wide highways, and hundreds of coal company workers would be interrupting a thousand years of desert solitude. Hundreds of residents would be displaced. The air, water, and land would be polluted. And the mesa, considered sacred ground by many of the local Hopis and Navajos, would be badly disfigured. As the land went, Loeffler feared, so would go the people—and, most likely, what was left of the traditional Navajo and Hopi cultures. According to Brown, the whole thing was imminent.

According to Loeffler, the whole idea was so wrong it was almost unbelievable. He had to see it for himself.

Loeffler knew Black Mesa as well as any white man alive. He'd driven every dirt road, walked almost every trail, and spent dozens of nights sleeping under the biggest, clearest, starriest sky he'd ever seen. He discovered the high desert land around the mesa in the 1950s, when he was wandering the Southwest, playing jazz and living the life of a beatnik. He became friends

31

with some of the Navajo and Hopi Indians who lived on the vast reservation around the mesa, and in 1965, Lee Udall, the wife of Interior Secretary Stewart Udall, hired Loeffler to teach Navajo and Hopi children their own history. The job took him to every school on the reservation. Year after year, he came back, and year after year, very little on the Mesa changed. Today promised to be different.

After a full day's drive, Brown and Loeffler saw their destination come into stark relief. Its steep walls rose sharply out of the rocky sands and sun-baked clay and formed a mammoth rock tabletop, a barren, 3,300-square-mile island in the sky, 1,500 feet above the surrounding countryside.

The mesa's raw beauty had a harsh and unforgiving side. Winter days were bitterly cold, and with the frigid nights came a stiff and steady wind. After a short spring, long, blistering summer temperatures routinely broke one hundred degrees. The annual rainfall was barely enough to support the sparse cover of crackly bushes and spindly trees that clung to the surface. For anything more, water had to be brought up from wells deep below the surface.

In spite of the rugged conditions, the southern part of the mesa was home to the longest continuously inhabited village in North America. The town called Oraiba was settled more than a thousand years ago by Hopi Indians. Carefully cultivated crops of beans and corn, along with water from several wells, provided a thin margin of survival.

After five centuries, Navajo Indians also showed up at Black Mesa. The two groups had considerable cultural differences, and sharing the mesa for the next five hundred years wasn't easy. But a fragile peace sprung from a common reverence for the land: to traditionalists from both tribes, the mesa was considered the spiritual center of the universe. It was a great place to pray, they believed, but a very bad place to do battle.

For the first white people who arrived in the Southwest in the 1800s, Black Mesa, like the deserts around it, seemed to offer nothing. No trees, no gold, no large herds of game, and no water. Then in the early part of the twentieth century, U.S. government geologists discovered that the center of the Hopi universe lay atop the only significant coal deposit in the state of Arizona.

At first, the proposed mining project that would carve up Black Mesa received virtually no news media attention. Jack Loeffler didn't know anything about the Peabody Coal Company's plans until Bill Brown passed along a rumor he'd been hearing at the office. Brown worked for the National Park Service, which kept tabs on major projects that might affect park land, and Black Mesa was close enough to be on the list. The agency hadn't made any formal announcement, but the grapevine was always active, and Brown had picked up enough information to make him nervous. Loeffler was furious at the prospect, and had insisted on a personal visit to determine whether the bad news was true.

Loeffler had never believed that mining companies and government agencies would actually bother to go after the mesa's rich veins of coal. As far as he knew, cheap hydroelectric power from the Colorado River would provide all the energy the region could ever want—enough, even, for the Central Arizona Project.

Born in the industrial boom years of the 1940s, the Central Arizona Project was meant to harness the mighty Colorado and make the deserts bloom. Arizona was on the verge of explosive growth. Cities like Tucson and Phoenix were poised to become major regional metropolises, and with the gentle climate and long growing season, project designers imagined that the state's agriculture could come to rival California's. The only thing missing was water.

Arizona had extensive water rights on the Colorado River, but the rights had always seemed useless—the river was far from the cities and farms, and pumping billions of tons of water hundreds of miles across the desert would take huge amounts of power.

Shortly after World War Two, Floyd Dominy, the chief of the Federal Bureau of Reclamation, took on the challenge. He envisioned a string of dams along the Colorado, each one backing up the river into huge artificial lakes. Stored water released back downstream from those reservoirs would spin large turbines and generate substantial hydroelectric power; enough power, if Dominy had his way, to pump a good bit of the precious water east to the deserts. And enough to generate millions of dollars in water and power sales. He called his project the Cash Register Dams.

But in the late 1950s, Dominy and his dam projects ran into a roadblock by the name of David Brower. Ultimately, the bureau was able to build only one dam, at Glen Canyon. The new reservoir held plenty of water for the Central Arizona Project, but not nearly enough to generate the power needed to pump it to Phoenix and Tucson. So leaders of governments and industry in Arizona began looking hard for other sources of cheap electricity, and before long, their sights came to rest on Black Mesa. Although David Brower didn't fully understand it at the time, Black Mesa was part of the deal that saved the Grand Canyon and Dinosaur Monument from Floyd Dominy's Cash Register Dams. While Brower was stirring up the conservation movement to fight against the dams, Interior Secretary Stewart Udall and Senator Carl Hayden of Arizona were working behind the scenes to find alternative power sources for the Central Arizona Project—and Black Mesa was at the top of the list. When Udall and Hayden proposed that the government subsidize a new coal-fired power plant instead of building the infamous dams, the conservation groups responded with applause. It seemed to many activists that the Congress and the Interior Department had finally adopted the principles of a sound environmental policy.

Udall never explained what would happen to Black Mesa when all the coal was gone and all the walls were dry. He never discussed what the coal-burning plant would do to the crystal-clear southwestern air. He never explained why the nation had to plant thirsty crops and build air-conditioned houses with swimming pools in the middle of the Arizona desert.

Nobody ever asked the Indians.

In 1964, the Peabody Coal Company began to negotiate for mining rights on the mesa. The company's plan was simple: heavy equipment could easily tear open the land and extract raw coal. The coal would be pounded into a powder, and the limited supply of water beneath the mesa would be pumped to the surface and mixed with this pulverized coal dust. The liquid mixture, known as a slurry, would then be piped to a new generating plant in Bullhead City, Nevada, 286 miles to the west. A consortium of utility companies, along with the federal government, joined forces with Peabody, and the plan was set in motion. The electricity generated by burning the coal would light up Las Vegas—and help move to southern Arizona some two million acre-feet of Colorado River water a year, enough to supply the residential water needs of roughly fourteen million people.

However, the negotiations over the coal lease were complex. It wasn't clear who actually owned the Black Mesa land—the Hopi and Navajo tribes both had credible claims to parts of it. Nor was it clear who or what group among the Indians had the authority to sign the rights away.

Since 1934, federal law required Indians to elect tribal councils, which would oversee the government of reservations and represent the tribes in negotiations and contracts with private businesses and public agencies. But many of the Navajo and Hopi elders considered themselves part of an independent sovereign nation, bound by old tribal laws, not new American laws. So they refused to accept the councils' authority.

Shortly after the 1934 law took effect, tribes like the Hopi and Navajo began to split into two distinct factions—traditionalists, who rejected any form of assimilation, and progressives, who sought to ease the Native American population into modern American society. The most enlightened progressive council leaders were looking for ways to bring some degree of prosperity to the nation's most economically depressed ethnic group, and they saw the mineral resources on tribal land as a tremendous opportunity. Selling or leasing mineral rights could provide the money for better schools, houses, infrastructure, health care, and other pressing needs; it could create job opportunities that could reduce the Indians' reliance on government welfare programs and build self-reliant communities.

To traditionalists, progress came at a steep price: once the land was sold off, or torn open, it was gone forever. The land, they believed, belonged to nobody—the plants and animals that lived on the earth and the rocks and minerals that lay below it had as much right to exist as did people, and nothing justified the destruction of the natural world. White man's civilization, they insisted, was way out of balance; the constant need for more resources was unhealthy. Why would the Indians want to participate?

But since the traditionalists didn't actively participate in official tribal council business, their arguments never had much of an impact. Peabody's chief lawyer, John Boyden, negotiated directly with the Hopi tribal council, contending (correctly, the courts would later determine) that the council had full authority over the land the company wanted. In 1966, Peabody Coal closed a deal with the Hopi council, securing the rights to strip-mine parts of Black Mesa for the next thirty-five years. The tribes received a small cut of the revenue, and a few modest promises that Indians would be considered for jobs in the mining operation. The company promised to return the land when the lease expired, "in as good condition as received, except for the ordinary wear, tear, and depletion incident to mining operations."

Critics of the deal would later suggest that Peabody had an unfair advantage: while Boyden was representing the coal company, another member of his law firm was representing the Hopi council.

The plight of the Indians on Black Mesa stirred up questions that most of the white man's environmental movement was still afraid to touch. The notion of preserving land and wildlife for its own sake, above and beyond its utilitarian value to humans, would not even begin to come into the mainstream of environmental politics for at least another decade. It would take even longer for the major environmental groups to begin discussing something Jack Loeffler sensed from the moment he learned of the fate of Black Mesa: the connections between racial inequality and environmental destruction, between poverty and pollution.

Eight hours out of Santa Fe, Jack Loeffler and Bill Brown stood together in the early evening light, looking across the mesa. For the first time in twenty years, Loeffler didn't like what he saw. The preliminary operation was well under way. Land had been cleared, trees cut down. Heavy earth-moving equipment was in place. Within months, possibly only weeks, Loeffler guessed, the strip-mining of Black Mesa would be under way.

Loeffler wasn't much of a political organizer. He didn't like playing the game; he had trouble obeying the rules. He couldn't even embrace a consistent political philosophy: the peaceful spirituality of the Hopi elders made tremendous sense to him, but he still liked to carry a .357 magnum pistol, and he dreamed of blowing up construction equipment before it could be used to defile the wilderness. He lived from one day to the next, changing his plans when the spirit moved him and trying at all costs to avoid getting stuck with a full-time job. On some level, he'd always been an environmentalist; wilderness was deep in his soul, and he did what he could to save it. But he did it on his own terms, when he wanted to, how he wanted to. He couldn't imagine working in an office, filing forms, answering phone calls, raising money, and talking to lawyers.

And yet, he knew, the Hopi and Navajo elders couldn't save Black Mesa alone, and neither could he. The coal miners were getting away with their scheme for exactly one reason: the residents of the mesa weren't in any position to fight back. The worst environmental problems, he suspected, would always wind up getting dumped in the backyards of people the government officials and the press and the major political groups ignored. Places like Black Mesa.

There was only one choice, and Loeffler knew it. He had to go back to Santa Fe and do what he hated most in the world. Somebody had to give Peabody Coal and the Central Arizona Project a run for their money. Somebody had to start an organization. And as he looked across the darkening desert, Jack Loeffler didn't see any other volunteers.

6

TWO TONS
OF GADGETS

April 20, 1970
Atlantic City

A thousand delegates were on their feet, clapping and cheering wildly as the president of the United Auto Workers took the stage. The spontaneous demonstration was more than just a show of respect: it was sign that, after twenty-four years in office, the leader of one of America's largest and most powerful labor unions was still a working-class hero. Chunky, red-haired, and still boyish-looking despite his sixty-three years, Walter Reuther cast a shadow far beyond the world of organized labor.

When Reuther joined the UAW in 1935, as a high-school dropout struggling to make ends meet in Depression-era Detroit, his West Side UAW local had exactly 78 members. A year later, the local's membership had reached 2,400, and Reuther had become its president. By 1969, the delegates in the Atlantic City Convention Hall represented more than 1.3 million unionized workers, and the numbers were growing every day.

Reuther was a formidable negotiator, a scrappy street-fighter who could be as smooth and articulate as the best public relations man. Under his leadership, the nation's autoworkers had seen a dramatic expansion in their union's bargaining power—and with it, a rise in their standard of living. The days when a man could be fired for daring to breathe the word "union" were long over; so were the thirteen-hour shifts, the forced overtime, the random layoffs, and the violent sit-down strikes. Thanks in no small part to Walter Reuther, the autoworkers, and the rest of the nation's unionized industrial workers, had job security, benefits, pensions, and wages that put many of them comfortably in the nation's secure, home-owning middle class.

But Reuther wasn't ready to stop there. His social agenda went far beyond the assembly lines and corporate boardrooms of the major automobile manufacturers. Over the past few years, he'd begun to argue that the entire manufacturing sector of the United States economy was in grave danger. The current high standards of living were an illusion, he told his friends; the nation couldn't continue devouring natural resources and degrading the environment without eventually paying a heavy price. The implications for his labor force were serious: the next generation of autoworkers and their children would be the ones who would inherit the mess. They would foot the bill to clean it up—and they would suffer when the cheap raw materials and energy supplies ran out, and the high-paying manufacturing jobs disappeared.

Reuther knew what he had to say to the 1969 convention would not be popular. It was hard to talk to autoworkers about the environment. They worried about jobs; they had kids to support, mortgages to pay. And the way many of them saw it, all the environmentalists seemed to want to do was to stop making so many cars that burned so much gas—and created so many unionized jobs.

But somebody had to say it: making more cars designed to carry just one or two passengers was simply not the answer. In the long term, big, gas-eating American cars would become obsolete—and so would American autoworkers. The sooner they started thinking about that day, Reuther had decided, the less painful it would be. If they started now, the next generation of union workers would still have good jobs in twenty or thirty years. They'd be making buses, and trains, and smaller, more-efficient cars—or a lot of them would be making nothing at all.

In less than forty-eight hours, the nation would be celebrating Earth Day— and if Reuther's old friend Gaylord Nelson was right, for at least a little while there would be unprecedented interest in the environmental issues that had been so badly ignored for so long. America had to take a new approach to its industrial future. And Reuther thought the United Auto Workers ought to be fighting for it. Most union leaders—even the more popular ones—might be thrown out of office for that kind of talk, but Reuther was in a different class. He'd fought off death threats and corruption, taken on big industry, big government, and organized crime, all in the name of the people on the assembly line. When Walter Reuther spoke, the rank and file listened.

"We must recognize," he told the convention, "that in our complex technological world in which we are fighting for the very survival of our environment, we cannot rely on the selfish, socially irresponsible forces of the marketplace. . . .

"It is asinine (I don't know of a better word to describe it) to have hundreds of thousands of people going to the same place at the same time for the same purpose, and all of them dragging two tons of gadgets with them. . . ."

7

EARTH DAY

April 22, 1970
Washington, D.C.

From his seat on the stage at the Sylvan Theater, Denis Hayes could see the last empty seats filling up. A full house, packed with reporters from across the nation: not bad for the crack of dawn. In a few hours, the entire Capitol Mall would be packed with more than 200,000 people, more than Hayes could ever have imagined. But even at this early hour, as he stepped up to the microphone for the sunrise speech that would kick off Earth Day, the director of the first National Environmental Teach-In knew the event was going to be a stunning success.

It was beginning to seem as if every politician in America wanted to get on the bandwagon. Both houses of Congress had decided to adjourn for the day, since so many members were going to be making Earth Day appearances. Mayors, governors, aldermen, city council members, and village trustees, from Florida to Alaska, from southern California to northern Maine, had agreed to march in parades and make speeches. Boy Scout troops, grade school students, college radicals, labor unions, and business groups were planning activities.

In fact, the only major political figure who wasn't going to celebrate Earth Day was the president, Richard Nixon, who had declined to issue any formal proclamation of support. The only organization that had come out against the event was the Daughters of the American Revolution. ("It is planned," Mrs. Samuel M. Neill explained to a DAR convention. "Subversive elements plan to make American children live in an environment that is good for them.")

All day long, across the nation, millions of people were taking to the streets. In most cases, the tone was decidedly civil, the political message

39

remarkably moderate, just the way Senator Gaylord Nelson had wanted it when he first conceived the idea. In forty-two statehouses, legislators passed Earth Day resolutions and governors made statements of support. In Knoxville, Tennessee, students scoured local streams and rivers for garbage to see if each of them could reclaim the five pounds of garbage the average American discards every day. The Albuquerque, New Mexico, city commission lowered bus fares to a penny for the day to encourage people to leave their cars at home.

Here and there, activists took a more militant stance. About two hundred demonstrators carried coffins into Logan International Airport in Boston in a "die-in" to protest the expansion of the airport, an expansion that would bring noise-polluting supersonic transport planes. A twenty-seven-year-old man in Key Biscayne, Florida, showed up at the headquarters for the local power company with a cart of decaying fish topped off with a dead octopus. A dozen self-styled Yippies at Indiana University had poured concrete stolen from a nearby construction site into the sewage pipes that polluted the Jordan River. A crowd of protesters in Clarksburg, West Virginia, collected more than a ton of garbage from local highways and dumped it on the courthouse steps.

In New York City, Major John Lindsay led a march that shut down parts of Fifth Avenue, one of the busiest commercial strips in the world. Lindsay was in a jovial mood: "This is the first time I've walked down Fifth Avenue without getting booed half the distance," he told a reporter. A few blocks away, several thousand more people gathered in front of the Forty-second Street library. Kurt Vonnegut, Jr., addressed the crowd from a lectern beneath a giant paper sunflower, and added a note of cynicism to the proceedings. "Here we are again, the peaceful demonstrators," he said, "mostly young and mostly white. Good luck to us, for I don't know what sporting event the president may be watching at the moment. He should help us make a fit place for human beings to live. Will he do it? No. So the war will go on. Meanwhile, we go up and down Fifth Avenue picking up trash."

Denis Hayes missed Kurt Vonnegut's speech, but when he read the text later, he recognized a lot of his own sentiments. The organizer of the largest demonstration in the history of the United States was feeling a bit cynical, too.

By day's end, there would be twenty million people participating in Earth Day activities, in two thousand communities and on twelve thousand high school and college campuses. By almost any standard, it was a huge political success. But Hayes still wasn't happy. It was all so nice, he thought, so comfortable. So utterly devoid of any real political action.

Denis Hayes had always seemed destined for success. Eagle Scout, class president at Stanford, one of the elite handful of students in the nation admitted to Harvard's joint program in law and public policy, the kid from the tiny lumber-mill town of Camas, Washington, was on the fast track to the top. Along the way, he'd become something of a campus radical, influenced, like many of his classmates, by the leftist writers and thinkers of the 1960s. He spent a good deal of his time fighting the burning crusade of the day, the struggle against the Vietnam War. He had never thought of himself as an environmental activist. Not until the morning of October 27, 1969, when he sat down in the kitchen of his cramped student apartment a few blocks from Harvard and read about a senator named Gaylord Nelson and his plans for a national environmental teach-in.

Hayes had become a bit disillusioned with the antiwar movement: the crusade was torn by factional infighting and seemed to be degenerating rapidly into violence. Besides, he needed some kind of respectable job in the public-policy arena to complete one of his course requirements. He called Senator Nelson, offered to help organize part of Boston, and asked for an interview. Nelson met with Hayes, checked a few references, and gave him a job—as national coordinator.

From the start, the senator had been very clear: Earth Day was not going to be a Vietnam Moratorium. It was not going to endorse any form of violence, property destruction, or civil disobedience. Everything the Earth Day office sanctioned was going to be perfectly legal, perfectly proper. In fact, Nelson had incorporated the Environmental Teach-In as a nonprofit entity; if the organization engaged in any partisan politics, it would lose its tax status. To ensure that Hayes and the staff stayed in line, Nelson sent two of his aides over to the Earth Day office to keep an eye on the day-to-day operations.

All year long, Hayes had done his job, sitting in an office in Washington, D.C., living on stress and caffeine, generating huge volumes of paper about the upcoming national event that would probably never be recycled, calling politicians and Boy Scout leaders, sending out press releases, and generally making it clear to all concerned that nothing about Earth Day was radical or militant. And the response had been staggering: hundreds of groups, in small towns, big cities, college campuses, and neighborhood school districts wanted to plug in.

The staff members Hayes had recruited to work for him, many of them friends from Harvard and Stanford, were even less happy. Back in January, the staff had rebelled against the decision to call Earth Day an "environmental teach-in," since it implied that nothing dramatic or important would actually *happen.* Hayes couldn't ignore Gaylord Nelson's mandate—but he could sidestep it. So Hayes and a few of the other Earth Day staffers began to put together a new organization, the Environmental Action Foundation. It would technically be separate and distinct from Earth Day, and would continue for years after the teach-in was over. In the meantime, however, it would give the Earth Day organizers a vehicle for promoting more controversial positions.

In practice, the Environmental Action Foundation operated out of the Earth Day office, and in the minds of a lot of people (including most of the reporters who covered Earth Day) the two were interchangeable. Tomorrow, the Environmental Teach-In would begin the process of going quietly out of business, and the Environmental Action Foundation would be able to act freely, openly, on its own.

It was too late now to get fired, too late for Nelson to stop him. As Earth Day dawned, Hayes decided, it was time to demonstrate that the environmental movement was not just part of a nice antilitter campaign.

"I suspect," he began in a speech to a rally on the Capitol Mall, "that politicians and businessmen who are jumping on the environmental bandwagon don't have the slightest idea what they are getting into. They are talking about filters on smokestacks while we are challenging corporate irresponsibility. They are bursting with pride about plans for totally inadequate municipal sewage treatment plants; we are challenging the ethics of a society that, with only six percent of the world's population, accounts for more than half of the world's annual consumption of raw materials."

He mentioned Vietnam (as an ecological catastrophe), the garbage crisis (a "reverse King Midas touch"), and the lack of individual accountability for America's environmental problems. And as he approached his conclusion, he launched into the point he had been itching to make for months:

"You simply can't live an ecologically sound life in America. That is not one of the options open to you. . . . We are building a movement, a movement with a broad base, a movement which transcends traditional political boundaries. It is a movement that values people more than technology, people more than political boundaries and political ideologies, people more than profit.

"It will be a difficult fight. Earth Day is the beginning."

From sunrise to sundown and into the evening, Denis Hayes traveled the country, appearing at rallies in half a dozen cities and towns and making speeches to audiences that were always big, and always enthusiastic. But as he arrived at Chicago's O'Hare Airport for his final speech of the day, the nagging questions remained. Were all these people going to join environmental organizations, fight city hall and Congress, march in the streets again— and again, and again? Were Americans ready to make personal sacrifices to bring about lasting changes, or would they settle for better trash collection?

Would the new movement be largely white, middle-class people, like those who participated in Earth Day? And how many more tragedies like the Santa Barbara oil spill would it take to keep the attention of the nation focused on the environment?

Hayes hailed a cab outside the airport and gave the driver a downtown address. He tried to talk to the cabbie—about Earth Day, the environment, the sorts of issues that seemed to be on everyone's mind that day—but the guy wasn't a bit interested. After his attempts at conversation failed, Hayes began going over the notes for his last speech of the day.

Half an hour later, the driver pulled over to the curb and turned off the meter—nine dollars and change. Hayes reached for his wallet. It was empty. Then he opened his briefcase, and began searching his pockets. With a terrible sinking feeling, he moved on to his pants, shirt, jacket . . . it was no use. Denis Hayes had overseen the logistics of the largest demonstration in United States history, and somehow, he'd arrived in Chicago completely broke.

He tried to smile as he gave the driver the bad news. Left in a rush, big day of speaking all over the country, a lot on his mind, picked up the tickets at the office and somehow forgot to get any cash. He asked for the driver's address and promised to mail him the fare as soon as he got home.

The cabbie just glared as Hayes opened the door and got out. Hayes could see the message in his eyes: Kids today. They talk about changing the world, but they just want a free ride.

PART 2

THERE OUGHT TO BE A LAW

We should not tolerate incremental additions to
stratospheric pollution, whether they equal those
produced by two Volkswagens or five hundred
Mack trucks. For these will accumulate over time.
And fifty years from now, we will look back and ask
ourselves why we did not dig our heels in and say
"No" when it really could have counted. We will
ask ourselves, "Suppose we simply didn't build the
albatross?"

—*Senator George McGovern*

In the spring of 1969, with outrage over the Santa Barbara oil spill and the rumblings of a broader environmental constituency starting to reach the nation's capital, two powerful Democrats—Senator Henry Jackson of Washington and Congressman John Dingell of Michigan—introduced a pair of bills that came to be known as the National Environmental Policy Act, or NEPA. It was one of the least-controversial laws Congress enacted that year: the bills sailed easily through the often-contentious process of committee hearings, and cleared both the Senate and the House with strong bipartisan support. A consolidated version went to the White House, and President Nixon quickly signed it into law.

Most big-business lobbyists on Capitol Hill saw the legislation as essentially harmless—it didn't put any tough new restrictions on industrial pollution. All NEPA did was require studies—any time a project under the jurisdiction of the federal government might affect the environment, some federal agency had to issue an "environmental impact statement," outlining the potential problems and possible solutions. Environmental activists didn't pay much attention, either: none of them had much time for a law that looked toothless.

Both sides were wrong. NEPA turned out to be one of the most important pieces of environmental legislation ever enacted by the federal government. Congressional records suggest that even the sponsors had no idea that they were about to give the environmental movement a vast new arena: the federal courts.

NEPA was a major political milestone, too. It marked the last time the members of Congress would make any important environmental policy decision without a sizable crew of environmental lobbyists breathing down their necks.

In the months after Earth Day, a growing number of activists began to take their campaigns out of the streets and into the mainstream political system—from the halls of Congress to state legislatures and city halls across the country.

8

A LEG TO STAND ON

April 23, 1970
Washington, D.C.

Thursday morning dawned cool and cloudy in the nation's capital. A few thousand activists slept peacefully after their Earth Day labors. Jim Moorman still hadn't been to bed.

While the rest of the nation was marching and celebrating, the thirty-two-year-old lawyer had been holed up in a cramped office in a seedy part of town, staring at the text of two obscure federal laws, and preparing a radical argument that was just too good to be true. There had been no time for sleep: Moorman was about to face off against a team of more than twenty experienced lawyers representing two government agencies and three major oil companies, over a project worth more than a billion dollars.

This was not how Moorman had planned to spend his legal career. A small-town southern boy, he'd made his way to Duke University and law school, served a brief stint in the Army, and moved to New York to join a prominent Wall Street law firm. But he'd always loved the outdoors; he spent as much time as he could hiking in the wilderness areas north of the city. And just as he was settling into a comfortable corporate-law practice, he met someone who would help him turn his personal interest into a professional crusade.

In the late 1960s, the entire field of environmental law could be summarized in a few pages. As far as most law schools and legal journals were concerned, the field didn't even exist. But a few lawyers were starting to change that—and their undisputed leader was David Sive. Like Moorman, Sive was a corporate lawyer; like Moorman, he was also a wilderness buff. And he had just done something truly astounding: he'd convinced a New

York court to accept a lawsuit to preserve a wilderness area on behalf of a group of people whose interest in the place was entirely aesthetic.

Since the birth of the American legal system, people who wanted to file a lawsuit had to show they had "standing"—and generally, that meant they were facing the threat of some sort of financial loss. The plaintiffs in Sive's case didn't own any property near Storm King Mountain, a spectacular rise overlooking the Hudson River, and they would suffer no economic damage if a private utility, which did own the land, went ahead with its plans to build a power station on the site. But that didn't matter, Sive argued—not all losses were material. The people who hiked through the area and enjoyed its natural beauty had a right to challenge a project that threatened to destroy it.

To the surprise of almost everyone, including David Sive, the court accepted Sive's argument and allowed the case to proceed—and Consolidated Edison Company was forced to give up its project. The Storm King case would soon be described as the birth of modern environmental law, and Sive as its father.

Moorman and Sive were both members of the Sierra Club, and the local chapter sponsored regular hiking trips through the Catskill Mountains. The two lawyers got to know each other, and before long, Moorman asked Sive to help him find a job in environmental law. With Sive's help, he landed a job doing water-rights litigation in the Interior Department.

After Richard Nixon became president, Moorman realized the prospects for an aggressive young Democrat in a Republican administration weren't too promising; by early 1969, he was looking to move on.

On a sweltering day in June, Moorman received a call from Bruce Terrace, a lawyer who was chairman of the District of Columbia Democratic party. Terrace was putting together a public interest law firm, and he was looking for someone to handle environmental cases.

Moorman had never heard of a "public interest" law firm, and had no idea what such an organization would do. But he agreed to meet with Terrace and his partner, Charles Halpern, at the posh downtown offices of the prominent firm Arnold & Porter. Terrace and Halpern outlined their plans: the two were prepared to set up a nonprofit legal organization that would represent citizens' groups who couldn't afford private lawyers, and take on the sorts of cases the government, especially under Richard Nixon, would be sure to avoid. Terrace was interested in consumer law; Halpern wanted to work on legal issues in public health. A third potential associate, Geoffrey Cowan, would pursue communications law. The fourth member, they hoped, would represent environmental groups.

Moorman was instantly sold. He arrived home drenched in sweat and told his wife that a couple of guys had just asked him to retire, so they could pay him to pursue his favorite hobby.

With a grant from the Ford Foundation, the Center for Law and Social

Policy set up shop. Moorman spent his first few months wrangling with pesticide regulations and attempting to get the Department of Agriculture to ban the use of DDT. Toward the end of 1969, he got a call from David Brower.

Moorman had stayed active in the Sierra Club after he left New York. He helped start a Southeast Chapter in Washington, and when the furor over Brower's leadership exploded, Moorman was strongly in the Brower camp. He'd even flown to San Francisco for the fateful meeting at which Brower resigned. He knew Brower was building a new organization called Friends of the Earth; a few months earlier, David Sive had filed the incorporation papers. If David Brower needed legal help, Moorman was happy to do what he could.

Well, Brower said, he did have a legal question, something Moorman might find interesting. He was wondering if there was any way Friends of the Earth could file a lawsuit to stop the Alaska pipeline.

Alaska's northern coastal plain was an odd place for an environmental battle. Two hundred miles above the Arctic Circle, cut off from the rest of the state by the steep mountains of the Brooks Range, the area known as the North Slope was a vast, barren expanse of frozen tundra, a featureless land where temperatures routinely dropped to eighty below zero in the long winter months and the sun stayed below the horizon for fifty-six dark days. It was some of the wildest territory in North America, for the most basic of reasons: very few people had any cause to go there.

Since the turn of the century, however, geologists had known there was oil—maybe a lot of oil—under Alaska's snow and ice. By 1957, oil explorers were drilling lucrative wells; when Alaska became a state in 1959, 90 percent of its budget came from oil revenue.

In 1968, the Atlantic Richfield Company struck oil near the tiny North Slope fishing town of Prudhoe Bay. ARCO geologists quickly determined that the company had made a major find: trapped in the porous sandstone beneath the Arctic tundra was the largest oil field in North America. The excitement reached all the way to Washington, D.C., where President Nixon, the secretary of the interior, and congressional leaders agreed the rich, new oil reserves would help reduce the growing amount of money the nation was shipping off each day to oil-producing nations in the Middle East.

There was only one problem: the oil was a long, long way from anywhere. Prudhoe Bay had only primitive port facilities, nothing that could handle even small oil tankers, but that was the least of the problem. The infrastructure could be upgraded easily enough, but for much of the year, it would be entirely useless: the Beaufort Sea was locked in thick polar ice between early September and late May. In fact, the nearest deepwater port open to shipping all year round was on Prince William Sound, more than seven hundred miles to the south.

ARCO executives quickly agreed that the problem was far beyond the capability of any one company. Besides, a few other companies, including Exxon, had claims on part of the new oilfield. Within months, several major oil companies had joined together in a consortium and announced plans to construct the most ambitious single project ever attempted by private industry: a 789-mile pipeline that would carry the Prudhoe Bay oil across the entire state of Alaska, from the North Slope to the port of Valdez. From there, it could be shipped by tanker to refineries in Seattle, Los Angeles, and San Francisco.

Building the pipeline would be a gigantic feat of engineering. The forty-eight-inch pipe would have to cross three mountain ranges, three earthquake faults, and more than eight hundred rivers and streams. More than half of the line would be elevated, on steel pilings that would be driven deep into the frozen ground.

The project would require an extensive support system. Hundreds of miles of new roads would have to be built through the Alaskan wilderness to bring workers and supplies to the construction sites. Entire towns would have to spring up, to provide thousands of workers with housing, and food, and recreation. The oil consortium, known as the Trans Alaska Pipeline System, would have to win the right to use a lot of land—the land below the pipeline, the land alongside it, the land where the roads would go, the land for the new towns and construction facilities. Some was available easily, for a price, from private owners. But most of the pipeline's path—641 miles of it—passed over public property, land owned by the United States government.

In June 1969, the pipeline consortium applied to the Interior Department's Bureau of Land Management for a right-of-way—a permit to use public land. The application requested the consortium be given a fifty-four-foot-wide strip of land for the pipeline itself, another forty-six-foot-wide strip for construction and support facilities, and an additional one-hundred-foot-wide strip for new service roads. The application also asked for the temporary use of between two hundred and five hundred feet on either side of the major river and stream crossings to set up transient camps for the construction crews.

Interior Secretary Walter Hickle established a North Slope Task Force to evaluate the pipeline permits, and in September 1969, it submitted a preliminary report, directly to the president. The report was generally favorable, but it identified a few serious problems. Among them was a clause in the Mineral Leasing Act of 1920, the statute that authorized oil companies to apply for the use of federal land for pipeline construction. The law was fairly clear, the staff report said: oil pipelines were limited to a single right-of-way, and the maximum was fifty-four feet.

David Brower had plenty of reasons to oppose the Alaska pipeline. For starters, Alaska was a treasure, one of the last great untouched wilderness areas in the United States, where bald eagles, caribou, bears, and wolves lived in a natural state found almost nowhere in the lower forty-eight states. Alaska still had pristine and fertile breeding grounds for hundreds of species of fish and birds. The pipeline would disturb, maybe destroy, the habitat of countless creatures—and if a serious accident should happen, and giant gushers of oil should burst from a crack in the pipeline, thousands of acres of virgin wilderness would be damaged beyond repair. The oil spill in Santa Barbara had shown how devastating that scenario could be.

Besides, Brower felt, the oil from Alaska would just feed a culture that was already too dependent on fossil fuels. It would encourage the automobile manufacturers to build bigger cars, and the highway builders to construct wider highways, and the electric companies to generate more, cheaper electricity. It would all encourage the rush of industrial civilization, which Brower thought was moving far too fast already. Brower had a very different vision for the future, one that seemed outlandishly radical at the time but would soon seem a lot more practical. If we stopped producing more and more energy, he argued, we would have to learn to live smarter, to develop smaller vehicles and appliances that did more with less. We'd have to recognize that, ultimately, oil was a vanishing resource, one that would have to be replaced sooner or later with energy sources that were renewable. We'd have to find a national life-style that was sustainable over the long term, and kicking the petroleum habit was a good way to start.

At Friends of the Earth, Brower was free to do almost anything he wanted. The organization was his personal platform; the only real agenda was supporting his crusades. The staff was made up largely of refugees from the Sierra Club, people who had joined with Brower in the final, fateful days and left their jobs, voluntarily or involuntarily, shortly after he walked the plank.

Jim Moorman knew the legal system wasn't quite so compliant. Brower could gripe about the Alaska wilderness all he wanted; he could generate plenty of publicity, and get thousands of his supporters to write to Congress. But when it came to a lawsuit, none of that would mean a thing. The courts were somewhat insulated from public opinion; they operated on very different, very technical rules. One of those rules was called "standing"—and although David Sive had cracked open the door a bit at Storm King, Moorman feared the Alaska pipeline was a very different case.

It might well be possible, he told Brower, to find a flaw in the application, or to uncover a key legal issue that could be used to challenge the governmental approval. But in order to sue, one would still have to claim damages. Under the Storm King decision, those damages could be "aesthetic, conservationist or recreational" in nature—but as far as Moorman knew, neither David Brower nor any of the members of his new organization had any visible recreational interest in the remote northern Alaska tundra. Certainly, nobody in Friends of the Earth owned any property near the proposed pipeline right-of-way. None of the members depended on the preservation of Alaskan wilderness for a livelihood. None of them hiked or camped in the area; in fact, almost nobody Brower or Moorman knew had ever actually been there. In real, down-to-earth legal terms, the construction of the pipeline wouldn't injure Brower or Friends of the Earth in any tangible way.

Brower wasn't happy with the explanation, but he accepted Moorman's word. Moorman wasn't happy, either, but he didn't see any alternative. Both agreed to think things over, and stay in touch.

Over the last few weeks of 1969, Moorman did some research into the pipeline application, and it didn't take him long to notice the same thing the Interior Department task force staff had noticed: the oil companies were asking for a right-of-way under an obscure law written in 1920, when the nation, and the oil-drilling business, were very different. But no matter: the application sought considerably more land than the law allowed. He called Brower to let him know there was a potential problem with the application, but it didn't seem to be grounds for a lawsuit. After all, the extra 146 feet of land along the pipeline route wouldn't damage Friends of the Earth any more than did the pipeline itself.

Then one morning early in January, Moorman started reading the text of another largely unknown law, one that had taken effect the first of the year. He'd heard about the bill when it was making its way through Congress, but like most environmental lawyers, he hadn't paid much attention. It didn't sound like anything terribly important—just another way for the politicians to convince the folks back home that they were doing their jobs. In this case, the politicians were hearing rumblings about the environment. So they'd passed the National Environmental Policy Act.

As far as Moorman knew, the act didn't contain any new restrictions on environmental destruction, just studies of "environmental impact." The whole thing, Moorman figured, would create a lot of jobs for a lot of bureaucrats, and the studies would sit on a lot of shelves in a lot of obscure offices, gathering a lot of dust.

But as he worked his way through the text, he began to change his mind. There was something fascinating about this innocent-looking bill: it had the potential to solve the sticky problem of legal standing that environmental organizations had been struggling with all these years. The way Moorman read it, the National Environmental Policy Act gave almost anyone the right to sue.

Every citizen, no matter where he or she lived, had the legal right under NEPA to demand a valid environmental impact statement on any project under federal jurisdiction. David Brower didn't have to own land in Alaska, or live in Alaska, or ever go to Alaska, to demand a legally adequate environmental analysis of the pipeline project. The mere lack of a legally valid report could force the project sponsors to stop in their tracks. It wasn't clear yet what constituted a legally valid report—but if Moorman and Brower could find the slightest potential flaw in the Alaska pipeline environmental impact statement, Moorman was sure they could take the matter to court.

For a project the size of the Alaska pipeline, Moorman knew, the environmental impact statement would have to be quite extensive—at least a few hundred pages, maybe more. Collecting and analyzing that much data would take time—maybe as much as a year or two. And until the report was complete, and the courts agreed it was adequate to meet NEPA standards, the oil companies couldn't build an inch of pipe. And once the court accepted a lawsuit over the validity of the EIS, Moorman expected to have little trouble bringing up the additional issue of the illegal right-of-way.

On March 26, 1970, Jim Moorman filed the nation's first National Environmental Policy Act lawsuit, asking a federal judge to block the secretary of the interior from approving the pipeline right-of-way or issuing a permit for construction. Moorman and Brower had worked quickly. It wasn't hard to find some possible defects in the pipeline EIS: the document was prepared hastily, and it failed to address all sorts of potential environmental issues. The Wilderness Society and the Environmental Defense Fund joined Friends of the Earth as plaintiffs in the case. The lawsuit was based on two issues: the defect in the right-of-way application, and the failure of the Interior Department to prepare an adequate environmental impact statement on the pipeline project.

The United States District Court House for the District of Columbia was on C Street, just off Pennsylvania Avenue. The courtrooms where most federal cases were heard occupied the lower part of the building. Appeals went upstairs, to the fifth floor.

Judge George L. Hart, Jr., a scholarly, sixty-four-year-old jurist with twelve years on the federal bench, had initially scheduled oral arguments in the pipeline case for April 22. But a conflict arose at the last minute, and the hearing was delayed.

As far as Moorman knew, Judge Hart had not been celebrating Earth Day. In fact, he didn't know how well the judge really understood environmental issues, or whether he would be willing to break some new ground on a legal argument that had no precedent in any United States court.

But if Moorman was a bit nervous, his main counterpart was a complete wreck. Herbert Pittle, the elderly, white-haired solicitor from the Justice Department, was visibly shaken as the judge entered the courtroom and the bailiff called the case. When Hart asked the government to present its case, Pittle's hands were twitching so badly he was unable to hold his pleading papers, and the sheaf of carefully organized documents fell in a heap on the floor.

The courtroom was crowded with lawyers—Pittle and his assistants were the official representatives of the defendant, Interior Secretary Walter Hickle, but the eight oil companies that had joined the pipeline consortium were working closely with the Justice Department, and all eight had legal teams on hand. Moorman counted two dozen lawyers in the opposition camp, but he thought he missed a few—oil company lawyers and legal assistants had been shuttling in and out of the courtroom, and there was no way to keep track of them all.

Hart listened intently as Moorman explained why the pipeline application violated NEPA, and why the court should issue an injunction against any pipeline approval until a valid EIS could be completed. It was late in the morning by the time he finished, and the windowless room was starting to get warm. Moorman was exhausted and a little bit dazed, and as Hart leaned forward to speak, he felt his heart start to pound. He'd expected the judge to take the case under submission; if he was ruling from the bench, it was probably bad news.

But Hart wasn't ready to rule, not yet. First, he had a question for Mr. Pittle. Would the government voluntarily agree to delay issuing any pipeline permits until Hart had time to conduct a thorough review of the new law and the issues that the plaintiffs had raised?

Pittle asked for a brief recess, and for several minutes, a small army of government and oil industry lawyers huddled in the hallway and discussed their plan of action. When the meeting broke up, Pittle strolled into the courtroom and informed Hart of his decision: the Interior Department would accept no delay. The secretary was prepared to issue the permits, and unless the court wanted to accept this unusual argument from these crazy environmentalists, that was exactly what he planned to do.

Judge Hart looked out at Herbert Pittle and the army of oil company lawyers. "In that case, gentlemen," he said, "I guess you're going to have to take this up to the fifth floor," where the appellate judges held court. Then he picked up his pen and signed Jim Moorman's injunction.

The battle over the Alaska pipeline would continue for years, and ultimately, the oil companies would prevail. But Brower and Moorman had already won a major victory, one with implications far beyond the Alaskan tundra. From now on government officials and big business executives would have to pay close attention to the environmental impacts of their projects—and environmentalists who disputed those projects would have a new way to fight back. Over the next twenty years, some of the movement's most successful crusades would take place in the courts.

9

TWISTS OF FATE

May 9, 1970
Pellston, Michigan

Walter Reuther's Earth Day euphoria wore off all too quickly. His speech denouncing the "two tons of gadgets" had won accolades from environmental leaders, and cautious but growing support within the United Auto Workers. But his campaign to bring union members into the environmental fold was stagnating, bogged down by the more immediate social and political crisis of the lingering Vietnam War. President Nixon's decision to invade Cambodia on April 30 turned the United States into a battlefield; on the campus of Ohio's Kent State University, National Guard troops shot four student protesters dead.

Reuther immediately tried to bring a new coalition of labor, industry, students, and clergy together to protest the escalation in Southeast Asia and work for a peaceful solution. The most important problems facing the United States, he announced, were not in Vietnam but back at home. If the resources of war could be poured into domestic needs, the nation could develop sound ecological and industrial policies that would lead to both a cleaner environment and a more prosperous economy. It was probably the most important, most radical organizing effort the legendary union leader had ever undertaken. It was also slow going. Early in May, Reuther told his wife he needed to take a break.

The United Auto Workers owned a rustic vacation complex on the edge of Black Lake, deep in the wilderness of northern Michigan; Reuther often used it as a retreat, a place to relax with friends and associates and discuss new ideas and strategies. He arranged to use one of the cabins for a few days, and invited a couple of guests to join him.

Reuther made no secret of his plans. A few years earlier, somebody had fired shots through his kitchen window, and although he never found out who had done it or why, he'd stepped up his personal security afterward. But Black Lake was union territory; he went there all the time.

Early in the evening of May 9, the Reuthers drove to Detroit's Metropolitan Airport. As usual, the union had chartered a Learjet to fly them 220 miles north, to the town of Pellston. A union car would meet them at the Emmet County Airfield, about an hour's ride from the shores of Black Lake.

The twin-engine jet took off at 8:44 P.M. The pilot, George Evans, and the copilot, Joseph Karaffa, had taken passengers to the Black Lake retreat many times before; their company, Executive Jet Aviation, did a lot of work for the union. Evans was forty-eight years old and in perfect health. He had more than 7,700 hours of commercial flight time, 2,000 of those hours at the command of a twin-engine Learjet. A steady rain was falling as he guided the craft into the sky, but that didn't cause the passengers much concern. Evans was fully instrument-rated, and he'd flown the same plane, with Reuther aboard, through far worse conditions.

The flight to Pellston took about forty-five minutes. By 9:15, Evans had made radio contact with the Emmet County Airfield tower, and at 9:28, he announced he had the runway in sight and was turning on his landing lights. The rain was still falling, although a bit more lightly; winds were from the east at ten miles an hour. Visibility was seven miles.

At 9:30, as Evans began his final landing approach, the Learjet suddenly and rapidly lost altitude. Three miles short of the runway, it clipped the top of a fifty-foot elm tree; both engines caught fire, and the plane slammed into the ground, exploding into a hot fireball. The bodies of Walter and May Reuther, another passenger, and the two pilots all were burned beyond recognition.

Inspectors from the National Transportation Safety Board investigated the accident and filed a report; the results received only brief mention, buried under reams of glowing obituaries extolling the virtues of the late great Walter Reuther. The investigation was routine, the newspapers said. The crash was a bit odd, the government experts concluded, but nothing that unusual; every now and then, this kind of accident happened. It was, they reported, probably the result of pilot error.

Twenty years later, National Transportation Safety Board records would shed little additional light on the incident. A brief computer printout would repeat the conclusion—probably pilot error, perhaps a minor instrument failure. The investigators' original reports were all destroyed, officials would explain, as part of a routine effort to reduce the volume of paper in the federal government archives.

Still, the timing of the accident would continue to bother a few environmental activists—and although he almost never talked about it, the event would haunt David Brower for the rest of his life.

In political terms, Brower knew, Reuther's loss was devastating. No other labor leader alive had the courage and the vision to suggest that autoworkers campaign against building more cars, and encourage the manufacturers to start making trains and buses. No other labor leader had the reputation, the charisma, and the rank-and-file credibility to have even a remote chance of bringing the labor and environmental movements together at a time when war and social unrest were tearing the nation apart. Over the next twenty years, to the delight of big industry executives, labor unions and environmentalists would continue to squabble over whether a cleaner environment would cost union jobs. Nobody would ever come forward to take Walter Reuther's place.

But that wasn't all that haunted David Brower. He knew as well as anyone else alive what Reuther had planned for that Black Lake retreat. The nation's most important labor leader wanted to spend some time with the nation's most important environmental leader. Brower was in Detroit the evening of May 9, and he promised to meet the Reuthers at the airport. At the last minute, he had to change his plans; the Learjet took off without him.

10

LAY WASTE THE SKY

May 12, 1970
Washington, D.C.

The Senate Subcommittee on Economy in Government was at the end of a long, complicated, three-day hearing when the president's environmental adviser dropped his political bombshell.

The issue before the panel was an item in the Federal Aviation Administration's 1971 budget request, a $290 million allocation for the development of an experimental aircraft, the sort of thing congressional committees studied, debated, and resolved every working day. In this case, though, the matter was anything but trivial. The FAA was seeking authorization to continue work on the supersonic transport, better known as the SST—a high-speed commercial aircraft that was caught up in a fierce environmental storm.

The SST project had started out years earlier as a simple government subsidy for the advancement of American technology. But for the emerging environmental movement, the SST had turned into a symbol of a wide range of problems with the direction of national policy. It had also become the first major chance for the environmental movement to show it could do more than turn people out for rallies and marches. It was a chance to prove that the popularity of Earth Day was not a fluke—and that some of that grassroots energy and enthusiasm could be put to work effectively in the complex world of high-stakes lobbying on Capitol Hill. In the course of the battle, a new generation of environmental lobbyists would come of age.

A new generation of liberal activists would also learn to face an important fact: the environmental agenda often clashed with the interests of other traditional liberal constituencies, like organized labor—and sometimes it fit in well with the ideology of old-fashioned conservatives.

And in the middle of the fray, a star witness would throw a startling new issue into the environmental debate.

William Proxmire, the committee chairman, was a seasoned Washington veteran. Bright, hard-working, disciplined, and in excellent health, he could boast the establishment credentials of a Harvard education and the populist sensibilities of a small-business owner from the town of Waterloo, Wisconsin. The voters of that state had just given him a third six-year term, by a landslide margin of 72 percent. On paper, the fifty-five-year-old lawmaker seemed the picture of political success.

But after thirteen years in the Senate, Proxmire had little to show, save a reputation for cantankerousness and a penchant for lost causes. He despised the traditional Senate collegiality. He angered liberals with his conservative stands on social issues, infuriated conservatives with his attacks on the defense industry, and made enemies on both sides of the aisle with his constant opposition to congressional salary increases and other perks of office. His colleagues generally viewed him as a minor pest, someone who could make life difficult, but hardly a force to be reckoned with, and certainly not an effective policymaker.

But Proxmire was sensing a change in the political landscape. Under the banner of environmentalism, people all over the country were starting to discuss some radical-sounding ideas, like natural limits to growth and the need for a slow, cautious approach to technological advances—ideas that Proxmire had always considered plain old conservative good sense.

The SST program, first proposed in the early days of the Kennedy administration, embodied almost everything Proxmire opposed. Proponents, led by Kennedy's energetic FAA director Najeeb Halaby, wanted the federal government to spend huge sums of money to help private industry develop a commercial airliner that would travel across the country faster than the speed of sound (about 750 miles an hour). Eventually, supporters said, the supersonic jets would be able to carry passengers from New York to Los Angeles in just two hours.

Even the airline industry was a bit dubious when Halaby first launched his campaign. Military jets had broken the sound barrier years before, but the technical problems of commercial supersonic flight were still somewhat daunting. And the costs of operation had to be low enough to make the fares attractive in the marketplace. Developing a commercially viable SST would require a fairly sizable capital outlay; the major airlines and aircraft companies were reluctant to take the risk. So most of money for the development of a workable SST prototype would have to come from Uncle Sam.

Of course, if the project was successful, and a fleet of SSTs began carrying thousands of paying customers from coast to coast and overseas, the manufacturers and the airlines would keep all the profits. And since seats on the high-speed aircraft would be far more expensive than those on other flights, only a tiny percentage of the populace would ever be able to take advantage of the service. But Halaby and his allies insisted that the investment of public funds was justified: France and Great Britain were building an SST, and so was the Soviet Union; and if the U.S. didn't build its own model first, American industry could lose its competitive edge. Labor leaders, who saw tens of thousands of union jobs on the line, quickly joined the crusade. In August 1961, Congress agreed to spend $11 million to get research efforts under way.

Seven years and some $250 million later, Boeing, which had won the government contract to develop a prototype, finally came up with a workable design. The B-2707-300 would carry 298 passengers at a top speed of 1,800 miles an hour. Each plane would cost about $52 million; if everything went well, Boeing estimated, the SST would be available for commercial use in 1978.

From the start, however, everyone involved in the project knew it had a serious problem: when a plane flew faster than the speed of sound, it created a sonic boom, a powerful shock wave that could rattle nerves, break windows, frighten animals, crack building foundations, and cause all sorts of other damage to anyone and anything in its path.

Sonic booms were an unavoidable side effect of supersonic flight. When an airplane flew at normal speeds, it pushed the air in front of it aside for a moment; the air molecules slid over the top and bottom of the plane, causing a minor change in air pressure. That pressure change gave the plane its lift. But under the basic laws of physics, air molecules could only move as fast as the speed of sound. When a plane reached supersonic speed, the air in front of it didn't have time to move smoothly aside. The molecules were compressed tightly together as the aircraft pushed its way through them, creating a powerful shock wave that extended outward for forty to sixty miles in every direction.

The shock wave didn't stop after the plane broke the sound barrier; a supersonic aircraft produced a sonic boom trail as long as it continued to fly faster than sound. A person on the ground felt the boom only once, as the plane passed overhead, but the impact could extend over a vast area. An SST flying at sixty thousand feet from Chicago to Los Angeles would leave a shock wave trail fifty miles wide and roughly two thousand miles long, affecting a total land area ten times the size of the state of Massachusetts.

SST supporters argued that the intensity of the boom decreased over distance; as long as the planes were flying at a high-enough altitude, they insisted, the actual impacts of the booms on the ground would be minimal. The evidence, however, suggested otherwise. In 1964 and 1965, the FAA conducted a series of test flights over major population centers. Since no commercial SSTs existed, the tests used supersonic military jets, which were much smaller and lighter and produced less intense shock waves. Still, when the planes flew over Oklahoma City, residents complained that the booms shattered windows, cracked plaster walls and caused fragile objects to fall off shelves. Tests over Chicago, Pittsburgh, St. Louis, and Milwaukee yielded similar results. Over all, the government was forced to pay out some $400,000 in damage settlements to residents of the test areas.

Beyond the physical damage to property, the sudden unexpected sonic booms left people nervous and irritable. To some—doctors and dentists in the midst of a delicate operation, musicians in a recording session, actors, teachers, and others trying to hold the attention of an audience, for example— the potential impacts of even what the government considered a fairly mild boom were unacceptable.

By 1966, a few sporadic magazine articles had appeared questioning the SST, and a few members of Congress, most notably Senator Proxmire, had begun taking a hard look at the program's ever-expanding budget. The interior secretary, Stewart Udall, announced he was appointing a departmental commission to study the environmental impacts of SST flights over wilderness areas; the move infuriated President Johnson, and almost cost Udall his job. But overall, public opposition to the program was limited, and none of the major national environmental groups had shown more than token interest in the issue.

Then a fifty-eight-year-old Harvard physicist named William A. Shurcliff happened to read an article in the *Bulletin of Atomic Scientists* that outlined the sonic boom problem and presented a detailed scientific case against the SST. Shurcliff was no aviation expert—his background was in radiation and optics. He had never been terribly interested in politics, and he didn't spend a whole lot of time worrying about threats to the environment. A series of patents on optical devices left him fairly well-off, and with his children all grown, he was beginning to think about a nice, peaceful retirement.

But the sonic boom article intrigued him. In October of 1966, he began writing to the FAA, requesting information about sonic boom tests and asking how the agency's scientific advisers responded to the questions raised by the SST critics. The answers disturbed him; the data didn't seem to add up. He began writing to a few key members of Congress, outlining what he saw as inaccurate and biased conclusions in the government's scientific reports on the SST.

Early in 1967, Shurcliff read a pair of letters to the editor in *The New York Times* complaining about the sonic boom. He recognized the name of one of the letter-writers immediately—John Edsall was a colleague in the Harvard Physics Department. Shurcliff called Edsall, suggested he start an organization to fight the SST project, and offered to donate $20 to get things rolling. "I'm much too busy for that," Edsall replied. "You start it, and I'll give the twenty dollars."

The second letter was signed by a woman named Elizabeth Borish, who lived in a small town in Vermont. Shurcliff tracked her down through the phone company. Her response was almost exactly the same: Go ahead, you start it. I'll give the money.

On March 9, the Citizens League Against the Sonic Boom was born, with Shurcliff as director and Edsall as deputy director, and with a staff made up of Shurcliff's sister, Mrs. F. J. Ingelfinger, and his son, Charles. Shurcliff had no idea how to run a political organization, but he'd done a lot of technical writing, and he was an expert typist. So he began writing letters—to Congress, to the administration, to the FAA, and to the news media. Soon, he was producing detailed fact sheets, packed with information about the costs of the SST program, the technical problems involved in building the aircraft, and the environmental impacts of sonic booms. Shurcliff had a passion for scrupulous organization, and he paid careful attention to every detail. He compiled extensive research files, all cross-referenced and cataloged by subject. The information he sent to the news media was based on established scientific sources. Often, he sent drafts to the FAA for comment before releasing them; the agency rarely bothered to reply.

He was also persistent. When a subcommittee of the National Academy of Sciences released a study minimizing the dangers of the SST and endorsing the FAA's program, he personally addressed more than a thousand letters to prominent members of the academy, outlining the flaws in the report and demanding a retraction. When 330 wrote back to endorse his position, Shurcliff told the academy chairman he was planning to send out a press release announcing a rebellion in the ranks of the prestigious institution and naming the many leading scientists who thought the SST report was shoddy and inaccurate. The academy quickly issued a statement disavowing the report.

Toward the end of 1969, Shurcliff got a call from a fellow in San Francisco who seemed to be intensely interested in the SST battle. He was somewhat new to the issue, but he was impressed with Shurcliff's work, and he'd just founded an environmental group that was ready to jump into the fray. He also had a good friend in the publishing business, and was wondering: Would Shurcliff like to write a book?

Shurcliff had never met David Brower, and knew nothing about Friends of the Earth. But there weren't a whole lot of national environmental organizations that wanted to help fight the SST, and he could use all the help he could get. Shurcliff agreed to take a shot at it, and Brower said he'd have his friend Ian Ballantine call to work out the details. Ballantine was already working with Brower on an environmental handbook for Earth Day, and he agreed to take on the SST project as well, especially if the two could be printed at the same time.

In February 1970, the *SST and Sonic Boom Handbook* rolled off the presses, priced at 95 cents. Its basic message was devastating: If all went as the FAA and Boeing planned, as many as 1,200 American SSTs would be taking to the air each day. Add the 200 SSTs planned by the Soviet Union and 400 from the French and British and you wind up with 1,800 planes, pounding 400 million square miles of land with sonic booms and causing an estimated $24 million worth of property damage. Every day. Not a single major city would be safe from repeated daily booms.

Shurcliff asked the publisher, Ballantine Books, for a special rate on a bulk order; Ballantine offered to sell him all the books he wanted for 16 cents each. On the spur of the moment, Shurcliff ordered ten thousand. Over the next few months, he mailed copies of the book everywhere: to all 435 members of the House, all 100 senators, hundreds of administration officials, thousands of environmental activists, reporters, editors, and columnists. Anyone who had ever contacted Shurcliff to ask about the SST was listed on a file card in the office; most of them wound up with a book.

On the other side of the country, Brower was proving true to his word: Friends of the Earth had taken on the SST as its first major campaign. Brower's full-page newspaper ads against projects like the Grand Canyon dam had been a great success in the Sierra Club campaigns, and with the help of a San Francisco advertising genius named Jerry Mander, he put the same tactic to work again. In March, Mander's ads appeared in *The New York Times* and the *San Francisco Chronicle*. In big, bold type, the headlines proclaimed the case against the SST: "BREAKS WINDOWS, CRACKS WALLS, STAMPEDES CATTLE AND WILL HASTEN THE END OF THE AMERICAN WILDERNESS."

The response was overwhelming. The San Francisco office was swamped with calls and letters. Contributions for the SST campaign came pouring in to Brower's group, and the membership rolls of the new organization began to swell.

By the time Proxmire convened his hearing, the SST controversy was making headlines across the country. Local organizations opposed to the project were springing up everywhere. In Boston, members of the hastily formed Massachusetts Committee Against the SST held a "die-in" at Logan Airport. In Los Angeles, the UCLA Ecology Action Council prepared a statement denouncing the SST as a "gross" national product. Even the Sierra Club, which had always been reluctant to take a stand on the issue, announced its opposition to the SST and urged its members to take action.

Proxmire had lined up an impressive array of anti-SST witnesses for the critical Senate hearing. They produced scientific data, financial reports, and perhaps more important, a wide range of public opinion polls and personal statements suggesting just how angry the voters would be when the sonic booms started shaking up their lives. But the final witness, Russell Train, was Proxmire's secret weapon: the chairman of the Council on Environmental

Quality was part of the administration, an important adviser to the president. And although President Nixon was strongly supporting the SST, Train had some serious reservations.

Train acknowledged that the sonic boom would be at least a minor annoyance, and that the noise problem would have to be addressed before the planes could begin commercial flight. But there was another problem, too. A few SST opponents had mentioned it over the years; government scientists, and most of the news media, had always dismissed them as crackpots. Train had come to the hearing room to say something else.

The SST, he told the committee, would fly at seventy thousand feet, and would release large amounts of water vapor, carbon dioxide, nitrogen oxides, and particulate matter into the region of the upper atmosphere known as the stratosphere. Over time, five hundred supersonic planes could increase the water content in the stratosphere by 50 to 100 percent. That, he said, would "affect the balance of heat in the entire atmosphere, leading to a warmer average surface temperature" on the planet. In addition, the emissions might damage the ozone layer, which helped protect the Earth's surface from ultraviolet rays.

Ultimately, Train told the senators, the SST fleet could bring on a worldwide temperature increase—a global warming.

Train's testimony was probably the first time members of the United States Senate heard a government expert warn about damage to the ozone layer. A lot of scientific experts were dubious; much of the news media was skeptical. At first, Proxmire's colleagues were generally unimpressed. But to environmentalists, the matter was cause for serious alarm.

Proxmire's hearing was the turning point in the SST campaign. By the end of 1970, the Sierra Club, the Wilderness Society, the National Wildlife Federation, and Zero Population Growth were all standing firm with the opposition. Proxmire picked up some other important allies, too: Ed Muskie, the senator from Maine who was gearing up to run for the presidency, and Gaylord Nelson, the father of Earth Day, took leading roles in the battle, giving Proxmire and the anti-SST cause a tremendous boost of credibility.

For some senators, though, the most important issue may have had little to do with the environment. Proxmire took every opportunity to wrap his crusade in populist rhetoric, portraying the aircraft as an elitist waste of the taxpayers' money—exactly the sort of thing that always embarrassed politicians when they went back home to the voters. "We are being asked to spend $290 million this year," he proclaimed on the floor of the Senate, "for transportation for one-half of one percent of the people—the jet setters—to fly overseas, and we are spending $204 million for urban mass transportation for millions of people to go to work. Does this make sense?" His logic helped bring on board an entirely new lobbying force—the conservative National Taxpayers Union.

On March 18, 1971, the House of Representatives approved a measure killing all funds for the SST. The final decision was up to the Senate; the vote was set for March 24.

The lobbying reached a fever pitch. Gary Socie, executive director of Friends of the Earth, sent out a mailing to the group's membership—now more than five thousand strong—and urged everyone to flood the offices of local representatives and senators with letters opposing the project.

Supporters of the SST cranked their efforts up, too. The stakes were high: the government had already spent more than $700 million on research and development, and Boeing and its subcontractors had kicked in another $197 million. Potentially, insisted William Magruder, the Transportation Department's SST point man, the SST would create 150,000 jobs and improve the nation's balance of trade by $22 billion. In February, the National Committee for an American SST, backed by Fairchild-Hiller and the International Association of Machinists, even adopted one of David Brower's favorite tactics: the group began taking out full-page ads in major national newspapers promoting the project as a boon to the economy and downplaying the importance of environmental issues. The committee spent $350,000 on the advertising effort in just a few weeks.

For environmentalists, the involvement of organized labor in the pro-SST campaign became a big problem. A lot of the SST's staunchest critics in Congress came from blue-collar districts, and the threat of layoffs at companies like Boeing and General Electric was making them nervous. George Meany, the powerful AFL-CIO chief, personally contacted several undecided senators to urge them not to kill the project.

The SST foes, try as they might, were unable to find any prominent labor leaders to come out publicly against the project. The loss of Walter Reuther loomed larger every day.

To make matters worse, in the weeks before the final vote, Senator Proxmire suffered a serious public-relations setback. In what seemed to be an important move to bolster the case against the SST, the senator trotted out an atmospheric scientist from the University of Arizona named James McDonald, who announced that his research showed that a fleet of SSTs would deplete the ozone enough to cause as many as ten thousand new cases of skin cancer in the United States every year. McDonald's assertions attracted considerable media attention.

Then a few days later, SST foes discovered that McDonald had a few unorthodox scientific theories that Proxmire apparently hadn't known about. In 1968, for example, in testimony before a congressional committee, he had suggested that flying saucers, manned by humanoid-type creatures, might have been responsible for a widespread power failure in the northeastern United States. SST supporters immediately tried to use the incident to cast doubt on the rest of the evidence Proxmire had presented on the negative environmental impacts of SST flight. The news media had a field day.

But Proxmire lined up statements from twenty-one prominent biologists and atmospheric scientists who all agreed that the SST could do such serious damage to the ozone layer that it could lead to a significant increase in skin cancer rates. In fact, Dr. Gio Gori, who worked for the National Cancer Institute, appeared with Proxmire at a press conference and said that McDonald's estimates might even be low. According to Gori, the total number of new skin cancer cases resulting each year from a fleet of eight hundred SSTs could reach 103,000.

The Senate debate began before noon and continued well into the day. Amid the lofty rhetoric, the obligatory quotations from constituent letters and hometown editorials, and the lengthy citations of contradictory scientific and economic evidence, the senators on the floor and the spectators in the gallery got a glimpse of the deep and profound questions underlying the fight over the future of the SST.

"Regarding whether the environmental doubts raised by critics of SST have been laid to rest, or will be at the time that the airplane goes into production," Senator George McGovern of South Dakota noted, "I ask you to view the issue from a different perspective—a perspective assumed by David Brower, president of Friends of the Earth. . . . Brower asked the question: 'Suppose we simply don't build the albatross?,' not 'What noise levels, or what boom frequencies, or what emission levels can we tolerate in the SST?'

"Toleration is at best a very shaky relationship. . . . No doubt the first liter of environmental pollutant introduced to Lake Erie was tolerable to the trout and swimmer alike. And the second and the third liter, too. But now, consider what toleration has done to Lake Erie. . . .

"We should not tolerate incremental additions to stratospheric pollution, whether they equal those produced by two Volkswagens or five hundred Mack trucks. For these will accumulate over time. And fifty years from now, we will look back and ask ourselves why we did not dig our heels in and say 'No' when it really could have counted. We will ask ourselves—'Suppose we simply didn't build the albatross?' "

The vice president of the United States, Spiro Agnew, made a rare personal appearance to preside over the Senate and cast the tie-breaking vote, if necessary. The majority leader asked him to direct the clerk to call the final roll. Agnew looked out over the packed chamber, and sternly warned the spectators in the gallery that Senate rules forbid any applause or other outbursts during the roll call. Then the clerk began calling out each senator's name, in alphabetical order, and recording his or her vote. George Aiken of Vermont came first, and, as expected, he voted against the SST funding. The clerk moved on, to Senator James Allen (against) and Senator Gorton Allott (in favor). No surprises.

The next name on the list was Clinton Anderson, a New Mexico Democrat;

both sides considered him a strong SST supporter. In a clear, firm voice, Anderson announced his vote—to discontinue funding. Proxmire couldn't believe his ears. A few minutes later, John Sherman Cooper, a Kentucky Republican who was generally listed in the pro-SST camp, also voted to cut off the funds. Proxmire was elated: for the first time in thirteen years, he was actually headed for a major political victory. By the time he cast his own vote, the outcome was almost certain; the final tally was 51–46 to eliminate funding for the program. The SST was history.

And for a moment, the era when bigger, faster, and higher were synonymous with the American way of life seemed as if it might be going the way of the supersonic albatross.

11

THE MAN IN
THE GRAY SUIT

November 1971
Columbus, Ohio

In a cheap roadside motel room on a warm, Ohio night, an exhausted traveler tossed and turned in a restless sleep, as images of violent destruction flashed through his head. In his unconscious imagination, the man saw himself pull a big pistol from his belt and pump six bullets into the engine of a dump truck. The truck became a giant earth-mover, the pistol a bag of sugar that the man poured into its gas tank, silently sentencing the expensive machine to death. Then suddenly, he was standing by a railroad track, watching as a train roared over a hefty monkey wrench that he'd wedged between the rails. He watched, spellbound, as the Peabody Coal train derailed, twisting into a mangled piece of wreckage.

Jack Loeffler awoke with a smile. He had a speech to make shortly, at Ohio State University, but he took the time to savor a good dream. It helped get him through the real-life nightmares of his hopeless political campaign.

By now, the fight to save Black Mesa had turned the laid-back former beatnik into the organizational madman. The phone at his house rang constantly—sometimes, to get a little relief, he'd stick it in the freezer. He spent long days out on the mesa's Hopi reservation, trying to educate and organize the Indians. He supervised an underpaid, overworked crew of local activists who were plowing through mountains of complicated legal research for his new group, the Black Mesa Defense Fund. He harassed politicians, took calls from the press, spoke to rallies, and had even gone to testify before a congressional subcommittee. He scrambled constantly to raise money: a Jerry Mander ad in *The New York Times* soliciting support for the Black Mesa battle brought in $20,000, but that barely covered the overdue bills.

More than anything else, though, Loeffler filed lawsuits. The lawyers he pulled into the fray, primarily through the nonprofit Native American Rights Fund, would ultimately bring six different cases to court on behalf of the Black Mesa Defense Fund and the Navajo and Hopi peoples. One case would make it all the way to the United States Supreme Court.

The litigation would bring to light serious flaws in the Peabody Coal lease. The lawyers would break new legal ground by incorporating the rights of Native Americans into the field of environmental law. Loeffler would break new political ground by putting the struggle of a nonwhite community onto the national environmental agenda.

And one by one, all of the legal cases and political campaigns would go down to defeat.

No matter how solid his evidence, no matter how hard he worked, Loeffler was starting to think he couldn't do anything to stop the Black Mesa mine. It wasn't improving his attitude toward the laws of his native land.

Loeffler's staff and Native American Rights Fund legal team spent hundreds of hours researching the Indian Reorganization Act of 1934, the federal statute that established tribal councils and gave them the authority to enter into contracts. The law formed the basis for Peabody's contention that the Hopi and Navajo councils had the right to sell mineral leases on reservation land.

Loeffler's researchers found a critical flaw in Peabody's claim: the 1934 law never actually authorized tribal councils to sell or lease Indian land. In fact, the legislation did just the opposite—it only gave the councils power to prevent land sales. In other words, there was no need to question the validity of the Indian Reorganization Act, as some traditional tribal elders had done. The lawyers could happily accept the authority of the act—then show how it rendered the Black Mesa mining contracts legally void.

Meanwhile, the defense fund was coming up with clear evidence to show that the promises of wealth and prosperity for the Indians—the political basis for the mining agreement—were nothing but empty lies. Officials from Peabody Coal and the Interior Department pointed to a coal-fired power plant in the Four Corners area as a prime example of how Black Mesa's coal, burned in another new plant, would create lucrative Indian jobs. But the plant, researchers learned, employed just 240 people, and only 80 were Native Americans. With 130,000 Navajos and 5,000 Hopis living in the region, another 80 jobs would be no great bonanza.

In 1969, as the mining operations got under way, an official of the Bureau of Indian Affairs put the actual benefits from the mining into perspective. If the Hopi tribal council members had known Peabody was just "going to pile mountains of dirt and leave it," the official said, "you couldn't have got that lease for any amount of money."

What the new power plants did provide was serious air pollution. Before the Four Corners plant went into operation in 1964, Shiprock, a famous natural landmark in the area, was visible from 125 miles away. Within a year, locals were complaining that when the wind was wrong, visibility dropped to one hazy mile. In 1966, their complaints were confirmed from the sky: astronauts discovered the plume of smoke belching from the power plant to be the only phenomenon in the United States that was visible from outer space.

The information Loeffler found most disturbing was the role of the federal government in promoting the Black Mesa mine. The Interior Department, which by law was supposed to protect the environment and watch out for the interests of Native Americans, turned out to be a partner in the deal.

The Bureau of Indian Affairs, which approved Black Mesa lease deals, answered to Interior Secretary Stewart Udall. But so did the Bureau of Reclamation—which had a 25 percent partnership in the Navajo Power Plant. The bureau put up part of the cash for construction, and in exchange got a share of the electrical output, which it could sell on the open market. Revenue from the sale of that power provided a significant part of the bureau's budget. The cheaper the plant could buy coal, and the less stringent the air-quality standards, the more power it could generate—and the more money the government could take in.

In other words, Udall would be undermining his own interests by interfering with the Black Mesa coal mine or demanding strict controls on the emissions from coal-burning plants. There was no point asking the government for help, Loeffler decided: the system was rigged against him.

His instincts were only confirmed when he traveled to Washington to testify before the congressional subcommittee. He'd been asked to outline the problems with the Black Mesa agreement, but when he walked into the hearing room, Sam Steiger, a conservative Republican from Arizona, seized the floor and spent forty-five minutes attacking Loeffler, calling him "the arch-enemy of the environmental movement." By the time the congressman finished, the committee was running short on time; Loeffler never got a chance to speak.

After a bit of reflection, he decided to back off from the courts and Congress for a while, and take his case to a very different forum. Just as Gaylord Nelson had done when frustration with Washington overwhelmed him a few years earlier, Jack Loeffler decided to hit the college lecture circuit.

The message Loeffler would deliver to the next generation of environmental activists was very different from anything Senator Nelson—and for that matter, much of the rest of the environmental movement—had ever really imagined, certainly not as a serious political strategy. Loeffler had decided to share some of his wildest dreams and present them as a legitimate form of environmental action. When he thought about it, the concept didn't seem that wild at all.

The audience at Ohio State University was fairly typical—mostly young, mostly white, and easily bored by abstract political theory. Loeffler watched some of their eyes glaze over as he launched into the semantic underpinnings of his thesis—the distinction between terrorism and sabotage. Terrorism, he explained, was always bad, like the indiscriminate bombing of Vietnamese civilians. It was killing and destruction for no reason other than personal or political gain. Sabotage, on the other hand, could have a sound moral basis. Destroying a gun to keep terrorists from shooting someone might be a very good idea.

And in that case, he continued, it might be entirely reasonable, even proper, to go out some night and sabotage the engine of a bulldozer, so that coal miners couldn't use it to destroy the spiritual center of the Navajo and Hopi universe.

As a matter of fact, Loeffler announced with a twinkle in his eye, ecological sabotage was not only morally correct—it was sometimes a whole lot of fun. As always, at the mention of fun, the collegiate audience began to perk up.

For many of the students who attended Loeffler's lectures, violent property destruction in the name of ecology sounded like a crazy, radical concept. Loeffler had long considered the Fox—the mysterious saboteur who had plugged the chemical waste pipe in Illinois—as something of a hero, even a role model. But the assault on Armour-Dial's sewer line was relatively mild, easily repaired—the act was symbolic, designed to attract attention. Nobody had ever heard the Fox stand up in public and proclaim the moral imperative of destroying construction equipment or derailing coal trains.

In ten years, however, the idea of "ecotage" would be gaining widespread attention, and considerable respect, within the mainstream of the environmental movement. And the leading eco-saboteurs would count Jack Loeffler (along with his old friend, a writer named Edward Abbey) as the source of their earliest inspiration.

Students and future activists weren't the only ones paying attention to Loeffler. As he spoke to the Ohio State students, he kept watching the man in the gray suit, standing at the back of the auditorium. He recognized him instantly: the same man showed up at all of Loeffler's lectures. He always wore the same gray suit, and his face was always expressionless. He always stood in the back of the room, staring at Loeffler and occasionally taking notes.

In the spirit of political fun, Loeffler stopped his speech and pointed the man out to the audience. "This gentleman must be a serious fan," Loeffler deadpanned. "He follows me everywhere I go." The students turned and stared. The stranger stayed at his post, stone-faced as ever.

You can always tell an FBI guy, Loeffler told himself. They've got no sense of humor.

PART 3

POLITICAL SCIENCE

Science will overcome all things,

even the human emotions.

—Ming the Merciless

If only I had known,

I should have become a watchmaker.

—Albert Einstein

The U.S. environmental movement had a strange relationship with science.

Some of the earliest American environmentalists were scientists. John Muir, the legendary Sierra Club founder, was a brilliant inventor who studied geology and botany at the University of Wisconsin. Five of the first nine directors of the Sierra Club worked in the natural sciences. Gifford Pinchot, who founded the U.S. Forest Service, studied scientific forest management at Yale. Rachel Carson, whose book helped spark the modern environmental movement, was a biologist.

But at the same time, environmentalists recognized early on that science had created many of the problems facing the planet—and the nation's unbounded faith in modern technology had allowed the ecological crisis to get out of control.

Since the Age of Enlightenment, scientists had, by and large, taken the position that humans could be divorced from the natural world. Over the next three centuries, science took an increasingly mechanistic view of nature, breaking the world down into smaller and smaller parts and looking at creatures, objects, and events as individual items.

In the early 1970s, however, as the environmental movement began changing American politics, American science was undergoing a revolution of its own. Increasingly, scientific experts were taking the side of the environmentalists in crucial policy debates. Some were even making a truly radical statement: average citizens, not just experts, should be making the tough choices about scientific and technological developments like genetic engineering, nuclear power, and chemical production.

No hazardous material could ever be contained safely 100 percent of the time—and if that material were sufficiently deadly, shouldn't the general public, not just the scientists, decide if the potential value was worth the risk?

But on some of the broadest scientific issues, the experts—even the staunchly environmentalist experts—remained bitterly divided. The divisions reflected the classic, historic splits in the scientific and environmental communities: Could improved technology allow industrialized nations like the United States to continue enjoying a life-style based on unlimited, cheap energy and abundant natural resources? Was the world approaching natural limits to growth?

12

THE CRACKPOT

The *Shackleford* pitched and rolled in the heavy North Atlantic swells. On the damp, windy deck, the lone passenger steadied himself against a railing and began waving a small metal box in the air, letting the stiff ocean breeze blow through the holes he'd cut in the sides. The routine had been going on for days, in all kinds of weather, ever since the ship steamed out of London. He was taking measurements, Jim Lovelock told the crew—atmospheric measurements. The box was a sensitive scientific instrument that picked up tiny changes in the air. It worked perfectly, he said; after all, he made it himself. He called it a "gas chromatograph."

If the sailors on the *Shackleford* weren't impressed by the device, Lovelock could take it in stride. His family had never been too impressed, either. When he pulled his invention out on a vacation trip to the Irish countryside, the relatives called it a "gas pornograph." Then they laughed, a good-natured version of the ridicule he'd heard so many times, from so much of the scientific establishment.

For a physician, biologist, and professor with impeccable academic credentials, Lovelock had built quite a reputation for sounding like a nut. He'd also shown flashes of creative genius. The gas chromatograph turned out to be one of the most important environmental research tools of the era— Rachel Carson, for example, used it to collect the data for *Silent Spring.* Royalties from Lovelock's patents on other unconventional devices were enough to support his wife and kids and pay for the upkeep on a modest home and lab.

In the early 1960s, the United States space agency hired him away from an English university to work at the prestigious Jet Propulsion Laboratory, which was looking for life on Mars. The project was somewhat unusual; Lovelock's methods were entirely weird. While his colleagues tried to study the Martian landscape, Lovelock pretended he was living on the Red Planet, and set out to study the Earth. By the time the government called off his research, Lovelock was well on the way to developing a radical new theory that had nothing to do with extraterrestrial life—and that would push him to the fringes of modern scientific thought. He decided that the Earth was alive.

The concept was startling in its logic and simplicity. From an imaginary seat on Mars, it looked as if the Earth were regulating itself, making minute internal adjustments to maintain its internal health. It was acting like a living thing.

Lovelock hadn't finished writing up his living planet theory when he set sail for South America aboard the *Shackleford,* a converted freighter that Britain's Natural Environment Research Council was sending on a voyage to Antarctica. The theory was on hold for the moment, while he pursued another, more immediate venture. A class of artificial chemicals called chlorofluorocarbons, Lovelock was convinced, had escaped from the major industrial regions of Europe and North America and were circling the globe, floating on air currents thousands of miles from their point of origin. If he could track the chemicals across the Atlantic Ocean, maybe he could convince others that he was right. The last time he tried, he'd gotten nowhere.

Lovelock had been thinking about chlorofluorocarbons—CFCs—for several years, ever since he started seeing a smoky haze appear over the remote Irish countryside where his family had a vacation home. When Lovelock was growing up, he remembered, the air at the cottage had always been crystal clear. He brought the homemade gas chromatograph up to the cottage, and it revealed some interesting evidence: There were traces of CFCs in the air outside the cottage. The closest factory that made the material was in London, far beyond the range most scientists believed airborne pollution could travel. The CFCs weren't causing the smoky haze; as far as Lovelock knew, they were basically harmless. But they were easy to identify—and unlike coal fumes or most other industrial emissions, they could be traced back to a limited number of sources. The chemicals were nice atmospheric footprints, tracks that would let researchers follow dirty air from a city like London as it made its way around the world. It seemed like important news.

But when Lovelock called London to discuss his findings, government officials insisted his claims were impossible. All the major scientific journals rejected his papers on the subject. The foundations and universities refused to underwrite any further research. When he finally convinced a small academic magazine to publish his article, the response was a deafening silence. Everyone seemed to think he was crazy.

Lovelock was sure he was onto something. If the evidence from Ireland wasn't good enough, he decided, then he'd go even further from the centers of civilization, and look for even more. If he could find CFCs out in the Atlantic, hundreds of miles from anywhere, he'd have evidence that nobody could ignore. He took a leave from his teaching job, packed up the gas chromatograph, and convinced the government-sponsored Natural Environment Research Council to give him free passage on a ship bound for Antarctica.

The results of the voyage were all he could have hoped for. The evidence was strong, consistent, and clear: from the English Channel to the South Pole, the air was littered with chlorofluorocarbons. This time, *Nature,* one of the world's leading scientific journals, would publish Lovelock's conclusions: a harmless chemical used in everything from refrigerators to Styrofoam provided startling new information about atmospheric circulation patterns and the spread of industrial pollution.

At the time, Lovelock had no idea that he'd overlooked one of the biggest environmental crises of the twentieth century.

13

TOO MANY PEOPLE

June 4, 1972
Stockholm, Sweden

Jack and Katherine Loeffler stood nervously with the four Hopis and two Navajos at the Swedish customs and immigration counter. The customs official, looking perplexed, examined Thomas Manyaka's passport. The document was distinctly not issued by any major government agency: it had the homemade look of a grade-school arts and crafts project, a couple of pieces of cardboard wrapped in buckskin, with an eagle feather hanging off the edge. Handwritten letters on the back of the leather cover asserted that "The Owner of this Passport is a Citizen of the Hopi Independent Nation. This Passport is Valid as Long as the Sun Shines, the Water Flows and the Grass Grows."

The official shook his head and asked where this motley crew might be going. To Stockholm, Loeffler said; they were headed for the United Nations Conference on the Human Environment.

The customs officer smiled and waved them through.

The Stockholm conference held the promise of being the most important environmental gathering in history. The United Nations had finally recognized the importance of environmental issues; that alone was a major breakthrough. With delegates from more than a hundred countries and dozens of heads of state on hand, the attention of the world would be focused on the environmental crisis. Some advocates called the conference a turning point in global politics, a moment when civilization woke up to a looming threat and began taking action to stop it. Nobody in the young movement wanted to miss it.

When Loeffler heard about Stockholm, he decided the Hopi nation needed to be represented. The rest of the world had to know how the United States government was treating the Indians at Black Mesa, he insisted—and more important, the concerns of native peoples needed to be part of the environmental agenda. He just had a little problem: the Hopis from Black Mesa considered themselves citizens of a sovereign nation; they refused to get United States passports. So Jack and his wife Katherine sat with the Hopi leaders and fashioned some passports of their own. The approval of the Swedish customs authorities was a small victory, but Loeffler was jubilant— the way the Black Mesa battle was going, any victory at all was cause for celebration.

The Black Mesa Defense Fund wasn't the only unofficial delegation arriving at the conference. Hundreds of other activists had the same idea: more than four hundred "nongovernmental organizations" would be on hand when the conference opened, many without any formal invitation. Conference organizers initially worried about security—mixing large numbers of unaccredited, unsupervised, and probably uncontrollable people with ambassadors, dignitaries, and world leaders was a security official's nightmare. But they realized there was no point in trying to stop the influx, so they arranged for camping and meeting facilities and established an "Environmental Forum" outside of the main conference to allow the uninvited guests a chance to join the debate.

For two weeks, Stockholm was the center of the environmentalist world. The roster of unofficial visitors from the United States read like a who's who of the young environmental movement—everybody who was anybody, or could round up the price of a plane ticket, seemed to have made the trip.

The official U.S. delegation was much smaller, and its makeup reflected the lukewarm interest President Nixon had shown toward environmental issues. The senior delegate, EPA administrator William Ruckelshaus, wasn't even a member of Nixon's Cabinet. The United States ambassador to the United Nations, George Bush, missed the entire event. In fact, the most powerful American at the conference was probably Robert McNamara, president of the World Bank, an agency notoriously unconcerned with environmental issues.

Inside the official conference, discussions were bound by cumbersome diplomatic protocols, and progress was slow. Still, by the end of the conference, the delegates had established the United Nations Environmental Program, marking the first time in history that the world's major governments gave their formal support to an international environmental watchdog.

Outside, the talks were faster, less organized—and to the participants, far more exciting. An international community of grassroots environmentalists met for the first time in the conference rooms and campsites of the Stockholm Environmental Forum, and the connections they made would last for years. The staff of David Brower's Friends of the Earth published a daily conference newspaper, called *ECO,* reporting on the leading speeches and debates; it quickly became the unofficial conference record.

The issues at hand were almost endless, from the fate of the SST (still a raging battle in Europe) to ocean pollution and international whaling regulations to an emerging crisis called "acid rain," which was poisoning the European countryside. But on every level, from the formal conference chambers to the late-night campfire circles, the same single problem came to dominate discussion: the explosion in human population. Grassroots activists, government officials, and scientific experts asked the question over and over: Could ever-increasing numbers of people, and the economic and industrial expansion needed to feed, clothe, and shelter them, peacefully coexist with a healthy environment?

Two American scientists, Paul Ehrlich and Barry Commoner, took center stage in the debate.

For a man who was fast becoming a media celebrity, Barry Commoner acted remarkably staid and reserved. He spoke with a slow, deliberate style, shuffling around Stockholm in rumpled suits and looking for all the world like an obscure college professor.

But Commoner had always been something of an enigma. Over the years, the brilliant, cagey biologist had earned a reputation as a strong environmental advocate who advanced some radical theories. He was also known for backing up his arguments with rock-solid scientific research. Commoner had a way of packaging tantalizing bits of his work that were just right for newspapers and magazines—he'd recently been featured on the cover of *Time* magazine. At Stockholm, he set off a furor that showed some of the deep divisions in the way environmentalists approached science and technology.

Commoner had just published a book called *The Closing Circle,* a frightening account of impending ecological disaster that was selling like hotcakes. The United States, the author argued, was rapidly poisoning itself with the toxic by-products of industry. Many plant and animal species were already dying off. Soon, the book proclaimed, the American way of life would lead to widespread human death.

Commoner wasn't the only scientist issuing dire warnings about the fate of the Earth. A group of eminent researchers known as the Club of Rome, with the backing of the Massachusetts Institute of Technology, had just released *The Limits to Growth,* a dense, scholarly work that was creating quite a stir in political and academic circles.

"If the present growth trends in world population, industrialization, pollution, food production, and resource depletion continue unchanged," the book asserted, "the limits to growth on this planet will be reached sometime within the next one hundred years. The most probable result will be a rather sudden and uncontrollable decline in both population and industrial capacity."

A lot of people were impressed by the academic credentials of the Club of Rome, and were alarmed by the group's predictions. But not Barry Commoner.

On the second day of the Stockholm Conference, Commoner told a large crowd that the Club of Rome had reached bogus conclusions by failing to take into account some "fundamental" economic factors. His own research was much more thorough, he insisted, and his conclusions were much more reliable.

Although his speech focused on the obscure sort of details that often framed scientific debates—questions over the accuracy of data and the quality of analysis—it marked a more fundamental schism in the environmental movement. Commoner, for all his radical claims, held closely to one of the deepest traditions of American philosophy. Growth was good, he argued. Limits on population and industrial expansion would only lead to economic decline and human misery. The problem wasn't a lack of resources—we were just using our resources badly. Better technology could change all that: more could be made with less. Pollution could be reduced and environmental damage repaired without any reduction in living standards. With a little help, Third World countries could share in the wealth.

Commoner argued, for example, that with the right economic incentives, American ingenuity could easily produce cars that ran on electric power instead of gasoline. The same thing could happen with solar energy, and recycling, and pollution-free consumer products.

Nobody from the Club of Rome was in Stockholm to answer Commoner, but Paul Ehrlich made sure the remarks didn't go unchallenged. Although the two never met face-to-face, their scientific and political dispute was one of the highlights of the conference.

Ehrlich was almost as famous as Commoner. He hadn't made the cover of *Time,* but he was fast becoming a regular on television talk shows, and his landmark 1968 book *The Population Bomb,* a grim look at the prospects awaiting uncontrolled population growth, had sold several hundred thousand copies.

Ehrlich took issue with Commoner's basic premise. He argued that science and technology, no matter how enlightened, would never save the day. The problems were too basic: the planet was running out of raw materials. Minerals, oil, and gas reserves—nonrenewable resources—dwindled every day. Most animal populations showed signs of severe stress, as did the land, water, and air they lived on. The planet couldn't support many more people, not without widespread famine and ecological disaster.

The dispute reflected two fundamentally different views of the way human civilization fit into the natural world. Barry Commoner's scientific training gave him faith in limitless human potential; Paul Ehrlich's demanded acceptance of finite natural resources. To Commoner, people represented the best hope for an ecological future; to Ehrlich, people were the single biggest problem.

That same philosophical debate, although often smothered under religious intolerance and political ignorance, would simmer beneath some of the most important environmental issues of the next twenty years. Almost always, Commoner's scientific view would prevail—and almost always, his policy suggestions would be ignored. The world's population would keep growing rapidly and political leaders would continue expressing their faith in the next generation of scientific advances to solve the world's problems. Ehrlich's dramatic projections of resource scarcity would turn out to be somewhat overstated, and would be dismissed by critics as hysterical and unfounded.

The millions of people who starved to death every year would be noted as a tragic loss.

On the day the conference ended, a rented truck pulled up to the door of the empty meeting hall that had hosted the environmental forum. A small mountain of unread fliers and pamphlets covered the floor, offering at least a hundred ways to save the planet from at least a thousand environmental ills. Most of the material was in English.

The collective leadership of the U.S. environmental movement had gone home and left a giant mess behind. Jack Loeffler decided to stick around and clean it up.

Something about the trash heap annoyed him, and as he opened the truck doors, he realized it had been bothering him for the whole two weeks. So many activists had put so much energy into the conference, and after two weeks, the only obvious result was a giant wastepaper mound.

Loeffler had been as excited as anyone when the conference started, and he found the discussions fascinating. But as the days wore on, he began to wonder whether all the precious time and money he'd devoted to the event could have been better spent back home. Congressman Sam Steiger, according to the latest reports, had just introduced a bill that would take even more Black Mesa land from the Navajo and Hopi tribes, and drive thousands of Indians away from their traditional homes to make way for even more strip-mining. By now, Loeffler figured, Steiger probably had all the votes he needed to pass the bill—and none of the lofty resolutions or stimulating debates in Stockholm would make the slightest bit of difference.

In fact, Loeffler was beginning to wonder whether any of the environmental organizations he'd seen were making any real difference. Organizations got bogged down in details, and wasted a lot of time arguing over internal politics. Organizations tried too hard to preserve their own existence, and lost track of their original goals. Organizations held conferences and printed leaflets that wound up in somebody's garbage.

On a fundamental level, Loeffler decided, the Black Mesa Defense Fund had done what it set out to do. The Navajo and Hopi had learned a good bit about fighting with the white man's system. The struggle had become a political issue within the environmental movement. The Indians could speak for themselves on Steiger's bills, and the rest was in the hands of the lawyers. Jack Loeffler was ready to shut down his office and start doing his political work alone. Quietly. In the middle of the night.

Loeffler shoveled all the environmental literature into the back of the truck. Then he hopped in the cab and took off for the Stockholm city dump.

14

GENESIS

November 1972
Honolulu

One of the most important scientific breakthroughs in modern history began with a couple of corned-beef sandwiches in a delicatessen 2,500 miles from home.

Herbert Boyer was a rumpled thirty-six-year-old veteran of Berkeley's antiwar movement who taught at the University of California in San Francisco. Stanley Cohen was ten years older, an intense, driven researcher with a lab at the Stanford University Medical Center in Palo Alto. The two gifted biochemists lived and worked less than an hour's drive apart; they barely knew each other's names.

But both happened to attend a scientific conference in Honolulu, and on a typically balmy night, after a long day of listening to detailed presentations, they happened to meet for a midnight snack in a Waikiki deli. The conversation turned to work—and within minutes, Boyer and Cohen were scribbling notes on a paper napkin, laying the groundwork for a genetics experiment that would startle the world.

Four months later, a single microscopic bacterium from a harmless species called *E. coli* that lived in the human intestine was doing something few of its natural relatives had ever done before: it was surviving an assault of streptomycin, an antibiotic that normally killed bacteria on contact. The microbe Boyer and Cohen had created wasn't a mutant, or a hybrid; it didn't have any biological parents. The tiny organism was a totally new form of life.

Inside its genetic material, the bacterium carried a genetic implant, a piece of reproductive material plucked from another species. In this case, part of the gene that made a different bacterium resistant to antibiotics was spliced into an *E. coli*—and when the experiment was over, the new creation was vigorously producing the chemical that rendered streptomycin ineffective. Soon, the two researchers would go even further—they'd splice a gene from a toad into a bacterium, giving a tiny microbe some of the cellular characteristics of a hopping, breathing animal.

Most important, when the altered bacteria divided and reproduced, they reproduced the implants, too.

The physicists who turned Albert Einstein's theory of relativity into a controlled nuclear reaction gave the human race control over the most powerful force in the known universe, the energy of the atom. Cohen and Boyer were unleashing a technology far more profound—and in some ways, far more frightening.

The experiment they had concocted looked on the surface to be relatively simple. They just spliced together two unrelated pieces of genetic material. Chemists routinely spliced different atoms together to form artificial substances, like plastics; biologists routinely combined different types of seeds and crossbred different types of animals to create better strains of plants and bigger, stronger livestock. But those scientists only tried to tinker with nature, to work with natural processes and improve on the final products—and even so, as Rachel Carson pointed out, the results were often disastrous. Cohen and Boyer were going a big step further.

The roots of Cohen and Boyer's breakthrough went back to 1957, when two British scientists named James Watson and Francis Crick discovered the structure of the genetic material called DNA, the basic building block of life. Scientists had known for years that molecules of DNA, or deoxyribonucleic acid, contained the entire genetic code that allowed living things to reproduce. Somehow, within the structure of the complex molecule, millions of pieces of information were stored—information that determined the precise characteristics of every living entity. The DNA code determined precisely which characteristics an individual would inherit from its ancestors; it controlled everything from whether an embryo would develop feet, wings, or hooves to the eventual color of its hair, skin, and eyes.

If scientists could crack that code, and figure out how to change it, they could, in theory, create monkeys with wings—or fruit that would never rot, or bugs that would eat oil spills. Potentially, they could find the human genetic code that caused blindness or diabetes, and alter it before an infant was born. Watson and Crick took the first step: they figured out what a DNA molecule looked like. It was shaped like a long, twisted ladder, a "double helix," with two strands of material connected by millions of different "rungs." When a cell reproduced, the ladder "unzipped" down the middle, and the precise chemical structure of each of the rungs provided the template for the genetic makeup of the offspring.

It took the scientific world sixteen more years to make the next big leap, to turn the Crick and Watson theory into working technology. But once Cohen and Boyer figured out how to cut open a section of DNA and splice in a new piece of coded material, the information spread quickly. The technology was still very crude: scientists barely understood how the genetic code worked, and had no idea which bits of information stored in which parts of which DNA molecule would affect which characteristics of a species or individual. Philosophically, the implications were profound—the basic foundation of the modern science of biology, Darwin's theory of evolution, would become irrelevant if people could mix and match pieces of genetic material from plants and animals at will.

Environmentally, the potential impacts were just as staggering—if inorganic chemicals like DDT could wreak havoc on an ecological system, what could the accidental (or intentional) introduction of a new living creature do?

One of Cohen's colleagues at Stanford, Paul Berg, who worked in a lab upstairs, was pursuing a similar experiment on similar bacteria when he began to wonder about that exact question. The *E. coli* bacteria that were used in both experiments multiplied at a dizzying rate; within twenty-four hours, a population of a few artificial bugs could turn into tens of thousands. Since they thrived in the human intestine, any strange new form of the bacteria could spread through contact with food or water, breeding rapidly and potentially infecting millions of people in a short period of time.

As far as Cohen, Boyer, and Berg knew, the engineered life-forms they were trying to create would be completely harmless. But no matter what the scientists said in public, most agreed privately that they had no idea exactly what they might be setting loose on the world.

Stanley Cohen wasn't terribly concerned—biologists worked with dangerous materials, including disease-causing microbes, on a regular basis. Careful lab techniques, he believed, would make the chances of any outbreak minimal. "What we're talking about," he told reporters at one point, "are hypothetical dangers that have never happened."

But even the thought of it scared the hell out of Paul Berg. By the time Cohen and Boyer made their historic leap, Berg had decided to stop playing God. He would soon be spending a good deal of his time trying to convince the rest of the scientific world to think about this fabulous new advance—and to take it slow and easy.

15

OUT OF COURT

July 13, 1973
Washington, D.C.

By the time Gaylord Nelson took the floor, every member of the United States Senate had heard almost every possible argument for and against every version of the bill known as S. 1081. Every member understood the complex political stakes—the oil companies and labor unions supported one version of the bill, and they were among the biggest campaign contributors and most influential lobbyists in the nation. Some big midwestern industries and regional newspapers supported a different version, and for hometown senators, they were an equally powerful force. Some environmentalists opposed the entire bill; some realized it was going to pass, and were fighting for the best possible amendments.

But even after months of public discussion, a series of committee hearings, and volumes of expert testimony, Senator Nelson was convinced that the real issues were being ignored. "To this day," he told his colleagues, "energy, economic and environmental factors of great public concern in the Alaska oil issue have not been fully and comprehensively addressed by the oil industry or the U.S. government.

"Instead, the facts have been clouded and confused by a massive oil industry propaganda campaign designed to scare Congress and the public into rubber-stamping the Alaska pipeline, granting energy fuels price increases, and permitting a stronger industry monopoly.

"In short," he concluded, "the whole history of the Alaskan oil pipeline proposal is a classic study of how not to make an intelligent, publicly responsive energy policy decision."

*　　*　　*

The issue before the Senate was a direct result of the lawsuit Jim Moorman and David Brower filed over the Alaska pipeline. Several other organizations had joined the fray, and the legal wranglings had been immensely complicated, but the bottom line was simple: the federal courts agreed that the plaintiffs had standing to sue, and that the secretary of the interior had no right to issue the pipeline permits. The Mineral Leasing Act of 1920 set limits on the size of a pipeline right-of-way, and the one the oil companies wanted to build in Alaska clearly didn't comply.

In February 1973, the U.S. Court of Appeals for the District of Columbia Circuit issued a permanent injunction blocking the pipeline; the Supreme Court refused to hear the case, letting the decision stand. The pipeline was dead—for the moment.

But Senator Henry Jackson of Washington, the powerful Democrat who chaired the Interior Committee, took up the cause, introducing a bill that would supersede the old Mineral Leasing Act and give the interior secretary sweeping authority to approve rights-of-way for oil and coal pipelines and to authorize the construction of oil shipping terminals on federal land.

That would eliminate the only major obstacle the courts had put in the pipeline's path—so far. In its original form, however, the bill wouldn't solve what the oil companies and administration officials thought was a potentially larger problem: the threat that environmentalists would continue to challenge the adequacy of the pipeline's environmental impact statement.

Moorman, and the lawyers from the Environmental Defense Fund and the Wilderness Society who joined the suit, had raised that issue from the start, and it played a key role in Judge Hart's original injunction. But the 1973 appeals court decision, the one that had the final force of law, didn't even address the matter. There was no need to evaluate the environmental impact statement, the court concluded, "since the project will be enjoined in any event under our ruling on the Mineral Leasing Act issues."

The oil company lawyers and their allies knew full well that the pipeline foes would take that as an opening to raise the issue again if the Jackson bill passed. Already, the companies and the Interior Department had spent more than $9 million preparing an EIS; the lengthy report was packed with technical analyses and scientific conclusions, any of which could be challenged in a lawsuit. Experts from one side would argue with experts from the other; the litigation could drag on for years. The longer it dragged on, the more expensive the pipeline would get, and the more time opponents would have to find ways to block it. For political reasons, too, delay was the last thing the oil companies wanted. The summer of 1973 was a perfect time to mobilize public opinion in support of the pipeline. For the first time since World War Two, Americans were waiting in long lines for gasoline. Without new oil supplies, the companies warned, the lines would just get longer.

Most environmentalists knew that the Mineral Leasing Act of 1920 was ripe for revision, that the size of the pipeline right-of-way was one of the less-important problems with the project. It was a legal gimmick, and chances were good that Congress would overturn it. By July, the real fight wasn't so much over the Jackson bill as over a series of amendments that would exempt the pipeline from any further legal challenges brought under the National Environmental Policy Act.

There were two major alternatives. An amendment offered by Senator Mike Gravel of Alaska would simply take lawsuits out of the picture; it gave the interior secretary authority to approve the Alaska pipeline and issue the necessary permits "without further action under the National Environmental Policy Act of 1969 or any other law." Senators Walter Mondale and Birch Bayh, with the support of some environmentalists, offered a competing proposal—in place of NEPA, Congress would ask the National Academy of Sciences to undertake an extensive environmental study on the pipeline and report back its findings within eleven months. Then Congress would have three more months to approve or reject the pipeline on the basis of the scientific evidence.

As the debate dragged on, the impacts of the pipeline on Alaska's caribou herds received some limited attention; so did the possibility of a pipeline rupture in the arctic wilderness. But there was virtually no discussion of the possibility that one of the tankers might run aground in the rocky sound just off the port of Valdez. That seemed the least of the Senate's concerns: Interior Secretary Rogers Morton had already announced that the Alaska oil tankers would all have double hulls, and the pipeline consortium insisted it would be able to contain any spill quickly and easily.

The decision came down on July 17, and like many critical Senate votes, the official question on the floor seemed ridiculously technical. Formally, the issue was a motion to table a call for reconsideration of a vote on an amendment that took place when several senators were out of the room. In reality, everyone knew the outcome would determine whether Gravel's amendment would become law, whether NEPA would take a serious beating, and whether the pipeline would go ahead without any environmental delay. The battle was so close that Vice President Spiro Agnew made a rare personal appearance shortly before the vote; for a few minutes, he assumed his formal position as president of the Senate—with the power to cast the deciding vote in the event of a tie.

As the packed gallery watched, with all one hundred senators in their seats, the clerk called the roll. And when the last senator had spoken, the count was even—fifty for, fifty against. The vice president put the pipeline over the top.

David Brower immediately called Moorman. The director of Friends of the Earth was sure the bill was unconstitutional, that the one-time NEPA exemption would never hold up in court. Moorman agreed there might be a case, but it would take a lot of money, and since Friends of the Earth didn't have anywhere near the resources, the Wilderness Society and the Environmental Defense Fund, which funded much of the earlier litigation, would have to be on board. It wouldn't be an easy fight—politically or legally. Very few Americans had ever been to Alaska, and not many cared that much about its icy wilderness. But everyone was sick of the lines at the gas stations.

The two big organizations didn't want to discuss it. They'd already made a decision: the fight was over.

16

COMMUNITY
SERVICE

July 1973
Montgomery, Illinois

The five men met around eleven P.M. They were mostly strangers—the sailor didn't know the biologist, who didn't know the teacher, who didn't know the off-duty police officer. But they all knew the person who had brought them together this evening to assist in performing a small community service. They all knew the Fox.

The pollution coming from the asphalt plant on the edge of town constantly violated air-quality standards. The owners received repeated citations, paid them off, and continued fouling the most communal of properties, the air. For the good of the greater society, the members of the group agreed, the plant owners needed to be disciplined.

The Fox and the cop had made an agreement. If his police colleagues showed up while the crew was at work, the cop would begin arresting them, as though he'd just caught them by surprise. If they were going to get busted anyway, there wasn't any point in a cop who supported them taking a fall, too.

The Fox grabbed a padlock out of his bag and headed for the electrical box on the side of the factory wall. He opened the box, threw the switches that cut off all power to the plant, and then locked the box shut. The others were busy locking up the doors and plugging the smokestack. The whole process only took a few minutes; by midnight, the five had finished their work and had dispersed.

When the police investigated, they'd never trace the locks back to the Fox or anyone else in the group. The cop had gotten them from an ex-convict, who had filed off all the serial numbers.

Of course, it wouldn't take long for plant employees to hacksaw their way inside. Most likely, the factory would be back in business the same day. The asphalt inside would have cooled down during the night, with all the power off, and it would take a while to heat up. The delay would cost the owners a few bucks; maybe it would send them a message. Just to be sure, Ray left a note with his trademark foxhead signature, advising them to clean up their operation if they wanted to keep making money in Montgomery.

The scheme might not work. The company might just absorb the cost, go on with business as usual and get a night guard, maybe even hire a private detective to try to track the Fox down. On the other hand, the technique had worked before.

The Armour-Dial discharge pipe was running a lot cleaner than it had been before the Fox plugged it back in 1969. The river was making a little recovery. It might not have been all the work of the Fox, but certainly the attention he'd focused on the problem had helped considerably. And the response from the community had been remarkably positive.

The Fox had become a modern outlaw legend. At Armour-Dial, he'd done what the politicians wouldn't do, and the law-abiding people of Montgomery couldn't help but notice it. His actions hurt nobody, save for the red-faced company officials. The diverse crew he had assembled tonight was a sign of the widespread support a conservative midwestern town could muster for this new style of environmental action.

Years later, when other groups would come together hundreds of miles away to plan what they called "monkeywrenching" and "ecotage," they'd look back at the mysterious character called the Fox, and wonder who he was and why he'd been driven to his unusual line of work. They'd wonder how he managed to do what nobody else ever could—convince upstanding, con-servative midwestern citizens to take the law into their own hands in the name of environmental protection.

None of the prominent activists who followed in his footsteps would ever get to meet the Fox. None of them ever knew his real name. But many would agree that he was their first inspiration, the one who set the standard for a generation of monkeywrenchers that would change environmental politics forever.

17

A FISHING TRIP

August 12, 1973
Knoxville, Tennessee

Professor David Etnier had no idea what he was about to unleash on a warm summer afternoon when he and a student strapped on diving masks and snorkels and waded into a shallow stretch of the Little Tennessee River, near a place called Coytee Springs. For the most part, it was a routine field trip. Etnier was an ichthyologist—a fish scientist—and he was constantly sticking his head under the waters of the abundant streams and rivers of eastern Tennessee to see what sorts of aquatic creatures were living there. In this case, there was just a touch of urgency: no ichthyologist had ever bothered to investigate the aquatic life of the Little Tennessee—and since the Tennessee Valley Authority was preparing to build a new dam on the last free-flowing stretch of the river, there wasn't a lot of time left.

Fish fascinated Etnier—fish you could catch, fish you could eat, and fish that were just obscure entries in scientific textbooks. He'd grown up with a fly rod in his hand, on the edge of one of Minnesota's twenty thousand lakes, and by the time he was ready to finish his graduate work in zoology at the University of Minnesota, he was fishing for national trophies. When the University of Tennessee at Knoxville offered him a teaching job in 1965, he considered the pay, the reputation of the school, and the prospects for advancement. Then he read the rules for a major fishing contest in *Field & Stream* magazine, and made up his mind right away.

The contest was open to all anglers who had landed a ten-pound trout—except those from Tennessee, who had to land a fifteen-pounder. In Tennessee, apparently, ten-pound fish were no big deal. It sounded like Etnier's kind of place.

And in fact, the new assistant professor of zoology quickly learned that he was living in one of the richest, most diverse fish habitats in North America. It was also rich in human history.

More than eight thousand years before the white settlers arrived, Cherokee Indians had found their way to the hickory and oak forests of the Little Tennessee Valley; they named one of their villages Tanasi, "the place of flowing waters." The great Cherokee leader Sequoyah was born in a village called Taskigi, a few miles upstream, near the ancient town of Chota, the last great spiritual center of the Cherokee nation. In 1838, the United States government forced most of the tribe to leave, driving thousands of men, women, and children along the legendary "Trail of Tears" to a reservation in Oklahoma. But a few Cherokee slipped away, hiding out in the Great Smokies, and more than a century later, their descendents still made pilgrimages to the valley's ceremonial landmarks and ancient gravesites. In the late 1970s, a report by government archaeologists would label the valley a place of "worldwide historical significance."

In the meantime, several generations of American farmers had taken advantage of another priceless asset: the valley's rich, fertile topsoil. In some areas, the layer of dark, moist earth was as much as twenty-five feet thick, and it provided some of the most productive cropland in the eastern United States. In fact, the quality of the topsoil had helped preserve the quality of the river: since the farmers needed virtually no artificial fertilizer, there was virtually no chemical pollution running off from their land.

By the late 1970s, the quiet valley would be the center of one of the most emotional environmental battles in American history. The conflict would turn an obscure little minnow into a national celebrity and set off a bitter, divisive debate over the value of endangered species, the appropriate use of environmental law, and the role that environmental concerns should play in the nation's economic development.

It would also become one of the most misunderstood, poorly reported, and grossly sensationalized political issues in modern American history.

The Tennessee Valley Authority was one of the great success stories of Roosevelt's New Deal, and after four decades, it still held legendary power over the Appalachian region. The architects of the New Deal set out to bring a deeply depressed, backward region into a new era of modern prosperity, and to a considerable extent, they succeeded: vast public-works projects put hundreds of thousands to work. A string of giant dams tamed the wild rivers, ending the constant devastation of floods and providing cheap hydroelectric power to millions of homes, farms, and factories. The TVA directors had unusually broad authority to create and approve their own projects, and they pursued their mission with considerable zeal: the agency dammed more than 2,500 linear miles of river, creating dozens of giant reservoirs and giving the state of Tennessee more fresh-water shoreline than all five Great Lakes combined.

For an entire generation, TVA was the largest employer in the state of Tennessee; in 1973, it still had 58,000 people on the payroll. But the aging engineers and bureaucrats who so proudly ruled such a vast domain for so many triumphant years were starting to face an ominous problem: they had succeeded. Appalachia had all the dams and electric power that it needed. The economic development business had changed; there wasn't much left for the old-fashioned TVA to do. But the old guard wasn't ready to retire, and didn't want to listen to criticism. One agency staffer called it a case of "institutional menopause." The TVA directors insisted that there were still some big projects on the drawing boards, and they went to considerable lengths to justify those conclusions. The Tellico Dam, proposed for the mouth of the Little Tennessee River, was by far the most outrageous example.

At first, the agency described Tellico as a flood-control and hydroelectric dam, but floods were no longer a problem, and the dam itself would generate no electricity. Then the agency declared that the area was blighted, and promoted the dam as an economic development project. But that made no sense, either: even by TVA's own initial figures, the loss of a vast strip of productive, fertile farmland and the costs of buying out the farmers, rerouting local roads, and building the dam far outstripped any discernible economic benefits. Ultimately, staff economists were given a clear directive to find some conceivable reason to justify the dam—and after a few left the agency in disgust or disgrace, the rest came up with an alternative plan, resting on the notion of a new resort community called "Timberlake."

The idea was as bold and daring as anything TVA had attempted in years. The agency would buy up 38,000 acres of land, and flood 16,500 behind the dam. The remaining 21,500 acres would be resold to private developers, who would turn the former farmland into industrial parks and recreational facilities, all surrounding a new town of fifty thousand people, which would spring up on the edge of the artificial lake and "demonstrate the latest concepts of a high-quality urban environment." The Boeing Corporation was slated to build Timberlake, with extensive public subsidies, which TVA officials promised to extract from Congress. The total bill would run between $250 million and $800 million—none of which was included in TVA's cost estimates for the Tellico Dam project.

The whole thing sounded foolish to a lot of people, including the governor of Tennessee, who initially urged TVA to scrap the plan. But the state's congressional delegation saw a big advantage to the project: by the time it was finished, more than $60 million of federal money would pour into Tennessee. And a lot of construction companies, cement contractors, road builders, engineering firms, trade unions, and real estate developers would be very grateful to their benefactors in Washington. With the help of Howard Baker, Tennessee's powerful Republican senator, Congress approved initial funds for the Tellico Dam in 1967, and appropriated more money every year. By 1971, TVA had spent $29 million; the concrete foundation was finished and new roads were under construction.

Late that year, the Environmental Defense Fund and two local conservation groups filed suit under the National Environmental Policy Act, charging that the project's environmental impact report was inadequate. The evidence was fairly clear: in its rush to promote the benefits of economic growth, the TVA had paid little heed to the environmental costs and ignored any realistic alternatives. Even the East Tennessee Economic Development Association, not a particularly conservation-minded group, complained that the EIS ignored the impact of sudden, large-scale urbanization on a distinctly rural area that lacked sufficient utilities and services to handle another fifty thousand full-time residents. Federal Judge Robert Taylor issued an injunction on January 11, 1972, halting all work on the project until a new, acceptable environmental review was complete.

The injunction lasted sixteen months. When Taylor dissolved it, environmentalists were deeply frustrated—they'd hoped the delay would give them time to find another cause of action. They'd hoped something else would come up.

David Etnier had testified as an expert witness in support of the NEPA suit. He'd always considered the dam a bad idea—after all, it would ruin a world-class trout fishery—but when he appeared in court, he went a step further. He told the judge that he'd heard of some eight or ten types of rare and unusual fish that lived in the Little Tennessee. The issue wasn't mentioned in Taylor's written decision, but it put Etnier's scientific mind in a new gear: the truth was, he realized, he didn't really know exactly what was living in the Little Tennessee. By August, he couldn't put it off any longer. For the scientific record, and his own curiosity, he had to go take a look.

The scientific fishing trip didn't take long.

On his first dive, Etnier noticed a tan, three-inch fish nestled into the sandy river bottom—and in the clear, shallow water, he could tell immediately that it was one for the record books. It was clearly a member of the family Percidae, and was a type of fish known as a darter. More than a hundred varieties of darters had been identified, eighty or ninety in Tennessee alone. It took years of training to recognize them all—and it took Dr. Etnier about three seconds to recognize that this one was distinctly different.

Etnier scooped the wiggling creature up in his hands, and by the time he got back to the lab, there was no doubt in his mind: a unique little fish was swimming around in the Little Tennessee River. By the time a panel of scientists from the Smithsonian certified his discovery, Etnier had learned a lot more. The species lived on tiny snails, and survived only in clear, cool, well-oxygenated water. The entire population in the Little Tennessee numbered roughly ten thousand; it had been seen nowhere else on the planet Earth.

Etnier's scientific colleagues called it by the formal Latin name of *Percina tanasi*. Everyone else called it the snail darter.

18

OUT OF GAS

November 8, 1973
Washington, D.C.

The president of the United States was in serious trouble. All summer long, millions of Americans were glued to their televisions, watching a special committee of the United States Senate investigate a second-rate burglary that turned into a first-rate political scandal. The Watergate hearings dominated national news like no event in years—and as summer turned into fall, Richard Nixon was on the ropes, clinging to the presidency with a grim determination as a growing number of opinion leaders began calling for his resignation.

But early in November, Watergate was suddenly pushed off the front pages. The nation—and for the moment, the president—had something more important to worry about. A foreign crisis was threatening the American way of life.

For the first time in peacetime history, the United States was running out of a key natural resource. For the first time ever, the citizens of a peaceful United States were going to have to accept limits on their standard of living. The crisis would become a defining event in environmental politics.

At 7:30 P.M., Eastern Standard Time, Nixon stared into the television cameras and began to talk. He looked haggard; his skin was puffy, and his eyes were sunk deep in their sockets. But his voice was clear and firm, his manner confident as he wished the nation good evening.

"I want to talk to you about a serious national problem," he said. "A problem we all must face together in the months and years ahead.

"We are heading," the president explained, "toward the most acute shortages of energy since World War Two."

When Richard Nixon was born, in 1913, the United States produced all its own energy. The leading fuel was coal—the mines in Appalachia, the Great

Lakes region, and the western hills provided almost 70 percent of the nation's energy needs. Petroleum—oil—made up less than 10 percent. But since the turn of the century, coal usage was in decline, and oil consumption was growing fast.

At first, the United States seemed to have abundant supplies of oil. The plains of western Texas and Oklahoma were tremendous oil fields. The underground pools were so full that you didn't have to pump: the oil burst out of the wells in "gushers," and the biggest problem was trying to contain the flow for long enough to put a tap on the end of the pipe. Until 1947, the United States exported more oil than it bought from abroad.

By the early 1970s, though, a substantial portion of U.S. oil was imported. The nation was using more than sixteen million barrels of oil a day—and domestic fields were producing less than ten million barrels. But although the nation's appetite for oil had grown immensely, American oil wells were still capable of meeting most of the demand. The steady growth in imports was largely a matter of economics: crude oil from the Middle East or South America was cheaper than the oil produced at home.

When the war between Egypt and Israel closed the Suez Canal in 1967, tankers from the Persian Gulf had to travel all the way around the tip of Africa to get to the United States, and prices temporarily soared. Some critics warned that the incident showed how dangerous it was for the United States to rely so heavily on the Middle East for such a crucial commodity. But demand kept rising, and importing Middle Eastern crude was the most profitable way for the oil companies to meet it.

Military clashes were not the only threat to the nation's oil supplies. Economic and political factors were starting to shape up as even more of a hazard. In August 1960, after Standard Oil of New Jersey brazenly announced it was cutting the price it paid for imported crude, the Venezuelan oil minister called together leaders of thirteen major oil-producing countries and convinced them to engage in collective bargaining. The Organization of Petroleum Exporting Countries became perhaps the largest and most powerful cartel in the world, and as the United States and other industrial nations of the West increased their reliance on imported oil, OPEC's power continued to grow.

On October 17, 1973, in the bustling metropolis of Kuwait City, the leaders of ten Arab nations issued a stunning communiqué: unless the United States agreed to stop helping its ally, Israel, which was at war with its Arab neighbors, the flow of oil to the West would be slowly cut off. In the meantime, the price would almost double, effective at once.

Oil company profits were probably not the only reason the United States had been doing more and more business with OPEC. The oil companies gave a succession of White House officials a back-door way to do something the American public would probably never tolerate: fund a massive arms buildup for both Israel and the Arab states.

Israel had tremendous political support in the United States. The tiny Jewish nation had few natural resources, and was surrounded by hostile enemies. So Congress sent billions of taxpayer dollars to the Israeli government every year, to aid civilian projects and equip a sophisticated military machine. But protecting Israel wasn't the only goal of U.S. foreign policy in the Middle East. As the Cold War dragged on, Washington officials became increasingly worried about Soviet expansion in the region; after all, it was right on the Soviet doorstep. Some argued that a well-armed bloc of Arab nations, with growing, healthy economies that depended on continued commerce with the United States, would provide a powerful bulwark against the Communist threat.

Of course, since the Arabs were constantly fighting with the Israelis, the United States government couldn't openly help them buy weapons or build modern industrial facilities—and since U.S. foreign policy officially condemned the Arab nations for trying to wipe out Israel, government officials couldn't openly act too friendly.

The oil companies, however, were another matter altogether. Under the laws of the United States, private corporations were generally free to do business with anyone they wanted. When it came to doing business overseas, those corporations often worked very closely—and very privately—with the State Department and the CIA. In the case of oil imports, the companies had a special incentive to do business in the Middle East: a little-known tax loophole allowed them to pay large royalties, or export fees, to the OPEC nations—and write those fees directly off their U.S. tax bills. Every dollar that went to the oil-producing countries was a dollar the U.S. companies didn't have to pay to the federal government; the "royalties" were, in effect, a direct transfer of money from the U.S. treasury.

By the early 1970s, the oil companies were sending $150 million a year to Saudi Arabia, Iran, and Kuwait, courtesy of the American taxpayer. A lot of money went to pay for an unprecedented Arab military buildup; a lot of the weapons came from private arms manufacturers in the United States. The higher the price of oil, of course, the higher the royalty payments. It would not be much of an exaggeration to say that the oil price hikes of the 1970s amounted to a huge subsidy by the American people for a covert foreign policy most of them bitterly opposed.

President Nixon didn't talk about the politics of the Middle East, or the ways his administration had left the country open to just this sort of attack. He did what millions of his fellow Americans would do in the years to come: he blamed OPEC. "The Middle Eastern oil producers have reduced overall production and cut off their shipment of oil to the United States," he explained. "By the end of this month, more than two million barrels a day of oil we expected to import into the United States will no longer be available. Our supply of petroleum this winter will be at least ten percent short of our anticipated demands, and it could fall short by as much as seventeen percent."

Then he set out a series of proposals that would change the lives of virtually every man, woman, and child in the United States.

Temperatures in all public buildings would be reduced to 68 degrees. Gasoline would be scarce, and more expensive. Speed limits on major highways would be cut to fifty-five miles an hour. Daylight savings would be extended into the winter; children would walk to school in the dark so electricity would be saved for the peak hours of business use.

Nixon insisted that many of those conservation measures, and the suffering they caused, would only be temporary. The United States, he told the nation, was not going to accept a reduced standard of living. The nation would soon become energy self-sufficient—by increasing its domestic energy supplies. Environmental standards would have to be relaxed, so that new domestic energy projects, like the Alaska pipeline, could move forward faster. More nuclear power plants would have to be built more quickly. American know-how would ultimately solve the problem, he asserted, just as it always did. If all went according to plan, he announced, by 1980 the United States would not need foreign oil to meet its energy needs.

In reality, the oil price hikes of the 1970s would devastate the United States economy, fueling steep inflation, reducing disposable income, and destroying tens of thousands of jobs, mostly in blue-collar industries. The goal of energy independence would remain elusive. The oil companies would reap record profits.

But the energy crisis would also force the American public to begin facing a fact that much of the nation had tried to ignore: oil was a limited resource, and someday the industrial world would have to learn how to live without it. As oil prices kept rising, the environmental movement would be able to make some significant advances by showing that "alternative energy" sources, like solar and wind power, were not only cleaner but cheaper. And slowly, grudgingly, government agencies and even private utilities would start to recognize that the best and cheapest alternative of all was simple conservation.

For the moment, though, much of the United States was stunned by the crisis, and willing to take the president at his word. "My concern has been to lay before you the full facts of the nation's energy shortage," Nixon announced. Then he spoke briefly about Watergate, vowed to remain in office, and bid the nation good night.

19

KILLER CANS

December 1973
Irvine, California

Mario Molina kept checking the numbers in front of him, looking for some embarrassing mistake that would explain how he'd gone so far astray. The figures couldn't be right; it was too unbelievable. Simple research projects didn't generate such startling results. Young chemists with freshly minted doctorates certainly didn't jump to profound conclusions like the one that kept spinning around in the back of Molina's head.

And yet, time after time, the numbers told the same exact story. There was nothing more he could do by himself. Heart pounding, he took the paperwork and went to find Dr. Rowland.

Sherwood Rowland was the chairman of the Chemistry Department at the University of California's Irvine campus. He was known all over the world for his work in radiation chemistry, but was losing interest in that field, and had been looking for something else to pursue. He stumbled on to a potential subject in 1972, at an atmospheric research conference sponsored by the Atomic Energy Commission; when he got back to campus, he put his post-doctoral assistant to work on it.

What Rowland had picked up was an early version of a paper scheduled to be published several months later in the highly respected journal *Nature*. The paper discussed the atmospheric levels of a class of compounds known as CFCs; the author, a maverick British biologist named James Lovelock, said the chemicals might provide an excellent way to trace the way air pollution moved around the globe. The CFCs themselves, he noted in passing, posed "no conceivable hazard."

Rowland wasn't so sure. He'd done some research a few years earlier on the way chemicals reacted to light, and he suspected that CFCs might start to break apart in the upper atmosphere, under the bright glare of the sun—and some of the chemicals that were left over might not be so harmless at all. The more he thought about it, the more the question intrigued him: Where did all those chemicals end up, anyway?

Rowland listened carefully as Molina described what he'd found. It was certainly surprising, the professor agreed; it was probably just a mistake. But all night long, and all the next day, both men kept checking the work—and finally, like Molina, Rowland admitted he could find no errors. The research was all straightforward, the chemistry relatively simple, the math completely correct. Unless something was terribly wrong—something he couldn't see or imagine—Rowland was on the verge of announcing the most important discovery of his long and productive career. It would bring the two men lasting fame, make Rowland a superstar in the world of science and Molina the envy of his peers. But neither seemed terribly happy.

"The work is going very well," Rowland told his wife that evening. "But it looks like the end of the world."

Rowland was deadly serious. What he and Molina had discovered was frightening: CFCs, which poured out of factories, air conditioners, and spray cans by the ton in cities all over the industrialized world, were rapidly destroying the Earth's natural sunscreen.

A thin layer of ozone in the upper atmosphere was all that stopped powerful solar rays from frying the planet's surface to a crisp. Ozone, a natural, relatively unstable form of oxygen, collected miles above the Earth, where the air pressure was low and the particles spread far apart: at sea level, the entire ozone layer would be less than half an inch thick. But this sparse veil of molecules filtered out ultraviolet light—an invisible, high-energy form of solar radiation that could potentially wipe out most forms of life on Earth. Even a relatively small amount of damage to the ozone layer could have a dramatic effect: the increased radiation could kill the microscopic ocean plankton that were the basis of a significant part of the global food chain. The radiation could destroy agricultural crops, too—and it would almost certainly cause a marked increase in the amount of human skin cancer.

Rowland and Molina weren't the first to notice that the vital protective shield was in possible danger. In the late 1950s, a few scientists measured the ozone layer, and found it thinner than they'd expected. In 1970, a meteorologist named Paul Crutzen published a paper suggesting that nitrous oxide, a common chemical released by burning flares, animal flatulence, and the anesthesia used in medical and dental offices, appeared to break down ozone. The theory never got much attention—there wasn't that much nitrous oxide around, and if anything, its use was tapering off. The issue made a big political splash during the SST debates, but once the SST died, so did a lot of the interest. After all, the plane wasn't going to be flying, so the ozone wasn't in danger.

The new information was very different. CFCs were considered a technological wonder, used in everything from hair spray to refrigerators. So much had already been released into the air that a fair amount of ozone damage was probably unavoidable. Preventing a major global disaster would require a political effort of immense proportions, an immediate, drastic reduction in one of the world's most popular chemicals.

Millions of people would have to take the scientists' word and give up useful products that had no visible impact on the environment—and at best, if the effort was completely successful, nobody would be able to tell the difference.

20

POISON POWER

September 17, 1974
Greenfield, Massachusetts

The Franklin County Superior Court hadn't seen this much attention in years. Day after day, from the opening gavel to the final recess, Judge Kent Smith's courtroom was packed. Reporters from all over the country were showing up early to be sure to get a seat.

It wasn't a sensational murder case or a celebrity divorce. The defendant was charged with a fairly small-time felony, and he didn't have a famous lawyer or a prominent family name. The crime was property destruction, dismantling a steel utility tower that housed meteorological instruments. The perpetrator had turned himself in minutes after completing the deed.

But something very unusual was happening in Judge Smith's court. A young organic farmer from a small hippie commune was trying to put commercial nuclear power on trial. And after nine days of emotional testimony, Sam Lovejoy was starting to think he might actually get away with it.

Lovejoy was never the crusader type. He had been a quiet, introspective child, the son of an Army officer. He grew up moving from base to base, never spending more than a couple of years in the same town. When Lovejoy's father was killed in combat, the family settled on a small farm near Springfield, Massachusetts.

Sam developed an interest in science and spent most of his high-school years studying math and physics. He enrolled at Amherst College, and when he took his degree in 1968, he joined a group of young back-to-the-land hippies who were setting up a commune in a quiet rural town on the edge of the Connecticut River.

Montague, Massachusetts, was a relic of a bygone era in New England

109

history, a community that had outlived the textile mills and factories of the nineteenth century and never quite found a new niche in the modern economy. Twenty miles south, a cluster of colleges and universities helped Northampton grow and prosper, but the benefits didn't extend up the river; Montague was too far away to become a suburb. Unemployment was epidemic. The population was aging; most of the kids moved away as soon as they were able. Long-term economic prospects were bleak. Farming was difficult.

For the young and idealistic folks who founded the Montague Farm, these weren't serious drawbacks. The farm was big enough to support at least thirty people, and even in the summer, the population never went much beyond twenty. The commune-dwellers were all healthy, educated people, devoted to an alternative life-style and a radical social vision; they grew crops without fertilizers or pesticides, heated their houses with wood-burning stoves, and shared all the wealth equally. They put a tremendous amount of energy into making the operation work, and after a rough year or two, it did just fine.

Early in 1973, while folks at Montague Farm were busy cutting wood for their stoves and planning the summer's crop, a delegation from Northeast Utilities Corporation paid the town of Montague a visit. The utility executives met with village selectmen and business leaders, and over steak dinners on the company tab, they floated out a proposition.

Northeast Utilities was looking to build a large nuclear power plant along the Connecticut River. Montague could be the perfect place.

The way the executives described it, the project would be a tremendous boon to the local economy. Construction would create thousands of jobs, and operation and maintenance would create hundreds more. The plant would generate millions of dollars in tax revenue for city government, and the company would pour countless millions more into building new streets, water pipes, and sewer facilities.

It would solve all of Montague's problems, well into the next century.

The site that NU had in mind was a barren square-mile tract overlooking the river on the western side of town. Montague Plains, as the lot was known, had just what a nuclear power plant needed—plenty of space and a virtually limitless supply of water. The plains were also a natural aquifer: a deep bed of sand and gravel underneath the land filtered the runoff from rain and snowstorms and fed clear, clean water into the river below. When a company from Boston tried to turn the site into a garbage dump, the townspeople rebelled, citing possible damage to the fragile ecology of the Connecticut watershed.

But the landfill project had only minor economic benefits. The nuclear plant would increase the local tax base by a factor of thirty. Property values would soar.

The civil leaders of Montague embraced the plan wholeheartedly.

In December 1973, Northeast Utilities made it official. Montague, Massachusetts, would be the home of a major nuclear power station. In fact, announced the company proudly, the project would be even bigger than originally planned: with two reactors and a generating capacity of 2,300 megawatts—enough to provide electricity to more than three million homes—it would be the largest plant of its kind ever constructed. The projected cost: $1.52 billion.

The local newspaper published an aerial photo with an artist's rendering of the plant superimposed on the site.

When Harvey Wasserman picked up the *Greenfield Recorder* and saw the graphic image of a giant power plant looming over the Montague Plains, he had a sudden feeling that his life was about to change.

Wasserman hailed from Columbus, Ohio, the scion of a relatively prosperous family and the heir-apparent to a moderately successful business selling uniform clothing and shoes through a mail-order catalog. But the family business didn't excite him; by the time he finished college, he'd decided to pursue a career as a journalist and historian. He signed on with a journalistic experiment called Liberation News Service, designed to provide an alternative to the Associated Press; when it all blew up in a factional dispute, he moved to the Montague Farm, with the modest goal of rewriting American history.

Wasserman had become friends with Sam Lovejoy at the farm, and the two of them quickly agreed that this nuclear power business needed a lot more study. At the quiet hippie commune, the high-school science whiz and the radical historian spit on their hands and went to work.

The nuclear power business, Wasserman and Lovejoy came to learn, was born in a frosty Cold War dawn, when the scientists and political leaders who developed the atomic bomb went looking for a peaceful way to harness the awesome power of their frightening new technology.

Since the late 1930s, physicists had known that a tremendous amount of energy could be released—in theory, anyway—by splitting atoms.

The concept was fairly simple. Atoms were made up of three types of particles: electrons, protons, and neutrons. Electrons were wisps of electrical energy, orbiting like vaporous moons around a central core made up of protons and neutrons. The particles in the core, known as a nucleus, clung tightly together, bound to each other by an unknown force far more powerful than anything else in the universe. If those subatomic particles could be broken apart, the energy of the binding force would be released, all at once, in a fire hot and bright as a microscopic sun.

If millions of atoms were split at once, in a giant chain reaction, with broken fragments flying off in all directions and shattering everything in their path, the energy released would be incredible—greater than anything science fiction writers had ever imagined. It would be an inexhaustible power source, one that could transform society forever.

*   *   *

In the summer of 1939, Albert Einstein, at the urging of several of his colleagues, warned President Roosevelt that Germany was building an atomic weapon that could let Hitler rule the world. Neither Einstein nor Roosevelt knew that the threat was greatly exaggerated, that Germany was years away from developing an atomic bomb. So Roosevelt did the obvious thing. He marshaled the military, industrial, and scientific resources of the United States for the most ambitious technological effort in human history. The code name was "The Manhattan Engineering District," but it quickly became known as the Manhattan Project.

At a cost of $2 billion, the top-secret research and development team created the bombs that destroyed Hiroshima and Nagasaki, and ended the Second World War.

By then, Germany had surrendered, and Adolf Hitler was dead.

The American public was slow to react to the human carnage at Hiroshima and Nagasaki. After all, the Japanese had launched a sneak attack on Pearl Harbor and forced the United States into the war; tens of thousands of American soldiers died in the Pacific Theater, at places like Guadalcanal, and Okinawa, and Iwo Jima. If the Japanese didn't want to get bloodied, they never should have picked a fight.

But the carnage from the Hiroshima blast was awful. More than 100,000 died, the lucky ones instantly incinerated, the less lucky condemned to a slow, agonizing death from radiation sickness. Vast stretches of what was once a major city were reduced to ashes and dust.

It was hard to imagine the Japanese missing the point at Hiroshima. And it was hard to imagine a valid military reason for dropping the second bomb on Nagasaki.

Truman swore to his dying day that he never felt any guilt for ordering the two bombs. But he was unusual; many of his advisers—and quite a few of his constituents—felt at least somewhat queasy about unleashing such a terrifying force of destruction. Even before the bombs fell, some of the scientists and politicians were beginning to look for a brighter, more noble mission. There had to be a way to harness the power of the atom for a peaceful and prosperous world.

The same thoughts were floating around the executive offices of some of the nation's largest industrial corporations—for a very different reason.

By some estimates, as many as half a million people were involved in building and operating the industrial infrastructure that produced the Hiroshima and Nagasaki bombs. Three entire cities had been constructed from the ground up. And when the Japanese surrendered, the whole operation ground to a sudden halt.

There had to be a way to turn that tremendous wartime investment into a profitable peacetime business.

By 1953, several major companies, including General Electric and West-inghouse, had figured out the commercial potential of generating electricity with nuclear reactors. The next year, under intense pressure from industry, Congress amended the Atomic Energy Act to allow private ownership and development of nuclear power plants.

The nuclear plants that Westinghouse and General Electric developed had the same basic structure as the old-fashioned plants that burned coal and oil. Essentially, the nuclear reactors were a fancy way to boil water.

In theory, nuclear reactors had some obvious advantages over coal and oil burners. The fuel would be cheap—a small amount of uranium lasted a long time. And reactors wouldn't release clouds of black smoke into the air.

Potentially, nuclear reactors could power cars and trains, and even rockets to explore the cosmos. The power of the atom could change the world, eliminate the human suffering that resulted from the scarcity of energy and the resources to produce it.

But there was a serious drawback. Reactors used, and created, large amounts of radioactive material. And that radioactive material was some of the most poisonous stuff on Earth.

The private companies that would build and operate the nuclear power plants knew just how dangerous this new technology could be. The insurance companies did, too—when the underwriters started imagining the potential of a reactor accident, they refused to issue liability coverage.

In 1957, the nuclear industry solved the problem neatly. Industry exec-utives convinced Congress to pass the Price-Anderson Act, which limited the total liability of any company operating a nuclear power plant to $60 million. If an accident did occur, and claims were higher than that, the government would pick up the tab.

On February 22, 1974, Sam Lovejoy got out of bed early. The fields of northern Massachusetts were still deep in their winter slumber; ice covered much of the Connecticut River, and the frozen ground was buried beneath a thin layer of dry, crusty snow. The night air was clear and crisp as Lovejoy left Montague Farm. It's Washington's birthday, he told himself: a great time to start a revolution.

Lovejoy stayed off the road as he made his way toward Montague Plains, an empty, six-hundred-acre tract on the eastern edge of the river. Even on a cold night, it wasn't a bad walk—maybe a couple of miles, no more—and Lovejoy knew the area well enough to get around it blindfolded. At about three A.M., he slipped onto the plains; a few minutes later, he reached the base of the tower.

Lovejoy leaned back and took a long look at the giant iron skyscraper that loomed over the quiet little New England town. Four big legs anchored the tower to a cement foundation; a latticework support structure zigzagged upward, 550 feet into the air, where a bright red beacon blinked on and off, bathing the dark landscape in an eerie light.

Somewhere up there, Lovejoy knew, a set of fancy instruments and meters was hard at work, recording every last scrap of data about the local weather—wind, temperature, humidity, air pressure, and anything else the engineers at the electricity company might find useful when they set out to build their nuclear power plant.

It's the beginning of the end, Lovejoy told himself. The power company was going to ruin his life—and he wasn't going to make it any easier for them. He pulled a crowbar and a wrench from his shirt, and got down to work.

He was amazed how easy the job was. A few bolts here and there, a little twisting and prying, and by sunrise, the mighty tower of utility power was reduced to a pile of tangled wreckage.

Lovejoy gathered his gear and ran down to the nearest road. He stood there for a few minutes, catching his breath in the frosty morning sun and thinking about the future of a nuclear-powered world. Then he flagged down a passing patrol car and asked for a ride to the nearest police station, so he could turn himself in.

The case of *Massachusetts* v. *Sam Lovejoy* got under way September 17. From the start, Lovejoy refused legal counsel, and insisted on representing himself.

Prosecutor John Murphy called a series of witnesses who testified to the basic facts of the case: The tower cost Northeast Utilities $42,500. On the morning of February 22, it was destroyed. And according to police, a man identified as Sam Lovejoy—the defendant—had appeared at the Turners Falls station and confessed to tearing it down.

But as the officer on duty that morning took the stand and read the written statement Lovejoy had given the police upon his arrest, the jurors and the gallery could sense that the case would not be quite so simple. "As a farmer concerned with the organic and the natural," the statement read, "I can find no natural balance with a nuclear plant in this or any community. . . .

"There seems to be no way for our children to be born or raised safely in our community in the near future. No children? No edible food? What will there be?

". . . It is my firm conviction that if a jury of twelve impartial scientists was impaneled, and following normal legal procedure they were given all pertinent data and arguments, then this jury would never give a unanimous vote for deployment of nuclear reactors amongst the civilian population. Rather, I believe they would call for the complete shutdown of all commercially operated nuclear plants."

Lovejoy's defense rested on the legal description of the crime for which he was charged: "Willful and malicious destruction of personal property."

The way Lovejoy intended to present the case, his act was entirely willful—but not the least bit malicious. His goal, he set out to tell the jury, was to prevent the far greater destruction of Montague Plains and the surrounding area that would result from the operation of a nuclear power plant.

When the prosecution rested, Lovejoy called his first witness: Dr. John Gofman.

Gofman's presence in the courtroom attracted tremendous media attention. He was one of the nation's most eminent scientists, a physician and physicist who played a central role in the Manhattan Project by isolating the first pure samples of the material used in the core of the bomb. And over the past few years, he had become one of the nation's most controversial scientific figures.

In 1962, the chairman of the Atomic Energy Commission, Glenn Seaborg, asked Gofman and a colleague, Arthur Tamplin, to conduct a rigorous study of the effects of nuclear radiation on human health. Gofman had all the right credentials—a medical doctor with a background in atomic physics, he had been one of Seaborg's best and brightest students at the University of California in the 1930s, and one of the famous Berkeley success stories in the postwar era.

Seaborg had chosen carefully—it was a critical assignment. Since the first radioactive material was discovered at the turn of the century, scientists, doctors, and government officials had debated the hazards and benefits of the mysterious and powerful force. By the early 1960s, the debate had become an uproar—and just about everyone involved was operating on a dearth of solid, scientific facts. To Gofman, the assignment was a clear mandate: find out the truth, and tell it to the world.

The bailiff swore John Gofman in, and Sam Lovejoy began his questioning. He asked the scientist to state his name, address, and occupation, and Gofman complied.

Then Lovejoy asked Gofman to define the term "nuclide."

Prosecutor Murphy objected immediately. The trial, he argued, was about a case of vandalism, property destruction. What possible relevance could this testimony have to the issue at hand? Judge Smith sent the jury out of the room, and asked the defense to explain.

Lovejoy launched into his carefully prepared argument. The case, he told the judge, is actually about malice, and malice was not in his mind when he tore down the Northeast Utilities tower. Long before he decided to destroy the tower, Lovejoy said, he had done some research into nuclear energy, and had read a book by Gofman, called *Poisoned Power*. The information in that book had influenced his decision to topple the tower; if his state of mind at the time was at issue, the testimony of the author was obviously relevant.

Smith was dubious, but clearly intrigued. He called a short recess, then returned with an unusual decision: Gofman could testify, for the record, while the jury remained out of the room. If Lovejoy was convicted, the testimony could provide the basis for an appeal.

In the meantime, it provided a great show for the media. Gofman had a powerful story to tell, and to those who had never heard it, the conclusion was absolutely stunning.

Radiation, Gofman acknowledged, was not a simple subject.

All sorts of radiation existed in nature. Visible light, the stuff that allowed us to see, was a form of radiation. So were heat, and radio waves, and the ultraviolet emissions from the sun that gave people nice tans, and awful burns. But the kind of radiation that concerned Gofman was a special type, called "ionizing radiation." It differed from heat, and light, and radio waves, and most other forms of radiation, in one very basic way: it had enough energy to make very strange things happen when it came into contact with living cells.

As Gofman explained, the natural chemistry that governed the processes of life was gentle and orderly. In the cells of plants and animals, atoms of various elements and compounds gradually interacted; big, complex molecules of sugar and starch were slowly broken down into smaller, simpler molecules, and as the bonds that hold the big molecules together broke, energy was gradually released. Some of that energy was used to bring other small molecules together, into the proteins and fibers that allowed living organisms to grow and develop.

Radioactive materials released a constant stream of tiny, high-speed, high-energy particles—"ionized" particles. When one of them burst into the delicately balanced system of a living cell, it could create what Gofman called "chemical and biological mayhem." The ionized particle became a microscopic "bull in a china shop," upsetting the natural balance and causing all manner of unpredictable damage.

Early research showed that ionizing radiation burned skin, made bones brittle, and caused hair to fall out. But those were only the immediate, surface effects. The most insidious danger of radiation was its ability to disrupt the sensitive process of cell division and reproduction, leading to runaway tumors, many of them fatal. Ionizing radiation caused cancer.

A certain amount of ionizing radiation occurred naturally—from radioactive elements and a few high-energy rays bombarding the Earth from outer space. So it was hard to say just what exposure to what level of radiation—from what artificial sources—would cause an individual to come down with cancer.

That was the problem federal officials were trying to grapple with when the Atomic Energy Commission asked Gofman and Tamplin to determine what level of exposure to radiation was an acceptable health risk—in the lab, in the workplace, and in the overall environment. Commission chairman Glenn Seaborg assured Gofman that the government was seeking a fair, unbiased scientific study. "All we want is the truth," Seaborg told his former student; whatever Gofman and Tamplin found, he promised, would be published verbatim.

By 1968, Gofman and Tamplin had reached a conclusion: No amount of radiation exposure could be considered "safe." Every bit of radiation added to the natural environment increased the chances of somebody getting cancer—and over a large enough population, like that of the United States, those chances could be measured in the statistical certainty of an increased number of deaths.

The numbers were frightening. The levels of radiation exposure that the government considered acceptable were at least twenty times too high, Gofman and Tamplin wrote. If the government continued to use those standards, 32,000 Americans would die of radiation-induced cancer—every year. A lot of those deaths would be directly linked to the expansion of the nuclear power industry.

The Atomic Energy Commission quickly disowned the report and cut off Gofman's funding. But in 1970, an editor named Robert Rodale, whose family publishing business specialized in organic gardening pamphlets, convinced Gofman to put his conclusions into a book. That was how Sam Lovejoy first learned about the dangers of nuclear power.

Gofman testified that nuclear energy could never be completely safe. The materials used to fuel the power plants—uranium and plutonium, for example—were so toxic that a few tablespoons could kill everyone on Earth. The by-products created by the nuclear reactors were almost as toxic.

Between the fuel and the by-products, hundreds and hundreds of pounds of radioactive material would be used every year by the growing nuclear power industry. Some of it would be dangerous for hundreds of centuries—and to prevent the kind of cancer levels Gofman and Tamplin predicted, 99.9999 percent of it would have to be handled flawlessly.

Year after year, from the first stages of mining, processing, and transportation to the eventual disposal in still-undetermined locations, less than one ten-thousandth of the myriad types of radioactive material from nuclear plants could be allowed to escape into the environment. It would have to be guarded perfectly, in peace and in war, through natural disaster and human error, for a thousand generations.

And that, Gofman told the Franklin County Superior Court, was just not humanly possible.

Lovejoy's trial ended a week after it began, when Judge Kent Smith returned from a lunch recess and suddenly sent the jury home. The indictment, he ruled, was legally flawed. The case was dismissed. The defendant was free to go.

After seven days of emotional testimony, with experts in science, history, and political philosophy discussing nuclear power, civil disobedience, and private property, the trial had come down to a legal technicality. Lovejoy was charged with "destruction of personal property," a felony that carried a sentence of up to five years in prison. But the local tax collector testified that the Northeast Utilities tower was assessed as "real property," and by law, destruction of real property was just a misdemeanor. The state had charged Lovejoy with the wrong crime. The jury of twelve ordinary citizens from Franklin County, Massachusetts, would never have the chance to decide whether Lovejoy had done the right thing, whether the dangers of nuclear power justified what would normally be called an act of vandalism. The deep, moral issues of individual action in the face of environmental disaster had been swept aside by the wording on a county tax bill.

Sam Lovejoy was furious.

The next day, Northeast Utilities made a startling announcement. Construction of the Montague Nuclear Power Station would be delayed for a year, perhaps a little more.

The problem, company president Lelan Sillan explained, was entirely financial. Projected costs had risen to $1.5 billion and the company only had about a third of that in available cash. With interest rates getting so high, the prospect of borrowing a billion dollars was a bit troubling; the company would need a little time to find the most attractive financing.

Charles Bragg, the chief public relations official at Northeast Utilities, told the *Greenfield Recorder* that political opposition just wasn't a factor: "We would have to go ahead with it, even if there was a protest movement mounted by the citizens of the area."

PART 4

THIS LAND IS OUR LAND

We abuse land because we regard it as a commodity belonging to us. When we see land as a community to which we belong, we may begin to use it with love and respect.

—*Aldo Leopold*

The pilgrims who arrived on the shores of America in the 1600s found a vast wilderness stretching west. As soon as they had carved out a stable society along the coast, they began to expand the frontier.

Every step was a struggle. Forests had to be cleared for farms and towns, rivers dammed for water and power, prairies plowed under to plant crops, hills mined for coal and minerals. Building a nation required a tremendous amount of raw material, but there was always more beyond the horizon—more lumber, more water, more fuel. And always, there was plenty of land.

It took almost three hundred years to settle the United States "from sea to shining sea." By the early 1900s, a few people were starting to realize the price we were paying for that progress.

The early debates over land use gave rise to one of the most important divisions in U.S. environmental history. The conservationists, like Gifford Pinchot and Theodore Roosevelt, argued that public land should be used as much as possible for human benefit. They agreed that some of the most choice and beautiful parcels, like Yosemite Valley in California, should be set aside as national parks. But they insisted that most of the land should be managed for "multiple use"—logging, mining, hunting, and cattle grazing, for example, along with hiking, fishing, and other forms of recreation.

The preservationists, like John Muir and Aldo Leopold, thought of nature less as something to be managed for human use than as something to be preserved for its own inherent value. The preservationists saw people as stewards of the land, not its conquerors and masters.

After the passage of the 1916 National Parks Act, the conservationist approach dominated environmental politics. It wasn't until 1964 that Congress passed the next major piece of preservationist legislation, the Wilderness Act. The law established that a few large tracts of public land would be forever wild, closed to any form of human activity other than the appreciation of nature.

By then, millions of acres of public land were open to use by private individuals and businesses looking to make a profit off its resources. Loggers cut trees in public forests. Miners staked claims on public hillsides. All over the West, ranchers let cattle loose to graze and fatten on the public range.

Until the early 1970s, not many people seemed to care.

21

THE COWS
COME HOME

December 15, 1972
Palo Alto, California

Johanna Wald put away the last pile of legal briefs and pulled out a copy of *Reader's Digest*. It wasn't her normal reading material, but on a Friday afternoon, after a long week of complicated research, a nice, simple magazine seemed like a welcome break. Besides, a friend had told her the latest issue had a story she might find interesting. Something about cows.

Wald skimmed the table of contents and flipped to a piece called "The Nibbling Away of the West." It was everything her friend had promised: the article described in clear, graphic detail how a simple farm animal was becoming one of the nation's most serious environmental disasters. Cows were turning the last great open spaces of the West into an ecological wasteland, the author argued. If the devastation continued at its current rate, millions of acres of land—public land—would become a new Sahara Desert.

The article was packed with statistics and documentation, material Wald had never seen before. More important, it quoted a former federal employee who seemed to know exactly what was going on—and why the government was letting it happen. It was exactly the break the young lawyer needed, the clue that would help her bring an obscure, old-fashioned land-use problem into the forefront of the new environmental struggle.

The campaign would also help the environmental movement make some new and powerful enemies.

For the first twenty-seven years of her life, Johanna Wald didn't know much of anything about cows. In the 1950s, in suburban Croton-on-Hudson, most people didn't bother to ask how the milk and hamburgers got to the store. Even in the stormy 1960s, when Wald went to Yale Law School, became a serious political activist, and pursued all sorts of political causes, the last thing she ever thought about was a cow.

She thought a lot about public interest law, however, and after graduation, when her husband landed a job in Palo Alto, California, Wald began looking around for a way to put her legal education to work for a better world. It didn't take her long to find out that a local law firm called the Natural Resources Defense Council was looking for another lawyer—or that the three cofounders, Ed Strohbehn, John Bryson, and Gus Speth, had been classmates of hers at Yale. And it didn't take long for them to offer her the job.

Wald's new colleagues had plenty of work. The firm was dedicated entirely to environmental law, and the roster of issues that might be addressed through the legal system was growing rapidly. Air pollution, wilderness, pesticides, toxic waste—Wald could take her pick of some of the most high-profile legal battles of the day. Instead, she decided to take on the most obscure environmental problem most lawyers had ever imagined: the effects of cattle grazing on public land.

It didn't take her long to realize she was on to one of the biggest scandals in the country.

The federal government, Wald learned, owned more than 600 million acres of land—about two and a half acres for every citizen. It ranged from the lowest point in the nation, on the floor of Bad Water Basin in Death Valley, to the highest, atop Alaska's Mount McKinley.

The largest holdings were scattered throughout the eleven western states, and were designated National Resource Land. These 177 million acres—an area the size of the entire eastern United States from the Mississippi River to the Atlantic Ocean—served what government officials called "multiple uses." Vacationers fished, rafted, hunted, and hiked in the wilderness. Lumber companies harvested millions of board feet of timber from the forests. Mining conglomerates leased the right to extract minerals and fuels like gold, silver, copper, nickel, gas, and oil.

But for the most part, the National Resource Land provided a grazing range for thousands and thousands of cows.

Cattle had been grazing on public lands since the 1800s, when the first wagon trains headed west. Through purchases and annexation, the United States had acquired billions of acres of empty land, and the government was eager to settle it. The Homestead Act of 1862 offered 160 acres to any citizen who would occupy it, and thousands lined up at the "land office" to take advantage of the deal.

The settlers claimed what seemed by eastern standards to be huge tracts, but quickly realized the land was too parched and rocky for crops. Cows and sheep could survive, but even a modest herd required thousands of acres of grazing land. At first, that didn't present much of a problem; most of the land was empty. The ranchers just let their herds roam freely across the open range.

By 1865, grazing on public lands in the West was a free-for-all. Cattlemen claimed large sections of land as their own, building giant ranches and running huge herds of cattle on public property. The laws were vague and poorly enforced. Border disputes were settled by gunfire; most of the time, the bureaucrats and politicians back in Washington never heard a thing about it. Before long, westerners came to see the use of federal land for unrestricted grazing as a right, not a privilege.

The years between 1865 and 1895 were known as "The Great Stampede." Ranchers let millions of cattle and sheep loose to forage. Cowboys became big businessmen, building giant ranching empires and snapping up hundreds of Homestead Act parcels under phony names. Some ranches gobbled up more than a million acres each, claming as many as 150,000 cattle under their brands. The infamous cattle baron Charles Goodnight illegally fenced three million acres of public range before President Theodore Roosevelt personally intevened and ordered the fences cut.

In 1934, Congress passed the Taylor Grazing Act, which gave the secretary of the interior the power "to stop injury to the public grazing lands by preventing overgrazing and soil deterioration, to provide for their orderly use and development, and to stabilize the livestock industry dependent upon the public range." But the law was enforced loosely, when it was enforced at all.

By then, the millions of cattle had taken their toll on the dry rangeland, transforming much of it into desert.

Herds of grazing cattle did more than just eat plants and grasses. Thousands and thousands of hooves trampled on the dry plains, crushing everything in their path and compacting the soil to the point where it couldn't hold water. The bacteria, mosses, and tiny plants that kept the soil spongy and moist died off. The larger plants and animals that depended on the moist fertile soil didn't last much longer.

The heavily grazed and compacted land lost 98 percent of the rainfall. Instead of soaking into the ground, the water formed pools and lakes that finally overflowed. Flash floods carried away precious topsoil, along with sharp sand and rock chips. Over the years, erosion gullies became trademark scars on the western landscape.

The implications, Wald discovered, were alarming. In the late 1960s, overgrazing in North Africa triggered the sudden growth of the Sahara Desert. It spread to the productive areas of six nations, killing most plant and animal life and causing a famine that cost hundreds of thousands of lives. By 1972, the same conditions were apparent on public lands in the West.

*   *   *

For six months, Wald studied cows and grazing. She figured out right away the people responsible for managing huge pieces of public land were more interested in helping out a few well-to-do ranchers than in preserving the western plains for future generations. But the more she learned, the more it confused her. The politics of grazing and western land use was immensely complicated; it would take her years to figure it all out. Before she could hope to pursue any form of legal action, she needed some expert advice.

The problem was, everyone she called—Bureau of Land Management employees, Department of Agriculture scientists, ranchers, professors at the land grant colleges—told her the same thing: nothing.

The *Reader's Digest* article told a very different story. The writer, James Nathan Miller, explained that the U.S. Bureau of Land Management was charged with making sure ranchers only grazed a safe number of animals on public lands. But the BLM reported to the secretary of the interior, who, Miller claimed, did everything corporate ranchers demanded. The article quoted a former BLM employee describing how the system worked: "In the words of range ecologist William Meiners (who last year quit the BLM in disgust), 'The rabbits have been put in charge of the pea patch.'"

Wald felt the case begin to crack open in front of her. The name of the writer even seemed familiar—she remembered that years ago, she'd sold her house in New York to a man named Nathan Miller. She called directory assistance, and got the number for her old address. Nathan Miller answered the phone.

Of course he remembered her. Yes, he wrote the article. Sure, he would be happy to help, and he thought William Meiners would be happy to help, too. He gave Wald Meiners's home phone number, and told her she should feel free to call.

Meiners was exactly the sort of expert Wald was looking for. He had forty years of experience as a range conservationist, starting with a degree in range management from Oregon State. He worked with the Forest Service in the 1930s and 1940s, then with the Soil Conservation Service and the Bureau of Indian Affairs, managing somehow to squeeze in a master's degree from Utah State. By the time he was hired by the BLM, he was a national expert in range conservation.

But these days, Meiners had nothing but time on his hands. After ten years with the BLM, ending in a stint as director of the Boise district, he had officially retired. In reality, he'd left because he'd been unable to settle a long-standing dispute: he believed the BLM was doing a rotten job monitoring grazing. In some areas, the situation was completely out of control. And his superiors wouldn't do anything about it.

Meiners listened patiently as Wald identified herself and explained what she was doing. The politicians and bureaucrats—Meiners's ex-bosses—might be violating the law, she said. With a little luck, she might be able to file a lawsuit under the new National Environmental Policy Act. It might even force the government to start protecting the public interest, instead of the ranchers' profits. She just needed someone on the inside, someone who could talk in detail about what was really going on on the open range. Would he be willing to help?

Sure, Meiners told her. He'd be happy to talk about grazing. It was all he ever talked about anyway.

22

THE OUTCAST

March 1973
Lincoln, Montana

Cecil Garland watched the most beautiful place in the world fade away in his rearview mirror. A few miles down the highway, and he missed it already—the Blackfoot Valley, the Scapegoat Wilderness, the snow-capped peaks of the western Montana Rockies . . . and the tiny town of Lincoln. He'd always think of it as home, he knew. If he hadn't picked a fight with the Anaconda Mining Company, he would never be leaving.

For years, Garland had been trying to stop the giant company from opening a new mining operation at a long-abandoned site called the Mike Horse Mine. In some ways, he'd been remarkably successful: so far, the mine was still closed, and a big chunk of the land around it had been designated a federal wilderness area. A freshwater stream had been saved, a toxic waste dump halted. A lot of towns would have called Garland a hero.

But not Lincoln. Closing down mines wasn't a popular cause in western Montana: the region was in a deep economic slump, and mining was one of the few industries that seemed to be creating any jobs. Garland's neighbors cared about wilderness and clean water, but the threat didn't seem so immediate—the northern Rockies were still pretty far from the crush of civilization. Everywhere you looked, there was plenty of wilderness left. But none of it did the people of Lincoln any good if they couldn't buy groceries and pay the rent.

In fifteen years, mining would be a major environmental issue in the western states, and a whole generation of activists would look back at Cecil Garland as a pioneer. But in 1973, Garland was caught in one of the environmental movement's most troubling dilemmas. His crusade was costing his community jobs—and that was costing him friends.

*   *   *

Much of the mountainous American West was settled by hard-rock miners. California was the first to attract attention; at the height of the Gold Rush, in 1849, a hundred thousand people flocked from east to west in search of their fortunes. Within twenty years, Montana and most of the other Rocky Mountain states were pockmarked with gold, silver, lead, and copper mines and the towns that grew up to serve them.

Like the cattle ranchers, the miners operated largely on public land. Thanks to a remarkable piece of legislation, the General Mining Law of 1872, miners had almost unlimited rights to stake claims, drill for minerals, and take anything valuable away, all for just a few dollars a year in fees.

The mines did horrible damage to the mountains around them. The hillsides were stripped of their trees to make room for enormous open mining pits, which left entire mountainsides unprotected against the ravages of erosion. Frenzied miners built roads, dug tunnels, and dumped waste with no regard for anything except the prospect of instant riches. The stampede into the mountains was without precedent: the numbers, the lack of planning, and the utter disregard for the local environment dwarfed any other single event in modern United States history. But the 1872 law made no provisions for cleaning up the mess.

The Mike Horse Mine was a typical example. From the 1880s until about 1940, miners sporadically extracted silver, lead, and zinc. In the course of carving out the underground shafts, the miners also brought up an assortment of other metals, like mercury, cadmium, and arsenic. Since there was less of a market for those metals, the miners just tossed them aside, in huge piles of rock and rubble.

A lot of those waste metals were extremely toxic—and over the years, the sun, wind, and rain leached them from the exposed piles, carrying the poisons into the streams and aquifers of the Scapegoat National Wilderness, and eventually, into the Blackfoot River. By the time Cecil Garland got into the act, the Blackfoot was in serious trouble.

Garland owned a general store in Lincoln, and the Mike Horse mess infuriated him: years before, Anaconda had closed the mine and walked away, leaving the people of Lincoln to deal with the contamination. Through much of the 1960s, Garland tried to force the company to clean up the site. He never had much success: under the General Mining Law, what Anaconda did was perfectly legal. But the campaign taught him a lot about politics, and when Anaconda came back with a new plan for the Mike Horse in 1968, he put that knowledge to work.

After more than twenty years, the company decided to reopen the mine. Under the new plan, miners would dam a portion of Alice's Creek, a Blackfoot River tributary, to form a pond that would hold the next generation of mining wastes. The clear, freshwater stream would become a toxic sludge pool; the area around it would be turned into waste pits, silted streams, and eroded hillsides. Instead of getting a badly needed cleanup, the Blackfoot was to take a new round of environmental insults.

As far as Anaconda officials were concerned, the Mike Horse deal looked smooth and easy—in Montana, mining projects rarely ran into political snags. The site was on state land, but that didn't matter: state land, federal land, the game was all the same. Company lawyers filed a few forms, company executives stroked a few political egos, and the permits arrived as fast as the bureaucrats could stamp them. Nobody ever complained.

But this time, Cecil Garland was determined to make a fight of it. He learned that four state officials were required to approve Anaconda's mining lease. At first, the situation looked bleak: the governor, Forrest Anderson, fully intended to support the company, and there was no reason to believe the attorney general, the secretary of state, and the superintendent of schools wouldn't go along.

But Garland plugged away, telling everyone who would listen about the toxic wastes that would contaminate the Blackfoot River. He convinced the Montana Wilderness Association to petition Congress to designate the land around the mine as a federal wilderness area. He stirred up environmental sentiment around the state, and when the final meeting on the issue was convened on a cold, snowy day in March 1969, Governor Anderson was shocked to find his chambers jammed beyond capacity. Anderson was in for an even bigger surprise when he called for a vote on the Anaconda lease: both the attorney general and the superintendent dissented. The lease request was denied.

Anaconda representatives were dumbfounded. Since the day Montana joined the Union, state officials had never denied Anaconda a mining lease. The company went back to lick its wounds and figure out a new strategy, and Cecil Garland went home to his wife, his daughter, and his general store. Another surprise was waiting for him.

Lincoln was totally polarized by Garland's crusade. A few people strongly appreciated his efforts, but most people had been anticipating the money the mine would bring into town, and they weren't going to forgive Garland for driving it away. Within weeks, Lincoln residents organized a boycott of the Garland store. Old friends stopped talking to him. People avoided him on the street.

For three years, Garland tried to stick it out, hoping the anger would wear off, the economy would pick up, and things would return to normal. Instead, the situation got worse. His business started failing. A lot of his neighbors began blaming their financial problems on him. His wife and daughter began feeling the effects, too.

By 1973, Garland had won his environmental battle, but lost his home in the process. The people of Lincoln had spoken, loudly: they'd rather have Anaconda Mining, and its jobs, than Cecil Garland, and his cause. Garland packed his car, bid his family good-bye, and left Montana forever.

23

HIGHWAY ROBBERY

Fall 1973
New York City

Marcy Benstock sat in the back of the room, watching a powerful city official tell community leaders how he wanted to transform the West Side of Manhattan Island. The guy was incredibly annoying, Benstock decided: he didn't seem to have the slightest concern for what anyone in the neighborhood thought about his grand proposal. He acted as if the community meeting were just a formality, a little, insignificant step on the road to one of the largest real-estate development projects in the history of New York. Years later, a federal judge would call it "contempt for democracy." For the moment, though, it seemed like business as usual.

The man on stage was Lowell Bridwell, the director of the West Side Highway Project. The way Bridwell described it, the project was far more than a highway: it was, he insisted, a solution to some of the city's worst problems, a way to create new jobs, new apartments, new stores, new offices, and new tax revenue.

The way the plan went, eight million cubic yards of rock, soil, and industrial garbage would be dumped into the Hudson River, extending the Manhattan shoreline sixty feet into the water. It would literally create new land, 170 acres of virgin real estate, in one of the most crowded, land-hungry places on Earth. In a tunnel underneath the new landfill, a six-lane highway would run for four miles, connecting the lower tip of Manhattan with midtown. With any luck, the road would be declared an interstate highway, and the federal government would pay for the whole thing.

The entire New York power structure—the governor, the mayor, both senators, all three daily newspapers, the big New York banks, the major real estate developers, and all the construction unions—had lined up behind the project. Most other New Yorkers either supported it, ignored it, or seemed prepared to accept the inevitable.

Fighting the highway was a hopeless cause. Marcy Benstock couldn't resist.

New York City was hardly a vision of ecological paradise: the largest, densest urban area in the nation, New York was everything environmentalists seemed to fear. It was overdeveloped, overpopulated, and badly polluted. The air was foul with exhaust fumes. The rivers were thick with sewage and industrial waste. Save for a few parks, every available scrap of space was either paved over or built up.

But the use of public and private land was as much an issue in the inner cities as it was on the open range. In the prairies, deserts, and mountains of the interior, miners and ranchers were exploiting public land for private gain. On the crowded, urbanized coasts, real estate developers were doing exactly the same thing, and often they left the same legacy of destruction.

Highway builders had tremendous influence over the way land was developed. They could cut great swaths through existing communities, turn quiet residential neighborhoods into busy commercial centers, and encourage private industrial expansion everywhere along the way. And they did almost all of it at the taxpayers' expense.

The West Side Highway Project would eventually involve billions of dollars in public money. It would become a symbol of some of the most fundamental clashes in national priorities—mass transit against private cars, clean air against economic growth, the short-term interests of people against the long-term limits of nature.

Supporters of the highway project would use every weapon in their arsenal to undermine the opposition. They would buy off politicians, squelch dissenting journalists, and create phony environmental organizations to confuse the public. But the battle would drag on for more than ten years, in city hall, the state legislature, Congress, and the courts. Along the way, environmentalists would master a powerful weapon: the politics of delay.

Without Marcy Benstock, the fight might never have happened.

She wasn't a native New Yorker. Marcy Benstock grew up four hundred miles to the northwest, in a blue-collar city on the edge of Lake Erie. Buffalo and New York City were part of the same state, but that was an accident of political geography: for all practical purposes, Benstock's home town was part of the industrial Midwest, a lot closer to Cleveland and Detroit than Manhattan.

Her father was a successful jewelry manufacturer, and Marcy lived a life of relative comfort, attending private schools and eventually Radcliffe College, where she majored in English literature and largely ignored the outside world. When she graduated, in 1963, she was blissfully unaware of the emerging civil rights movement, the extent of the nation's military involvement in southeast Asia, or the problems a biologist named Rachel Carson had recently revealed in a book called *Silent Spring*. For most of her college career, Marcy Benstock never read a newspaper.

But she knew about New York City. Her father had spent a brief part of his young life struggling to make it as an actor on Broadway, and whenever he could, he took the family to Manhattan. New York was everything Buffalo wasn't—exciting, alive, full of hope and adventure. When she graduated from college, Benstock never even considered going anywhere else. She took a job in the publishing business and found an apartment on the Upper West Side of Manhattan.

West One Hundredth Street wasn't exactly what she had pictured in her dreams of the big city. For one thing, the air was full of soot. It was everywhere, staining the sides of the brownstone buildings, hanging hazy in the summer air, turning the winter snow black and foul, and seeping through her open apartment windows. After a while, it would start to build up, forming a filthy layer on the bookshelves, the table tops, and the bathroom sink. Some days, the dust would get so thick that she couldn't get her contact lenses clean enough to put them in her eyes.

For a lot of New Yorkers, dirty air was a part of life. So were noise, crowded streets, big buildings, and high prices. New York had Wall Street, Broadway, Fifth Avenue, the Empire State Building, the Statue of Liberty, Rockefeller Center, the Metropolitan Museum of Art. New York was the center of the world; if the air wasn't always pure, that was life in the big city. If you wanted fresh air, you could move to the country.

Benstock was different. With the civic pride of a recent immigrant and the outraged energy of a stern, middle-class reformer, she set out to attack the scar on the city of her dreams. She quickly became obsessed with her work: every project took over her life, every detail had her constant attention.

The clean-air crusade first took her to Washington, where she spent two years working for Ralph Nader, editing a pair of books on air and water pollution in major American cities. By 1971, she was back in Manhattan, applying to the Fund for the City of New York for a grant to study the primary sources of air pollution in Manhattan and evaluate possible ways to address the problem. The executive director, Gregory Farrell, was interested enough to arrange a meeting, but a little impatient with the project's scope. "I'm sick of studies," he told the slender, dark-haried woman with the girlish voice sitting across his desk. "I want to fund somebody who is ready to stop studying, and start acting." Farrell gave Benstock six weeks to put together a compre-hensive plan for reducing air pollution in the two-hundred-square-block area around her apartment.

Benstock's research quickly revealed the major culprit in the Upper West Side's air-quality problems: dozens of small incinerators and furnaces, built into private apartment houses, were spewing huge clouds of dirty smoke out of short exhaust stacks—and most of it was not only illegal, but a terrible waste of the landlords' money. With a few cheap, simple improvements and a little bit of operator training, the owners could easily comply with the city's air-pollution codes and cut down their fuel bills at the same time.

With the foundation money, Benstock established the Clean Air Campaign. The campaign moved into a tiny office on 106th Street, with a telephone, a couple of chairs, and one employee, Executive Director Marcy Benstock, who made $7,500 a year. If Greg Farrell wanted action, he got his money's worth: by 1973, the level of particulate matter in the Upper West Side air had dropped by a third, and for the first time in history, that corner of Manhattan was coming close to compliance with federal air-quality laws.

Then one spring day, the phone rang in the Clean Air Campaign office, and Benstock found herself on the line with a mid-level city employee named Brian Ketcham. The guy sounded almost as manic as she did; the message he was passing along would change the future of New York City and send Marcy Benstock's life into a new and lasting obsession.

Ketcham was a traffic engineer, a bureaucrat who might have spent a long career stashed away in a concrete cubbyhole, drawing lines on pieces of paper and projecting the number of cars that would flow in and out of an ever-changing city into an unpredictable future. But he'd recently landed a critical assignment: he was in charge of drafting a plan to bring New York City into compliance with the Clean Air Act, which mandated a comprehensive traffic management plan to reduce the number of cars on the streets of the city.

Benstock listened as Ketcham described the basic outlines of his plan. The young engineer had tried to design a transportation system that relied on private cars only as a last resort, and did everthing possible to encourge mass transit. To make it all work, Ketcham concluded, the city would also have to make driving less appealing to people—by raising the tolls on the bridges into and out of the city, by charging higher rates at parking meters, and maybe most important, by reducing the number of parking lots.

At the same time, he explained, New York would have to pour a considerable sum of money into improving mass transit. It would take millions and millions of dollars—the same kind of money the city was planning to spend on a new highway along the West Side of Manhattan.

Instead of fixing the subways, New York was going to bring more cars into town. The director of the Clean Air Campaign decided to take a look at this West Side Highway Project.

Marcy Benstock loved the New York subways. They were part of the New York she had seen as a kid, the steel pulse of the city, wild, noisy cars racing through dark tunnels underneath the busy streets. The subways were also one of the most extensive public transit systems in the world: for a 30-cent token, you could enter a vast network of train lines that would take you within a few blocks of almost anyplace in the five boroughs of New York. And they didn't pollute the air like cars.

After fifty years, though, the system was falling apart. Like most parts of the country, New York City had been losing interest in mass transportation. Since the end of the Second World War, city planners had been looking away from the cheap, crowded public trains of the past and building dreams of the future that rode open highways, in sleek, powerful, private American cars. To a certain extent, the change was driven by force of the market: a booming economy gave millions of working families the money to buy cars, and low gasoline prices made it relatively cheap to travel in style.

But more than the invisible hand of Adam Smith was at work. Long before the United States entered World War Two, the automotive industry and the oil companies saw the potential to create a virtually guaranteed market for their products. Beginning in 1939, Standard Oil of California and Phillips Petroleum began conspiring with General Motors, Firestone Tire, and Mack Truck to buy up mass transportation systems in cities across the nation— systems that depended largely on electric-driven rail cars. As soon as the consortium, operating through a series of dummy corporations, got control of the transit lines, the trains would be shut down, the rails torn up and sold for scrap. Before long, cities all over America were forced to replace their electric streetcars with buses—buses built by General Motors, with tires by Firestone, fueled by gasoline. Industries found it harder to ship their goods into and out of cities by rail, so they began turning to trucks. Most important of all, with the demise of the efficient, cheap, and popular rail transit systems, millions of urban dwellers found reason to purchase gasoline-powered cars.

In 1947, the companies that orchestrated the systematic destruction of urban mass transit in the United States were tried in federal court for violations of the Sherman Antitrust Act. They were found guilty, and fined $5,000.

The New York subways survived the assault from Detroit. But a more serious danger was lurking right around the corner. Steel, rubber, and oil weren't the only big money-makers of the automotive revolution: there was also concrete.

A lot of political power grew out of concrete. For years, highway projects were a politician's dream. The voters generally loved to drive, and nobody minded spending money on more and better roads. So cities, counties, towns, states, and anyone else with a claim to represent the public sold bonds, raised taxes, and collected tolls to pay for new pavement. With all that loose money around, highway construction looked like the best thing since war profiteering, and contractors big and small found ways to cash in.

The richest concrete gravy train was the interstate highway system. First proposed in the waning days of the Truman administration, the network of superhighways was designed first and foremost as a military strategy. With rail systems falling into decline, the armed forces needed a reliable way to move men and matériel rapidly around the country in times of emergency. A network of wide, smooth, high-speed roadways connecting all the major cities in the continental United States seemed like a perfect solution. Under President Eisenhower, civilian and military engineers sketched out a rough web on a map, and Congress appropriated several billion dollars to get the project rolling.

For the most part, the program was wildly popular, especially in the statehouses and city halls. The way Congress designed it, state and local politicians got to oversee the new highways and hand out the massive construction contracts—and the federal government paid 90 percent of the tab.

But back in the neighborhoods, the projects sometimes stirred up a bit of controversy. In the late 1950s, San Francisco residents rebelled against a plan to build an elevated freeway through Golden Gate Park. In the Bronx, low-income residents tried to prevent Interstate 95 from destroying neighborhood communities that had been around for more than a century.

In 1973, New York congresswoman Bella Abzug gave highway opponents an important new tool—she introduced a bill that allowed cities and states to trade in their federal highway money for mass-transit programs. It was a critical change in policy that would undercut one of the highway lobby's most powerful arguments: for years, local politicians had been warned that the only way to get all that big federal construction money into town was to go ahead with an interstate highway. Otherwise, the money—and the jobs— would go to another part of the country. Around the same time that Marcy Benstock was listening to Lowell Bridwell describe what he hoped would be the latest piece of the interstate system—the West Side Highway Project— Abzug's bill became law.

Benstock learned about it a few weeks later, from a short article buried in the back of *The New York Times,* and the concept hit her with the force of a high-speed locomotive: the West Side Highway money could be traded in and used to fix the New York subways.

For the next ten years, she would think of almost nothing else.

24

LET'S MAKE A DEAL

December 31, 1973
Washington, D.C.

The federal government shut down early on New Year's Eve. Most of the members of Congress and the Senate were home, celebrating the holidays somewhere far from the Capitol. Even the frenetic lobbyists took some time off to relax.

For Lynn Greenwall, the director of the United States Fish and Wildlife Service, the break couldn't have come at a better time. Greenwall had a horrible case of the flu and was too sick to care about official business; for the next twenty-four hours, he hoped, the phone wouldn't be ringing and the office wouldn't be sending messengers to his house with important papers to sign. Nobody tried to get any work done on New Year's Eve; even the head of a major federal agency would have a chance to catch up on his sleep.

But Patrick Noonan had other ideas. As the clock ticked down on 1973, Noonan, one of the most unusual real estate brokers in America, was trying to put the final touches on one of his biggest and hottest deals: he was buying 343 square miles of remote New Mexican wilderness—today. And he needed Lynn Greenwall to help him.

Like most of his colleagues in the business, Pat Noonan had a real estate broker's license. Like the best and the brightest in the field, he had a natural instinct for making deals. But Noonan wasn't getting rich; his office never made a profit. He bought some of the most attractive parcels of land in the country, but he never tried to develop a single acre. In fact, he sold off most of his best property at far less than its market value. His goal in life was just the opposite of most real estate brokers—he was trying to take land off the market, forever. And at the age of thirty, the president of The Nature Conservancy was having tremendous success.

As little as Noonan had in common with other real estate brokers, he had even less in common with a lot of the activists who made up much of the growing environmental and conservation movement. He had no interest in protests or sit-ins. He'd never wanted to rebel against the system. In fact, as a matter of policy, he didn't lobby or take positions on environmental issues. But he was doing something that in its own way was profoundly radical: he was using private money to create public wilderness preserves, saving vast tracts of land from the logger's ax and the developer's bulldozer. And in the process, he was making a place for the conservative business community in the environmental movement.

Noonan looked like a typical young business leader, on the fast track to success. After earning an undergraduate degree from Gettysburg College and a masters in business at American University, he went on to a second masters degree, this one in urban planning, from Catholic University. Along the way he became a professional appraiser and a licensed real estate broker. With his wall full of degrees and certificates, the clean-cut Noonan went to work for the federal government, helping plan for future national parks. The job paid well, and it gave him good professional experience and contacts, but after three years, it started to seem pointless. Park planning was a fine idea in theory, but in practice it was mostly an exercise in frustration. Noonan participated in study after study, showing time and again what was needed to improve urban environments and how parks fit in to the solution. But nothing ever happened. The hamstrung government agencies moved slower than jellyfish, and Noonan, with the head and heart of a deal-maker, couldn't take it anymore.

For two years, he tried the private sector, selling real estate for a Washington firm. Then in 1969, he joined The Nature Conservancy as a trainee, earning $10,000 a year. Within three years, he became the organization's youngest president.

The Nature Conservancy that Pat Noonan inherited was an old-fashioned, conservative organization, founded in 1951 by a small group of ecologically minded scientists. It had evolved out of a committee formed in 1917 by the Ecological Society of America, which worried that untouched land, especially near major urban areas, was disappearing fast, and that soon little nature would be left for scientific study. So the society began buying up parcels of wilderness and setting them aside as laboratories, for research into natural biological systems.

Over the years, as The Nature Conservancy grew, it became less interested in scientific study. The goal became broader: the group bought land that might otherwise be developed, then left it in its natural state, whether the parcel was worthy of research or not. The organization's strength was speed.

The wheels of law and politics ground slow: changing laws and fighting development plans could take many years and a lot of cash. But if you bought land on Tuesday, you could halt development on Wednesday. And since The Nature Conservancy was a charitable organization, people who sold their land to the group at less than its market value could get a substantial tax break.

By the early 1970s, the organization owned hundreds of lots, big and small, spread across the East Coast, and increasingly, the rest of the country. Most were donated by philanthropists, companies needing tax breaks, or rich people who didn't want to see a shopping center spring up underneath their windows. The acquisitions were largely random: as far as The Nature Conservancy was concerned, more land was always better. As long as the group owned it, the land would stay wild.

By the time Noonan took over, the operation was slowing down. The money needed to manage the hundreds of tiny parcels scattered around the country was draining the organization. The staff was getting spread thin. And some of the parcels, small as they were and sandwiched in by development, were beginning to look useless as any sort of wildlife or plant preserve.

The basic approach that evolved under Noonan's guidance was simple— and creative. Like his early predecessors, he picked his shots, using scientific studies to determine a potential site's ecological significance and concentrating on saving the most important wilderness areas. Then he put some of the tricks of his trade to work—and revolutionized the land conservation business.

Instead of looking for cash donations, Noonan's fund-raisers started soliciting loans. They promised to pay the money back, with interest; they warned the lenders that the process might take some time, but they explained that there was no chance of default. The money would go directly into large land purchases—and since Noonan always got the best, most valuable property at the lowest possible price, the loans were completely secure.

The Nature Conservancy would use its borrowed money, its tax-exempt status, and Noonan's real estate savvy to do what slow-moving state and local governments often couldn't: snap up endangered wilderness lots at bargain-basement prices. Then the organization would try to convince a public agency to buy the property at roughly the same price, and hold it off the market until the agency could round up the money and political support to proceed.

If it worked, everyone would come out ahead. Landowners would get a tax break for selling their land to a nonprofit organization. The public would get important wilderness or park preserves that would otherwise have been developed. And government agencies that were in the business of buying up parks and wilderness areas would get the land cheaper and easier than they could ever manage alone.

Noonan worked out another creative scheme that laid the groundwork for saving millions of acres of land over the next twenty years. Instead of buying parcels of land outright, The Nature Conservancy would buy certain rights to the land—like the right to develop it, or mine it, or use it for a hunting ground—and never exercise that right.

For example, a railroad might own a forest that was home to a locality's last breeding pairs of wolves. In order to help offset the cost of owning the land, the railroad might auction off a few hundred very expensive hunting permits each year. Even if the hunters didn't kill the wolves, they could scare off enough of the deer and small game to deprive the predators of their food supply.

The Nature Conservancy could offer to buy the whole forest and discontinue the sale of hunting permits. But that would cost a small fortune. Besides, the railroad didn't care about hunting; it just wanted income. So for a fraction of the price of the land, the conservation group could simply buy up all hunting rights on the property—and then refuse to let anyone hunt. In the same fashion, it could buy the right to develop the land, or mine it. The railroad would keep its title, and could keep running its trains through, but the wolves, and the trees, and the natural beauty of the area would be preserved forever.

The deal Noonan was finishing on New Year's Eve looked like exactly the sort of project he loved: everyone would come out a winner.

Under the 1965 Land and Water Conservation Act, the federal government was supposed to identify and acquire enough land to satisfy park and recreation needs of the public over a twenty-five-year period. Funds for purchases came primarily from oil and gas leases on the federally owned outer continental shelf. But the congressional committees that oversaw the land program identified a lot more parcels than the appropriations committees found money to buy.

The Sevilleta de la Joya land grant was one of the parcels that fell through the cracks. The 228,000 acres of arid New Mexico ranchland had been overgrazed for years, but were still home to puma, bald eagles, roadrunners, and endangered peregrine falcons, among other species whose habitat was rapidly vanishing. The land was valued at around $12 million, and the owner, the Campbell Family Trust, had offered it to the United States Forest Service for a few million less. But Noonan, who was always a first-rate salesman, managed to convince the head of the wealthy Campbell family, who considered herself an environmentalist, to sell the property to The Nature Conservancy for only a few hundred thousand dollars. Then the organization could pass it on to the Fish and Wildlife Service for practically nothing, and the family could take a tax write-off of more than $11 million.

But the family matriarch, Elizabeth Campbell, wanted a few guarantees. She wanted to be sure that a handful of Mexican families who lived on a remote corner of the land wouldn't be evicted; she wanted a promise that the land would never be sold for private development; she wanted all the cattle removed, so the land could recover. She wanted a few other things, too, things that Noonan couldn't promise—and she didn't trust the nameless bureaucracy of the federal government. So she wanted the head of the Fish and Wildlife Service to meet with her and give her his personal word that the agency would take good care of her property. If Noonan couldn't arrange that, she was going to back out. And since she was determined to take the tax deduction for 1973, she insisted that they close the deal by midnight.

It was, Noonan realized, the largest single parcel of land ever purchased for conservation by a private organization. It was also everything a deal-maker dreamed of: he would get the land at a fire-sale price, the public would get a major new addition to the federal wilderness system, the owner would get her wish for preservation and a hefty tax write-off to boot . . . everybody would be a winner, everybody would walk away happy. If that meant poor Lynn Greenwall had to be dragged out of his sickbed on New Year's Eve, Pat Noonan could live with it.

Greenwall had worked with Noonan on several earlier deals, and he knew the man was not one to give up. So when the phone rang and his wife told him Pat Noonan was on the line, he realized he had no choice: he was going to see Mrs. Campbell, flu or no flu. And if he refused to get in his car and drive the fifty miles from his house to Noonan's office, Noonan was going to come over and get him.

So a pale and shivering Fish and Wildlife director bundled himself up in warm clothes, fought his way through the holiday traffic, and as most of official Washington was starting to pop champagne corks, patiently convinced a reluctant property owner to give Pat Noonan the deed.

And on the first day of 1974, the central New Mexico sun rose over 343 square miles of Nature Conservancy land.

25

GOOD NEWS, BAD NEWS

December 31, 1974
Palo Alto, California

It was late in the day and Johanna Wald was alone in the office when the call from Washington finally came in. But the moment she heard the tone of her colleague's voice, she knew it had been worth the wait. Roger Beers could barely control his excitement. The federal-court decision was a total victory, he told her: on every single count, Judge Thomas A. Flannery agreed with the public interest lawyers. The federal government was mismanaging 170 million acres of public land, letting herds of privately owned cattle literally trample it to death.

Wald allowed herself a quiet pat on the back. Two years of work was paying off. She thanked Beers for all his help—the guy was a prize, a court-room litigator as good as they came. Without such a smooth, eloquent advocate to present Wald's complicated theories in court, the case might have been doomed from the start. But both of them knew the real credit belonged to Bill Meiners.

Over the past twenty-four months, the retired range manager had transformed Wald from a suburban lawyer with an Ivy League education into an expert on cattle grazing and western land management. He'd explained how his former employer, the Bureau of Land Management, worked on behalf of corporate ranchers, not the taxpayers. And he became the NRDC's premier witness on the state of public rangelands, his affidavit testifying to years of federal neglect—and sometimes, corruption.

Judge Flannery's ruling, based heavily on Meiners's expert testimony, reflected the growing importance of the National Environmental Policy Act as a legal tool for environmental change. But as Wald would soon discover, the case also reflected NEPA's serious limitations.

Roger Beers and Johanna Wald fought the federal government's grazing policies on essentially the same grounds Jim Moorman had used to fight the Alaska pipeline: the Bureau of Land Management hadn't done an adequate environmental impact report. A few years earlier, the case, *Natural Resources Defense Council* v. *Morton,* would probably have been thrown out of court for lack of standing. But following the groundwork Moorman had done on the pipeline case, and the Supreme Court's precedent-setting Mineral King decision, Judge Flannery found reason to grant the environmental group the right to pursue its complaint.

The BLM had put together an overall study on the environmental impacts of its grazing policies. Wald and Beers charged that it badly underestimated the damage the cattle were doing. But the lawsuit went a crucial step further: even if the study were perfectly accurate, the lawyers argued, it still wouldn't have been good enough. To satisfy the requirements of NEPA, the lawsuit stated, the BLM had to prepare a separate, individual report for every single area on which it allowed grazing.

Beers and Wald presented extensive evidence to show that the public land was in imminent danger—and the government, they charged, was well aware of the situation. Meiners's testimony was even more dramatic. "I have observed widespread and obvious degradation of the Juniper Mountain Unit," a 220,000-acre site in Idaho, Meiners's affidavit stated, "including serious and extensive depletion of the native vegetative cover, active and accelerated erosion, destruction of wildlife habitat, water pollution, and general impairment of scenic and aesthetic values. In my opinion, the major reason for this degradation is the severe over-utilization of vegetative cover by domestic livestock which has been permitted by the BLM. The particular BLM practices which have contributed to this situation are many and can be summed up as an almost complete lack of meaningful management of any sort."

The government's legal defense was essentially technical. The BLM itself had confirmed the validity of Meiners's complaints: an internal report introduced as evidence in the lawsuit stated that "uncontrolled, unregulated or unplanned livestock use is occurring in approximately 85 percent of the state (Nevada) and damage to wildlife habitat can be expressed only as extreme destruction." But agency lawyers argued that the plots of land in question were too small to require individual environmental impact reports.

Judge Flannery ruled that the BLM procedures violated both the letter and the spirit of NEPA. The evidence presented by the NRDC clearly showed a pattern of widespread environmental abuse—and the government had not done its duty of revealing that fact to the public. Flannery ordered the agency to prepare and publicly circulate environmental impact statements for each and every parcel of grazing land, and discuss alternatives to its permits. Within thirty days, the bureau had to propose a timetable for completing the reports that was acceptable to the NRDC—or the court would do it instead.

But the real issue behind the case was much larger than the scope and validity of an environmental study. Wald and Beers wanted to use the courts, and the grazing problems, to challenge the overall federal policy of "multiple purpose" land use, the idea that public land should be exploited for its highest value, not protected as wilderness. The NRDC wanted the government to put long-term environmental preservation at least on a par with short-term economic returns. Wald and Beers even raised the question in their court briefs, along with the technical claims about the validity of the environmental impact statements.

But the court completely ignored the larger issue, ruling only on the narrow legal grounds of NEPA compliance. And for all her elation in victory, Wald knew the real battle had only just begun. NEPA was a powerful tool for bringing environmental issues to court. It was good for delaying projects like the Mineral King ski resort until the political will to block them emerged. But by itself, the law was limited: Judge Flannery had ordered the BLM to write reports about environmental damage, but once the reports were finished—and all the problems duly noted—nothing in NEPA required the agency to correct the problems. And nothing in Flannery's decision would force a shift in federal land-use policy.

The larger battle would be political, not legal, and the immediate prospects weren't very good. Few environmental activists knew or cared about cows and the threat to rangeland—at most major organizations, the problem was far from the top of the political agenda. But the issue hit home on the range: the ranchers were motivated, organized, and loaded with money. And they had been getting their way for the past hundred years.

The news on New Year's Eve was generally good, Wald decided. But it wasn't quite time yet to break out the champagne.

26

WRONG SIDE UP

February 1977
Salina, Kansas

Wes Jackson kept staring at the chart on his desk. He'd been looking at it for days, holed up in his little office at the Land Institute, listening to the wind blow across the Kansas plains and wondering what to do with the rest of his life. And all of a sudden, he was starting to see an answer.

To a genetic biologist like Jackson, the chart was as simple as a grade-schooler's multiplication table. He'd sketched it out on scrap paper in a matter of minutes. But hidden in its rows and columns, Jackson was starting to think, were answers to all of the problems of modern agriculture. If he was right, he knew, the discovery would usher in a new environmental era, allowing abundant crops to be grown and harvested without topsoil loss or chemical contamination.

It was almost too much to believe. The whole thing was so simple.

Across the top, the chart Jackson had drawn divided plants into four categories—annual, perennial, seed-bearing, and vegetative. Annuals, like wheat and corn, lived and died in a single year; perennials survived many years. Vegetative plants, like carrots and apple trees, bore edible fruits and vegetables; seed-bearing plants, like wheat and beans, gave their bounty through their seeds. Down the side, the chart listed four more categories: woody plants and herbaceous plants—trees were woody, lettuce herba-ceous—along with monoculture and polyculture systems. A field of wheat was monoculture, a single crop; ancient forests, wild prairies, and most do-mestic gardens were polycultures, mixes of all sorts of different plants.

The four-by-four grid created sixteen boxes. Four of the sixteen described hybrid plants that didn't exist in the natural world—woody annuals, for example, hypothetical trees that would reach maturity in a single year and die off like sunflowers. Eleven of the twelve remaining boxes described plants long established in the world of agriculture and forestry.

But the last box was empty, a tantalizing hole that kept staring back at Jackson, driving him to a wild conclusion that wasn't the least bit crazy.

The missing combination was a perennial, seed-bearing, herbaceous polyculture. To most people, even a lot of farmers, those words didn't mean a lot, but to Jackson, they suggested a fascinating possibility. The way he saw it, modern agriculture relied either on seed-bearing or vegetative annual plants—crops like wheat, corn, or potatoes that grew, yielded a harvest, and died in one season. Every year, farmers had to plow up their fields, turn over the earth, and, more often than not, pour on huge amounts of chemicals to kill bugs and weeds and to fertilize the soil.

The field Jackson envisioned—the one described in the empty sixteenth box—would be a mixture of grasses, like the native tall-grass prairies of central Kansas, which had thrived for centuries with no insecticides, no irrigation, no cultivating, and no planting. He imagined a domestic version of the wild prairie—one with seeds people could eat. The plants from the sixteenth box would yield instant granola, year after year, with no plowing, no chemicals, and no irrigation.

The Land Institute of Salina, Kansas, was a long way from the comfortable, cosmopolitan world of Sacramento and the California State University Jackson had left just three years before. He'd been following the traditional path to academic security, teaching biology, coaching football, and earning a tenured position as a full professor. He was also heading up a new department, called the Environmental Studies Program.

It all sounded good, but somehow it wasn't enough. At the end of the 1973–74 school year, Jackson took a sabbatical to think about what he wanted to do with his life. He, his wife Dana, and the three kids piled into the family car and headed east—back home, more or less, to Salina.

Salina was as close as you could come to the geographic center of the continental United States. Jackson was born a hundred miles to the east, on a farm outside of Topeka, but in the great Midwest, a hundred miles was nothing. Salina was where Jackson had gone to college, at Kansas Wesleyan. He owned a few acres of land on the outskirts of town, uncultivated prairie that he had acquired for a song back in his college days. He'd always liked the feel of the area, its openness and sense of potential; the future, it sometimes seemed, stretched out before him, across the flat fields of the grain belt.

Kansas had a checkered history. The Spanish discovered it in 1500, the French claimed it two hundred years later, and in 1803, the United States bought it as part of the Louisiana Purchase.

In the 1850s, the Mennonites arrived in Kansas. For the previous century, many of the deeply religious farmers had been living in Russia. When they came to Kansas, they brought with them a hardy variety of Russian winter wheat called "red turkey," which took very well in the Kansas soil. Soon, the Sunflower State didn't have many sunflowers, but it was the leading wheat-growing region of America.

Growing all that wheat required enormous fields. Acre by acre, the settlers turned over the prairie by shovel and plow, bringing up virgin, black soil and sending down the native grasses.

That, Wes Jackson believed, was one of modern civilization's biggest mistakes. He liked to tell the tale of an Indian who watched a pioneer plowing up the prairie many years ago. When the pioneer proudly asked what the Indian thought of the wet, black furrows, the Indian replied simply: "Wrong side up."

By the 1960s, a growing number of environmentalists were starting to realize there were serious problems with American agriculture. Since the dawning of the postwar Chemical Age, the use of insecticides had increased radically, from 15 million pounds a year to more than 100 million pounds. Although DDT was banned in 1972, plenty of other dangerous substances had moved in to take its place—and as rain washed them off the plants and topsoil, they were making their way into rivers, streams, and underground water supplies.

Soil and water contamination weren't the only problems caused by chemical farming. Research was starting to show that common farm fertilizers threatened the ozone layer. The fertilizers used heavy amounts of nitrogen, an element that plants needed for healthy growth. Unfortunately, the heavy amounts of nitrogen in the fertilizers combined with oxygen to form nitrous oxide—laughing gas. And nitrous oxide was murder on ozone.

More than a few farmers were responding to the fear of chemical backlash on their farms. Experimental organic farms began springing up around the country, small-scale operations meeting with limited local success but seemingly economically nonviable on a large scale. Rather than buying fertilizers, the farmers composted organic material and used the compost to enrich the soil. They also rotated their crops, every third or fourth year planting, say, sorghum, which restored nitrogen to the soil, instead of planting wheat, which tended to use up the nitrogen. They set bugs loose on their farms—ladybugs and spiders—to catch and eat pests instead of crop-dusting their fields with chemicals. Predictably, air, water, and soil quality improved, and the nontoxic farming gained the endorsements of many environmentalists.

Wes Jackson knew the organic farms were more environmentally sound—and thus more sustainable—than their more traditional counterparts. They used a lot less energy, and the food was largely uncontaminated by pesticides, herbicides, insecticides, and fungicides. But there was a larger problem, one that even the organic farmers weren't addressing, one that the modern environmental movement seemed to have all but ignored.

Every season, the organic farmers did just what the rest of the nation's farmers were doing: they brought out their tractors and tilled the earth. That left the topsoil—the basis for all plant life—constantly exposed to the wind and rain. And every season, countless tons of this precious soil were washing away. By the late 1970s, the average farm was losing two bushels of soil for every bushel of corn it produced.

Wes Jackson wasn't the only one concerned about soil erosion. A small group of scientists, farmers, and government officials had known about the problem for years. In 1935, in the wake of the Dust Bowl, President Roosevelt created the Soil Conservation Service to seek solutions to the problem, and for much of the past forty years, the agency had paid farmers to leave some of their land idle, in the form of pastures that held the soil or belts of trees that sheltered tilled fields from the wind.

But in the early 1970s, the market for U.S. grain began to boom overseas. The Soviet Union purchased a huge volume of wheat in 1972, when the Russian wheat crop failed, driving up demand and prices—and giving farmers a strong incentive to grow as much as they could. Federal officials, looking at the exports as a way to improve a declining balance of trade and boost the U.S. economy, encouraged the increased planting. In 1973, Agriculture Secretary Earl Butz announced that farmers everywhere should plant from "fencerow to fencerow."

In 1975, a little-noticed report prepared for the Senate Committee on Agriculture and Forestry by the Council for Agricultural Science and Technology suggested that the problem of soil erosion was so serious that, even without a severe drought, it could trigger another Dust Bowl. One of the main problems, the report noted, was that farmers, taking advantage of inflated wheat prices, had stopped rotating wheat with fallow seasons and sorghum seasons. "Maximizing short term crop yields has taken precedence over long term advantages of conserving soil," the report concluded.

Unfortunately, the report was ignored during all of the hype over increased agricultural exports. By the 1970s, the United States government had spent more than $15 billion on soil conservation—and still, by some estimates, more than two thirds of all cropland in the Grain Belt urgently needed protection from erosion.

Wes Jackson was a practical man, and he knew that solving the soil erosion problem was not going to be easy. There was too much money to be made—in the short term, anyway—by doing agribusiness as usual. Agriculture was the nation's largest industry, employing millions of people and feeding hundreds of millions more. There were tremendously powerful interests at work, protecting their valuable turf; anything that threatened to reduce all that bounty was politically hopeless.

But it was just the sort of problem Jackson thought the Land Institute should be working on.

* * *

For three years, planning the Land Institute had been Jackson's life. When his sabbatical ended, he and Dana had decided not to go back to Sacramento and the life of a tenured professor. Instead, they started their own school, one that would be everything the big university wasn't. It would be small, tuition would be low, and the students would work with both their heads and their hands. Within the walls of the modest schoolhouse they'd built, he and his wife had hoped to change the ways of America's biggest business—farming.

Beyond that, the Jacksons weren't sure exactly what their school was going to do. With a handful of students and no money, the renegade geneticist commenced classes in September of 1976—and on October 17, in a freak fire, the school burned to the ground.

Five months later, with winter blowing in strong and his dream a pile of cold ashes, Wes Jackson needed an insight, a vision of what, exactly, he and Dana were trying to do in the middle of Kansas. In his new, makeshift office, he thought, and he read, and he thought some more. And every now and then, he looked up at the chart he'd stuck on the wall.

He'd just finished reading another depressing report—this one by the General Accounting Office—when the idea began to hit him. The GAO study showed just how badly American topsoil was being eroded: some 6.5 billion tons a year—the equivalent of an inch of topsoil spread over an area the size of Kansas. Something had to be done, Jackson told himself, and it had to happen soon.

Then he thought about his missing plant, the sixteenth block on the chart.

The one type of crop that was unknown to American farming could be the answer to the whole agricultural problem. Prairies didn't require cultivation; they clung tightly to the topsoil. And since they were made of a mix of different plants, there was no need for crop rotation. Of course, you couldn't eat the prairie—the grasses didn't produce any form of seeds that humans could eat. But Jackson was a geneticist, and he knew that, with a little crossbreeding, all sorts of things were possible. Maybe even a domestic, seed-bearing prairie.

The prairie of Jackson's dreams would fit in fine with the modern, large-scale farming business. Farmers could harvest the seeds over giant expanses, with the same sorts of machines they used to harvest wheat. They could make plenty of money doing it. Other than the chemical manufacturers, everyone would be happy.

Of course, Jackson realized as he sat down to map out his plans, a project like that might take some time. Maybe fifty years. Maybe a hundred. He wouldn't finish it in his lifetime. On the other hand, if it worked, it would be the most significant event in agriculture since the invention of the plow.

PART 5

THE MORAL EQUIVALENT OF WAR

Nuclear power is a feminist and lesbian
issue. . . . The struggle against the rape of our earth
by rich, white males is the same struggle as the
struggle against the rape of our bodies and the
rape of our lives.

—*Laurie Holmes*
Clamshell Alliance Rally, June 25, 1978

The day Sam Lovejoy toppled the Montague weather tower, the event barely registered on the Richter scale of general political awareness. Five years later, when a plant called Three Mile Island came close to a nuclear meltdown, it set off a political earthquake of enormous magnitude.

Between 1974 and 1979, nuclear power emerged as the single biggest environmental issue in the country. Tens of thousands of people turned out for rallies against nuclear plants. Hundreds were arrested for blocking construction sites. Across the country, millions voted for antinuclear propositions. The accident at Three Mile Island turned even mainstream politicians and groups against the technology.

At Seabrook, New Hampshire, the strengths and weaknesses of the antinuclear movement became clear.

The battle over nuclear power was closely linked to an increasingly critical environmental issue—the nation's energy policy. As the energy crisis of 1973 flared up again four years later, that issue was on the top of the political agenda.

But the antinuclear crusade kept raising issues that went far beyond energy policy, or the safety of one commercial technology. The activists were talking about transforming the entire structure of American society. They saw the fight against nuclear power as a fight against capitalism, sexism, racism, homophobia, patriarchy, militarism, and the United States political system.

And the more the antinuclear groups advanced that agenda, the harder it was for mainstream Americans to work with them.

In 1975, as many as 28,000 people occupied the construction site of a nuclear plant in Wyhl, West Germany. They stayed for months, setting up an encampment that the authorities couldn't evict; eventually, the plant was abandoned. It was probably the worst thing that ever happened to the U.S. antinuclear movement. Over and over again, starry-eyed activists evoked the image of Wyhl; over and over again, they fooled themselves into thinking they could reproduce the event in the United States, where political, social, and economic conditions were entirely different. When friendly allies tried to explain the facts of life, they were rejected summarily.

In the meantime, a little-known physicist named Amory Lovins was developing an approach to energy policy that would challenge all the established thinking on the issue.

The United States, Lovins argued, didn't have to accept nuclear power plants, more oil wells, or a less affluent life-style. We didn't have to glow from radioactive emissions, and we didn't have to freeze in the dark. We didn't even have to live slower and simpler—we just had to live a little smarter. And we didn't need a lot of dangerous technology to do it.

27

MODERATION IS FOR MONKS

April 1976
Los Angeles

The conference room at the Los Angeles International Airport was packed. Dozens of reporters, wearing plastic badges and holding notebooks and tape recorders, jostled each other and squeezed toward the front, stepping over the maze of cables that stretched across the floor and fed the lights, microphones, and cameras. It was a major national news event.

The object of all the attention sat at a folding table, wearing a simple, conservative suit and a plain striped tie. His shirt looked a bit wrinkled under the hot glare of the television lights, and his hair was slightly mussed. But his eyes were clear and sharp, and he looked remarkably relaxed as the men and women of the national press began shouting questions at him, five or six at a time, each reporter trying to speak louder than the next, hoping to be heard above the din.

"It's okay," the governor of California said, raising his hands in a futile attempt to calm the raucous crowd. "It's okay. I'm not going anywhere."

Not for the moment, anyway. In less than an hour, Edmund G. Brown, Jr., the thirty-six-year-old governor of the nation's largest and fastest-growing state, would take his seat in the economy-class cabin of a commercial jetliner and head for Baltimore, Maryland, the first stop in his sudden, last-minute campaign for the presidency of the United States.

"I know I'm coming to this race late," he told the pack of reporters, answering the question that everyone was trying to ask. "But I'm going to bring my energy and all my heart to it.

"I've brought a different kind of leadership to Sacramento," he continued. "I run a tight ship. I've avoided new taxes and I've tried to promote social and economic justice. I've tried not to kid people, and I've told them that we face very serious ecological and human limits to what we can do."

After seventeen months in office, Jerry Brown was already something of a legend, a pop political superstar in the state where the trends of the future were born. A slender, pale man of average height, Brown would never be mistaken for a Malibu beach boy. He talked more like a philosophy professor than a movie star and acted more like a monk than a major politician. But in ways that even Brown didn't fully understand, he was coming to represent a new wave of American politics.

He was also coming to represent the best potential, and the worst problems, of environmentalists seeking to move up in elected public office.

Brown grew up in one of California's most powerful political families. His father, Pat Brown, rose through the ranks of the Democratic party, becoming district attorney, then attorney general, and finally governor of the state. Pat Brown was a natural politician, a glad-hander who made the right friends, cut the right deals, and retired to private life with a string of important, unglamorous accomplishments, a healthy popularity rating, and very little in the way of scandal or controversy.

Young Jerry didn't seem at all like his father. Moody, introspective, given to fits of unpredictable behavior, he was never much of a high school socialite. When he graduated from Saint Ignatius Catholic High School in 1955, he had become deeply religious and quietly intellectual; he spent a year at Catholic University in Santa Clara, then enrolled in the Jesuit Seminary, where he prepared for a life in the priesthood.

In 1960, just before he was scheduled to take the first of his sacred vows, Brown left the seminary and enrolled at the University of California at Berkeley. A year and a half later, he graduated and moved on to Yale Law School.

By 1966, the young lawyer was back in his home state, working as a clerk at the state Supreme Court, then spending a couple of years in private practice with a Los Angeles law firm. In 1971, riding on his father's name and his born political instincts, he won a seat on the Los Angeles Community College Board. The next year, he was elected secretary of state; in 1974, he ran for governor.

Brown swept into office easily, as voters in California and most of the rest of the nation rejected the party of Nixon and Watergate and replaced the old Republican guard with a new generation of young, activist reformers.

From the start, Brown insisted he would not live in the fancy, million-dollar governor's mansion that Ronald Reagan had built. Instead, he moved into a small, $400-a-month apartment in downtown Sacramento, a short walk from the governor's office. He furnished it sparsely, sleeping on a mattress on the floor; he hired no housekeepers, cooks, or orderlies to pick up after him and tend to his needs. He avoided the official limousine whenever possible, driving himself around the state in an aging Plymouth.

In fact, for a man with a liberal image, Governor Brown turned out to be quite a fiscal conservative. He cut back on any government spending he could see as excessive or wasteful, held the line on tax increases, and won the respect and admiration of a good part of the once-skeptical business leaders and conservative Republican taxpayer groups. But the young governor quickly showed that he was also ready to make some fundamental, even radical, changes in the state's social, judicial, economic, and environmental policies. He went out and found an astonishing collection of interesting, unusual, and visionary people and appointed them to the highest posts in his cabinet.

Huey Johnson was a well-known environmentalist, a man who had helped found the Trust for Public Land and who generally had little interest in, or respect for, powerful politicians. One afternoon, his office phone rang, and he found himself talking to the governor, who wanted him to join the new administration as director of the Department of Natural Resources. When Johnson declined, Brown launched into a lecture about the ease of sitting outside and griping about everything the government did. "If you really care about policy," Brown said, "and you have the guts to try to change things instead of complaining all the time, then you ought to give up your cushy job and come work for me." He had a point, Johnson decided.

Sim Van der Ryn, a radical architect and urban planner, wrote a letter to Brown one day early in 1975, suggesting that what the state really needed was an Office of Appropriate Technology, a branch of the governor's office that would study and implement ways to reduce wasteful energy uses, obsolete industrial systems, and other public and private practices that needlessly damaged the environment—and replace them with simpler, more efficient systems that would accomplish the same goals. A project like that would promote solar energy, wind power, and conservation, and work to phase out nuclear energy, private cars, and oil-burning power plants. Even Van der Ryn knew it sounded like a radical concept, far beyond anything the government would accept—but a few weeks later, Brown's office called to set up a meeting, and before long, the OAT was one of the governor's favorite showcase projects.

Brown's policies turned the traditional Democratic party line upside down. Since Franklin Roosevelt and the New Deal, many mainstream Democrats had stuck to a fairly cautious, traditional stance on social issues, and spent public money with liberal abandon. The new governor of California was doing just the opposite.

It was working, too. After his first year in office, polls showed that 85 percent of the state thought Jerry Brown was doing a good job, a stunning approval rating for any politician. His ideas were striking a powerful chord—Californians were ready to look to the future, to try new ideas, to preserve the environment, reduce waste, accept a simpler, cleaner life-style, and de-

28

THE ROAD NOT TAKEN

August 1976
Northern Maine

Lightning crackled across the New England sky. The afternoon rain was coming down in sheets, drenching the hot pavement; small rivers were flowing past the phone booth where a young physicist named Amory Lovins sat on the floor, squinting at the damp sheaf of typewritten text on his lap and arguing about sentence structure with the editor of a prestigious academic journal.

Five hundred miles away, William Bundy sat in the air-conditioned offices of *Foreign Affairs* magazine, cradling the phone to his shoulder and scrawling down the last of the last-minute changes. The author had been on the line for almost six hours; every word, every comma had to be exact before he was willing to hang up and go back to whatever woods he had hiked out of. Not your normal energy analyst, Bundy must have thought. Not normal at all.

In about six thousand words, Amory Lovins had torn to shreds the basic premise behind the energy policies of the modern industrial world, and offered a devastatingly simple, eminently practical, and remarkably inexpensive alternative. It would become the single most popular article *Foreign Affairs* ever published. And it would vault the soft-spoken, bespectacled scientist into the forefront of environmental politics.

Amory Lovins was born with the mark of genius. He was writing complicated piano sonatas at age ten; at sixteen, he was raising eyebrows at Harvard; and by twenty-one, he was a physics don at Oxford University, the youngest person to hold that chair in four hundred years. Everything seemed to come easy for the frail son of a scientific-instrument maker from Silver Spring, Maryland: the math, the science, the music, it all just fell into place.

But Lovins had more than academics on his mind. To strengthen his congenitally weak knees, he spent a lot of time hiking in the remote Snowdonia National Park in northern Wales. The haunting beauty of one of the last truly wild places in Britain had a powerful effect on him, and when he learned that a copper-mining company was planning to tear the place apart for its mineral wealth, he was drawn into the world of environmental politics.

In 1970, a mutual friend in London introduced him to a visiting American named David Brower. Brower was fascinated by the tale of the Snowdonia Park, and asked Lovins to put his concerns into a book; the result was *Eryri: The Mountains of Longing,* one of the most popular and influential books Friends of the Earth ever published. It showed a side of Lovins nobody had ever known, a deep, spiritual appreciation for the wilderness that went far beyond the horn-rimmed glasses and complex blackboard equations that made up the typical image of the Oxford physicist. "The light . . . pours molten across the ridge, level with the flowing sky," Lovins wrote. "It makes the ice and the rocks rise up. . . . I am here, drunk with light."

More important, perhaps, was that the release of the book had a profound impact on British policy. The public outcry was tremendous; the copper mine was abandoned. And Amory Lovins learned the power of the pen.

About the same time, he began learning the limitations of an academic career. The Oxford administration was thrilled with its young genius, but disappointed in his apparent lack of direction: at a time when scientists all over the world were pursuing ever more narrow disciplinary niches, Lovins didn't seem to want to specialize. He told the department head that he wanted to study "energy policy"; but the university decided it wasn't a proper field of study in the physical sciences, so his request was denied. In 1971, he abruptly left Oxford.

Brower had stayed in touch with Lovins, and when he heard the physicist was unhappy with Oxford, he decided to bring him on board immediately. So Lovins began a lengthy tenure in the newly created position of energy specialist for Friends of the Earth. He stayed in London most of the year, working out of a tiny apartment and traveling regularly to speak to environmental groups, government agencies, and even business leaders across the Continent. He read voraciously, teaching himself enough about geology, biology, economics, and political science to bring his understanding of energy policy out of the narrow world of physics. At the same time, he pored through reams of obscure technical journals and reports. He read thousands of pages of detailed records from Atomic Energy Commission proceedings. He digested volumes of congressional testimony. He analyzed everything the experts from the electric utility industry, the oil companies, and the regulatory agencies had to say. And by 1976, three years after the oil embargo had made the study of "energy policy" seem a whole lot less obscure, Lovins had come to some remarkable conclusions.

American energy policy, Lovins decided, had been driven by one rule: more power was always better. Through government grants, favorable tax programs, and sometimes direct public-works programs, the United States had encouraged the development of a gigantic electricity-making machine, a complex of coal, oil, gas, hydroelectric, and nuclear plants capable of producing far, far more electric power than the nation really needed. At first, the program seemed to be based on a sincere belief that electric-power reserves were the lifeblood of industrial society; after a while, though, the electric juggernaut just seemed to keep growing of its own accord, without any rational justification. With such a tremendous oversupply of power, people in the United States were being encouraged to use electricity for the most absurd, ridiculous tasks—like heating their homes. That, Lovins argued, made about as much sense as cutting butter with a chain saw.

Electricity was by far the most expensive form of energy. It was well suited to a few jobs—say, running televisions and making light bulbs glow—but it was a terrible waste to use it for heating and cooking. A staggering amount of electricity was needed to make the burners glow on a stove, or warm the air in a room; heating with electricity was equivalent to paying $100 a barrel for oil that normally cost $20. Natural gas was much more efficient for those tasks; often, solar energy was even better.

Debating whether nuclear plants or hydro plants were the best way to generate electricity, Lovins contended, was like discussing where to get the cheapest French brandy to burn in your car, or the cheapest antique furniture to chop up as fuel for your wood stove. The entire premise was wrong; we were asking the wrong question.

Energy planners, he decided, ought to be looking at the other end of the equation. Instead of worrying about supply, they should be looking at end use—and figuring out the most inexpensive, efficient way to deliver the appropriate form of energy for each different task. And in many cases, the best way to meet the nation's energy needs was not to generate any more electricity, or drill any new oil wells, or explore for any more natural-gas fields. The best and cheapest source of energy in the United States was conservation—using what we had more efficiently. The United States was like a bathtub full of hot water that kept leaking out through a hole in the side. What we needed wasn't a bigger, more expensive water heater. And we didn't need to stop taking hot baths. We just needed a plug.

Insulating houses so that heat didn't escape would cost about half a cent for every kilowatt-hour of electricity saved. Building a new plant to send even more heat out the old, inefficient windows and the leaky doorframes would cost five times as much. Lovins had great faith in technology: he knew that changes in design could make car engines far more efficient—and the price tag would be cheaper than the cost of finding, tapping, refining, and distributing new sources of oil.

The energy crisis didn't mean Americans should freeze in the dark. They

29

A SLOWER, SIMPLER
AMERICA

January 21, 1977
Washington, D.C.

The new president of the United States stood in a solar-heated reviewing stand and looked out across the cold winter land that he had just sworn to lead. Beyond the cheering inaugural crowds, the picture wasn't entirely pretty.

Since the energy crisis of 1974, the economy had taken a beating: for the first time in modern U.S. history, inflation and unemployment both rose at the same time. Although the recession appeared to be ending, its impacts continued to linger.

Jimmy Carter had told the voters that he wasn't a Washington insider. He was just a peanut farmer from Plains, Georgia, a citizen-politician who wanted to serve his country, a decent man who could promise his fellow citizens that "I will never lie to you."

There was a brief moment when it looked like the governor of California, Jerry Brown, might steal the Democratic nomination away—even after a late entry, Brown had startled the nation by winning a string of state primaries, including Maryland and California, sending the Carter campaign team into a near panic. But there just weren't enough primaries left for Brown to build the base he needed, and when convention time arrived, Carter held on to enough delegates to lock up the nomination. Still, the popularity of the young governor, with his talk of alternative energy and environmental limits, made Carter pay attention.

In a seventeen-minute inaugural address, the new president talked of a country returning to its roots, coming home to the basic principles that a young James Earl Carter had learned growing up in a small town deep in the Bible Belt. Honesty, hard work, and a concern for others would be the watchwords of Jimmy Carter's administration. The nation that he led would be a slower, simpler America, with a foreign policy based on human rights, not political expediency, and a domestic agenda bound by a spirit of humility and moderation. "We cannot afford to do everything," he announced. "We must simply do our best."

Then, in the midst of the edgy, insecure winter of American discontent, he did something that left the Secret Service, the national press corps, the crowds along the inaugural parade route, and most of the watching world absolutely stunned: he decided to walk home.

It was a simple sort of gesture, and to thousands of environmental activists around the nation, it carried a simple, clear message: the man in the White House would rather walk than drive. He valued simplicity. He didn't think bigger was always better.

But here and there, a few people couldn't shake the feeling that something was wrong with the picture. While Carter devoted his inaugural address to issues like human rights, disarmament, and justice, nowhere in the speech was there even a single phrase that could possibly be interpreted as a statement of environmental policy.

30

WAR AND PEACE

*

April 18, 1977
Washington, D.C.

President Carter spoke softly, in a measured tone, looking straight into the camera, never once flashing his trademark toothy smile. He wore a sober, conservative, pin-striped suit. The casual air of his earlier White House speeches, when he sat by the fire in a cardigan sweater and chatted in a friendly tone, was gone.

"Tonight," the president said, "I want to have an unpleasant talk with you about a problem unprecedented in our history. With the exception of preventing war, this is the greatest challenge our country will face during our lifetimes. The energy crisis has not yet overwhelmed us, but it will if we do not act quickly.

"It is a problem that we will not solve in the next few years, and it is likely to get progressively worse through the rest of this century."

Over the next few years, the president warned, almost every United States citizen would have to make sacrifices. Homes, schools, and offices would be colder in the winter and hotter in the summer. Gasoline would cost more. Prices on a lot of other consumer goods, ones that required energy-intensive manufacturing processes, would rise sharply. Transportation costs would rise, too, so food that had to be hauled from the farm to the store would get more expensive.

It would, Carter proclaimed, be the "moral equivalent of war."

A warm April day in 1977 seemed an odd time for the president to be declaring any sort of war. The world was mostly at peace. And the energy crisis was mostly invisible.

The gas lines of 1974 were gone; car companies were switching rapidly to smaller, more efficient models, which could travel as much as thirty-five miles on a single gallon. The days of 29-cent-a-gallon regular were over, but even at 60 cents, gas was a bargain. In most other countries, people paid three times as much. Heating bills were putting a strain on a lot of family budgets, but with spring in the air, furnaces were shutting off and memories of the cold were melting away fast. The oil embargo had been a shock to everyone's system, and the effects still lingered, but Americans were adaptable people.

And that, President Carter said, was exactly the problem. Since 1973, energy use had continued to rise. Every year, the United States used five percent more oil—and domestic production was falling just as fast. In 1970, the nation paid $3.6 billion for imported oil. In 1976, it paid $36 billion. Even more frightening, the supplies were running out: at the rate consumption was rising, by the end of the next decade all the proven oil reserves in the world would be used up. The way the world was burning through oil, a new Texas would have to be found every year, a new Saudi Arabia every three years. Not even the most optimistic geologists thought that was possible.

The last time a president spoke sternly to the nation about energy, Carter said, he had given the wrong message. Carter didn't mention Richard Nixon by name, but the implication was clear: Nixon's upbeat approach had been wrong. The shortages were not temporary, and the sacrifices wouldn't be, either. Drilling for more oil at home—on the continental shelf, or the North Slope of Alaska, or anywhere else—would not solve the problem. Burning more coal was better than burning more oil, but that wasn't the answer, either; coal would run out sometime, too. Nor was a vastly expanded—and vastly expensive—nuclear power program. Those options would only prolong the inevitable. Besides, Carter said, they would "plunder the environment."

This time, the president insisted, the United States couldn't just try to build its way out. The only effective way to address the energy problem was to cut back. To conserve. To use less energy. And to rely increasingly on "renewable" sources of energy, like solar power. Even with renewable energy, though, there was no getting around it: Americans were going to have to make do with less.

It was the beginning of a long downward slide in Carter's popularity, a road that would lead to the end of his presidency. Carter had done his best to present what he thought was the right position, but it just couldn't work: Americans didn't want to live with less. As soon as somebody came along who promised another golden age of growth and prosperity, they would abandon Carter in droves.

If he had listened to Amory Lovins, it might have made all the difference.

31

NO NUKES

May 2, 1977
Hampton Falls, New Hampshire

All morning long, Harvey Wasserman sat on the couch in Shirley Gustavson's farmhouse, with a phone on his lap and a blanket over his head, trying to block out some of the din so he could concentrate on his interviews. Reporters were calling from all over the country; Wasserman was trying to answer as many of their questions as possible, but it wasn't an easy task. About a hundred people were milling in and out of the tiny room that served as a temporary office for the Clamshell Alliance; everyone had a different story, and nobody seemed to know what was really going on.

By daybreak, Wasserman knew, more than 1,400 people had been arrested on the grounds of the partially completed Seabrook nuclear power plant. Most of them should have been released hours ago, receiving citations for trespassing and giving written promises to appear in court; that was what always happened at this sort of demonstration. They should have been streaming back to the makeshift headquarters at the Gustavson farm and letting the support staff know they were okay.

But somehow, only about 150 had checked in. The others were missing in action, 1,300 of them. There was no way the local jails could hold that many people, not for more than a few hours. They should have been out a long time ago, Wasserman told himself. At the very least, they should have been able to call the office or talk to a lawyer.

Something was wrong. Very wrong.

Thirty miles to the west, Rennie Cushing climbed off a chartered school bus and followed a National Guard officer through the door of the Manchester Armory. The place was huge. The thick stone walls were fifty feet tall, enclosing at least a square block of land. It was almost like a sports arena, except the floor was concrete, and guns and ammunition were stacked all over, and armored vehicles were parked in the corners.

About seven hundred very confused people were milling around, trying to figure out what they were doing in an armory, and when they might get some food or water, or a chance to make a phone call. A few of them still had their handcuffs on.

Cushing looked over at the National Guard troops who were trying to keep track of their new charges. They're not like real prison guards, he decided; they seem even more confused than we do.

All across the country, newspapers and television stations were getting the word from their reporters in New Hampshire: the biggest antinuclear demonstration in history was under way at Seabrook. More than a thousand demonstrators had occupied the plant grounds and were now under arrest. The New Hampshire authorities seemed to be completely overwhelmed by the turnout.

New Hampshire was the most conservative of the six New England states. The slogan on its license plates read "LIVE FREE OR DIE." It wasn't the sort of place where environmentalists could stop economic development just to save a few birds or fish.

The town of Seabrook, along the New Hampshire coast, had once been home to a small community of successful farmers. By the 1960s, the town's main asset was its beachfront—during the summer, thousands of tourists flocked to the clean, white sands and the quaint cottages adjoining the Hampton Beach State Park. But the tourist trade wasn't enough to sustain a healthy economy through the long winter months. Seabrook was stagnating.

In 1972, the Public Service Company of New Hampshire asked the Atomic Energy Commission to grant it a license to build a nuclear power plant at Seabrook. Utility officials had already convinced local political leaders that the plant was exactly what the little town needed to stimulate its economy and revive the tax base. The project described in the application was anything but conservative: the two reactors would each generate 1,150 megawatts of power, far more than the little utility could possibly use. PSCO had taken on several partners—a consortium of other utilities from the New England area would own half of the Seabrook plant. But even a 50 percent share would more than double PSCO's capacity; at full power, just one of the Seabrook reactors would generate almost twice as much electricity as the entire state of New Hampshire used, even during the busiest times of the day.

The price tag was impressive, too. At $973 million, Seabrook would dwarf the combined annual revenues of the utility partnership, and force PSCO to go heavily into debt.

Still, the company promised that the plant would pay for itself. By 1979, when the first unit was ready for operation, New Hampshire would need all the cheap, dependable energy it could get, and nuclear power was the best way to provide it. The Seabrook project, PSCO officials vowed, would not mean any new rate hikes.

In the small towns around Seabrook, along the rustic stretch of coastline where New Hampshire meets Massachusetts, news of the nuclear power plant slowly started to make people nervous. The more the residents learned about the plant, the worse it sounded. The plans called for a pair of 590-foot-tall cooling towers, concrete behemoths that would loom over the rural landscape, taller than most of the skyscrapers in Boston. Towns like Seabrook and Newburyport and Hampton Falls would turn into cities.

The scenic beauty and quiet life-style of the seacoast weren't the only things the plant would threaten. The construction site was part of an extensive and delicate ecosystem, a five-thousand-acre expanse of salt marshes, estuaries, tidal mudflats, and shallow coastal waters that supported a diverse collection of plant and animal life. The largest soft-shell clam bed in New Hampshire lay just offshore.

If PSCO had its way, a fifty-foot-wide ditch would slice more than two miles through the marsh, providing a conduit for a pair of giant pipes that would suck up more than a billion gallons of seawater a day to cool the reactors and turn the turbines. The ditch would damage the wetland, but the used cooling water would be even worse: when the water was returned to the ocean, it would be forty degrees warmer. That, some marine biologists argued, would shatter the fragile ecosystem, drive away the fish, and kill almost all the clams.

On May 27, 1975, the Atomic Energy Commission's licensing board began hearings on the PSCO application. Although the commission was responsible for protecting the public, it operated in much the same way as any number of other regulatory agencies that oversaw permits and licenses for hundreds of other types of businesses. The licensing procedure for nuclear power plants was long and complex, but it was essentially a technical procedure, designed to address scientific and economic issues, and to avoid any large political ones. The utility had to prove that its plans met a wide range of detailed requirements for design, engineering, and safety, and show that it had the financial resources to complete the plant and the technical expertise to run it. If the company met all those criteria, the license was approved.

By the time the hearings began, several local groups had lined up to oppose the plant. The New England Audubon Society called the site "the worst place in the United States for building a nuclear power plant," and along with an old, established local conservation group called the Society for the Protection of the New Hampshire Forests, it hired a lawyer to appear at the hearings and argue against the plant. The Seacoast Anti-Pollution League joined the fray.

Three months later, despite all the objections, the newly reorganized

Nuclear Regulatory Commission's Atomic Safety and Licensing Board ruled that the Public Service Company of New Hampshire had met all the necessary requirements, and authorized the utility to begin construction of the Seabrook nuclear plant.

Before the ink was even dry, bulldozers began clearing the site, and the company announced plans for its official ground-breaking ceremony. Through a bizarre coincidence, or perhaps some utility executive's perverse sense of humor, the ceremony was set for August 5; news that the Seabrook plant was under way would appear in the papers the next day, on the thirty-first anniversary of the Hiroshima bomb.

By then, the opposition had begun to take on a very different form.

On a warm Sunday afternoon in July 1975, about twenty people gathered in a field near the intersection of two rural roads in the tiny village of Jaffrey, New Hampshire, to form an organization to fight the Seabrook plant. The network of activists had been growing for several years, ever since Sam Lovejoy's trial vaulted the obscure commune of Montague Farm onto the center stage of environmental politics. Only a few of the people at the meeting actually lived near Seabrook. But the rest, including Lovejoy and Harvey Wasserman, saw the Seabrook plant as the next logical step in what was emerging as a nationwide movement against the expansion of commercial nuclear power. The two men from Montague Farm had even come up with a slogan that would come to define the crusade: "No Nukes." It fit nicely on a bumper sticker.

The loose-knit coalition followed the Seabrook hearings with interest. The intervenors, the activists agreed, were raising some good issues, and making some important points. But something about the process bothered them. The intervenors were fighting on the nuclear industry's turf, playing by rules that were stacked against them. By participating in the hearings, they were tacitly accepting the Atomic Energy Commission's basic premise—that there was such a thing as a safe nuclear plant, that there were conditions under which nuclear energy could be tolerated. The new organization would be different. It would never accept nuclear power, under any conditions. In memory of the clams that the plant would threaten, they called it the Clamshell Alliance.

The early Clamshell discussions had a somber, serious edge. As a few of the organizers were quick to point out, a civil-disobedience strategy involved considerable risks. In Europe, antinuclear demonstrators routinely faced tear gas and water cannons, and some had been seriously injured. Just a few years earlier, civil rights marchers and antiwar activists in the United States had been beaten, gassed, and even shot. If the Clamshell Alliance became at all successful, a couple of hard-core members warned, the authorities might attempt to use undercover agents to infiltrate and disrupt the organization.

The ghosts of the 1960s hung heavy in the air. For many of the Clamshell founders, the antinuclear movement was something of a political rebirth.

From the start, the Clamshell Alliance was more than just a new environmental group, and its agenda went far beyond the fate of a power plant on the New Hampshire coast. The Clams, as they called themselves, were out to dismantle American capitalism, and transform the nature of government, and halt the arms race, and end sexism, racism, the class structure of society, and the exploitation of nature. They were out to change the world, again. And this time, they were determined to get it right.

On August 1, 1976, right before the Atomic Energy Commission gave the green light for Seabrook, the Clams burst onto the scene with six hundred protestors gathered in the marshland near the site of the "nuke." After an upbeat rally and a picnic lunch, eighteen New Hampshire residents set off for the Public Service Company property. With forty reporters in tow, they strolled into the open area where the company was slated to build the reactors, and announced plans to "beautify" the site with pine and maple saplings. After a brief discussion with utility executives, who offered an alternative site for the tree-planting project, the demonstators sat on the ground and refused to move. A squadron of state police moved in and dragged the eighteen off to the Hampton Falls police station. They were charged with criminal trespass, disturbing the peace, and resisting arrest, and were released on their own recognizance, pending a court appearance later in the month.

On August 22, another Clamshell rally drew 1,500 people, and 180 of them marched onto the Seabrook site. This time, the demonstrators were held overnight in a National Guard armory in nearby Portsmouth. Most were released the next morning; ten "repeat offenders" from the August 1 action spent six days in jail before the state Supreme Court ordered them set free.

The Clamshell Alliance wasn't even two months old, and already it was growing faster than anyone had imagined. On dozens of college campuses across New England, new Clamshell chapters were springing up, and idealistic students were clamoring to join the occupation. In cities like Hartford, Boston, and Springfield, frustrated activists from across the left-liberal spectrum were showing up at meetings, offering to get arrested, and asking how to set up affinity groups.

All winter long, they organized and spread the word: the next occupation would take place on April 30.

Harvey Wasserman had worked with the news media long enough to know that predicting the turnout for an upcoming event was always a risky proposition. But the first two occupations had left him so excited that when the newspapers started calling the Clamshell media committee, he couldn't contain himself. "We had 18 people at the first event, and 180 at the second," Wasserman announced. "On April 30th, we'll have 1,800."

A week before the occupation date, the Clamshell Alliance announced publicly that more than a thousand had signed up to do civil disobedience at Seabrook. A Clamshell delegation visited the head of the New Hampshire state police, Colonel Paul Doyon, and outlined exactly how the occupation was planned—when it would start, where the people would meet, how they would enter the site, and where they would make their stand. Doyon was quite reasonable: he decided to let the demonstrators enter the site, since a confrontation on the edge of the utility property could interfere with traffic on a busy road that passed through the area. If they refused to leave when ordered, he would direct his officers to begin making arrests.

But Governor Meldrim Thomson had no interest in accommodating the antinuclear demonstrators in any way. Neither did his friend William Loeb, the irascible publisher of the *Manchester Union Leader,* New Hampshire's largest daily newspaper. In the days just before the occupation, Thomson and Loeb created an atmosphere bordering on hysteria. The newspaper painted the demonstrators as a gang of Communists and perverts. The governor announced that the Clamshell Alliance was a front for violent terrorists, who were determined not to leave the site without bloodshed.

In the office of the New Hampshire attorney general, Tom Rath and Jim Kruse had been meeting regularly with Colonel Doyon, local authorities, and members of the governor's staff to discuss law-enforcement procedures for the April 30 demonstration. The protest would overwhelm the small Seabrook police force; it might even prove to be more than the state police could handle. As the chief law-enforcement officer in the state of New Hampshire, the attorney general was responsible for coordinating all the various agencies that might play a role in responding to the situation.

On Monday, April 25, Rath, who held the post of deputy attorney general, met with his boss, David Souter, and gave him a status report. Rath had formally invoked a New England and regional law-enforcement compact and requested backup troopers from neighboring state police forces. The governor had put the National Guard on alert. The county prosecutor for the Seabrook area was conducting an inventory of all jail facilities in the state, to determine how many cells would be available to hold the protesters, but just to be safe, Rath had asked the National Guard commander to prepare the Portsmouth Armory for use as a temporary holding pen.

Attorney General David Souter didn't need a survey to tell him that the New Hampshire prison system was filled close to its capacity. The state had been sued recently over prison conditions, and Souter's office had handled the defense. At most, the county jails and the state penitentiary had a hundred free cells; the armory could probably hold a few hundred more.

But Souter didn't seem terribly worried. Forget the Clamshell Alliance numbers, he told Rath; you can't believe a word those people say. At most, the attorney general figured, two hundred people might get arrested. And most of them would get out on bail in a matter of hours.

*   *   *

Saturday, April 30, dawned clear and mild on the southern New Hampshire coast. A gentle breeze blew off the Atlantic as 1,500 Clamshell Alliance members crawled out of sleeping bags and packed up their tents. From three different campsites on the outskirts of Seabrook, the protesters slowly converged on the access road that led to the nuclear power plant construction site. At the Gustavson farm, where the friendly owners had let the demonstrators set up camp, a few hundred new arrivals checked in and went through last-minute training sessions.

By early afternoon, an occupation force more than two thousand strong had assembled in a dusty parking lot deep in Public Service Company territory. While roughly two hundred reporters watched, the protesters spread out across the site where the plant would be built. They pitched their tents, dug latrines, and began to settle in. By nightfall, they had elected a representative council, which quickly passed a series of proclamations designating the entire area as "Occupation City" and banning all nuclear material within city limits.

David Souter arrived at Seabrook a little before noon. Until a few days before, he'd left most of the day-to-day work on the demonstration response in the hands of Rath and Kruse, but on Thursday or Friday, he decided he should make a personal appearance. The event was obviously attracting a lot of attention; Governor Thomson would be there, and a horde of reporters would be following him around. If by some chance the Clamshell Alliance managed to deliver on its wild promises, and a thousand people showed up for the occupation, Souter knew the state police would have a serious problem: there was no way New Hampshire could handle that many arrests, not without creating a legal and political nightmare.

The attorney general had the authority to call off the police, and halt any mass arrests. A decision like that would cause a political furor; if it had to be made, Souter would have to make it himself.

The governor was already on the scene when Souter arrived. To his relief, not much seemed to be happening; from the state police command post, a series of warehouses on the grounds of the plant, he could see a few protesters milling around a parking lot, but there weren't any signs of a mass occupation. After lunch, Souter took a ride over the area in a state police helicopter; he spotted a group of people marching toward the plant along one of the local roads, and a few more entering the utility property, but the demonstration still didn't look very big.

When the helicopter landed, Souter took a stroll around the plant site, past the parking lot where the demonstrators were gathering. From close up, he realized the numbers were a bit larger than he'd expected. But the folks he saw didn't seem to be the hard-core political type: they were just a bunch of kids, playing Frisbee and laughing, having a good time on a sunny afternoon. When night fell, and the air got cold, and the blackflies started to come out of the marsh, most of them were bound to go home.

He told Colonel Doyon not to bother making any arrests, not right away. Let the kids have their little campout tonight, he suggested; tomorrow afternoon, there won't be many left.

By late afternoon, David Souter was totally bored. While reporters and camera crews from the national television networks and the nation's major newspapers descended on Seabrook, and while the governor stormed around making threats and predicting bloodshed, Souter sat in a quiet corner of one of the company warehouses, writing up the minutes of the last meeting of the Concord Hospital board of trustees. At about seven-thirty, he drove back to the farmhouse he shared with his mother, drank a glass of sherry, fixed a light supper, and went to bed.

Souter was back at Seabrook Sunday morning, in time to have lunch with Governor Thomson and Colonel Doyon. From the command post, he couldn't tell exactly how many of the protesters had stayed through the night, but the encampment seemed to be a lot smaller. Doyon had been sending scouts up in the helicopter every fifteen minutes or so; if any of them had counted, they would have known that the Occupation City lost fewer than half its residents to the cold and the blackflies: almost 1,500 were still hanging on.

Doyon had devised a plan, and he outlined it to Souter and Thomson. The colonel wanted to give the protesters a final chance to leave; if they needed help clearing the site, he would offer the use of the fleet of buses the police had chartered to carry people to jail. By now, he argued, the Clamshell Alliance had made its point: the whole world knew about the controversy over Seabrook's nuclear power plant. Perhaps they could be convinced to declare victory and leave.

Souter thought that sounded fine. Thomson agreed to go along, provided Doyon made it very clear that this was the last and final offer before the police would start making arrests.

A two P.M., a spokeswoman named Elizabeth Boardman delivered the Clamshell response. The organization wasn't just out to make a statement, she said; the goal was to halt construction, by any peaceful means available. As long as the utility planned to continue construction, the occupation would continue, too. At 3:09, Colonel Doyon picked up a loudspeaker and made his formal announcement: Everyone on the construction site was trespassing, and should leave the premises at once. Those who refused to leave would be subject to arrest.

A few minutes later, a battalion of troopers from five New England states marched into Occupation City.

*   *   *

As Doyon delivered his ultimatum, Souter turned to a police lieutenant who happened to be standing nearby and asked how many arrests to expect. About 400, the lieutenant replied; at most, maybe 450.

Around five-fifteen, Souter and Kruse left Seabrook and drove up the coast to Portsmouth, where the National Guard armory had become a temporary booking center for the antinuclear prisoners. Portsmouth was less than twenty miles away, but the trip took close to an hour; Souter had never been to the armory before, and he had to stop for directions.

The officers at the armory didn't recognize Souter, and at first, they refused to let him in. When he finally convinced them that he had the authority to enter, it was close to six-thirty.

All over New England, the evening news shows were broadcasting pictures from Seabrook and reporting on the afternoon's events. All over New England, millions of people were watching the news and hearing the figures: roughly two hundred demonstrators had been arrested so far; at least 1,000 more remained on the site. By the time the whole thing was over, state police estimated, more than 1,200 people would be taken into custody.

If any of the cops at the Portsmouth Armory knew that number, they didn't mention it to Souter. There wasn't much of a chance: from the moment he walked in, the attorney general was busy trying to stop a county bail commissioner from releasing all the protesters on their own personal recognizance.

Commissioner Louisa Woodman had discussed the situation with one of the local judges a few days earlier, and the judge had agreed: the members of the Clamshell Alliance were not a threat to society, and since they were determined to get arrested to make a political statement, it was safe to assume almost all of them would show up in court, where they would have a chance to make their statement again. Even a small amount of bail might slow down the process; with hundreds of prisoners on their way to the armory, and nowhere for most of them to sleep, the last thing anyone needed was another bottleneck. Souter had other ideas. If the protesters were released immediately, without posting any sort of bail, they could go right back to Seabrook and start the occupation again. More important, he feared, people who walked away and left nothing more than a signature might never come back to court, especially if they faced a serious fine or a stint in the county jail.

And as far as Souter was concerned, people who broke the law to protest a nuclear plant deserved to pay some kind of price. Otherwise, the law would have no meaning—and there would be no way to discourage the Clamshell Alliance from coming back again, and again, and again, until the Public Service Company found it impossible to go about its lawful business in the state of New Hampshire.

The attorney general cornered an assistant county prosecutor and told him to stop the bail hearings immediately. The prosecutor passed the word to Woodman, and the releases ground to a halt. About 150 people had left the armory under the commissioner's grace; with the exit doors closed, the makeshift prison began filling up.

Souter found an empty office with a working phone, and placed a call to his top adviser. Tom Rath was at home, watching the television news.

"What's going on down there?" Rath asked. "I hear on the news that we're looking at twelve hundred arrests."

Souter could barely contain his disgust. "That's typical of the news media," he said. "Totally unreliable. I've just come from the site, and the figure is around four hundred."

Souter left the armory at nine-thirty. He'd disussed the situation with the local prosecutors, and had spoken to the governor, and had come to a clear decision: the state of New Hampshire would recommend that none of the protesters be released without posting at least $100 bail. As he walked past the holding area on his way out the door, he could hear the spontaneous response from the growing crowd of incarcerated Clams. They were chanting it over and over again: "No bail."

Colonel Doyon called Souter at home somewhere around eleven P.M. to ask about a technical change in the booking procedure the state police were using at the armory. Souter said the change was fine. Out of curiosity, he asked Doyon how many people were under arrest.

"More than twelve hundred," the colonel said.

"Can you handle that many?" Souter asked.

"For the moment," Doyon replied.

Souter thanked him for the information. Then he hung up the phone and went to bed.

32

SOUTER'S CRUSADE

May 5, 1977
Hampton, New Hampshire

Jim Kruse put the caller on hold and walked over to his boss's office. The attorney general was in.

Kruse didn't waste any time with small talk. Carlton Eldridge was on the line. Eldridge, who was the judge down in Hampton, had just let the first of the Seabrook people off, with a token fine and a suspended sentence. Even the fine was suspended pending appeal: for all practical purposes, the protesters were going to walk out the door without serving another day or paying a single dime.

David Souter wasn't happy. The local county prosecutor had made it very clear that the state of New Hampshire did not want these people to escape punishment. If the judge down in Hampton wasn't getting the message, perhaps Souter would have to deliver it himself.

Souter picked up the phone and told Eldridge what do do. He should make a motion to reconsider the sentence, then delay things as long as possible; Souter would be there in an hour.

David Souter wasn't a crusader. He had none of the political ambition or ideological fire that drove the likes of Meldrim Thomson; if he had any passion at all, his friends said, it seemed to be purely intellectual. Souter lived the life of an ascetic: he had never married, rarely dated, and spent most of his spare time reading nineteenth-century literature and studying the history of law. When Souter was eleven years old, his family moved into a ramshackle farmhouse outside of Concord; save for a stint at Harvard University and Law School and a Rhodes scholarship at Oxford, he never moved out.

Souter shunned the limelight. He normally let his deputy, Tom Rath, deal with the press and take the lead on high-profile cases. He even let Rath have the spacious central office that traditionally went to the attorney general; he took a smaller room, off to the side. When Thomson's right-wing initiatives got the state in legal trouble, Souter would do his job and defend the governor. But he did so without any visible zeal. And he rarely made headlines on his own.

For reasons nobody who knew Souter really understood, the Seabrook protest was a different story.

Shortly after eleven A.M., Souter called the governor's office and told Thomson what was going on. At Souter's urging, the Rockingham County prosecutor had asked for a sentence of fifteen days for all the Seabrook trespassers. He'd also requested that the prisoners not be released on bail if they tried to appeal the sentence. That way, even if an appeals court ultimately agreed with them, the protesters would already have done their time in jail. But the judge had spurned that request, and was setting the occupation force free; Souter was about to head to Hampton to make a personal plea for justice.

Thomson thanked the attorney general for his call. Then Souter phoned the state police, and asked for a cruiser to take him to Hampton with all deliberate speed. He arrived at the Hampton District Courthouse a little after noon. Judge Alfred Casassa had adjourned for lunch.

Seventeen defendants from the Somersworth Armory were scheduled to appear for trial that day. Under New Hampshire law, Casassa had the right to deliver a verdict and impose a sentence immediately; if the defendants wanted a jury trial, they would have to appeal to the Superior Court. Casassa knew most of the protesters intended to do just that; he also knew the cases could become incredibly complicated and politically explosive. The protesters would argue that they had a higher calling, that the threat of nuclear contamination outweighed their responsibility to adhere to the trespassing laws. As far as he was concerned, those sorts of issues were best sorted out by a jury, at another level of the judicial system.

When the first activist, Murray Rosenblith, a twenty-six-year-old pacifist who edited a political magazine in New York, was brought into the dock late in the morning, Casassa found him guilty as charged. Then he fined Rosenblith $200, sentenced him to fifteen days at hard labor, and suspended the sentence pending appeal. Bond was set at $200.

After Rosenblith posted bail, he hung around the courthouse, waiting for his friends to go through the process and be set free. It seemed remarkably routine, considering what the Clams had endured over the past four days.

Since Sunday night, the New Hampshire state prison system had become a jailer's nightmare. When the attorney general demanded an end to personal recognizance releases, the Clamshell Alliance members in the Manchester

Armory had adopted a spontaneous position: everyone who could afford to stay in jail would refuse to post bail. They would hold out as long as possible, overwhelm the system, and attempt to turn Souter's decision into a major political issue.

Word spread quickly as waves of prisoners were unloaded from an endless stream of buses and shuttled into the armory. Not everyone went along: a few hundred bailed out, and returned to jobs or classes or families that couldn't be ignored any longer. But more than a thousand stayed the first night, and most of them held out as Monday became Tuesday, and Tuesday became Wednesday, and the ordeal kept dragging on.

At first, the "bail solidarity" stunned state officials. Nobody had prepared for more than a few hundred prisoners; there wasn't anywhere to put them. Standard legal rights and procedures fell by the wayside. Phone calls were impossible. Beds were nonexistent. Kitchen facilities at the Manchester Armory were primitive, at best; after a while, the National Guard was forced to send out to McDonald's to feed the growing mass of people on the armory floor. On Sunday night, while David Souter slept, hundreds of protesters spent up to fifteen hours on buses and troop carriers, without food or water, while the authorities figured out what to do next.

Eventually, the National Guard opened three more armories, and the members of the Clamshell Alliance were dispersed across the state.

Inside the armories, communication was almost impossible. Outside, the papers began to report on the costs of the mass detention, and the frugal citizens of New Hampshire began to take note: the tab was running close to $50,000 a day.

When Judge Casassa returned from lunch and called the court to order, Souter was ready and waiting. The attorney general stood up and argued for half an hour, making the sort of emotional case he almost never made in public. A suspended sentence, he argued, was as good as no sentence at all. The appeals courts were so backed up that a year could pass before all 1,400 defendants made it to trial; a lot of cases might be dropped altogether. "Justice can only be done," he concluded, "by imposing sentence right now."

The Clamshell defense lawyer, Emmanuel Krasner, did his best to present the other side of the story, but it was useless. The attorney general never made a personal appearance on a minor criminal case. If the matter was important enough to bring David Souter himself down from Manchester, that was all Judge Casassa needed to hear. The remaining defendants were sentenced to fifteen days, to be served at once. Bond for appeal was set at $500, a highly unusual level for a misdemeanor case.

Then Casassa did a truly amazing thing. He called Murray Rosenblith back into the courtroom and rescinded his original order. The suspended sentence was erased, and bail was increased. Rosenblith was ordered back into custody; the bailiffs dragged him off to join his friends.

33

TO TELL THE TRUTH

June 1, 1977
Concord, New Hampshire

It wasn't often that an ACLU lawyer got to question the attorney general of New Hampshire under oath, and Rennie Cushing didn't want to miss it. Spectators generally weren't invited to legal depositions, but Cushing convinced Michael Avery to let him come along. He swore he'd be quiet; he just wanted to sit and listen.

Avery was part of an ACLU legal team from Boston that had shown up in New Hampshire the first night the Clamshell Alliance members were held in the armories. Within days, Avery and his colleagues filed a lawsuit against the state, charging that the law-enforcement authorities had intentionally failed to prepare enough jail cells and forced the Clamshell Alliance members to endure unacceptable prison conditions. David Souter was a key witness, and Avery had issued a subpoena demanding that he appear at a convenient time and place for pretrial questioning.

For several hours, Souter explained in painstaking detail his role in the planning and execution of the state's response to the Seabrook occupation. Over and over, he insisted that neither he nor anyone in his office had any knowledge of how many people the Clamshell organizers were expecting for the event. The turnout was a complete surprise, he testified: up until the day of the occupation, all he knew was what the Clamshell spokespeople were saying to the press. And he didn't believe any of it.

"Did you," Avery finally asked, "have any informants, to your knowledge, within the Clamshell organization?"

"I knew of none, no," Souter replied.

Something about that answer made Cushing very nervous.

PART 6

THE TOXIC TIME BOMB

Without chemicals, life itself would be impossible.

—Monsanto Corporation advertising slogan

The United States entered the Chemical Age in 1945, when a nation flush with victory put the resources and technology of a booming wartime industry to work in the civilian market.

The natural materials in old-fashioned consumer and industrial products decayed fairly quickly, especially under harsh conditions—iron and steel would rust, wood rotted, cotton, wool, and leather degenerated. But modern chemists created thousands of synthetic products that were much more durable. In some cases, they were nearly indestructible. A piece of nylon thread would last hundreds of times as long as the bolts of cloth it bound together. A plastic grocery bag wouldn't disintegrate in the rain.

But not everything the industry made was as harmless as nylon thread and plastic bags. Some of the most popular products were solvents, lubricants, insulators, and other compounds used in manufacturing. When the factories were done with the chemicals, they threw them away. And in the process of making all these new consumer products, the chemical companies generated a lot more industrial waste.

Year after year, American industry threw away hundreds of millions of gallons of chemical waste, much of it in liquid form. Sometimes, they dumped it in streams and rivers. Often, they loaded it into tank trucks and shipped it to remote parts of the country, where the drivers would pour it into ditches. Occasionally, sand or dirt would cover the ditch, in a token attempt to hide the poisonous garbage below. But like the plastic bags, the chemical waste didn't break down quickly. And much of it was poison.

The waste remained hidden for years, buried in trenches, pits, and ponds all over the country. Eventually it began to bubble up in fields or flow out of faucets, and people began to get sick.

The victims of this chemical disaster were often working-class people who lived near major industries, and low-income rural communities where land was cheap and plentiful; most of the people affected were ethnic minorities. At first, they were mystified by the strange rashes, cancers, and coughing fits, the miscarriages and birth defects, the sickly and deformed farm animals. When they complained, the authorities paid little attention.

That began to change in the late 1970s, when people all over the country learned the truth about toxic waste and started to fight back. Places like Love Canal became household names, and people like Lois Gibbs became a new kind of environmental activist. Unlike the activists who dominated much of the modern environmental movement, many of the toxic avengers were women.

For the most part, they weren't concerned with global ecological problems, and they didn't have time to argue about building a new and perfect society. They weren't interested in political careers, either. Something was making their families sick, and they just didn't want it in their backyards.

Their success would startle the nation.

34

NO PEACE, NO QUIET

June 16, 1977
Willow Springs, Louisiana

Southeastern Louisiana was about as wet as dry land could get. Hundreds of streams wound in and out of the marshes and bogs, draining runoff from the rain-drenched soil into swollen rivers that dumped their muddy water into the Gulf of Mexico. A vast underground aquifer filtered slowly southward, just a few feet beneath the surface. Some of the land was only a few inches above sea level, and it flooded continually.

The lush climate supported a semitropical jungle, teeming with life. The broad-leafed plants grew so fast that people living near the swamps struggled constantly to keep them at bay. Wildlife was abundant. Fishing was legendary. The state's official motto called it a "sportsman's paradise."

Two hundred miles west of New Orleans, near the edge of Lake Charles, the town of Willow Springs went about its business at a pace that had changed very little since the turn of the century. The stately antebellum mansions that lined the shores of the lake a few miles south were as far away as the tin-roofed shacks on the outskirts of town, where descendants of sharecroppers still lived off the land. For the most part, middle-class people owned modest homes, raised nice families, and stayed out of trouble. The streets were quiet at night; the churches were full on Sunday. When Ruth Shepard moved there in 1971, it had seemed like the kind of place where an aging hell-raiser could finally retire in peace.

Ruth Shepard had never been the type to be satisfied minding her own business. She left home at eighteen, at the outset of World War Two, making her way north from a tiny southern Missouri town to work in the factories of Kansas City. She married a railroad engineer and settled down in a working-class neighborhood. But she wasn't happy just keeping house; as soon as she stopped working, she started to join organizations.

At first, it was just church auxiliaries and the PTA, enough to keep her occupied. By 1967, she had taken on a powerful industrialist named J. A. Tobin, who was mining for limestone near her house, setting off dynamite blasts in the middle of the night and undermining the stability of her land. A few hundred meetings and several lawsuits later, Shepard's neighborhood association shut down Tobin's mine and drove his operation out of town.

Leo Shepard never tried to argue with his wife. Only fools argued with Ruth: she never gave up. So when she suggested they move away, to someplace quiet where they could both retire, he agreed.

And for six years, the retirement plan had worked. Ruth didn't exactly sit at home all day—she raised money for the local church, and volunteered for local charities, and got to know just about everyone in town. She even picked a fight with the local electricity cooperative, which had made the mistake of stringing a power line across her yard and cutting down a few of her trees. But it wasn't like Kansas City.

Not until that sweltering June afternoon, when she took her son Bob for a ride in the country and ran into a convoy of tanker trucks, heading out for the middle of nowhere on the empty High Hopes Road.

The men who were driving the trucks along High Hopes Road didn't know why the woman in the Jeep kept following them. They never had any trouble out on the edge of Willow Springs—the place was normally deserted. The nearest people lived miles away, and they were mostly old black farmers who kept to themselves. People out there had no money or political influence; if they tried to ask questions, nobody would pay much attention. That was probably the main reason Browning-Ferris Industries had decided to buy such a muddy old piece of backwoods land, so far off the major highways. Nobody knew what went on at the end of the unpaved private driveway, a few hundred yards off High Hopes Road. And so far, nobody seemed to care.

But something about all those trucks bothered Shepard. It didn't make any sense: there weren't any factories or construction sites out in those fields. The dirt road didn't go anywhere. What were so many big, heavy-duty tanker trucks doing out there? She stuck close behind the convoy, and when the tankers turned off on the private road, she parked her Jeep and she and her son followed on foot.

The smell hit her first. Just a few feet down the road, it was strong enough to make her gasp, and the closer she got to the trucks' destination, the worse the sensation got. By the time they were close enough to see what was going on, their eyes were burning and Ruth was holding her shirt over her nose and mouth every time she took a breath.

At the edge of a well-packed dirt cul-de-sac, the empty fields had been turned into broad, open pits, most of them filled to the top with a dark, gooey liquid. As Shepard watched, one of the trucks backed up to the nearest pit. The driver came out and uncurled a long, fat hose from the bottom of the truck's chamber, draped it over the edge of the pit, turned a big red handle on the truck, and hit a couple of switches. A nasty-looking stream began squirting out, mixing in with the unknown contents of the foul artificial pond.

The two hurried back to the Jeep and made tracks for home. Ruth didn't know exactly what she'd found, but she was sure it wasn't healthy—and she couldn't believe it was sitting out among the rural bayous of southern Louisiana.

When the floods came—and they came almost every year—everything on the ground got mixed together in a big, soggy mess. When the water receded, washed-out cars and televisions turned up miles away from where they'd last been seen. If the contents of those pits were dangerous, what would keep them from winding up in some fish pond, or swimming hole—or for that matter, in somebody's drinking water? There must have been some terrible mistake, she decided: once the authorities knew about it, the pits would be drained, and the place closed down.

She started with the local health department, but that didn't get her far. The health inspector told her he'd never heard of any smelly pits in the town of Willow Springs; he'd pass her story along, he said, and if his superiors needed any more information, they'd be sure to give her a call. The police jury, Louisiana's equivalent of a city council, wasn't much better: nobody in the office knew about a dump off High Hopes Road. Nobody cared, either.

Ruth Shepard hung up the phone with a sigh. She was fifty-eight years old, she told herself; all she wanted was a little peace and quiet.

Then she went to tell her husband she was going back to work.

35

THE AMERICAN NIGHTMARE

April 1978
Niagara Falls, New York

Halfway between Lake Erie and Lake Ontario, on the northwest edge of New York State, the Niagara River drops 175 feet straight down, creating one of the world's most famous and spectacular natural wonders and one of North America's most popular tourist attractions.

Most of the city of Niagara Falls, however, was anything but a resort. A few miles away from the clean, broad walkways, manicured lawns, and honeymoon suites overlooking the waterfall was a gritty, blue-collar town, a community of hardworking, no-nonsense families struggling with an economy that seemed to be in a constant state of decline.

Niagara Falls wore the scars of its labor with a certain amount of pride. The smoke from the factories was a part of life. So were the long lines of trucks that rolled along the oily roads, bringing supplies into town or hauling finished products away. Industry—especially the chemical industry—kept the town alive; that's the way it had always been. And for most of the 75,000 residents, that was just fine.

In a modest, three-bedroom bungalow on the southern edge of town, Lois Marie Gibbs picked up the latest edition of the *Niagara Gazette* and began scanning the local news. One of the stories caught her attention. It was all about chemicals, and the ways they could make people sick.

At twenty-eight, Lois Gibbs was living the American dream, married to her high school boyfriend Harry and the mother of two children. Since September 1973, the Gibbs family had lived in a modest house on 101st Street, a postwar subdivision filled with young, working-class people.

Lois loved her house, with its neat lawn, and clean sidewalks, and little backyard. She loved watching the local kids playing in the streets. And she loved the location—her children would be able to go to school just a couple of blocks away.

It was a lovely neighborhood. It even had a lovely name. Folks called it Love Canal.

Love Canal was the legacy of William T. Love, a turn-of-the-century entrepreneur who dreamed of capturing the water from the Niagara River before it fell over the falls and using it to generate electric power. In 1892, Love proposed building a navigable seven-mile canal that would redirect the river around the falls, guide it gradually downhill, and send it over a set of giant turbines before releasing it back into the original riverbed.

A few critics were skeptical of the concept, but the state's political leaders weren't among them. Love was given a free hand to go ahead with the canal, and with investors backing the project, he began construction. But the project was poorly planned, and Love wasted a lot of money. When the local economy went into a recession a few years later, the investors pulled out, and Love walked away in financial ruin. All that stood as testimony to his celebrated dream was a mile-long ditch, about fifteen yards wide and twenty-five feet deep, running through an undeveloped section of Niagara Falls.

In 1920, the city sold the canal and the land that bordered on it to the Hooker Chemical Company, a subsidiary of Occidental Petroleum. Love's canal was the perfect answer to one of Hooker's most pressing problems: the company needed a place to put the waste products from its local chemical plant.

Hooker's chemical waste was poisonous: some of it emitted noxious fumes. Some was extremely caustic, and would burn skin on contact. Some was so poisonous that exposure to a tiny amount could give a person jitters, nausea, or heart palpitations; a little bit more could be fatal.

Hooker started trucking barrels of waste across town, tossing them into the canal. Other local chemical companies used parts of the canal as a dump, too. So did the United States Army.

By 1953, the cavernous ditch was completely filled with waste. Hooker covered the whole thing over with dirt and, in a gesture of civic duty, sold the land for a dollar to the Niagara Falls Board of Education, which was looking for a place to build a new elementary school. In the official document transferring ownership, Hooker didn't mention in any detail what or how much had been dumped in the old canal. The company did, however, include a legal clause stating that Hooker was not responsible for any injuries or deaths that might occur at the site.

The school board wasn't concerned with what was underneath the ground. Neither were the real estate developers who were busy building new houses on the empty lots nearby. For the most part, the families that moved into the new neighborhood never knew anything about the toxic wastes buried beneath them.

As the years passed, Love Canal residents occasionally reported strange cases of black gook seeping through their basement walls, bubbling up from their backyards or coming out of drains on the bottom of a swimming pool. But aside from one incident in 1959, when three children received chemical burns on their skin while playing in the schoolyard, nobody complained too loudly or asked too many questions.

Michael Gibbs started kindergarten at the same school in September 1977. After a few weeks, he started having health problems. He developed rashes, and his face would swell up. His eyes always seemed to hurt. Lois and Harry were concerned, but not overly worried: children were prone to all kinds of bugs, rashes, and allergies.

In December, Michael began having seizures, and the doctor diagnosed him as having epilepsy. Two months later, his white blood cell count suddenly began dropping. Lois took him to the doctor frequently, sometimes several times a month, but nothing the doctor did would make the problems go away. It didn't make any sense—Michael had always been a healthy kid.

For more than a year, a *Niagara Gazette* reporter named Michael Brown had been writing stories about hazardous chemicals leaking out of an old dump site, but Gibbs had never paid attention. She always assumed it was on the other side of town.

In April, though, Lois learned from one of Brown's stories that the Ninety-ninth Street school where Michael attended kindergarten was built right on top of the old chemical dump. She'd started watching the paper for developments—and the article in today's edition scared her half to death. One by one, Brown listed the chemicals that he suspected were present in the dump. One by one, he described the health problems they were known to cause. And one by one, Lois Gibbs recognized her son's mysterious symptoms.

36

HIGH HOPES

April 18, 1978
Willow Springs, Louisiana

The Willow Springs Baptist Church was crowded, more crowded than on Easter Sunday. But this was a Tuesday, and the dozens of people still mingling outside had not come to worship God. The residents of Willow Springs had come to hear Ruth Shepard outline what she'd learned about the sludge pits outside of town.

Her story was frightening.

For ten months, since the day she discovered the pits on High Hopes Road, Shepard had been getting the runaround at town hall. She'd finally forced a few local officials to admit they knew the place existed. But no matter how hard she argued, the civic leaders insisted the chemicals were harmless.

The bits of information she'd managed to put together from her own research told a very different tale.

In 1968, she learned, a company called Mud Movers began dumping industrial waste on seventy-five acres of vacant land on the outskirts of Willow Springs. Four years later, the operation was bought by Browning-Ferris Industries, the second-largest waste-handling company in the country. Browning-Ferris began digging deep, broad ditches on the site. Soon, it was trucking in liquid garbage from all over the South. By 1978, the site contained seven large open pits, full of an unknown mix of chemical and industrial waste.

Browning-Ferris was making good profits on the operation, and wanted to take in even more waste. But the pits were starting to overflow and new pits would fill up almost as quickly as they were dug.

191

Recently, though, company engineers had been exploring a different type of waste disposal, one they contended would open up unlimited chemical dumping space. And they wanted to try it in Willow Springs.

The system was simple. In theory, all Browning-Ferris needed to do was drill a deep, narrow hole in the ground—deeper than the local water supply—then line it with concrete and hook up a powerful pump. When trucks full of noxious chemicals arrived, technicians would inject it, under high pressure, down the hole, out the bottom and into the bowels of the Earth. In Louisiana, the process was especially easy: the state was pockmarked with thousands of abandoned oil wells, already drilled and already lined with concrete. For a few more dollars, each could be turned into an "injection well." As long as the wells went deep enough, the theory went, the chemicals would just disappear.

In early 1976, Shepard told the crowd, Browning-Ferris had received a state approval to construct an injection well on the Willow Springs dump site.

The construction process didn't take long. The Willow Springs site had several abandoned oil wells. By late that year, one had been converted, and an injection well was in operation. The pits were still there, too, only now they were called "holding ponds." Trucks dumped the waste there, and it sat around for a few months. Then the technicians pumped it into the earth, and more trucks came, and the ponds filled up again.

Browning-Ferris officials promised the waste could never leak up to the aquifer or get back to the surface. But the more Shepard learned about the process, the more dangerous it looked. The land along the Gulf Coast was geologically fractured: hard rock, soft, porous rock, and underground rivers were piled in uneven, sometimes shifting layers. No matter how deep the injection wells went, liquid waste wouldn't stay in one place for very long. If enough waste went down there, some of it was bound to come back up. And a lot was going down: the Browning-Ferris well could handle tens of thousands of gallons a day.

Besides, the holding ponds weren't even lined with concrete, and they weren't covered on top.

When Shepard first found out about the possible dangers of the pits, she visited people who lived nearby. Herbert Rigmaiden, a farmer who'd lived down the road all his life, confirmed her worst fears. As far back as 1970, he recalled, the water and air around his farm had been dirty. By 1973, it got so bad he started buying his drinking water in town. Rigmaiden's porch was covered with plastic jugs used to lug home dozens of gallons of water a month. Besides the astronomical cost, it was a lot of extra work. But he worried that the stuff from the faucet would kill him. Since BFI had come to town, he'd watched his wife and mother fall victim to strange cancers.

A while back, Rigmaiden told Shepard, a storm had flooded his land.

Twenty cows wandered into a pool of floodwater, and within a day, they bloated up and started acting strange. When the first one died, he cut her open. Her insides were an odd shade of green.

Shepard urged Rigmaiden to help her organize the neighbors in an effort to get some answers from local officials. He agreed, and brought in his sister, Mabel Jones. A year before, Jones had circulated a petition against the foul-smelling pits, and a few Willow Springs residents signed it. She presented it to the Police Jury, and never heard of it again.

The meeting at the Baptist church this warm, Tuesday evening attracted a lot more attention. Most of the community had turned out. A lot of people had a lot to say about the Willow Springs dump site. Out of the raucous complaints and sympathetic conversations, the High Hopes Road Committee was born. Once again, Ruth Shepard had an organization; once again, she was stirring up trouble. This time, she was making history.

The High Hopes Road Committee would set off a political furor that would help turn the conservative Louisiana bayou towns into hotbeds of environmental action. It would also demonstrate something that much of the environmental movement was slow to learn: the immediate victims of industrial pollution were often the sort of people who didn't join the Sierra Club or Greenpeace. They lived in backwater towns or tough inner cities, they had very little money, they never went hiking in the wilderness—and in many cases, they weren't white.

The next morning, Herbert Rigmaiden was surprised to see Deacon Jones, the Willow Springs Baptist Church pastor, show up on his front porch. Generally, the only time he saw the deacon was at Sunday services. The deacon asked about Herbert's family, and how the farm was doing. Then he asked about yesterday's meeting at the church.

Rigmaiden explained what the group was doing, and how pleased he was with the turnout. The deacon hemmed and hawed for a moment, then told Rigmaiden why he had come. Browning-Ferris just gave the church a donation, he said, to be used for anything the deacon thought appropriate. There was just one condition that came along with the $200: no more meetings like the one held yesterday.

The deacon was very cordial and civilized. From now on, he said, his church was off limits to the High Hopes Road Committee. Perhaps, he suggested, the group could hold its meetings up the road, at the Houston River Baptist Church.

37

ANTINUCLEAR MELTDOWN

June 25, 1978
Seabrook, New Hampshire

It should have been everything the Clamshell Alliance had ever hoped for: the largest antinuclear demonstration in the nation's history.

For two days, the town of Seabrook was bathed in warm sunshine as the marshland around the Seabrook Nuclear Generating Station construction was transformed into an unusual sort of fairground. Big, colorful tents, food stands, concession booths, and demonstrations of the wonders of alternative technology lined the makeshift roadways, serving a steady stream of customers. On a temporary stage in an open, grassy area, Jackson Browne and Arlo Guthrie sang popular folk songs to a dancing, cheering crowd.

Over the weekend, close to twenty thousand people had poured onto the grounds of the Seabrook plant. The demonstration was a stunning show of support for Seabrook opponents and a signal that the movement against nuclear power was developing a far broader, more diverse constituency than anybody had imagined. The peaceful, legal demonstration was a compromise: a few Clamshell Alliance members had agreed to a deal with the New Hampshire authorities to avoid what could have been a bloody confrontation. They did it to preserve the good working relationship the organization had developed with the residents of Seabrook. It was a big step toward building a critical bridge between radical antinuclear activists and the more conservative, traditional people who lived around the plants—people who, like Lois Gibbs in Love Canal, were mostly concerned about somebody poisoning their kids.

The demonstration was front-page news in *The New York Times*. It should have been one of the antinuclear movement's finest moments.

Instead, it almost destroyed the Clamshell Alliance.

*   *   *

Six months earlier, the Clams were soaring, riding a wave of excitement and emotional energy that was building so fast it seemed almost magical. The activists thought it was only a matter of time before the power of the peaceful wave would surge over the nuclear industry.

The movement was exploding all over. From California to Maine, hundreds of antinuclear activists in dozens of new groups were using nonviolent, Seabrook-style tactics to block roads and occupy plant sites.

In November, more than three hundred representatives from fifty local affiliates showed up for a Clamshell Congress in Putney, Vermont, to plan the next occupation. It would be held on June 24, 1978, they decided; as a huge act of civil disobedience, peaceful protesters would take control of the site and restore it to its natural state. They would install windmills and other alternative-energy devices to demonstrate that nuclear power was completely unnecessary. Before the demonstration, all participants would undergo special nonviolence training, and would canvass door-to-door in the local communities to talk to neighbors about the plant.

But as the occupation training got under way, a few problems started to emerge.

For one thing, the Public Service Company had finally done what most security-conscious landlords would have done years before: it had finally surrounded most of the construction site with a chain-link fence. Although small, sensitive areas had been fenced at the time of the first protest, the Clamshell protesters had always been able to walk right onto the company's land and force the police to drag them away.

The fences were clearly an obstacle: as far as anyone could see, gaining access to the site would mean breaking though the steel mesh or pulling some sections down. Without a lot of expensive equipment, there was no way several thousand people could scale a twelve-foot fence topped with barbed wire. But the physical barrier quickly came to represent a much larger set of philosophical divisions, ones that cut to the heart of the emerging antinuclear movement.

To the Clamshell purists, the Seabrook nuke was only one manifestation of a profound social crisis. Nuclear energy, nuclear weapons, corporate power, capitalism, imperialism, racism, sexism, homophobia, rape, and a thousand other ills were all connected, and none of them could be addressed or solved properly without a complete restructuring of the entire world. Tearing down fences was violent, they felt, and thus unacceptable.

To another, equally committed Clamshell faction, the fences were a sign of the organization's weakness. It was silly to waste time fighting about abstract questions like whether the nonviolence code, which forbade the destruction of property, applied to chain-link fences, they argued; this was war, and the object was to win.

And somewhere in between, a third group tried desperately to carve out a middle ground. The internal peacemakers weren't worried about the ethical and philosophical sides of the fences; their concern was entirely practical. The Clamshell Alliance had worked hard to develop a base of support in the conservative Yankee towns along the New England coast. And a lot of those townspeople were very uneasy with the notion of cutting down somebody else's fence, and the prospect of violence that the destruction of property entailed.

The government of New Hampshire was pressing hard against the Clamshell Alliance. With an election year coming up, Governor Meldrim Thomson was determined not to appear soft on protesters; if the Clamshell Alliance tried to occupy the Seabrook plant again, he vowed, the state police would use tear gas, attack dogs, and, if necessary, live ammunition to disperse the protesters and clear the area.

The Rockingham County prosecutor, Carlton Eldridge, who had generally opposed the plant, started making the same sorts of noises. He warned that protesters who cut down fences could face water cannons, nightsticks, and maybe even bullets.

By early spring of 1978, the Clamshell Alliance was under tremendous stress; its delicate internal structure was collapsing.

The local Clamshell groups met openly, and anyone who walked through the door could be considered a member. The organization operated under the principle of "consensus"; there were no votes, no majority rule. Every single member had to agree before any decision could be made. So anyone who walked through the door—of a college dormitory lounge, or a YMCA community center, or a church basement, or any of the other places where Clamshell chapters met—could single-handedly halt the entire organization in its tracks.

Meetings could drag on for twelve hours or more; sometimes, the only way an issue could be settled was for all of the people with strong opinions to get so tired they would leave. Then the ones who remained—often, the college students, the unemployed, and the independent professionals, who didn't have to worry about going to work the next day—could finally have their way.

In the best of times, the process could be paralyzing. In dealing with politicians, it could lead to disaster.

Attorney General Tom Rath, intentionally or not, managed to capitalize on the problem. The new attorney general had taken office just a few months earlier, when David Souter was elevated to a post on the New Hampshire Superior Court. Rath had a keen political mind, and he wasn't all that fond of Governor Thomson. He knew that if he could broker a deal with the Clamshell Alliance, one that would keep the peace at Seabrook, it would please almost everyone in New Hampshire and give quite a boost to his career. It would also deprive the governor of a chance to play a tough law-and-order man on national TV. So Rath made an offer, designed, he said, to defuse the potential for violence. The deal was simple: The Public Service Company and the state police would allow the Clamshell Alliance to enter and occupy a sizable portion of the plant site, and stage an antinuclear rally—over the weekend, when no construction would be going on. In exchange, the protesters would promise to clear out, peacefully and without resistance, by the time the first shift arrived for work Monday morning.

At first, the Clams were almost unanimous in their response: the deal was a sellout. The state was trying to co-opt the power of the Clamshell Alliance's civil disobedience tactics. The occupations were not supposed to be symbolic media events—the idea was to take over the site and stop construction of the nuke, which was still moving forward slowly.

But before long, Harvey Wasserman and Sam Lovejoy, the two veteran activists from the Montague commune, found themselves making a case for accepting the Rath proposal. They weren't alone: within a week, a fair percentage of the membership—especially the older members, who had been through the antiwar movement—were lining up in favor of the deal. It had some distinct advantages, they argued. A violent police confrontation would play right into the hands of Thomson's hard-liners, and might leave a few of the protesters injured or even dead. A peaceful, legal rally would have the full support of the Seabrook community, and could help the Clams expand their local base. Besides, that way they would never have to decide the conflict over cutting down the fences.

It would also give the Clamshell Alliance a chance to start organizing around a new issue, one that could turn into fertile antinuclear turf: the Public Service Company's constant hikes in electric rates, hikes that were needed to pay for the nuclear plant.

While groups like the Clamshell Alliance were protesting over the safety hazards of nuclear power plants, economics was quickly becoming the nuclear industry's Achilles' heel. When Seabrook was first proposed, the Public Service Company had promised it would mean low electric rates for at least thirty years; within four years, PSCO had raised the price of electricity in New Hampshire by 112 percent.

The cost of building the Seabrook plant kept going up every day. From the original estimate of $973 million, the price tag soared to more than $2.5 billion, and there was no end in sight. As a 50 percent owner, Public Service Company was responsible for putting up half the construction money—more than a billion dollars by 1977. For a small local utility, that was a huge amount of cash. So PSCO borrowed heavily, mostly by selling bonds.

Before the Seabrook plant was proposed, Public Service Company had pretty good credit—the big Wall Street credit agencies gave it an A rating, which meant the utility would have to pay about 8 percent interest on its bonds. But the minute the company proposed to build a giant nuclear power plant, Wall Street started backing off.

PSCO lost its A rating in 1972. Wall Street analysts were nervous about the Seabrook project—even at a projected cost of $973 million, the analysts argued, it was far too big an undertaking for such a little utility. By 1976, the company's credit rating had fallen dramatically; big investors considered Public Service bonds too risky for comfort, and the company was forced to pay as much as 12 percent interest to find buyers for its bonds.

In the wake of the energy crisis of 1973, sales of electricity started to drop off all over the country, and New Hampshire was no different. All through the 1960s, PSCO sales had grown by almost 9 percent a year; in 1974, growth slowed to almost nothing, and by 1976, sales were actually starting to decline. With demand for electricity leveling off, a few people argued, the need for the plant was becoming more dubious; in 1976, an economist hired by the New Hampshire Public Utilities Commission concluded that the Seabrook project would leave PSCO with far more generating capacity than it could use. But the report was suppressed, and the economist was immediately transferred to another department.

In the fall of 1977, the company's financial situation was approaching a crisis. PSCO would need to borrow roughly $300 million over the next two years to continue construction at Seabrook. The bond-rating agencies were issuing warnings that Public Service bonds were "not of investment quality," and the utility's bankers had cut off its line of credit.

So the company went to the state Public Utilities Commission to beg for mercy. In October, a consultant for the utility told the PUC that that utility was "on the brink of financial disaster." The only way to recover, company lawyers argued, was to take a highly unusual step, and start billing customers directly for the Seabrook construction costs, even though the plant wouldn't generate a watt of electricity for at least another five years. A sharply divided PUC agreed to accept the proposal.

The decision turned half a century of utility regulation on its head. Normally, private electric companies could only start charging their customers for new power plants when the plants were finished and began generating power; until then, they were considered unproven investments, and like any private business, the utility stockholders had to bear the costs. The tightfisted New Hampshire voters were outraged by the prospect of paying for a private company's risky investment, and the state legislature quickly passed a bill outlawing utility charges for "construction work in progress." But Governor Thomson, long an ally of the utility industry, vetoed the bill, and the rate hikes went into effect.

The rate hikes were alienating even conservatives who had always supported nuclear power. A car salesman named Hugh Gallen, who had taken on the hopeless chore of challenging an incumbent Republican governor, was making tremendous headway all over New Hampshire by vowing to stop PSCO from charging its customers for the unfinished nuclear plant.

The economics of nuclear power had the potential for uniting the radical antinuclear activists with the conservative New Hampshire Yankees for the common cause of halting the Seabrook nuke. But the tactics and ideology of the Clamshell Alliance prevented it from seizing the opportunity. Neither could the Clams agree on how to react to Rath's proposal. Organizing efforts for June 24 ground to a total halt.

Three weeks before the demonstration, three hundred members of the Clamshell Coordinating Committee held a thirteen-hour meeting and crafted a statement that said essentially that any change would be impossible. Since the organization had reached a "consensus" agreement on the occupation back in November, any change in plans would also require a new consensus, and that was impossible. So the occupation would proceed.

But to mollify supporters of Rath's proposal for a legal rally, the committee agreed to accept the attorney general's offer—on the condition that the Public Service Company halt all construction immediately until it could prove that the nuclear plant was safe.

Rath had to acknowledge the offer for what it was—a silly public relations effort that amounted to a rejection. He announced that he was sorry, but plans for arresting the demonstrators would move forward.

Governor Thomson was elated. He berated the attorney general for making the compromise offer, and proclaimed that the Clamshell Alliance had publicly humiliated itself. The protesters, he announced, were a "gurgling, spurting bunch of nonproductive individuals."

On Saturday, June 10, the coordinating committee met for a final session, to wrap up some last-minute logistical details for the upcoming occupation. The turnout was unexpectedly small; the issues at hand were unexpectedly large.

Over the past week, virtually every local organization that opposed the Seabrook plant had withdrawn its support for the occupation, fearing violence. Clamshell members from Seabrook and Hampton Falls showed up to beg the committee to reconsider the Rath proposal.

Baffled and moved by the presentations, and unsure of how to proceed, the committee did something it technically had no right to do: with one member abstaining, it reached a consensus to overturn the Clamshell's previous decisions and accept the attorney general's offer.

A delegation quickly carried the message to Rath, and he quickly endorsed the plan. The occupation was off, replaced by a rally and "alternative-energy fair." It would be peaceful and legal; the Clamshell members would arrive Friday afternoon, and everyone would leave by Monday morning. Anyone who broke the rules, the delegation announced, "is not a member of the Clamshell Alliance."

The move set off a furor in the Clamshell ranks. This was exactly what the consensus process was designed to avoid; it was domination, hierarchy, and elitism. But it was too late to change. Nothing could be done but to go along and try to make the event a success.

In the state capital, the reaction among right-wing Republicans was far more vicious and divisive. The *Manchester Union Leader* ran a front-page editorial blaming Thomson for caving in to the antinuclear radicals and insisting that he should have forced the attorney general to withdraw the offer the minute the Clamshell Alliance failed to go along. "The Clams have achieved a propaganda victory of sorts by outmaneuvering both the state and the Public Service Company," the paper said. "It's not that the Clams are overly bright. It's just that when it comes to understanding their perverse mentality, state and company officials are just stupid."

Despite it all, Wasserman marveled, there were no signs of rancor among the Clams at the fair, no indications of a split in the ranks. All appeared to be well; the broad antinuclear coalition seemed to be holding. On the stage, Benjamin Spock, the legendary pediatrician whose books had served at least a million mothers, invoked the idealistic spirit of the sixties. John Gofman outlined the rational, scientific case against nuclear energy. And a woman from Boston named Laurie Holmes told the crowd that "nuclear power is a feminist and lesbian issue."

"The struggle against the rape of our earth by rich, white males," she proclaimed, "is the same struggle as the struggle against the rape of our bodies and the rape of our lives."

As the Clams broke down their windmill and geodesic dome and cleared away the physical impediments to the nuclear plant construction, the cool night air seemed full of hope and promise. But deep down, the divisions from the spring had never healed. The Clamshell Alliance would never recover.

38

WOMEN AND CHILDREN FIRST

August 1, 1978
Niagara Falls, New York

Lois Gibbs gathered the results of three months of research—newspaper clippings, scribbled questions, and articles from technical journals—and stuffed it all into a big folder as she ran out the door. She got in the car with her husband Harry and their friend Debbie Cerrillo, and they drove off toward Albany, the state capital. The New York State Department of Public Health was about to make an announcement about chemical contamination at Love Canal.

Over the past four months, Gibbs had talked to a lot of her neighbors and had put together an informal study on health problems in the area. The results were alarming—all around the old Hooker Chemical dump site, people who had no prior record of health problems were getting sick. At the same time, thanks to Michael Brown's newspaper articles, the state health department had started a study of its own. The agency had called a public meeting to announce its conclusions, and although Gibbs had never been to Albany before, she was determined to be on hand. If the state study didn't turn up anything, she figured, maybe she could talk about hers.

On the way out of town, the three travelers stopped to visit Wayne Hadley, Lois's brother-in-law. Hadley was a biologist, and he'd been helping Lois understand some of the scientific details of the toxic waste problem. This day, though, his advice was entirely political: "If you want the press to pay attention to you," he told the group, "make your bid within the first fifteen minutes." After that, he said, all the journalists would probably leave.

The drive to Albany should have taken about six hours, but Harry loved to stop at rest stops and chat over a cup of coffee. At three o'clock in the morning, after twelve hours on the road, the Gibbs party finally pulled into the capital and collapsed in the cheapest motel room they could find.

Michael Brown was also going to the health department meeting, but before he left, he had another meeting to attend. A Hooker Chemical executive had asked Brown and his boss to come by the company office to discuss the *Niagara Gazette*'s coverage of Love Canal. The tone of the invitation wasn't friendly, and Brown knew the meeting would be a nightmare, but the paper's publisher, Susan Clark, had made it clear she was going, and she wanted him to come along.

The minute Clark and Brown walked into the Hooker office, Clark went over to Charles Cain, the company's vice president for public affairs, and gave him a big hug. The meeting went downhill from there.

"Let me just say this," Cain told the visitors. "We just did a little survey, and we found Hooker is more popular in town than the *Niagara Gazette*." He went on to accuse Brown of shoddy journalism, and advised him to watch his step.

By the next morning, however, Brown was more committed to the story than ever. Hooker's warning made him more convinced that Love Canal was a big story, that the company had something to hide. The word was getting out, too: the morning edition of *The New York Times* carried a story headlined UPSTATE WASTE SITE MAY ENDANGER LIVES, based on Brown's work at the *Gazette*.

Brown arrived at the government building in Albany just a few minutes after the meeting began. Lois and Harry Gibbs and Debbie Cerrillo were already there, along with some other Love Canal residents.

Robert Whalen, the state health commissioner, opened the meeting by reading an order stating that residents of Love Canal should not eat food from their gardens, and explaining how the state was going to clean up the schoolyard. People nodded and sipped their coffee—none of this was news. Within minutes, though, the commissioner dropped a bomb: he urged the evacuation of all pregnant women and all children under two years of age.

"Love Canal," the commissioner said, "is a great and imminent peril to the health of the general public."

The small crowd sat in stunned silence. Panicked whispers spread through the room, as the people from Love Canal realized their worst fears had been confirmed. The place was poisoned, really poisoned. But Gibbs's panic quickly turned to anger. The state, she realized, was admitting the place was deadly, but the solution it offered was to split up families, leaving everyone but pregnant women and toddlers to remain in a toxic dump.

Remembering Hadley's advice about the press, Gibbs jumped to her feet. "You can't do that! That would be murder," she shouted. "Wait a minute," Cerrillo chimed in. "My kids are over two. Are you trying to tell me my children are safe?" As Gibbs and Cerrillo kept shouting questions, demanding to know why more wasn't being done, and why the state was unwilling to evacuate everyone, Commissioner Whalen abruptly adjourned the meeting. Dr. David Axelrod, who worked with the health commission, announced he would hold a public meeting in Niagara Falls in two days and explain the situation to residents. Outraged, Gibbs and her companions left the capital and immediately started for home. This time, they didn't even stop for coffee.

By the time the three arrived back at Love Canal, word of the commission's warning had already arrived. Lois's mother was standing on the Gibbses' sidewalk, jumping up and down, waving her arms. She said the whole place had gone crazy; everyone was at a big meeting on Ninety-ninth Street. All Gibbs wanted in the world right then was a little sleep, but she decided to check out the meeting anyway. She dragged her two companions along with her.

A block away from Ninety-ninth, the noise of the crowd reached them. It was a mob scene. Her mother had been right: everyone was going crazy. Hundreds of men and women were shouting furiously. At the front of the crowd, a resident named Tom Heisner was talking through a makeshift public address system, urging everyone to burn their mortgages and their tax bills. "Our homes are worthless," he yelled. "They're less than worthless. We can't get near them, can't live in them."

A few feet away, somebody had put a garbage can in the street and started a fire, and as Lois Gibbs watched, an unlikely group of revolutionaries— housewives, retired plumbers and welders, teachers and bus drivers— marched up and tossed piles of mortgages and bills into the blaze.

Then Heisner recognized Gibbs, and quickly handed over the microphone. Gibbs was terrified; she'd never spoken before this many people, and she'd certainly never used a microphone. The minute she touched it, it started to squeal.

The crowd fell silent. Gibbs calmed herself down, took a deep breath, and started to speak. She told the crowd exactly what Commissioner Whalen had said about pregnant women and children and how ridiculous his proposal sounded. The problem, she said, was clearly worse than the state was admitting. She asked everyone to write down all the health problems they'd had since moving to Love Canal, and promised that someone would come around soon to collect the reports.

As she spoke, Gibbs began to gain confidence. She stopped punctuating each sentence with a tentative "okay." She told her neighbors they'd have to work hard to make the government listen. If they had a cold or a headache or always felt tired, they had to call Albany. If their children had eye problems, trouble keeping up at school, or birth defects—call Albany. Before she left for a few hours of sleep, she reminded the still-frantic crowd to show up for the meeting with Dr. Axelrod, who had promised to be at the school the next night.

The Gibbses' living room, usually spotless, was cluttered with newspapers, dirty dishes, and trash. The floors were filthy. For the third night in a row, Lois Gibbs went to sleep at three-thirty A.M., numb with fatigue. By six A.M., the phone was ringing with calls from reporters on early deadlines.

The next evening, when the delegation of state officials arrived at the school auditorium, several hundred angry residents were on hand to greet them. So were reporters from television stations and newspapers all over the state. It was a hot night. Dr. Axelrod, Commissioner Whalen, and a few assistants sat on the stage, sweating, as people fired questions and accusations. But the officials never wavered from their position, and didn't disclose any new information.

Through it all, Gibbs felt Whalen staring at her, as if she were the one responsible for it all. As if the diseases and deaths were just a result of some housewife stirring up trouble.

Gibbs spent the next day on the phone, fielding calls from the press in her dirty living room and setting up another neighborhood meeting. More than six hundred people showed up at a local firehouse that evening for the birth of the Love Canal Homeowners Association. Lois Gibbs was elected president.

As the new group debated strategies, took dues, elected officers, and tried to create an organization out of chaos, Gibbs felt her head begin to spin. It all seemed so unreal, as if she were living somebody else's life. As she staggered home well after midnight, she wondered if she'd ever get a good night's sleep again.

39

A FEW SLINGSHOTS

October 1978
Baton Rouge, Louisiana

William A. Fontenot sat back in his big office, with its executive-style furniture, and wondered what he was supposed to do. No one had ever had a job like this in the Louisiana attorney general's office, or in any other office in Louisiana. In fact, he had the only job of its kind in the United States.

Fontenot's title was Environmental Specialist, Citizen's Access Unit for the Attorney General's Office, State of Louisiana. It was a long title, but the idea was straightforward. Fontenot was supposed to help citizens who wanted to fight pollution from a grassroots level. The man who hired him, Attorney General William Guste, had never offered any specific details; he just put Fontenot in an office and told him to get going.

Fontenot had no way of knowing he was about to become a major catalyst in the grassroots revolution that was brewing in Louisiana. Over the next ten years, he would help create some three hundred environmental organizations, by far the most of any state in the country.

It was an odd record for Louisiana, and the fact that someone appointed by a top-ranking politician helped make it happen was odder still. In essence, Fontenot's job was to use the resources of the state to help people fight the state—and to use the good graces of a politician to help people fight the most powerful political force in Louisiana, the oil and chemical industry.

The ties between politicians and the oil industry went back to the 1930s, when oilmen surged into Louisiana looking for "black gold" under the swamps and bayous. Huey Long, the populist "kingfish" governor of the 1940s, built his populist reputation by fighting the oil barons, sticking up for the "little guy." But he secretly cast his lot instead with the people he'd been

205

fighting. In 1934, Long and some buddies formed the Win or Lose Corporation. Using Long's already substantial political connections, they bought state mineral leases cheap, and resold them at large profits to oil companies in Texas and Oklahoma.

Most of the leases were sold to a little outfit called the Texas Company, and with the wealth of oil and gas under the bayous, the fledgling company grew quickly into a corporate giant called Texaco. As for Long and his heirs, royalty money poured in by the tens of millions.

The tradition of mixing oil and politics continued up to Fontenot's time. In fact, it may have gotten worse.

Governor Edwin Edwards, a three-term Democrat also elected on a populist platform, didn't see any need to disguise the fact that his oil-company investments earned him $100,000 a year in royalties.

By the mid-1970s, Louisiana was the nation's leading producer of natural gas, and second in oil. By all rights, the state should have been extremely wealthy. Instead, it was the fifth poorest in the nation, and had the highest illiteracy rate.

It also had some of the highest concentrations of chemical waste. Nearly a billion pounds a year of oil's toxic by-products went into the state's air, rivers, and land, more than twice the amount dumped in any other state except Texas.

Part of the problem came from the oil wells. Drilling a well required huge amounts of toxic sludge—as the drill bit bored into the earth, operators drenched it constantly with a substance called "drilling mud." The mud was a mix of asbestos, formaldehyde, and carbolic acid, combined with caustic soda (the active ingredient in Drano), and a few heavy metals, like barium and arsenic.

With four thousand new wells under way each year, the Louisiana oil and gas industry spent more money on drilling mud than all the other states combined. A single, typical well might require one million pounds of mud—and a third remained underground. What returned to the surface was often deadlier than what went down, having picked up along the way such things as mercury, selenium, and radioactive isotopes of potassium. Sometimes the used mud was sent to landfills, other times it was dumped into oil wells that had come up dry. Often, the waste mud was abandoned in small earthen pits around the drill site. Thousands of such pits pocked the Louisiana marshlands, almost all of them slowly leaking into the groundwater.

Most of the work involved in the oil business didn't even come from drilling—it came from the complex process of taking raw crude and turning it into more and more refined products. A hundred huge refineries and chemical plants lined the Mississippi River, from Baton Rouge to New Orleans, taking in crude and churning out fertilizers, plastics, gasoline, nylon—and tons and tons of poison.

When Attorney General Guste offered Willie Fontenot a job, he described it as a maverick position, one that would help citizens get involved in environmental efforts and encourage them to take charge of their communities. Guste promised to back Fontenot if he ever got into trouble. The attorney general may not have realized quite what he was starting, but he remained true to his word.

Fontenot wasn't a typical Louisiana politician—he wasn't a rabble-rouser, a womanizer, a gambler, or a thief. A calm, soft-spoken man with round, wire-rimmed glasses, Fontenot had a long history of environmental activism. In the late 1960s, he'd joined a mainstream civic organization that was fighting a highway bypass around New Orleans. That led to positions with the Sierra Club, the Ecology Center of Louisiana, and the National Wildlife Federation. Along the way, he'd lost any hope of a normal career. Fontenot was virtually incorruptible: he had no interest in personal wealth or political advancement. He had no interest in compromising with the oil or chemical industries, either.

The way Fontenot saw it, grassroots environmental activists in Louisiana were starting off with huge disadvantages. Without help, they couldn't successfully fight the oil and chemical companies, the major polluters and political operators in the state. It was like taking on Goliath with no hope of divine intervention.

Fontenot couldn't bring down the wrath of God. But at least, he thought, he could hand out a few slingshots.

40

LIVE AND LEARN

November 8, 1978
Hampton, New Hampshire

The first of the 1,414 Seabrook defendants arrived in Rockingham County Court prepared to be the next Sam Lovejoy.

By now, the man who toppled the utility tower in Montague, Massachusetts, had become something of a celebrity in antinuclear circles—his exploits were even the subject of a popular documentary film called *Lovejoy's Nuclear War*. Lovejoy had challenged his arrest in court, and in the process, put nuclear power itself on trial; now everyone who got arrested at Seabrook wanted to follow in his tracks.

The Clamshell Alliance fought hard for this moment. More than five hundred members spent two long weeks in crowded National Guard armories, demanding the right to make their case before a jury of their peers. The first defendant, Carter Wentworth, a twenty-six-year-old artist from the nearby town of Kensington, had prepared a "defense of necessity"; he would argue, as Lovejoy did, that the threat of a nuclear plant was so serious, so profound, that it justified breaking an ordinary law.

A citizen of New Hampshire could ignore the trespassing statutes and break down a neighbor's door if an elderly relative was trapped inside and the house was on fire; a motorist could dismiss the traffic codes and swerve across a double line to avoid running down a pedestrian. By the same logic, attorney Eric Blumenson would tell the jury, Wentworth had every right to trespass on Public Service Company land to save the people of New England from the horror of a nuclear accident.

Judge Wayne Mullavey would have none of it.

One after another, Blumenson called his expert witnesses to the stand, people who could testify, as John Gofman did at Lovejoy's trial, about the

208

dangers of this runaway technology. One after another, Mullavey ruled them out of order.

In his closing argument, Blumenson tried to tell the jury that the crime of criminal trespass required "knowing and willful" violation of the law. The jurors asked the judge to explain that part of the statute, but Mullavey instructed the jury to decide the case on the simplest of legal issues: Was the defendant on the company property? Did he leave when he was told? If not, the verdict should be guilty.

And guilty it was, three men and three women reaching a unanimous conclusion on the basis of facts that were hard to deny.

With the verdict in, Judge Mullavey pronounced sentence. The prosecution asked for essentially the same penalty the attorney general had sought back in May—fifteen days in jail and a fine of $100—but Mullavey had other ideas. The Seabrook occupation, the judge said, had been "a mob action," producing an "explosive situation." This sort of behavior should not be allowed to continue; the proper sentence could act as a strong deterrent to those who might contemplate similar actions in the future.

The defendant, he announced, would serve four months in prison. Then he banged his gavel and called the next case.

The message rang loud and clear for anyone in the antinuclear movement who was willing to listen: Sam Lovejoy had been lucky. Not many courts were prepared to play host to an antinuclear show trial. If that was what the demonstrators had in mind, they needed to take a hard look at their tactics.

But over the next five years, protesters all over the country would keep trying to "put nuclear power on trial." Lawyers would keep preparing "defenses of necessity." And judges would keep refusing to play along.

Construction on the nuclear power plants could continue.

In Manchester, New Hampshire, however, the Public Service Company had received a clear political message, too. On election day, Governor Meldrim Thomson, a strong Seabrook supporter, had gone down to defeat. Hugh Gallen, a Democratic car salesman, was the state's new chief executive.

Gallen's campaign had only one real theme: he ran against the Seabrook rate hikes. He opposed "Construction Work In Progress" charges, the utility's program of charging its customers for the costs of the unbuilt nuke, and Thomson supported them. That had turned the election. After all the Clamshell Alliance demonstrations, the people of New Hampshire had finally rebelled—against high electric bills.

PSCO president William Tallman was under no illusions: from now on, the company would have to find a whole new way of financing Seabrook.

41

GHOST TOWN

October 1, 1980
Niagara Falls, New York

The Niagara Falls Convention Center was packed with reporters, Secret Service agents, and politicians. Love Canal residents jammed the aisles, enjoying the spectacle: one after the other, public officials who had tried to avoid and stonewall the residents for years were making speeches praising their courage and persistence.

Lois Gibbs stood in the center of the stage, facing the crowd. She wore a simple dress, and had tucked a white carnation into her hair, symbolizing, she told reporters, her support for the hostages—the ones imprisoned in Iran, and the newly liberated ones of Love Canal. Standing next to her was the president of the United States.

Jimmy Carter put his arm around Gibbs and smiled for the cameras. Then he picked up his pen and signed the document in front of him. The federal government had just allocated more than $15 million to purchase every house in Love Canal.

For most of the residents, it was the end of an ugly chapter in their lives. For two years, they had lived with an awful dilemma: the place was too dangerous for anyone to stay, but since it was so dangerous, their property could never be sold, and the working-class homeowners couldn't afford to move. Now, with the government stepping in, they could start over somewhere else.

For Lois Gibbs, the battle had only begun.

Love Canal had transformed the quiet homemaker into a national political figure. For the past two years, she had been relentless. She organized her neighbors, taught herself enough chemistry to argue with the industry scientists, and pursued every possible channel of action. She worked her way up and down the political spectrum, moving from local and state health officials to the governor, congressional representatives and senators, and eventually, the White House.

The angry young mother with the sick children made great news copy, and Gibbs was always ready to meet the press. Her face was constantly on television. Her name was always in the papers. And all over the United States, she touched a nerve. She had book offers, movie offers, job offers, invitations to make speeches, and invitations to appear with political candidates. Now she was on stage with the president.

But Gibbs had done more than become a celebrity. She'd brought a little-known tragedy into the living rooms of millions of Americans. Almost by herself, she'd put toxic waste on the top of the national agenda. She had become an inspiration for people like Ruth Shepard all over the country.

And as she kept telling herself, there was still so much to do.

The federal government was only beginning to come to grips with the toxic time bomb. In October of 1976, just three months before Carter took office, President Gerald Ford signed the first major piece of legislation aimed specifically at the toxic-waste problem, the Resource Conservation and Recovery Act. The act gave the Environmental Protection Agency authority to regulate hazardous waste from "cradle to grave." A trail of documents would track every ounce of dangerous material from the manufacturing plant to the dump site. That way, nobody would build another school on top of another Love Canal.

But the law never had much effect, because the EPA never implemented or enforced it. In 1979, the House Subcommittee on Oversight and Investigations found that three years after the passage of the law, the EPA still hadn't adopted a single RCRA regulation. Some 260 million pounds of life-threatening chemicals were still being dumped every day, without federal oversight. A few EPA staffers went public with their complaints. Hugh Kaufman, the agency's chief toxic investigator, told reporters: "What do you expect? EPA lobbied against RCRA in the first place, and it has no intention of ever aggressively enforcing it." William Sanjour, head of the EPA's hazardous waste assessment branch, who helped draft and pass RCRA, told the *Philadelphia Inquirer*, "I've probably killed more people by passing that act."

But Jimmy Carter had a new law up his sleeve, a measure called "Superfund." The bill called for a new tax on the chemical industry, to pay for the cleanup of hazardous wastes. The way it was initially written, it would also make companies strictly liable for whatever damage they might cause in the creation, handling, transportation, and disposal of hazardous substances.

But under heavy lobbying from the Chemical Manufacturers Association, Congress utlimately passed a much-weakened version of the bill that left out all the liability clauses. Senator George J. Mitchell, a Democrat from Maine, raged: "This Senate has made the judgement that property is more significant than human beings, and none of us should delude ourselves or the people of this country that we have done anything more dishonorable."

The first day Carter took office, January 1, 1977, he had signed another piece of toxics legislation, the Toxic Substances Control Act. The original intent of the measure was to give the EPA a means to control the use and spread of poisonous chemicals. But like the RCRA, once it became law, it effectively vanished.

In theory, the bill gave the agency authority over the roughly 1,800 new chemicals that came on the market every year. By the time it got out of Congress, though, the law actually stipulated that the burden of proof in determining a new chemical's safety or potential toxic side effects lay with the EPA, not the chemical manufacturers. New pesticides, insecticides, and other lifeless compounds dreamed up in laboratories were innocent until proven guilty.

The EPA, of course, couldn't begin to test that many new chemicals. So the manufacturers kept making them, and nobody could do anything about it.

Lois Gibbs had been a key participant in the 1979 congressional Superfund hearings. She still had some hope for the law. But she had learned enough about the history of other toxic regulations to remain largely skeptical. As far as she could tell, Congress and the EPA would always be unwilling or unable to take on problems like Love Canal—unless enough people like her and her neighbors made enough of a fuss about it. From now on, that was how she planned to spend her life.

As for the tidy Niagara Falls suburb, with its green lawns and homes for young families, it would be fenced off and become a toxic ghost town. It would be many years before anyone would ever live in Love Canal again.

PART 7

THE CALL OF THE WILD

Have these people ever stopped to think what wilderness is? It is precisely what man has been fighting against since he began his painful, awkward climb to civilization. It is the dark, the formless, the terrible, the old chaos which our fathers pushed back, which surrounds us yet, which will engulf us all in the end. It is held at bay by constant vigilance.

—Robert Wernick, "Let's Spoil the Wilderness," Saturday Evening Post, *November 6, 1965*

Wilderness preservation was the first major environmental struggle. The early battles over wild areas helped define and shape the nascent conservation movement in the first part of the twentieth century, and in the late 1970s, the issue would come to dominate environmental politics again.

In the early days, most wilderness debates had focused on individual sites—a dam here, a forest there. When the issue resurfaced, the context had changed—the battle wasn't just over one parcel or project, but over a comprehensive plan for saving the last remaining roadless areas in the United States.

In 1977, the Interior Department began a complete survey of all the remaining roadless areas that weren't in the federal wilderness system, and recommended that some of those areas be protected from development. The project was supposed to be a victory for environmentalists, and the leaders of the major environmental groups accepted a compromise plan. But like David Brower at Glen Canyon, a few of them later decided it had been a terrible mistake.

42

THE WILD, THE INNOCENT

January 4, 1979
Washington, D.C.

In a comfortable office three blocks north of the White House, the chief lobbyist for the Wilderness Society propped his cowboy boots on his desk and cracked open another cold Stroh's. It was a gray day in the nation's capital; a big storm had blown in the day before, leaving the streets wet and the air chilly. Dave Foreman was in a foul mood.

About an hour earlier, a Forest Service official had announced the conclusions of the second Roadless Area Review and Evaluation study, a twenty-month program that had become the most important wilderness battle in a generation. The official statement was a jumble of big numbers and technical jargon, but there was no mistaking the bottom line: the environmentalists had lost. Badly.

Foreman was still numb from the shock. It wasn't supposed to happen this way. The big environmental groups had done exactly what the Washington insiders said they should do: they worked together, in coalition. Lobbyists from the Sierra Club, the Wilderness Society, the Audubon Society, the National Wildlife Federation, and a few other groups met regularly to devise common strategies. They kept their disagreements private, and when they met with administration officials, they spoke with a common voice.

And through it all, they had been so incredibly reasonable. They acted like professionals: they didn't issue threats or stage demonstrations. They didn't denounce their opponents in angry press releases. They didn't even demand what they really wanted—they gave in here, compromised there, and agreed to treat the logging, ranching, mining, and oil interests with respect, and to let the industries have a fair share. They acknowledged the

216

importance of economic issues, and the nation's energy needs, in setting wilderness policy. They kept the restless membership chapters quiet.

Somehow, Foreman realized, the environmental groups, representing maybe thirty million Americans, had gotten their collective butts kicked. Just what the hell had gone wrong?

As he thought over the history of the roadless area study, the answer started to become unpleasantly clear.

The Forest Service managed roughly 209 million acres of mountain, valley, plains, and prairie grassland. In 1964, Congress set aside a tiny portion of the national forest system as protected wilderness areas, places that have been, and must remain, relatively untouched by human civilization. The legislation directed the secretary of agriculture to review the holdings and recommend additional areas for wilderness designation, as he or she saw fit.

By the mid-1970s, the National Wilderness Preservation System was approaching twenty million acres, less than a tenth of the total Forest Service holdings. Another eighty million acres was still relatively untouched—largely because, for one reason or another, nobody had gotten around to building a road through it. But with the energy crisis on everyone's mind, the oil and gas companies were looking aggressively for new domestic supplies, and their petroleum geologists were looking at the federal land. The construction industry was also in a recession and trying desperately to keep down the price of building supplies—primarily lumber. So timber companies were being urged to cut more trees, and often the best place to find them was in national forests.

Since 1964, all of the additions to the National Wilderness Preservation System had been done piecemeal—Congress would add a few thousand acres in one state, then a few thousand in another, always over howls of protest from local industries that might have designs on the land. And slowly, but steadily, the remaining wilderness was slipping away.

The election of Jimmy Carter in 1976 elated the wilderness preservation groups. No president in seventy-five years had made wilderness so much of a concern. And after eight long years of fighting Republicans who seemed to consider industry their friends and environmentalists their enemies, even a moderate Democrat would be a welcome change. At first, the new president did little to dampen those hopes—in fact, veteran environmental leaders were finding themselves recruited for jobs in the Carter administration. Rupert Cutler, a former Wilderness Society staffer, was hired as assistant secretary of agriculture, and was running the day-to-day operations of the United States Forest Service.

With the support of environmentalists, Cutler launched an ambitious project: the Forest Service would undertake an extensive study of 62 million acres of roadless area that did not yet have wilderness protection. The study would determine which sites were threatened by development, which were appropriate for wilderness status, and which had such tremendous value for industrial use that they should be exempt from future protection. In one bold stroke, the agency would halt the slow, acre-by-acre erosion of the undeveloped national forests and put forward a proposal for a sweeping expansion of the wilderness system that would save environmentalists from continually fighting brushfires on a hundred different fronts.

In 1972, the Forest Service had made an abortive attempt at a comprehensive wilderness study, dubbed the Roadless Area Review and Evaluation. It was scrapped before it got off the ground, when a federal judge ruled that the project violated the National Environmental Policy Act; the agency had never bothered to prepare an environmental impact statement. This time, Cutler vowed, things would be different—he commissioned a detailed EIS to examine a range of possible alternatives for forest management, and in May 1977, the second Roadless Area Review and Evaluation, RARE II, got under way.

At first, industry leaders were distinctly unhappy with the project. With Cutler at the helm, they feared, the RARE II inventory would almost certainly be slanted toward wilderness preservation. Cutler would work with his environmental friends, and by the time the final report was done, the Forest Service would be recommending a tremendous expansion of the wilderness system.

But slowly, the lobbyists from the timber, mining, oil, and ranching associations began to see another side to the story. At private breakfasts and cocktail receptions, a few friendly congressmen and senators explained that a comprehensive wilderness bill might not be such a bad thing. If wilderness areas continued to be designated one at a time, business leaders could find themselves in a bind: it would be easy enough for a local lumber operation to pressure, say, a senator from Oregon to oppose an Oregon wilderness bill—but a senator from Texas, or Arizona, might not care a bit about the Oregon logging industry. And those senators might care very much about the endorsement and support of a few national environmental groups.

A national bill, with wilderness areas in almost every state, would be very different. The interests of a wide range of industries would be affected—and in every state, every senator and almost every member of the House would have some local business breathing down his or her back. The trick was not to oppose a wilderness bill, but to work from the start to ensure that it was as limited as possible—and that most of the remaining roadless areas wound up released forever from wilderness consideration.

The industry lobbyists got to work, conducting their own surveys of likely wilderness areas, organizing letter-writing campaigns from local business leaders in each area, and announcing to anyone in earshot—especially the news media—that extensive new wilderness protections would threaten the nation's energy independence, cripple the economy, and throw millions of Americans out of work.

The wilderness lobbyists were working, too, presenting the Forest Service with detailed, factual analyses of the various study areas, careful comments on the issues, and measured responses to the industries' concerns. They knew their friend Cutler was under tremendous pressure—from industry, from the Department of Energy, which was worried about domestic oil exploration, and even from Democrats in Congress, who were worried about the economy, the long lines and high prices at the gas pumps, and the ugly prospect of running for reelection as members of the incumbent president's party during a national recession. And the wilderness group knew they needed the support of the president and congressional Democrats on a host of upcoming environmental bills.

Some leading environmental lawyers suggested privately that the EIS Cutler had commissioned, while better than the 1972 version, was still clearly inadequate, but the lobbyists urged their organizations not even to threaten a suit. The last thing they wanted to do was make their friends in the administration and Congress angry.

Instead, as the study wound to a close, the major environmental organizations agreed to what they saw as an exceptionally reasonable compromise: they would seek wilderness protection for only about twenty million acres—a third of the land in the survey. A number of pristine areas with tremendous ecological value would be sacrificed; in exchange, many others would be saved. Cutler could take the plan to Congress with confidence; after all, nobody could accuse the environmentalists of being extreme or intractable.

And that, Dave Foreman decided, was a very big mistake. After all that work, all that compromise, all those awful moments when he and his colleagues had to tell the folks back home that the wilderness they loved wouldn't make the list. The professional lobbyists in their Washington offices had agreed to trade away two thirds of the remaining American wilderness to save the remainder and cover their powerful friends' asses—after all that, Jimmy Carter, Rupert Cutler, and the Forest Service had stabbed them in the back.

The final proposal released that morning had contained just 15 million acres of wilderness, and 5 million acres of that were in Alaska, in an area that Congress was about to set aside as wilderness anyway. Of the 62 million acres in the study, 47 million—75 percent—would soon be open to oil drilling, and clear-cut logging, and coal mining. In the lower forty-eight states, only 10 million acres would be protected as wilderness. The rest would be gone, forever.

This compromise business was a nice idea, but it obviously wasn't working. The way Foreman figured, the industry lobbyists hadn't compromised a bit— they'd been difficult and stubborn, and their proposals and comments were unreasonable and extreme. And in the end, they had gotten everything they wanted.

Maybe they were on to something.

43

A NUCLEAR ERROR

March 28, 1979
Middletown, Pennsylvania

A little after four A.M., on a small sandy island in the middle of the Susque-
hanna River, a pair of nuclear power plant technicians heard an electronic
alarm go off. Lights began flashing and meters spun: something was wrong
with Three Mile Island Unit Two.

From what the technicians could tell, a water pump had jammed, shutting down the main reactor cooling system. Without any water to cool
it down, the reactor core was starting to overheat; pressure was building
fast.

Within ten seconds, the automatic safety systems kicked in, and the reactor
shut itself down. The technicians breathed a sigh of relief: the fail-safe mech-
anisms worked. The readings were returning to normal. Craig Faust and Ed
Frederick had done their jobs.

But there were problems that didn't show up on the instruments in the
control room, problems that would turn the accident into a major environmental crisis that terrified the nation. The accident would demonstrate the
point John Gofman made at Sam Lovejoy's trial in 1973: no human activity is
foolproof.

The nuclear power industry would never fully recover.

The crisis at Three Mile Island was a case study in the fallacy of fail-safes.
All the controls, all the backups, all the sophisticated safety systems were no
match for a few little mistakes that happened to occur at the same time. The
brilliant physicists and top-flight engineers who designed nuclear power
plants didn't account for a factor that backyard mechanics have recognized

221

since the invention of the wheel: somehow, accidents always seem to come in bunches. Each additional glitch adds another complication to the picture; like radioactive particles, a few tiny problems can set off a chain reaction that quickly gets out of control.

In this case, when the jammed water pump shut down, an auxiliary pump was supposed to take over, keeping cool water flowing through the system. But a maintenance crew had been working on the auxiliary pumps, and had turned off the water. The operators in the control room didn't know that, and assumed the backup pumps were working.

Since no water was flowing through the secondary cooling system to carry heat away, the temperature of the water around the reactor core started rising fast, and some of it started to boil. When the temperature reached a certain level, an emergency relief valve automatically opened, releasing the pressure and sending a spurt of radioactive steam into a special containment area. Then the reactor itself shut down, and the nuclear reaction stopped.

At that point, the emergency relief valve should have closed again, to keep the rest of the core cooling water from escaping. But for some reason, the valve stuck in the open position. The control room operators didn't know that, either: a signal light showed that the valve had closed.

Within ten minutes, a sizable amount of the radioactive cooling water had escaped through the stuck valve and was starting to flood the overflow tank and pour onto the floor of the reactor building. The reactor core was heating up, fast.

In the control room, the sensors showed everything returning to normal.

By 4:50 A.M., the picture was changing. The temperature and radiation readings were starting to explode off the scales. The two technicians realized the situation was no longer under control, and called a senior engineer. In minutes, he was on the site.

From five A.M. on, a growing number of technicians and company officials crowded into the control room as the situation in the reactor kept getting worse. As more and more of the water in the reactor core boiled off into steam, the primary water pumps began to shake: after all, they weren't designed to pump steam. But the operators in the control room didn't know most of the water had boiled over into the room next door; the lights still showed that the valves were functioning, and the core was full of water. Fearing the pumps were overloading, the operators turned them off.

It was the worst possible thing they could have done. The last remnants of the cooling system were shut down; the core temperature soared.

At six A.M., two hours after the accident started, somebody finally thought to call an engineer from Babcock and Wilcox, the company that designed and built the Three Mile Island reactors. The call got the engineer out of bed; he listened for a few moments, then suggested that the pressure relief valve might be stuck. He told the operators to close off a secondary valve, which might keep a little bit of cooling water inside the core and prevent a total meltdown. When the control room crew agreed to give it a try, meltdown was less than thirty minutes away.

The Babcock and Wilcox engineer's early-morning diagnosis bought plant officials some time. When the valves were closed, enough water remained in the core to stave off a meltdown.

But with all that radioactive water spilling out, radiation levels in the reactor building were climbing. By nine A.M., intense radiation forced almost everyone to leave the control room; the last few technicians donned protective equipment.

Around the same time, utility officials informed the Middletown police that a small problem had occurred at the plant. But they said the situation had stabilized, and there was no cause for alarm.

In fact, the situation at Three Mile Island was anything but stable. Searing heat from the reactor core was causing the remaining water and steam to undergo a chemical reaction, releasing large amounts of hydrogen gas. A little after noon, some of the gas exploded; the thick concrete shell surrounding the reactor managed to contain the blast. Desperate to keep the pressure from building any further, technicians opened a valve in the dome and let some of the radioactive steam and gases escape into the air. The company issued no public announcement of the release, and made no effort to warn the people living and working nearby that a radioactive cloud was floating over their heads.

For more than forty-eight hours, officials from Metropolitan Edison, the state of Pennsylvania, and the federal government assured the American public that the Three Mile Island accident was minor, that everything was under control, and that nobody was in any danger at all. But the hydrogen gas continued to build up in the reactor building, and on Friday morning, the authorities decided they had no real alternative: large amounts of radioactive gas had to be vented to prevent a catastrophic explosion. Governor Richard Thornburgh swallowed two days of misleading promises, and urged pregnant women and children to evacuate the area at once. People began fleeing Middletown in droves.

The only ones going in the other direction were reporters, hundreds of them, from all around the globe. They were showing up to get a piece of what was fast becoming a world-class news event. When a Nuclear Regulatory Commission inspector announced that a reactor meltdown was still theoretically possible, banner headlines screamed the word to 200 million Americans: the nuclear industry lied.

Three Mile Island finally cooled down, but the message burned hot and bright on the political horizon: the fancy power plants weren't so safe after all. The companies that ran them couldn't be trusted. And in more than a hundred cities and towns from California to Maine, people looked out at their local nuclear power projects and shuddered at the same thought: it could happen here.

44

THE LAW OF THE SEA

July 16, 1979
Leixões, Portugal

The pirate ship *Sierra* was anchored about a quarter mile off the Iberian coast, rocking gently in the warm summer breeze. From a few hundred yards away, Paul Watson, captain of the *Sea Shepherd,* could see the crew sunbathing on deck, waiting nonchalantly for the Japanese cargo ship that would purchase its illegal treasure. It was the moment Watson had been waiting for for all these years: the legendary outlaw whaler was finally trapped.

Watson set a course straight for the bow of the big iron vessel, and cranked the *Sea Shepherd* up to twelve knots. Ramming speed.

Paul Watson took all his passions seriously.

From early childhood, he had loved animals. As a young teenager, he wrote to Cleveland Amory, the midwestern philanthropist who ran the Fund for Animals, and struck up a friendship that would last for years. He also loved the sea: at fifteen, he left his home in New Brunswick, Canada, to sign on with the merchant marine, sometimes neglecting his duties to stare out at schools of whales passing by his ship.

Five years later, in 1971, he enrolled in college at Vancouver, and quickly became caught up in the two leading issues of the day—the environment and the Vietnam War. He became a strict vegetarian and took to wearing a North Vietnamese flag on his jacket.

In Vancouver, Watson met a group of former Sierra Club members who were angry over the club's refusal to take a stronger stand against United States atomic bomb testing in the Pacific Ocean. The activists had hired a boat and had attempted to sail into the restricted zone near Alaska's Amchitka Island, where the test would take place, in the hope that their presence would

225

force military authorities to call off the explosion. U.S. Coast Guard interference and hostile seas forced them to turn back, but not before they had attracted international news media attention and established the groundwork for a new organization. They called it Greenpeace.

Greenpeace combined all three of Watson's strongest passions. The group was working both to save the environment and to stop war—and doing it on the open sea. Watson's personal intensity made some of the other founders nervous, but he was hardworking, committed to the cause, and a skilled, experienced sailor. When Greenpeace formally incorporated in 1972, Watson was on the board of directors.

In 1973, he found yet another passion. Fascinated by news reports of a Sioux Indian uprising at Wounded Knee, South Dakota, Watson traveled to the site, sneaked through the military blockade, and offered to help out. The Sioux leaders were so impressed by his dedication that they made him an honorary member of the tribe. During his initiation ceremony, in the heat of a traditional sweat lodge, Watson fell into a trance and heard a buffalo tell him to return to the sea and defend the marine mammals that were threatened with extinction.

Watson came back to Greenpeace with a new sense of spirituality and a driving vision that kept his intensity at a fever pitch. By 1975, he was helping to shift the focus of the organization away from nuclear testing and onto the plight of endangered marine mammals, starting with whales. His bold, adventurous campaigns would touch a nerve in the body politic. Watson had the stuff of American legend: Watson was the man in the white hat, riding outgunned into enemy territory and risking his life in a daring attempt to save the lives of some poor, helpless creatures. Whales made a popular cause, too: the giants of the deep were a part of national folklore—and almost nobody in the United States still depended on whaling to pay rent and put food on the table. The escapades attracted tremendous media attention and pushed marine ecology into the forefront of the U.S. environmental agenda in a way that nobody had done since Jacques Cousteau.

The oceans were a tough political battlefield. For centuries, nations had recognized that the waters outside of their own narrow coastal zones were common property. Everyone shared the rights to the shipping lanes and fishing areas. Everyone suffered if a few individuals abused those rights. But nobody had any authority to make sure the others acted responsibly.

Since the end of World War Two, the major nations had recognized that whaling was out of control. The issue was purely economnic: the whale population was dwindling, and if unlimited killing continued, there wouldn't be any whales left for anyone. In 1947, fourteen countries signed a treaty establishing the International Whaling Commission, with a mandate to "provide for the proper conservation of whale stocks" and "make possible the orderly development of the whaling industry."

Under the treaty, the commission would study the whale population every year and set annual limits for each country's catch. But the panel had no authority to enforce its decisions—and no ability whatsoever to force the rest of the world to abide by the same rules as the fourteen countries that signed the treaty. Faced with competition from nonsigners, whalers in the fourteen countries pushed for the highest possible limits, and the commission generally went along.

By 1972, the world population of blue whales, the largest creatures alive, had dwindled from 200,000 to about 6,000. Humpback whales were in a similar state. At the United Nations environmental conference in Stockholm that year, activists urged a ten-year moratorium on all commercial whaling, but among the official delegates, the idea won very little support.

Greenpeace moved full-tilt into the battle against whaling in June 1975, when the *Phyllis Cormack,* one of the organization's two oceangoing ships, confronted a Soviet vessel chasing down a school of sperm whales fifty miles off the California coast. Watson and Fred Easton, a documentary reporter and cameraman, climbed into a small inflatable boat called a Zodiac. Two other crew members climbed into another, and the four tried to get between the whales and the harpoonists. The Soviet sailors paid little heed: as Watson watched, and Easton's camera rolled, a harpoon zipped just over their heads, plunging into the back of a whale less than five feet away. A grenade attached to the harpoon instantly exploded, killing the whale and sending a geyser of blood in the air.

The film of the incident became an instant sensation, and the Greenpeace activists became immediate celebrities. Across the United States, dozens of new chapters sprung up. In the course of one year, membership in Greenpeace grew from a few hundred to more than ten thousand.

In 1976, Watson lead Greenpeace into another high-profile campaign, this time to save the harp seals, furry white creatures that lived in the Arctic Circle. The fur of the baby seals had become a hot commodity, and every year thousands of seal pups too young to swim or move by themselves were bludgeoned to death by fur trappers. Greenpeace crews traveled to the ice floes of northern Canada to spray a harmless, indelible die on the seals, rendering their pelts worthless.

The action, like everything Greenpeace did, was supposed to be strictly nonviolent. That was one reason the organization won so much sympathy and support—Greenpeace members didn't hurt anybody, didn't get in physical fights, and didn't destroy other people's property. But Watson pushed the rules a bit: at one point, he seized the wooden club from a trapper's hand and tossed it in the water. Then he carried a few seal pups away and hid them out of reach of the trappers, a clear violation of Canadian law. Finally, he handcuffed himself to a winch lifting seal skins onto a waiting ship. The winch operator repeatedly dunked him into the icy water, and by the time his colleagues rescued him, Watson was near death.

Again, the actions were first-rate media events. Even the French actress Brigitte Bardot showed up on the ice to lend her support, and dozens of reporters and camera crews followed. But Watson's confrontational tactics had become too much for the Greenpeace leadership. The group was facing stiff legal sanctions for interfering with the seal hunt: Watson's lawbreaking had already cost the organization its tax-exempt status in the United States. When Watson refused to back off, the board of directors voted to remove him.

Within a few months, Watson was back in the fray, this time under the banner of an organization he called the Sea Shepherd Society. His old mentor Cleveland Amory came up with $120,000 to purchase a 776-ton, 206-foot deepwater-fishing trawler, and in the spring of 1978, Watson and a twenty-member crew set sail from Boston, determined to track down a mysterious pirate whaling vessel called the *Sierra*.

The *Sierra* haunted Watson. It kept drifting in and out of his mind, a shadowy menace roaming the North Atlantic, killing hundreds and hundreds of whales, ignoring international laws, and escaping with impunity. Watson wasn't the only one angered by the pirate vessel: conservation groups all over the world complained about its ruthless slaughter. But nobody seemed to be able to stop it.

The 678-ton whaler was owned by Norwegians, but sailed uner the flag of Cyprus, a tiny nation that registered ships without asking too many questions. Its crew was mostly South African. Its customers were Japanese. For years, the *Sierra* had operated in waters that were off-limits to members of the International Whaling Commission, including Japan. The commission strictly forbade the hunting of endangered humpback and blue whales, along with juveniles and nursing mothers of any species, but the *Sierra* killed every whale it could find. Its crews harpooned more than five hundred whales a year, selling the meat at high prices to black-market profiteers.

The success of the *Sierra* had spawned other outlaw operations, and with the major nations of the world beginning to restrict legal commercial whaling, the number of pirate vessels was growing. For defenders of the marine mammals, who had struggled to win even limited international regulations, the outlaws were a source of tremendous frustration. On the high seas, no official agency had clear authority to interfere with a pirate whaler. And just to be sure the likes of Greenpeace didn't get any ideas, the owners of the *Sierra* had reportedly armed the entire crew.

But Watson wasn't terribly concerned about international law or gun-toting sailors. Since that day in the Sioux sweat lodge, he had been perfectly prepared to die for his vision, and if he wound up in prison instead, he wouldn't have any complaints. Besides, the *Sea Shepherd* was a weapon in itself—Watson had loaded one hundred tons of concrete into its bow, creating a powerful battering ram that could slice through the hull of a whaling ship like the *Sierra.*

The *Sea Shepherd* crew spent three weeks cruising the North Atlantic, following rumors and hunches and slowly closing in on the outlaw whaler. On July 15, Watson spied his quarry two hundred miles off northern Portugal—too far from shore to take any action that might risk the lives of the *Sierra*'s crew. The *Sea Shepherd* shadowed the vessel as it slid into port, and the next day, the target was in Watson's sights.

At first, the crew of the whaler seemed confused, unable to believe that another vessel the same size was heading directly for a collision. Those doubts disappeared in minutes, after Watson rammed his prow into the *Sierra*'s front section, just below the harpoon-launching platform. As the crew scrambled to get the engines started and escape, Watson backed up, circled once, and made another charge.

The second assault struck the *Sierra* broadside, ripping a six-foot gash in the hull. Seawater poured into a storage compartment filled with whale meat, and the *Sierra* began to list. In moments, the engines came to life, and the crippled vessel began limping away toward the harbor.

Watson turned north and made a dash for Spanish territorial waters. Eight miles from the border, a Portuguese gunship caught up and forced the *Sea Shepherd* back to port.

For four months, authorities held the ship in custody, although Watson and the crew were allowed to leave. In December, a decision came down: unless Watson could pay $750,000 in damages to the owners of the *Sierra,* he would forfeit his vessel to the whalers.

Watson had other ideas. On New Year's Eve, Peter Woof, the *Sea Shepherd*'s chief engineer, snuck aboard and settled the issue forever. He opened the valves that kept the seawater out of the engine compartment, and scrambled to safety just in time to see the flagship of the Sea Shepherd Society sink below the waves.

But it wouldn't be alone for long. On February 6, 1980, a bomb tore through the hull of the newly repaired *Sierra* as it sat in the Lisbon harbor. The empty craft sank in ten minutes. Watson and the rest of his crew were thousands of miles away at the time, and the bombers were never caught. But an anonymous caller told United Press International that the pirate ship "will kill no more whales. We did it for the *Sea Shepherd.*"

45

S O S U E M E

July 24, 1979
Sacramento, California

Huey Johnson had never felt quite so alone. For more than an hour, with a warm summer evening settling in, he walked the streets of Sacramento, hiding from his boss and thinking about the furor he was about to stir up in the offices of every big environmental group in the nation. In politics, Johnson liked to say, you were nothing but a Ping-Pong ball with a name—you got knocked around by every special interest that could swing a paddle. The only way to survive was to hold on to a solid base of support, a group of people that shared your views and backed you up when you got into trouble.

For three years, since he'd reluctantly joined Jerry Brown's administration, Johnson had been getting into trouble on a regular basis—and groups like the Sierra Club, the National Resources Defense Council, and the Wilderness Society had stood behind him. Now they were asking him, begging him, to accept the deal they had worked out with Congress, the deal called RARE II. And he knew he had to refuse.

In a few hours, Johnson would do what all of his allies dreaded. He would take RARE II to court. The outcome would haunt wilderness activists for the rest of the decade.

Huey Johnson didn't look like a troublemaker. A graying, middle-aged man of average height, he had the appearence of someone who had spent most of his life comfortably seated behind a well-worn desk. Actually, Johnson was an avid outdoorsman, a hiker, hunter, and fisherman with an environmental philosophy that was disarmingly simple. He liked wilderness. He thought as much as possible ought to be under the control of the public. And he hated to see a single square inch of it slipping away.

Johnson's first environmental fight came in the late 1960s, when he was living in Marin County, a scenic enclave across the bay from San Francisco. The real estate market in San Francisco was starting to explode, and Gulf Oil wanted to turn several thousand acres of open space in the hills overlooking the San Francisco Bay into a sprawling new community, with single-family houses, garden apartments, high-rise office buildings, shopping centers, and industrial parks. Johnson rounded up a few of his neighbors, including a pair of lawyers named Doug Ferguson and Martin Rosen, and filed suit against the county, arguing that the development violated state and local land-use laws; the suit kept the project tied up in court for years, and eventually, Gulf conceded defeat.

In the meantime, Johnson began looking around for a way to save small pieces of open land—urban land, like the Marin Headlands—from the growing pressures of development. The basic model was easy: Johnson worked for The Nature Conservancy, and he understood how a land trust worked. In 1972, he established the Trust for Public Land.

For four years, Johnson watched his new organization grow and prosper. Hundreds of community groups, small foundations, and loose-knit collections of individual neighbors worked with the trust to buy up the development rights to dozens of parcels of land, often a few acres at a time, and preserve it as parks and open space in dense urban centers. It worked so well that Johnson was getting bored.

Then Governor Jerry Brown called one day in 1976 and asked Johnson to take over the Department of Natural Resources, a major state agency with 1,800 employees and jurisdiction over a vast amount of forests, fields, rivers, wetlands, and deserts. He would report directly to the governor, who promised to let him do just about anything he wanted to preserve and protect California's vanishing wilderness.

Johnson said he had no interest in working for the government. Politics, he told Brown, was a corrupt and generally useless game. Anything worthwhile that he tried to do would be crushed by some type of special interest. Any important initiative would be watered down and compromised to death by the time it had passed through the bureaucratic and legislative maw. With all due respect, he told the young governor, he would have to decline the job.

Then Brown launched into a lecture of his own. Hiding in the private nonprofit sector was the easy way out, he told Johnson; government was only as good as the people who worked for it. Brown said he wanted to change the shape of California politics, to end the compromises and sellouts that had been the rule for so many years. He wanted people who would shake things up, bring in new ideas, cause a little trouble in Sacramento. He wanted someone like Huey Johnson—and if Johnson didn't have the guts to take on the job, he should stop complaining about Brown's environmental policies.

Johnson was so startled he couldn't think of anything else to say. So he said yes.

It didn't take long for the new secretary of natural resources to start making waves. Public and private utilities and state water projects were trying to expand the network of dams that created artificial lakes on almost every one of California's free-flowing rivers; one by one, Johnson refused to approve seven new dam projects, setting off a furor among business groups, labor unions, and municipal and agricultural water agencies. He fought bitterly with the chemical industry over pesticide regulations. As the state's population continued to rise, Johnson suggested that California offer widely expanded abortion services, set taxes on large families, consider state immigration limits, and restrict the construction of new housing. All over California, newspaper editorials began calling on the governor to fire him.

But Brown wasn't ready to abandon Johnson to the winds of political fate. When things got really tough, the governor would call and ask Johnson what the hell he was doing, but when Johnson explained, Brown would back down. "Well," he told Johnson at one point, when a controversial dam fight was under way, "from now on, you can talk to the labor union guys."

Those were heady days in the Brown administration. The governor was doing things no chief executive of any state had ever even considered, and some of them seemed to be working. He established a California Conservation Corps, to put eighteen- to twenty-year-olds to work setting up, maintaining, and restoring state parks and natural wildlife habitats. He poured millions of dollars into developing solar and wind energy.

And he listened. The Office of Appropriate Technology, one of Brown's most acclaimed projects, came out of a long memo written by Sim Van der Ryn, the visionary designer and planner whom Brown had hired for the normally obscure office of state architect. Van der Ryn was never one to let an opportunity pass: the minute he took office, he began designing a new state office building that would be heated and cooled almost entirely through natural air transfers—on summer nights, cool, heavier air would sweep down through special vents, driving out the heat of the day and leaving the offices fresh and pleasant for the next morning; in the winter, the vents would close, and large windows would capture the sun's heat to keep the building warm. Then he bought a fleet of bicycles and set up racks near all the downtown office buildings, to encourage state employees to use bikes instead of cars for their short official errands.

But that wasn't quite enough, Van der Ryn decided; the state needed a firm, top-level commitment to developing alternative ways of using simple technology to solve expensive resource problems. He put his ideas down on paper, mailed the letter off to the governor's office, and to his astonishment, Brown called to ask him how the operation should be run. The Office of Appropriate Technology came to symbolize the promise of the Brown administration, and Van der Ryn, as its first director, came to symbolize the vision of a California where small was beautiful, and technology was exciting, and just about any idea was worth consideration.

But Brown was also a politician, a skillful, ambitious politician, and he badly wanted to be president. And slowly, as his ambition grew, his politics started to change. He began to worry about the perception that California, with its growing environmental regulations, was bad for business. When Dow Chemical canceled plans for a major new factory in the state, claiming that the environmental rules were too costly, Brown took it seriously; when a major report named California one of the worst states in the nation to do business, he went into an angry depression that startled even his closest friends and advisers. In his first year, he won high marks from business for cutting the size of government and keeping taxes low; now, those same people were saying that his policies were costing jobs and hurting the economy. Environmentalists weren't exactly lining up to cover his flank, either—anti-nuclear activists were angry about Rancho Seco, and almost everyone else in the environmental community was mad about his support for shipping more water from the rivers of the north to the cities and farms of the south. Brown was getting nervous, and Huey Johnson knew it.

For more than a year, Johnson had been complaining about RARE II. His problem was as simple as his basic environmental philosophy. When Rupert Cutler brought together the heads of the major environmental groups and the leaders of industry for a conference on the project at the University of Montana, Johnson had taken the stage and torn into everyone. "What right," he asked, "do any of you have to deal away our natural heritage?"

His anger at the environmental groups was particularly keen. The Sierra Club, the Wilderness Society, and their cousins had sold out from the day they agreed to participate, Johnson believed; RARE II was a negotiation, a compromise that would inevitably lead to the loss of at least some roadless wilderness areas. Environmental groups had no business joining with government and industry in that sort of thing, he insisted. They belonged on the outside, where they could keep a sharp eye on the process and scream, shout, and howl about every lost acre.

But at a time when his tenure was increasingly shaky, those same groups were the one last stronghold of support that kept him in office and prevented Governor Brown from backsliding on his promises. So when the heads of the major environmental groups came to meet with him to discuss his pending lawsuit, Huey Johnson knew it meant trouble.

Johnson had made no secret of his intention to sue the federal government over the shape of RARE II. The compromise worked out in Washington left a lot of California wilderness open to potential exploitation. That was public land, Johnson insisted: once it was lost, it could never be replaced.

For some months now, Johnson had discussed the legality of RARE II with a friend in the state attorney general's office. The young environmental lawyer had uncovered what looked like a critical flaw in the federal proposal: the Forest Service had prepared a single environmental impact statement for the entire national wilderness program, and it looked badly inadequate. Besides, under the National Environmental Policy Act, there was certainly an argument to be made that a project of this magnitude required a whole series of EISs, one for each individual wilderness area. That would be a massive project; it could take years to complete. In the meantime, the wilderness would be safe. With any luck, the Forest Service would back off, like Gulf Oil did in the Marin Headlands, to avoid unending litigation; if not, at least Johnson would have time to figure out something else.

The state attorney general, George Deukmejian, was hardly an environmentalist. Deukmejian was a staunch, conservative Republican, and Johnson and his lawyer friend knew he would never agree to a suit over RARE II—and since the attorney general represented all state agencies, Johnson couldn't sue without his approval. But the two men had figured out a way around that, too: the environmental lawyer had prepared the legal papers, and when the time came, he would slip them into the middle of a thick pile of documents, all requiring Deukmejian's signature. The attorney general would never have time to read them all; he would sign the RARE II lawsuit without knowing it, and once it was filed, he wouldn't be able to back off.

The leading environmentalists didn't like Johnson's idea at all. To sue right now, they told him, would imperil the fragile compromise, worked out over more than a year. It would infuriate Congress, and maybe threaten some other important wilderness bills. Johnson listened patiently as they sat in his office and made their case; when they left, he told them he still wanted to go through with his plan.

Over the next hour, the phone rang twice: the two most important environmentalists in Congress came on the line, each of them repeating what the environmental leaders had said. Johnson had the utmost respect for Phil Burton, the San Franciscan who had carved out the Golden Gate National Recreation Area that preserved much of the Marin shoreline, and John Seiberling, the veteran Ohio liberal who chaired the Subcommittee on Public Lands. But he had to tell them both the same thing: with all due respect, he was going forward.

Then he realized what had happened. The environmental leaders had called Burton and Seiberling; now, the congressmen would call Jerry Brown. Soon, perhaps, the governor would buckle, and Johnson would be ordered to change his mind, or find a new job. He grabbed his jacket and dashed out of his office before the phone had a chance to ring.

And then, for an hour, he walked. He thought about his job, his friends, and how lonely he would feel without the people who had supported him through these years as a reluctant politician. Then he wandered over to a pay phone, and put in a dime. It was getting late; he hoped his friend in the Attorney General's Office would still be at work.

When the young lawyer answered, Johnson took a deep breath. "It's time," he told his friend. "Get the papers signed first thing tomorrow; next time I talk to you, it may be too late."

The lawyer took a deep breath, too. Then he told Johnson not to worry; by noon tomorrow, the state of California would have filed an action in court against the federal government, in the person of the secretary of agriculture, John R. Block. And there was nothing anybody could do about it.

46

THE KILLER RABBIT

September 25, 1979
Washington, D.C.

Frank Moore was a man who had always enjoyed life, but these days, he wasn't the least bit happy. The 210-pound former schoolbook salesman from Dahlonega, Georgia, had become one of President Carter's closest, most trusted advisers, his liaison to Capitol Hill—and right now, he knew his boss was in serious political trouble. With the 1980 election only a year away, unemployment, inflation, and fuel prices were soaring, and the Democratic congressional leadership was in open revolt. Some leading members of the majority party, including Senator Ted Kennedy and Governor Jerry Brown, were talking publicly about challenging Carter in the primaries. Worst of all, the president was starting to become something of a national political joke.

There were tough, important issues on the administration's agenda—Carter had just wrapped up negotiations on a treaty that would end United States control over the Panama Canal. Legislation to create a Cabinet-level Department of Education—one of Carter's major campaign promises—was working its way through Congress. But over the past two weeks, the news reports about President Carter had Americans alternately shaking their heads in worry over the chief executive's health and giggling over his strange encounter with a vicious swimming rabbit.

The health issue wasn't funny at all. In mid-September, Carter had collapsed from exhaustion while trying to complete a six-mile footrace. White House doctors insisted that Carter was basically fine—he was just tired and overworked, and had tried to push himself a bit too hard. But photos of the ashen, sweat-drenched president appeared on the front page of all the major newspapers; dramatic television footage led the network news.

The rabbit incident was the stuff of fishermen's clubhouse humor, a weird eye-roller of a tale that had little in the way of national significance. In most circumstances, most politicians would have shrugged it off without the slightest problem. The way the newspaper stories went, Carter had taken a brief vacation to go fishing on a quiet lake in Georgia, leaving the press corps and most of his staff far behind. But a few aides were watching from shore when what appeared to be a crazed rabbit leapt into the water and began swimming, teeth bared, directly toward the presidential canoe. Carter, startled and a bit confused, was forced to fend off the beast with his paddle. A White House photographer captured the scene on film, but the Press Office refused to release the pictures—so the media made do with a wide variety of creative, satirical illustrations.

Now Frank Moore was watching Carter's political future go down in flames—and when he walked into the Oval Office the morning of September 25, he feared the president was about to throw another big bucket of gasoline on the fire. And all for a few lousy snail darters.

Moore's pitch was simple and direct: the president needed some major new accomplishments, some headline-grabbing, crowd-pleasing victories, if he wanted to go into the primary season as a clear and convincing favorite. He couldn't afford to fight with Congress—and he certainly couldn't afford to be the butt of any more nasty political gags.

Right now, that meant that he had to sign into law a bill that made a mockery of fair play, legislative process, the rule of law, and a decade of environmental struggle. He had to reject his own common sense, the advice of his interior secretary, and the pleas of increasingly disillusioned environmental leaders.

He had to overrule the Endangered Species Act, and let the Tennessee Valley Authority finish work on the Tellico Dam.

"Mr. President," Moore explained, "if you veto this bill, every newspaper in the country will have a cartoon tomorrow morning showing you dropping out of a race, with a wild-eyed rabbit in one hand and a snail darter in the other. That's an image you just can't afford." Jimmy Carter got the message.

Like NEPA, the Endangered Species Act had slipped through Congress with very little controversy. Like NEPA, it seemed fairly harmless, the kind of bill nobody could possibly oppose. In fact, the impetus came from Richard Nixon, who was responding in part to public alarm over the possibility that a national icon—the bald eagle—was rapidly heading for extinction. He asked Congress in 1972 to enact strict legislation to outlaw the killing of any endangered species, and Senator Mark Hatfield of Oregon introduced an act that appeared to do just that. By December 1973, both houses had passed it by large majorities, and Nixon had signed it into law.

But the Endangered Species Act of 1973 did more than protect bald eagles from poachers. The bill contained what one observer would later call "snakes in the grass"—innocent-sounding language that was in fact carefully designed to make the act one of the most powerful environmental bills in history. It required the interior secretary to determine, on the sole basis of scientific evidence, when "any species" of plant or animal was threatened or in danger of extinction—and once a species was listed, the government was required to "use all methods and procedures" possible to prevent extinction and restore a healthy, stable population of the species. No government agency could do anything that would jeopardize that goal.

The implication, the courts would later rule, was completely unambiguous: the bill put Congress on record as determining that the preservation of any endangered species was the government's highest priority, overriding any other possible concerns. Whether or not the president and the legislators knew it, the law said that the most lowly, obscure form of life was worth more than the most ambitious human endeavor.

There were strong practical and philosophical arguments in favor of that position. Supporters argued that the human race had no right to "play God," to decide that the value of a new development, which would promote human prosperity, was more important than the survival of a tiny plant or animal. Others argued that the death of any species could turn out to be an incalculable loss to society: a strange type of dandelion, found only in one little corner of the planet, could hold the secret to a cure for cancer, or a microscopic bug could play an unknown but pivotal role in a major food chain. And once a species was extinct, its value—actual or potential—was gone forever.

Of course, there was another side to the argument, too, and even some leading environmentalists would come to agree that it had a lot of political appeal. Humans were part of the ecosystem, too—and when the choice came down to preserving or creating human jobs, giving people a way to feed their kids, pay for their homes, and build a better life, the fate of a few minor bugs and flowers could seem a lot less important.

The issue would come to play a central role in modern environmental politics, but it played no major role at all in the congressional debate on the bill. The overall theme cited by the witnesses who appeared before congressional committees to testify in favor of the act was the frightening loss of biological diversity on the planet, and the need to preserve not only creatures but the habitat that supported them. Most of the senators and representatives who rose to address the issue agreed with the basic principle, and few seemed to consider the prospect that their lofty goal would clash directly with a growing number of public and private development projects.

In fact, the Endangered Species Act didn't become a major national issue until after its passage, when a law professor at the University of Tennessee named Zygmunt Plater happened to learn that one of his colleagues in the Zoology Department, David Etnier, had discovered a new fish swimming around in the cool waters of the Little Tennessee River.

Plater came upon the snail darter early in 1974, and almost entirely by accident. He knew about the Endangered Species Act, of course, although the measure was still so new he hadn't paid much attention to it. He knew about the Tellico Dam, too—he'd helped local environmental groups file their NEPA claim. But he was also one of the first major law school professors to offer an in-depth course on environmental law—and by any standard, the only real environmental lawyer in eastern Tennessee. He had about twenty different cases begging for his attention, all of them important, all of them eminently worthy. Sometimes, he could barely keep track of the ones he'd actually agreed to take on; he didn't spend much time looking for more work. When a kid named Hiram Hill approached him early in the spring semester with a complicated fish story, Plater was initially dubious: after all, Hill had flunked out of law school the year before. He was obviously looking for some way to win a second chance. But after a few minutes, Plater realized that Hill had done his homework—and he was onto something important.

Hill had been too stubborn to leave campus after he failed his exams; he'd stuck around all semester, and to keep his mind off his troubles, he'd taken a class in zoology. The professor was David Etnier; the newly discovered snail darter was a big part of the syllabus.

Hill kept up with current events, too, and when the Endangered Species Act passed, he'd gone to the library and read it. He knew he hadn't been a brilliant student, but the law seemed remarkably clear. According to Professor Etnier, there were only a few thousand snail darters in existence, and they could live only in clear, shallow, free-flowing water. The act required the federal government to do whatever was necessary to protect any endangered species; the Tellico Dam would destroy the one place where the snail darters lived. The way Hill read the law, that meant Etnier's fish could put an end to the whole dam project. He thought maybe if Professor Plater would help him reenroll, he'd write it up as a term paper for the environmental law class.

Zygmunt Plater thought that sounded like an excellent idea.

On January 20, 1975, Plater and Hill filed the nation's first Endangered Species Act petition, requesting that the Interior Department formally list the snail darter as a species in threat of extinction—and the dam as a threat to its critical habitat. The Fish and Wildlife Service studied the situation, and decided the request was valid: "The snail darter occurs only in the swifter portions of shoals over clean gravel substrate in cool, low-turbidity water," the report stated. "The proposed impoundment of water behind the proposed Tellico Dam would result in the total destruction of the darter's habitat." A year later, in February 1976, Hill, Plater, and several conservation groups filed suit against the Tennessee Valley Authority, charging violations of the Endangered Species Act and asking for a permanent federal injunction to halt the dam.

TVA officials tried desperately to find someplace else that the snail darters lived. Divers searched more than fifty nearby rivers without success. With the help of Etnier, the agency tried to transplant some of the fish to a new home, in the hope they might establish a stable colony, but the short-term evidence was not at all encouraging. As far as the scientific world was concerned, there were only about ten thousand snail darters alive on the planet—and they all lived in the shadow of the unfinished Tellico Dam.

On May 25, 1976, after a two-day trial, Judge Robert Taylor ruled that Plater's suit was too late. He agreed that the snail darter was endangered, and that the law required its protection. But since the dam was 80 percent finished, and almost $80 million had already been spent on the project, and Congress had continued to authorize that spending even after the snail darter was listed as endangered, he concluded that the only fair and reasonable solution was to let the dam go forward. Plater filed an appeal, and in January 1977, the Court of Appeals reversed Taylor's decision, issuing an immediate injunction and bringing construction to a halt.

By the time the case wound up in the Supreme Court, the snail darter was big news all over the country—and the Tennessee Valley Authority wasn't the only organization that wished Zygmunt Plater would just pack up his briefcase and go away. When Plater arrived in Washington to argue the case, he met with a decidedly mixed reception from the leaders of some major environmental groups. Inside the Beltway, the snail darter was more than just a threat to the Tellico Dam: it was a public relations fiasco that had the potential to undermine the most important environmental law in history.

The Endangered Species Act came up for reauthorization in 1978, and even before the Supreme Court ruled on the snail darter case, some members of Congress were starting to say that the act had been a terrible mistake. The economy was bad enough, they insisted; the last thing America needed was a law that allowed environmental extremists to block almost any sort of economic development in the name of preserving wildlife, even species that were otherwise insignificant.

The environmental lobbyists agreed that in theory, the preservation of any species was critical; the environmental lawyers agreed that Plater had a pretty decent case. But they also had to face political reality: the snail darter made a lousy national mascot. It wasn't big and furry, like the grizzly bear, or dramatic and photogenic, like the gray whale, or majestic and symbolic, like the bald eagle. It wasn't the stuff of televised nature programs; you couldn't sell it on a poster or a T-shirt. Basically, it was a silly little fish—and the national news media had turned it into the laughingstock of America.

The whole thing was starting to drive Plater crazy. He was arguing a powerful case that would set critical precedents in the field of environmental law. The facts were all on his side, and the opposition had one of the least defensible projects an environmentalist could ever imagine. The issues were so obvious—and everyone seemed to be missing the point.

The Tellico Dam case wasn't about snail darters. It was about rational decision-making that took into account not only the immediate dollars and cents of a project, but the less tangible, long-term price. It was about forcing public agencies to add some new elements to their equations—to count the loss of a natural resource, or an archaeological or cultural treasure, or an endangered species, or a farmland so rich it needed no chemical fertilizers, or a fragile ecosystem that nobody fully understood, when they calculated costs and benefits.

It was also about exposing one of the great lies of the age—the supposed trade-off between economic development and environmental protection. Even by the old-fashioned way of figuring costs, the Tellico Dam wasn't just bad ecology—it was bad economics.

Even with huge taxpayer subsidies, the dam would destroy more jobs than it would create—and given the power of the TVA, it turned out that the only way to stop it was with an Endangered Species Act suit based on saving the snail darters. That didn't strike Plater as a bit unusual: after all, Al Capone was one of the most notorious criminals of his time, and the FBI had to settle for income-tax-evasion charges to put him behind bars. In the legal world, you used the weapons you had.

On June 15, 1978, the Supreme Court issued its ruling in *Tennessee Valley Authority* v. *Hill et al.* Just as Al Capone's long and brutal record was not at issue in his tax-evasion case, the best arguments against the dam never played a role in the decision. Almost every credible economist outside of the Tennessee Valley Authority (and many of those inside the agency) completely agreed that the way to create new jobs in the Little Tennessee Valley was to preserve the free-flowing river and the historic cultural artifacts along its banks, and use the rare, unique existing natural resources to promote recreation, agriculture, and tourism. But for the judges, it came down to the letter of the law, the intent and language of the Endangered Species Act, and the court sided strongly with the fish. "It is clear," Chief Justice Warren Burger wrote, "that Congress intended to halt and reverse the trend toward species extinction—whatever the cost." In other words, the court decided, the act required the TVA to sacrifice its dam to save the snail darter.

The reaction in Congress was swift and furious.

Howard Baker, the savvy Tennessee Republican who sat on the powerful Appropriations Committee, knew an outright repeal would be too politically difficult. Instead, when the act came up for reauthorization in 1978, he and Senator John Culver of Iowa introduced, and easily won approval for, an amendment adding what Baker and his supporters called a degree of balance to the act. It established a special seven-member Cabinet-level committee that could overrule the provisions of the law in cases of an "irreconcilable conflict" between economic development and species preservation. In simple terms, the committee could decide that the future of an animal or plant wasn't worth the economic cost of blocking a major project. It became known as the "God Committee."

Environmentalists, led by Senator Gaylord Nelson, fought an uphill battle to block or water down the amendment, and for the most part, the Carter administration supported them. But even with the president's tacit endorsement, their cause was ultimately hopeless: in the wake of the Supreme Court ruling against Tellico, nearly every member of Congress was terrified that some unknown species might cut off the flow of pork-barrel money to his or her home district.

But Baker's strategy wasn't foolproof: even Cabinet members with little interest in conservation were able to recognize a financial boondoggle when they saw it. On January 23, 1979, the six committee members—the secretaries of interior, agriculture, and the Army, the chairman of the Council of Economic Advisers, the director of the EPA, and the head of the National Oceanic and Atmospheric Administration—met to discuss the Tellico Dam, and something truly remarkable happened. The committee members took a hard look at the evidence and decided unanimously that the dam should be scrapped—because it was a horrible waste of the taxpayers' money. CEA chairman Charles Schultze denounced the dam in the strongest possible terms: "Here is a project that is 95 percent complete," he said, "and if one takes just the cost of finishing it against the [total project] benefits, and does it properly, it doesn't pay, which says something about the original design."

In other words, the committee accepted the precise arguments that Plater and others had been pushing for years—and that the news media had almost entirely ignored. "Frankly," Interior Secretary Cecil Andrus explained, "I hate to see the snail darter get the credit for stopping a project that was ill-conceived and uneconomic in the first place."

But for the most part, that didn't make the newspapers either.

Baker was furious—from the start, his main interest in changing the Endangered Species Act had been his determination to save the Tellico Dam. "If that's all the good the committee process can do," he fumed, "I will introduce legislation to abolish the committee and exempt the Tellico from the provisions of the act." A few days later, that's exactly what he did.

At first, the Baker bill went nowhere—a special exemption for Baker's pet Tennessee project wouldn't necessarily play in Peoria. Even Senator Culver, who had joined in the bill to create the God Committee, was an outspoken foe of the new bill. Baker's measure went down in committee, and when he tired to bring it back up on the Senate floor, he lost again.

But on June 18, 1979, Baker's chief ally in the House, Congressman John James Duncan, who hailed from the district where the dam would be built, pulled off a legislative trick that was astonishing even by the standards of the United States Congress. Late in the day, after a lengthy debate had concluded on a massive $10.8 billion public works appropriation bill, when most members had left the floor, Duncan rose to add another amendment. The clerk began to read the language, but before he could get to the word "Tellico," Duncan made a motion to waive the reading—and the handful of remaining legislators, confident that their leaders would never allow anything significant to pop up at the last minute, offered no objection. Then, in the course of forty-two seconds, on an uncontested voice vote, the House of Representatives agreed to exempt the Tellico Dam from the Endangered Species Act.

Baker spent another month twisting arms and making promises, and in September, the Senate approved the House version of the appropriation measure, 48–44. Interior Secretary Andrus promised to press for a presidential veto—but since there were dozens of other high-priced projects in the final bill, spread out through districts across the country, President Carter had an ugly choice. By law, the president couldn't veto individual "line items" in a bill; he had to accept or reject the whole thing. Meanwhile, the Senate and House leadership from both parties made the ultimatum clear: if Carter rejected the appropriation bill, he'd have a very hard time with the rest of his legislative agenda. He still might have sided with Andrus, if Frank Moore hadn't entered the Oval Office and explained the facts of political life.

In the major national news media, the snail darter had become a metaphor for an administration that seemed to be able to bungle or stop almost anything, and ask the American people for more and more sacrifice, but get almost nothing productive accomplished. As Congressman Duncan asked in a widely cited quote, "Should a worthless, unsightly, minute, inedible minnow outweigh the possible injustice to human beings?"

But the way most Americans saw it presented, the issue came down to a choice: a few thousand snail darters, or a few thousand jobs. And if that was the wrong way to frame the question, the embattled president couldn't seem to do anything to change it. On September 25, 1979, Jimmy Carter personally telephoned Zygmunt Plater and apologized. Then he signed the appropriation bill into law.

Among those who supported the Tellico Dam was a smart, attractive young congressman from central Tennessee, a senator's son who by all accounts had a bright political future. His name was Albert Gore, Jr.

47

THE BUG MAKERS

June 16, 1980
Washington, D.C.

In some ways, legal scholars argued, the case that made genetic engineering into a billion-dollar industry and sparked a decade of environmental controversy was just a run-of-the-mill patent dispute.

The basic facts were nothing unusual: a scientist working for General Electric in Schenectady, New York, had invented something the company might be able to market for a considerable amount of money. It was just the sort of technology the oil and chemical industry was looking for—a process that would break down oil spills, quickly and easily, and leave nothing toxic or unsightly behind. The inventor applied for a patent; when the United States Patent and Trademark Office rejected the application, he took it to court.

But the case of *Diamond* v. *Chakrabarty* had a twist that would make it one of the most important Supreme Court decisions in history: by the narrowest possible margin, 5–4, the high court ruled that a private company could patent a living thing.

In the majority opinion, Chief Justice Burger rejected the notion that the products of genetic engineering were legally the products of nature. Alive or not, he argued, something that didn't exist until an inventor created it was eligible for legal protection. Critics who raised concerns about the environmental implications, he wrote, were plagued by an irrational "fear of the unknown."

The inventor who set off the controversy was an Indian-born biologist named Ananda Mohan Chakrabarty, who had come to General Electric to develop a genetically engineered bacterium that would eat crude oil. Bugs that digested different types of petroleum-based hydrocarbons existed in nature, but no one creature would eat all the different compounds present in raw crude.

Slowly and painstakingly, Chakrabarty spliced the oil-eating genes from a variety of bacteria into a single new bug. The result worked well enough that the scientist quickly applied for the patent that would give him exclusive legal rights to the use of his invention for the next seventeen years.

In the case of an oil-eating bug—or for that matter, almost any genetically altered life-form—a patent was critical to commerical success. Once the bacterium was used for the first time, dispersed by the millions on a body of water, any rival company with access to a fishing boat could scoop up a jarful and breed its own stock.

Scientists and lawyers watched the case closely as it wound its way through the legal system. So did business investors.

In the eight years since Herbert Boyer and Stanley Cohen had hooked two unrelated pieces of DNA together, genetic engineering had become something of a rage in the business world. From the start, investors figured there was big money in new life-forms. Companies specializing in commercial genetic engineering were popping up around the country. Genentech, based in South San Francisco, was a classic example. It was founded in 1976, when venture capitalist Robert Swanson sought out Boyer at his University of California lab. Swanson convinced Boyer to become his partner in a venture that would produce and market genetically engineered pharmaceuticals. Among other things, they agreed, the company could use Boyer's expertise to splice into common bacteria genes that would spur the tiny cells to create rare and valuable substances—like insulin. The bugs would become microscopic factories; with a small supply of cheap nutrients, they could reproduce by the millions, churning out virtually limitless quantities of chemicals that sold for hundreds of dollars an ounce. Each man put up $500.

For the next four years, the company moved slowly forward, Swanson trying to scrounge up capital and Boyer looking around for possible products. But investors were nervous—like General Electric, they realized that any product made by living bacteria was hard to control. Scientists like Boyer and Cohen had always followed tradition, and shared their technological advances with others in the field; the two had reluctantly applied for a patent on their gene-splicing technique, but it was still pending when the ruling on the General Electric case came down.

Suddenly, the whole picture changed. In October 1980, three months after the *Chakrabarty* decision, Genentech took its case to Wall Street. The company went public at $35 a share, and within twenty minutes, the stock was up to $89. By lunchtime, Swanson and Boyer were worth $82 million. Over the next few years, dozens more biotechnology firms would appear all over the country, promising investors huge returns on products that existed only in the minds of a few scientists who had never worked in the business world, and a flock of venture capitalists who knew little about science. And it would all get under way without effective environmental controls.

The prospect made Jeremy Rifkin drop everything he was doing and launch a personal crusade that would raise some of the deepest philosophical questions of the modern era and turn bioengineering into a high-profile political issue.

Rifkin had picked up on the emerging technology long before most environmentalists even knew it existed. He was as much an intellectual as an activist, with graduate degrees in law and diplomacy. He never seemed to like working for anybody else either; from the moment he got out of school, he always seemed to have some sort of project of his own.

At first, it was the "Citizens Commission," which convinced Vietnam vets to report firsthand on war atrocities. Then the "People's Bicentennial Commission" worked to create an alternative to the Nixon administration's plans for the nation's two-hundredth birthday celebration. He was running the "People's Business Commission" in 1976 when he stumbled onto gene-splicing. He recognized instantly that the issue had political potential; it also tweaked his philosophical interest. Within a year, he had established the Foundation on Economic Trends, and published a book called *Who Should Play God?*

Rifkin knew how to get the news media's attention. He subtly invoked images of rogue genetic monsters, mentioning "dangers of an irreversible nature" in an amicus brief before the Supreme Court and arguing that "once out of the laboratory, there is no recalling a life-form." But on a deeper level, his critique of the new industry wasn't at all hysterical. Essentially, he would argue over the next ten years, the problem with gene-splicing scientists was that they were trying to expand the human race's control over nature. Already, that same philosophy had created ecological disaster; at a certain point, he insisted, the process had to stop.

Rifkin wasn't the only one sounding the alarm. In 1974, a group of scientists, led by Cohen's Stanford colleague, Paul Berg, called for voluntary restrictions on recombinant DNA research. In 1975, more than a hundred scientists gathered at the Asilomar conference center in Monterey, California, to adopt a set of guidelines requiring strict safety controls on all genetic-engineering experiments. Groups like the Environmental Defense Fund issued statements and pushed for legislation regulating the experiments; congressional committees held several hearings. But the issues were complicated, and the scientists vowed that they could prevent any serious mistakes.

48

OPENING DAY

March 21, 1981
Page, Arizona

The Carl T. Hayden Visitor Center perched on the edge of a sandstone cliff six hundred feet above the Colorado River gorge, overlooking the Glen Canyon Dam. The squat concrete structure was named after the longest-serving member of Congress on record, a man who spent fifty-seven consecutive years representing the state of Arizona in the nation's capital.

The Glen Canyon Dam was one of Senator Hayden's crowning achievements. He saw it as a symbol of mankind's conquest of nature, a testament to America's ability to harness the wild rivers of the West to provide limitless water and power for a growing nation. The dam rose 710 feet above bedrock, a thick wedge of concrete plugging a deep, narrow gorge, holding back the mighty Colorado and creating the world's largest reservoir, an artificial lake stretching for 186 miles. Construction crews worked for seven years to complete the project; along the way, they installed the world's highest steel-arch bridge, poured five million cubic yards of concrete, and built an entire new town from scratch, complete with thirteen churches, a nine-hole golf course, schools, shops, motels, restaurants, parks, and enough pastel bungalows to house more than six thousand people. The whole thing cost the taxpayers $272 million.

To Senator Hayden and other supporters, it was progress on a grand scale, a victory for the forces of modern civilization. To an entire generation of environmentalists, it had come to represent the grandest sort of disaster.

Glen Canyon was a landmark, the legacy of one of the most important environmental battles in the nation's history. Above and below the dam, long stretches of the Colorado still ran wild and free, thanks to conservationists like David Brower and Howard Zahniser. In the 1950s, they turned the fate

247

of the river into an emotional crusade, and their struggle brought postwar environmentalism to life. But the dam was the price Brower had paid for preserving the wilderness areas up and downstream. Like so many of those who later took up the environmental banner, he traded away one part of nature to save a few others. And on the first day of spring, 1981, with the desert sun driving away the last gasps of the chilly winter winds, a handful of activists came to Glen Canyon to announce that they would never accept another compromise.

In fact, the protesters were prepared to do something even the most forceful environmental groups had never imagined: demand that the plug be removed, and the Colorado once again be allowed to flow through Glen Canyon, free. Like the last generation that fought over the Colorado River, they would set off a political time bomb.

The Hayden Visitor Center was often crowded on Saturday. Since the floodgates closed in 1963 and Lake Powell began to fill up, the dam had been a big tourist attraction. Thousands of people came from hundreds of miles around to drive their speedboats and Jet Skis on the lake, or to fish in one of its quieter corners, or to hike along its rim. Quite a few stopped at the visitor center, to read about the dam's history, or pick up a map of the recreational area, or just to stare out at the imposing structure that dominates the canyon.

But on this Saturday morning, Park Service employees were visibly nervous about the seventy-five people wandering around in the parking lot. Despite its legendary status among environmentalists, demonstrations weren't a common event at the dam—and nobody had ever seen a demonstration quite like this. The protesters were carrying signs and chanting slogans that called for something almost beyond comprehension: they wanted the dam taken down.

Since the demonstrators hadn't announced their plans in advance, and hadn't applied for a permit, only a handful of Park Service police officers were on hand. Most were quickly dispatched to guard the sensitive electrical equipment at the generator stations deep inside the dam. The rest wandered around eyeing the unruly and unkempt crowd in the parking lot. None of the officers noticed as five of the demonstrators, carrying a large black bundle on their shoulders, slipped away from the crowd and walked out onto the concrete rampart atop the dam.

Dave Foreman, Mike Roselle, Bart Koehler, Ron Kezar, and Howie Wolke had been planning their caper for months. They made an unlikely gang of outlaws. Koehler was a singer and songwriter working as the Wyoming field representative for the Wilderness Society. Kezar, a librarian by training, was an expert in military history and an accomplished mountain climber who had a seasonal job with the National Park Service. Wolke, a native of New

Jersey, worked in restaurants and on construction crews to supplement the $75 a month he earned working for Friends of the Earth. Roselle was a vegetarian oil-field roughneck who had met Wolke at a salad bar.

Foreman, who brought this crew together, was the oddest outlaw of the lot. The son of an Air Force officer, Foreman grew up in Albuquerque, New Mexico, and dreamed of becoming a cowboy. In 1964, he worked on Barry Goldwater's presidential campaign, and became the New Mexico chairman of the right-wing Young Americans for Freedom. But the wide-open spaces of the southwestern desert were deep in his blood. Soon, he was working full-time for the Wilderness Society.

By 1979, Foreman was one of the rising stars of the environmental movement in Washington. His college degree in biology and his knowledge of natural systems won him the respect of the scientists who advised the Forest Service and the Interior Department. His natural skill at working the halls of Congress won him the respect of his colleagues—and a growing amount of political clout.

After he watched the RARE II deal go down, he decided his career in Washington was over. A few weeks after that brutal defeat, he resigned his Washington post, asked for his old job again, and moved home to the small town of Glenwood, New Mexico.

Ever since he was a teenager, Foreman had escaped to the wilderness when he needed to think, so he made plans to spend a week or two hiking and camping, to figure out what was wrong with the environmental movement and his career, and what he ought to do about it. He called a few old friends and told them he was heading off for the Pinacate Desert, a remote corner of Mexico on the edge of the Gulf of California; Koehler, Kezar, and Wolke all agreed to join him. Roselle convinced Wolke to let him tag along.

The Pinacate Desert was only about thirty miles south of the Arizona border, but it was one of the wildest, least-developed areas in Mexico, a rugged volcanic no-man's-land of cactus and mesquite, black lava flows and dry riverbeds. For a week, the five men hiked through the stark beauty of the desert; for a week, they talked about RARE II, environmentalists, and the future of the American wilderness.

There were plenty of horror stories to share. Foreman complained about the professional lobbyists in Washington. When he'd started with the Wilderness Society, he told his friends, environmental groups were built on volunteers, and the staff expected to work long hours for low pay in the service of a cause. Now, the folks in D.C. all seemed to be lawyers or businessmen; they made a lot more money, and they felt a lot more comfortable with the Beltway insiders than with the grassroots activists back home. Koehler, who worked on the other end of the Wilderness Society hierarchy, agreed. Just the year before, he explained, in the wake of the Three Mile Island accident, he'd written an angry letter to Senator Malcolm Wallop of Wyoming demanding a complete evacuation of Harrisburg. As soon as the new Wilderness Society executive director, William Turnage, learned about the letter, he dashed off an apology to Wallop, explaining that Koehler didn't speak for the Wilderness Society and that his demands should be ignored.

Wolke was as angry as Foreman about RARE II. One of his favorite wilderness areas, a part of the Gros Ventre Mountains on the edge of Yellowstone National Park, hadn't made the preservation list.

As the week wore on, RARE II kept coming back into the conversation, and as the five men talked about it, Foreman's thoughts became more and more clear. He decided he knew exactly what had gone wrong, he said, exactly where the environmental movement had failed. He and his colleagues had done their best to quiet the more radical voices in their organizations, and had come to the bargaining table with a fair and moderate proposal. The opposition had let the wild-eyed crazies howl all they wanted. When the deal went down, the industry lobbyists demanded just slightly less than the radical fringe—and came off looking reasonable by comparison.

That was the problem, Foreman told his friends: there was nobody out on the environmental edge, demanding it all, nobody pushing the rest of the environmental groups away from their concessions. Nobody who could make the most strident environmentalists look downright reasonable.

By the time the desert campers came out of the hills and sat down for a few cold Pacifico beers in a small-town Mexican tavern, the seeds of an idea were in place. It was time for a new organization, they agreed, one that would make no compromise in defense of Mother Earth. It was time for somebody to say out loud what so many environmentalists really believed, that any public policy ought to make the health of the planet the primary consideration. Any decision ought to start with a simple principle, one that the dusty, bearded gang sitting around the barroom table could describe in just two words: Earth First!

It sounded like a fine name.

High atop the Glen Canyon Dam, the charter members of the new environmental fringe tied the edges of their bundle to the parapets, tossed it over the side, and scrambled back to the parking lot. As they rejoined the crowd, a three-hundred-foot-long triangle of black plastic slowly unfurled down the side of the dam.

From inside the visitors center, the face of the dam was clearly visible through a broad panel of floor-to-ceiling plate-glass windows. It was a dramatic sight, but after a few weeks, every employee got used to it; after all, the dam never changed. So when Dave Foreman wandered in and casually asked the ranger on duty if she'd seen the dam recently, she thought he was making a joke.

As if by instinct, she glanced out the window. For a split second, she froze: right down the center of the concrete face, a huge, jagged crack had formed.

Then just as quickly, the ranger recovered, gave Foreman a nasty look, and went off to tell the police to cut down the plastic banner. When it was finally cut loose, it floated to a field below, where FBI agents later collected it as evidence of possible terrorist activity.

Out in the parking lot, a free-lance documentary filmmaker named Randy Hayes had recorded the action on camera and was trying desperately to get one of the mischief-makers to stand for an interview. Foreman and his crew were instantly suspicious—the earnest, clean-cut man with all the fancy equipment looked a lot like a federal agent. As the charter members of Earth First! traded barbs with his camera crew, Hayes started rummaging around under the piles of rented video gear in the back of his car. After a few minutes, he emerged with a case of home-brewed beer, and cracked open a bottle.

Mike Roselle smiled and stuck out his hand.

PART 8

THE CENTER CANNOT HOLD

Approximately 80 percent of our air pollution stems from hydrocarbons released by vegetation. So let's not go overboard in setting and enforcing tough emissions standards for man-made sources.

—*Ronald Reagan, quoted in* Sierra, *September 16, 1980*

In April 1980, the modern environmental movement turned ten with a re-sounding thud.

On the surface, the last half of the 1970s seemed to be a good time for liberal causes. The Watergate scandals swept Republicans from power at every level of government. Democrats moved into the White House, built decisive majorities in both houses of Congress, and took control of states like California, New York, and Texas. Dozens of important environmental bills became law, and leading environmental activists moved into top policy-making positions. As the tenth anniversary of Earth Day arrived, there should have been plenty to celebrate.

But the spirit Jimmy Carter called "malaise" had settled over much of the movement, and Earth Day 1980 pointed up the essential problem. Environmentalists didn't know whether to cheer or scream: with so many friends in public office, they had a hard time mounting angry protests against the government—but when they looked at the state of the land, air, and water, they realized they weren't making much progress.

Then the political tide turned.

By 1981, the environmental movement was on the defensive. The conservative new president, Ronald Reagan, insisted that "government was the problem, not the solution," and his staff quickly moved to undo as many regulations on business as possible and to slash funding for a wide range of programs.

But ultimately, the Reagan revolution was exactly what the movement needed. It jarred complacent citizens back to life, and forced environmental activists to go back on the offensive. In some ways, the Reagan team was its own worst enemy: the recruits from business and industry who took over key environmental positions, like Interior Secretary James Watt, were so radical they frightened people.

The center of environmental action began to shift away from Washington. The most important initiatives weren't coming out of the major organizations. The campaigns were emerging from the grass roots, from the rebels and the political amateurs—and to the astonishment of a lot of the old guard, they were actually working.

49

TEN YEARS AFTER

April 22, 1980
Washington, D.C.

In some ways, Earth Day 1980 looked just like Earth Day 1970.

Under sunny blue skies, environmentalists across the country marched, rallied, and held teach-ins. There were cleanup drives in Pennsylvania and educational programs in California. The Alternative Energy Resource Center made its grand opening in Anchorage, Alaska. In New York City, ten blocks of Sixth Avenue were cordoned off for a street fair.

But the tenth anniversary was a very different event. The crowds were a lot smaller—the twenty million who had once celebrated the birth of a new movement had shrunk to about three million. More important, the whole attitude seemed to have changed. The rabble-rousing attacks on industry and the talk of sweeping social change had vanished, replaced with subdued, cautious discussions of forming alliances with business and government.

In Washington, D.C., with the smell of tulips and azaleas hanging in the air, Douglas Costle, head of the Environmental Protection Agency and a former Wilderness Society lobbyist, told a muted rally that many of those marching in the streets in 1970 had made the shift "from the ragged squad of citizens' militia to disciplined platoons of lawyers, scientists and civil servants."

Former Oregon governor Tom McCall echoed Costle's words. "We're in an era where environmentalism...moves to a more intellectual level," he proclaimed. "Science, law, experience, maturity, eloquence—these factors have replaced taking issues to the streets."

Instead of sounding the call to arms, as they had ten years earlier, a lot of environmental leaders spent their time congratulating themselves on how much they had accomplished. Gus Speth was a classic example. One of the founders of the Natural Resources Defense Council, he had become chairman

257

of the White House Council on Environmental Quality. In a series of newspaper interviews just before Earth Day, he talked repeatedly about the legislative victories of the past ten years. He pointed to NEPA, the Clean Air Act, the Surface Mining Control Act, the Endangered Species Act, the Resource Conservation and Recovery Act.

But as if to mock everything Speth was saying, the big event in the northeast news media April 23 wasn't Earth Day—it was a chemical waste fire in Elizabeth, New Jersey. The night before, a spark ignited an illegal dump on the edge of the city, sending roaring flames hundreds of feet in the air. Plumes of thick, acrid smoke covered fifteen square miles. By the time firefighters brought the blaze under control, millions of gallons of water—turned crimson by its chemical contamination—had run off into the Elizabeth River.

50

ROAD WARRIORS

April 22, 1980
New York City

High above Manhattan, in a glass-and-steel tower of the World Trade Center, some of the most influential people in New York nibbled hors d'oeuvres and sipped bubbly drinks at the posh kickoff of a major political campaign. Everyone knew everyone else; this sort of event was standard fare for Manhattan's social elite. The only thing missing was a candidate. The object of everyone's attention couldn't put in an official appearance, but colorful photos and drawings helped fill the void; the movers and shakers were trying to promote a four-mile public road.

The slick press kits told the story: the new Citizens for Better Transportation was out to ensure that nobody in the city or state government would take seriously the prospect of trading in federal funds for the West Side Highway Project, known as Westway, and using the money for mass transit. If Westway was canceled, the glossy literature explained, New York would lose thousands of jobs, millions of dollars in tax revenue, and acres of new parkland. More ominous, it suggested, a Westway trade-in could threaten the future of the entire interstate highway system; if New Yorkers decided not to accept the federal funds for this interstate link, other cities might do the same, and before long, the whole national highway program would collapse.

The literature didn't bother to point out that twenty-four cities already had taken advantage of Bella Abzug's 1973 trade-in legislation and had exchanged interstate highway funds for transit programs. It didn't mention how much New York had to gain from a trade-in, either: just two months earlier, the secretary of transportation had informed city officials that Westway could be exchanged for its full projected cost, now more than $1 billion, plus inflation, and that the money could be used for any combination of other

259

roads and transit improvements that New Yorkers decided to make. For example, the federal highway money could be used to repair the New York City subways.

To the sponsors of the gala press event, none of that was important. Westway was the missing link in a vision of a new New York that was looking better every day. Looming bankruptcy was gone—under Mayor Ed Koch, tax incentives, outright subsidies, friendly zoning rules, and relaxed environmental standards had helped set off an honest-to-God real estate boom. A new midtown convention center was under construction; plans for a sweeping overhaul of the famous Times Square district were in the works. High-rise office buildings were springing up all over. On the presidential campaign trail, Ronald Reagan was preaching a similar gospel of growth and deregulation, and it warmed the hearts of the financial elite. The sad, dark days of Jimmy Carter, when America seemed to be bound by all sorts of controls and limits, were finally coming to an end. Already, New York was feeling like a world-class city again.

The supporters of Westway were finding a few unusual allies. Among the people who showed up to proclaim their support for the Citizens for Better Transportation were several prominent black and Latino leaders and the heads of three of the city's largest labor unions. They were sick of hearing about economic stagnation, too. Westway, they told reporters, would give their constituents what they wanted: jobs.

The name of the new organization was hardly coincidental. For years, a group called the Committee for Better Transit had been fighting for the rights of subway riders, who had the most to lose from Westway. The organizers of the well-funded Citizens for Better Transportation knew the name would create some confusion in the public mind—and it wouldn't hurt their cause at all. With a few prominent minorities and labor leaders on board, the whole thing could start to look like an actual grassroots coalition. That was becoming a popular tactic among business groups that fought environmentalists: in San Francisco, for example, an urban environmental group called San Francisco Tomorrow was trying to limit downtown office development; the Chamber of Commerce responded with a prodevelopment group called San Francisco Forward. Businesses and their lobbying groups were adopting the language of the environmental movement, too. The nuclear industry's Committee for Energy Awareness would soon begin broadcasting television ads promoting "alternative energy . . . like solar and nuclear power." An ad campaign by a major lumber company ended with the slogan, "Weyerhaeuser—the tree-growing people." On one level, it was a testament to the environmental movement's success—the corporate public relations experts recognized that environmental issues were a high priority to growing numbers of Americans. But the strategy was also creating serious problems for legitimate environmental activists, who didn't have the money to launch their own public relations offensive exposing the fraudulent claims.

*   *   *

The people in the World Trade Center meeting room were anything but a grassroots bunch. David Rockefeller, one of the world's richest men, brother of the former governor of New York, and chairman of one of the city's largest banks, was hosting the show, along with banker Felix Rohatyn, who had helped engineer the loan package that brought the city out of its financial morass, and former mayor Robert Wagner, now a partner in one of the nation's most powerful law firms, Finley, Kumble, Wagner.

There were many other important guests, but two in particular stood out. Among the people who had signed on to advise and direct the new Westway lobby were W. H. James, former publisher of the New York *Daily News,* and Marian Sulzberger Heiskell, sister of the publisher of *The New York Times.*

Ironically, those movers and shakers were forced to mount their well-financed, high-powered highway offensive largely because of the efforts of one frantic woman, who was sitting in a cramped office a few miles away. Marcy Benstock, the founder of the Clean Air Campaign and the major foe of Westway, was wondering how she would pay the next month's rent.

Benstock and the Clean Air Campaign had been fighting Westway for six years, and had turned the highway into a major political issue. The governor, the mayor, and both of New York's United States senators backed the highway, but Benstock and her allies had fought it every step of the way. She'd stirred up enough fuss that even David Rockefeller had to be fairly concerned. Still, Benstock was feeling more depressed every day—she'd managed to slow the Westway steamroller down, but she couldn't seem to stop it.

By 1980, the price tag for Westway was running well over a billion dollars, enough money to do wonders for the subway system. Although the old, elevated highway along the West Side had collapsed in disrepair seven years ago, traffic was flowing surprisingly well along the six lanes of surface street below. The city's own traffic studies showed the rush-hour drive time from the Brooklyn Battery Tunnel outlet at the southern end of Manhattan to Forty-second Street in midtown had increased from an average of about eight minutes to an average of thirteen. Westway supporters said the new road would cut it back to eight minutes again, but Benstock wasn't convinced: new highways, she realized, attracted new traffic. Westway would encourage more New Yorkers to drive down the West Side instead of taking the subway. Commuters who took the train in from the suburbs to avoid the West Side congestion would have an incentive to start driving to work. That would bring more traffic, more congestion, and more air pollution to the area.

Benstock spent almost every waking moment these days trying to present her case—to the public, to the governor, to the state legislature, to Congress, to city hall, and to the news media. She compiled volumes of information on the project, filling up file cabinets as fast as she could get them into the cramped office she shared with the New York Public Interest Research Group.

She wrote up lengthy, detailed analyses, taking the proposal apart piece by piece and pointing out every possible problem. She mailed her fliers out to everyone she could think of, and kept file cards on everyone who responded.

For the previous three years, the fight over Westway had focused mainly on two issues: air pollution and money. The central forum for the pollution debate was the hearing room of the state environmental conservation commissioner, who had to issue an air-quality permit before the project could begin. The hearings lasted a total of seventy-six days; hundreds of people testified, generating more than fifteen thousand pages of written record. The evidence convinced Commissioner Peter A. Berle to deny the permit, on the grounds that the city's estimates of the traffic Westway would generate were far too low. But under pressure from Westway supporters, Governor Hugh Carey dismissed Berle and replaced him with a commissioner who agreed to approve the permit.

Meanwhile, the Clean Air Campaign was trying to convince anyone who would listen that Westway was such an expensive proposition that even the federal government might not be able to pay for it—and the city and state of New York would unquestionably have trouble coming up with their 10 percent share. Westway, Benstock argued, would cost more than two hundred times as much per mile as the average interstate highway; with inflation and cost overruns, the total could reach $1 billion a mile. Congress would have to appropriate almost $4 billion, more than the entire annual budgets of most major states; the city and state would have to come up with another $400 million, and nobody seemed to know where it would come from.

But even that wasn't enough to kill Westway. The Tri-State Regional Planning Commission, which oversaw transportation projects for the Greater New York area, overruled its staff and agreed to endorse the highway. A special panel appointed by the governor and the mayor had done the same thing. The Federal Department of Transportation was on board, and the environmental impact statement was completed, approved, and certified.

There was only one minor hurdle to go: the Army Corps of Engineers still had to issue the city a permit to dredge the mud off the bottom of the Hudson River and dump several million cubic yards of landfill off the western side of Manhattan Island. The environmental impact statement suggested that there shouldn't be any real problems with the notion—as the secretary of transportation, Brock Adams, proclaimed, "There's not a living thing in that river."

Benstock knew that wasn't true. A few people in the lower levels of the EPA bureaucracy had raised questions about the marine life in the lower Hudson, and the damage the Westway landfill might do. But politically, Benstock worried, the landfill permit wouldn't strike much of a chord in New

York. When billions of dollars and thousands of jobs were at stake, she feared, New Yorkers wouldn't care about a few dead fish.

Still, the idea of pouring all that sand and gravel into the river bothered her more and more. As she scrambled to keep her organization from folding, Marcy Benstock kept thinking about the Hudson River, and wondering whether anything was really living underneath the rotting piers that hung off the Lower West Side.

51

LANDSLIDE

November 4, 1980
Washington, D.C.

Only a small fraction of the votes had been counted; the polls on the West Coast would still be open for another hour. But by 9:50 P.M., Eastern Standard Time, President Jimmy Carter was ready to throw in the towel. Loyal supporters greeted him with cheers as he climbed onto the stage at the Sheraton-Washington Hotel, looked into the television lights, and delivered the most painful address of his long political life.

"I promised four years ago I'd never lie to you," Carter said. "So I can't stand here tonight and say it doesn't hurt."

The concession speech was elegant, dignified, and graceful. But for thousands of environmental activists, it carried a brutal message: life may have been bad under Carter, but it was about to get a whole lot worse. Ronald Wilson Reagan, the sixty-nine-year-old former California governor who had insisted during the campaign that trees caused more pollution than cars, was headed for the White House.

Reagan seemed to see environmental programs as nothing but a drag on the economy. He vowed to relax restrictions on business and cut government spending on agencies and programs that enforced environmental laws. He promised to make the nation feel proud and strong again, to end the era of limits, to stop asking people to accept diminished expectations. In Reagan's America, bigger would be better again, just the way it was when he was a kid.

Most environmentalists voted for Carter, and a few campaigned actively for him. But even when they pleaded for votes, they had a hard time getting excited about a candidate who had let them down on so many issues, like nuclear power, RARE II, and the Tellico Dam. A lot of activists had campaigned

264

hard for Senator Edward Kennedy, the Massachusetts liberal who took on Carter in the Democratic primary. Kennedy had a decent environmental voting record, but his interests were largely in other policy areas, and his presidential bid was far from an environmental crusade—among other things, he endorsed offshore oil drilling. Unseating an incumbent president in a party primary was virtually impossible—ultimately, all the Kennedy campaign managed to do was divide the party, use up huge amounts of resources, and leave Carter badly wounded going into the general election.

Some Kennedy supporters still refused to back Carter, shifting their allegiance to John Anderson, a moderate Republican congressman from Illinois who mounted one of the strongest third-party presidential campaigns in years. Overall, 10 percent of the people who had voted for Carter in 1976 switched to Anderson four years later.

A front-page headline in *The Village Voice* summed up much of the liberal sentiment: "BOZOMANIA!," it screamed above pictures of Carter, Anderson, and Reagan. "MILLIONS DISAPPOINTED AS FOOLS VIE FOR HIGH OFFICE." A lot of those millions stayed home and voted for nobody.

With the economy on the skids, inflation rising, and a foreign nation holding American hostages for more than a year, the rest of the voters took to Reagan's message in droves. In the final few days of the campaign, Carter's support crumbled rapidly, and by the time the president conceded, Reagan was headed for a landslide victory. He would wind up with 50 percent of the popular vote, seven points ahead of Carter.

Barry Commoner, the famous biologist and environmental spokesman, was on the ballot, too, as the presidential candidate of the Citizens party. He received less than one half of one percent of the vote.

The Republican victory went beyond the top of the ticket: for the first time in twenty-six years, a Republican majority took control of the U.S. Senate. Among the senators swept aside by the Reagan landslide were two of the environmental movement's best friends—George McGovern and Gaylord Nelson.

52

TREE HUGGERS AND PRAIRIE FAIRIES

January 22, 1981
Washington, D.C.

The Department of the Interior was the closest thing to a Cabinet-level environmental agency in the federal government. Businesses had the secretary of commerce to argue their cause; farmers had the secretary of agriculture; soldiers had the secretary of defense. Environmentalists had only the secretary of the interior, the person charged with managing and protecting the natural resources of the nation.

Over the past fifteen years, under both Republicans and Democrats, the Interior Department had developed a reputation as a voice of caution and moderation. The political philosophy of the secretary changed with the administration, but the department staff moved slowly, cautiously. Although environmentalists didn't always believe the agency was headed in the proper direction, the people who ran it had generally considered environmental protection, at least in theory, an important part of the job.

Not anymore.

Nobody expected President Reagan to appoint a staunch environmentalist to the post, but even so, his choice for interior secretary came as a shock. James Watt seemed to have no interest whatsoever in protecting natural resources—he just wanted to find new ways to exploit them. It was like putting General Patton in charge of a peace march.

Even the most moderate environmental groups were outraged. Russell Peterson, president of the Audubon Society, denounced him as a man whose "actions and statements identify him as an aggressive, shortsighted exploiter rather than a farsighted protector of the nation's air, land, and water." The executive director of the Wilderness Society, William Turnage, called it "the most retrograde appointment since the appointment of Albert Fall [as interior

266

secretary] by President Harding"—a move, he reminded reporters, that led to the notorious Teapot Dome scandal.

James Gaius Watt was born in the tiny town of Lusk, Wyoming, in 1938. His father, William, was a lawyer with the good luck to set up shop in a town not far from a newly discovered oil field; the boomtown prosperity created plenty of work. Jim was an honest, hardworking boy with a passion for politics matched only by his strict Christian fundamentalism. Like his father, he saw the New Deal of Franklin Roosevelt as encroaching socialism; unlike a lot of his peers, he carried his strict social beliefs into his personal life. If underage friends brought beer to a high school party, Jim Watt would immediately leave.

Watt was a serious student, and by his early twenties, he had received a law degree from University of Wyoming and landed a job in Washington. Along the way, he married his high school sweetheart. Between 1962 and 1966, Watt worked as a legislative aide to Senator Milward Simpson, a Wyoming Republican. Then he took a job as a lobbyist for the U.S. Chamber of Commerce, and later became head of the Interior Department's Bureau of Outdoor Recreation—an agency he would abolish in 1981. In 1975, President Gerald Ford put him on the Federal Power Commission.

The rising star of this sharp, conservative Republican fell briefly in 1977, when Jimmy Carter came to the White House. But Watt had attracted plenty of attention; by the time he left the federal government, Joseph Coors, the arch-conservative Colorado beer magnate, had contacted him with an attractive offer. Coors and several friends wanted to start a "public interest" law firm of their own, to combat those like the Sierra Club Legal Defense Fund and the Natural Resources Defense Council.

If the environmentalists could sue to stop development under a Republican White House, Coors reasoned, then an opposing firm could sue to open up more land for development and oppose increased environmental protections under a liberal Democratic administration. Watt loved the idea. Soon, he was directing the new Mountain States Legal Foundation.

Watt was the perfect man to lead Coors's new venture. He was every bit as ideological as his mentor, and every bit as determined as the people he opposed. Some aides said there was even a touch of vengeance in his attitude: during the 1960s, when he first arrived in Washington, the liberal Democrats ruled the roost, and they treated him and his ideas with contempt. Watt wasn't one to forget.

For four years, Watt and his Mountain States Legal Foundation team worked to repeal or undermine environmental laws that hampered development. They fought federal strip-mining regulations. They opposed plans to designate parts of a Wyoming oil field as wilderness. They argued against a ban on motorized rafts in the Grand Canyon. In general, they took the position Watt had developed long ago: public lands weren't supposed to be just for wilderness and parks. They were meant to be used. Hikers and campers—the folks Watt's supporters liked to call "tree huggers and prairie fairies"—already had plenty of national parks, he insisted; the rest of the land should be available for hunters, ranchers, oil-drillers, off-road vehicle enthusiasts, and others—especially those who were willing and able to make money off the public bounty.

For all his fervor, Watt could be a keen political strategist. When the Interior Department began its RARE II inventory under Carter, Watt encouraged the ranchers, miners, and drillers of the western states to hang tough, act outraged, and make no reasonable compromises. He outfoxed the environmental leaders in Washington—and drove the likes of Dave Foreman and Huey Johnson away from the moderate center. It was a pattern that would be repeated in the years to come.

James Watt wasn't Reagan's first choice for the Interior Department. He'd wanted former senator Cliff Hansen of Wyoming, who was recommended to Reagan by Senator Paul Laxalt, one of Reagan's old friends. But Hansen turned the job down, fearing he would have to give up his grazing permits due to conflict of interest.

For his work as a senior adviser on the presidential campaign, Reagan had promised Laxalt two things: a chance to play tennis on the White House courts and the right to select the next interior secretary. When Hansen dropped out, Laxalt suggested Watt.

In December 1980, Watt met with the president. The two men discussed their views of the Interior Department—an agency that oversaw a vast empire of programs and projects, had a budget larger than that of some Third World countries, and controlled hundreds of millions of acres of land. The meeting took twenty minutes. Watt got the job. On January 22, 1981, the Senate, over the bitter objections of environmental activists, confirmed Watt's appointment. Only twelve senators voted no.

Reagan didn't know it, but he'd just done something Jimmy Carter was never able to do: he'd sounded an environmental call to arms.

53

SECRET SERVICE

January 22, 1981
Manchester, New Hampshire

The moment he walked into the courtroom, Kevin Lawless knew something was odd. The latest Clamshell Alliance trial was about to begin, but for some reason, the Clamshell lawyer, Jan Schlictmann, was sitting at the defense table in silence, lips pursed, staring ahead. The local prosecutor didn't look very happy, either. And as Lawless looked around at his antinuclear colleagues, he realized someone was missing.

Lawless was one of the founders of the Greater Newburyport chapter of the Clamshell Alliance, and the small-town antinuclear group had become the center of his personal life. The other members were his closest friends; the meetings were often as much social as political. The chapter stuck together and made all its decisions by consensus; when twenty-two members had been arrested several months ago at a demonstration at the headquarters of the Public Service Company, the prime sponsor of the Seabrook nuclear power plant, all twenty-two had decided to fight the charges in court. Over the past few weeks, all twenty-two had participated in legal strategy sessions with Schlictmann.

But on the day of the trial, only twenty-one defendants had shown up in court. The man they all knew as Lucas Macdonald had suddenly disappeared.

Before Lawless could ask Schlictmann why one member was missing, Judge Louis Wyman ordered the attorneys for both sides to meet with him in chambers. When they emerged about half an hour later, the judge looked out at the defendants and solemnly informed them that the charges were dismissed. He gave no further explanation.

*   *   *

The news that reached Jan Schlictmann early that morning was the stuff of defense lawyers' nightmares. One of the Clamshell defendants, who sat through every confidential legal strategy session, received copies of all Schlictmann's private legal memos, and knew every last detail of the case the defense would present, was really an undercover cop.

The infiltrator had reported everything he heard to the New Hampshire State Police and had shared a lot of it with the security department of the Public Service Company. Copies of some of his reports also went to the office of the state attorney general.

All of this, it turned out, had been going on for quite some time.

Lucas Macdonald, whose real name was James Nims, was assigned by the state police to infiltrate the Clamshell Alliance back in 1980. The bearded young officer took full advantage of the open atmosphere of the Newburyport Clamshell chapter. He started showing up at the regular weekly meetings, held at the local YMCA. He told everyone he lived in Hampton, a town just over the New Hampshire border. He worked at a gas station during the day, he said, and was trying to get his degree from the University of New Hampshire at night. He said he was worried about nuclear power, especially the Seabrook plant, and wanted to do something about it.

Lawless, one of the founders of the local Clamshell chapter, remembered him as a polite, respectful, working-class guy, always eager to help. He seemed like exactly the sort of person the alliance was trying to attract. Before long, Macdonald was dating a woman who was part of the Clamshell inner circle, sometimes spending nights at her place in Newburyport. He came to potluck dinners and birthday parties. Everyone accepted him into the Clamshell crowd.

But he was also taking careful notes on everything the organization did. At the annual Clamshell Congress in 1980, he even made a point of quietly walking around the parking lot outside the hall where the members were gathered, taking down every license plate number.

In May 1980, some of the Newburyport activists decided to split off from a demonstration at the plant site and try to occupy the Manchester headquarters of the Public Service Company. The decision was made quickly, and the action was planned with less than a day's notice. The idea was to catch the company by surprise.

But when the protesters, dressed in business suits, showed up in small groups at the high-rise office building, the place was surrounded by cops. PSCO security seemed to know every move in advance. By the time the Clamshell members had assembled outside the seventh-floor office of the company president, dozens of state police and security officers were on hand. Twenty-two protesters, including Macdonald, were arrested quickly; downstairs, a booking team and a fleet of paddy wagons were waiting.

Kevin Lawless and his Newburyport friends were baffled. They were baffled even more eight months later when Macdonald didn't show up for trial.

When Schlictmann hastily explained what had happened, the confusion turned to shock. The prosecutor had learned at the last minute that one of the defendants was an undercover cop, and had informed Schlictmann and the judge. Judge Wyman agreed that the informant's presence in confidential defense strategy meetings violated every legal canon and constitutional principle on the books and deprived the defendants of a fair trial. So he had to dismiss the charges.

Lawless left the courtroom with one of his best friends, the woman who had become Lucas Macdonald's lover. She was as confused as anyone, and a bit worried, too: nobody seemed to have any idea where Macdonald had gone. Whatever had happened, she told Lawless, she still cared about the man, and she wanted to talk to him.

Before they left the building, the woman happened to glance down the hallway, toward the offices of the district attorney. To her astonishment, the missing defendant was walking casually out of a prosecutor's door, and heading in her direction.

As he approached, she called out his name, the only one she knew. But James Nims walked right by, as if she didn't exist.

54

THE RAGGED EDGE

February 25, 1981
Niagara Falls, New York

Lois Gibbs left Love Canal early in the morning, with $10,000 in her pocket, two tired children on the seat next to her, and a U-Haul trailer hitched to the back of her old station wagon. Her mother chased the car down the driveway, shouting out one last time the same thing she'd been saying for weeks: it was crazy, leaving town like this, and moving to Washington, D.C.

Gibbs wasn't about to disagree. She didn't know anyone in the nation's capital. She didn't have a job. But she had a new project in mind, and Washington seemed like the place to give it a try.

From the first days of the Love Canal campaign, Gibbs had been frustrated. Fighting the chemical companies, and the bureaucrats, and the politicians was bad enough, but doing it alone, without any political advice or technical support, was almost impossible. All over the country, she suspected, people like her were facing the same problem: when toxic garbage from some hidden dump began showing up in the neighborhood, there was nobody to call for help. So hundreds of local activists were wasting hundreds of precious hours retracing the same steps, trying to figure out things that Gibbs could explain in a minute.

With all the media attention on Love Canal, Gibbs had practically become a full-time toxic-waste adviser. The phone in her apartment rang constantly. It was too much for her husband, Harry: he'd hoped that once the government agreed to buy the house and evacuate the neighborhood, the family could move somewhere else and life would get back to normal. But Lois kept getting involved in more battles, and after a few months, the couple split up.

When the house payment arrived from the government, Gibbs took her share and started looking for a new apartment, in Washington. The money would be enough to start a small organization, a citizens' clearinghouse for toxic waste information—and the closer she was to the people in power, the easier it would be to keep track of them.

Two thousand miles to the west, another recently divorced woman was packing up her belongings and heading for Washington. Anne Gorsuch, conservative Denver lawyer, former state legislator, and ally of James Watt, was about to take over the Environmental Protection Agency.

Like Gibbs, Anne Gorsuch was riding a wave of political success. Like Gibbs, she was smart and tough. But the similarities ended there.

Gorsuch grew up in a comfortable Colorado suburb, the daughter of a conservative physician. She earned her undergraduate degree at the University of Colorado at nineteen, a law degree two years later, and then traveled to India as a Fulbright scholar. When she returned to Colorado, she moved through a series of high-profile law positions, including the state real estate commission, before being elected to the state House of Representatives in 1976.

Colorado in the 1970s was racked by political controversy, much of it centered around the environment. The Rocky Mountain State had stunning natural beauty and a booming economy, both of which attracted a growing number of immigrants. Between 1960 and 1975, the state's population doubled, putting even more pressure on the natural resources. In the early part of the decade, liberal Democrats with strong environmental platforms took control of the governor's office and the legislature. At the same time, the oil, gas, mining, and timber companies that had been flocking to the state were running into problems—federal environmental laws were limiting their ability to expand.

By 1976, the young legislator helped put together a small band of antiregulatory extremists who called themselves the "crazies." At first they seemed unimportant, but their influence grew quickly. By 1977, led by the crazies, the Colorado legislature had refused to accept tight air pollution codes imposed by the EPA.

In the summer of 1976, she chaired a state legislative committee considering a measure to control toxic wastes. When the measure was killed, she got most of the credit. In 1977, Gorsuch's second year in the House, she earned a meager 8 points on the Colorado Open Space Council's 100-point environmental-consciousness rating of state legislators.

In 1980, with a messy divorce pending and her district angry over some of her far-right stands, Gorsuch decided not to seek reelection. But when Ronald Reagan swept into the White House, she saw a chance to return to public life. Always ambitious, Gorsuch decided to start using her contacts to lobby for a senior position with the EPA, perhaps even the job of deputy administrator.

James Watt, another antiregulatory extremist from Colorado, had noted her public record with approval. Her timing was perfect, too: the Reagan team was having trouble finding someone to run the agency. Watt set up a series of interviews for Gorsuch, and soon, instead of a deputy's post, she was offered the top EPA position.

The EPA was the most powerful regulatory agency in the United States government. When Gorsuch took control, the agency had 14,500 employees and a $1.3 billion operating budget. The Clean Water Act alone made the EPA responsible for controlling water pollution from nearly 100,000 different sources.

Lois Gibbs had a lot of problems with the EPA—as far as she could tell, it wasn't doing its job. Gorsuch had problems, too: she thought the agency was doing far too much. President Reagan had vowed that "there are tens of thousands of . . . regulations I would like to see eliminated"—and the way Gorsuch saw it, there was no better place to start than the EPA. The Office of Management and Budget had already begun the job: On February 17, just a week earlier, the president signed an executive order giving the OMB expanded power to, in effect, review and hold up all new regulations.

On President Carter's last day in office, he had signed the Comprehensive Environmental Resource Conservation and Liability Act—the so-called "superfund"—into law. The law allocated billions of dollars for cleaning up toxic waste sites. Although Gibbs hadn't lobbied for the law, it was a direct result of the Love Canal controversy, and once she was established in Washington, she was determined to see that the money didn't go to waste. Gorsuch was equally determined to see that the EPA didn't become another thorn in the side of the chemical industry. The battle would become a major focus of both women's lives.

Gorsuch, one writer suggested, "came from the ragged edge of environmental conflict . . . to a position of power and political visibility greater than either she or the White House understood." The same could easily have been said about Lois Gibbs.

55

THE PRIVATE SECTOR

March 1981
Washington, D.C.

Like most environmentalists, Dave Morine, vice president for land acquisition at The Nature Conservancy, had known the new administration would be bad. But he had no idea it would be this bad. Not for The Nature Conservancy.

Ronald Reagan had come to office on a promise to reduce government regulation, to set the economy free, to cut "red tape" that slowed industrial growth and development. From the start, he had shown an almost comical lack of understanding for environmental issues. But The Nature Conservancy seemed like Ronald Reagan's kind of organization. Much to the increasing chagrin of other major environmental groups, TNC didn't lobby for tighter environmental regulations or attack big business, or promote any sort of liberal social agenda. Shortly after the election, Reagan had even appointed Pat Noonan to an advisory board to help him set environmental policy.

Then came the other appointments: Robert Burford, a cattle rancher, to head the Bureau of Land Management. Anne Gorsuch, a chemical industry favorite, to run the Environmental Protection Agency. James Watt to head the Interior Department.

And today, with the stroke of a pen, Watt had wiped out the financial underpinning of almost everything The Nature Conservancy was trying to do. In the process, he'd killed the most ambitious land preservation project Morine and the organization had ever attempted.

It was bitterly ironic: Reagan spoke constantly of letting the "private sector" take over what government had once done—and now his own interior secretary was making it harder for a private conservation group to do exactly that.

*   *   *

The Rivers of the Deep South program was David Morine's baby, a vast, complicated, and groundbreaking deal that helped fill a tremendous vacuum in the organization. It evolved shortly after Noonan, who had built the organization into the wealthiest environmental group in the nation while saving millions of acres from development, decided to take a job with the wealthy Mellon Foundation. The directors of the philanthropic foundation wanted to move into land conservation in a big way—that meant millions of dollars a year—and they wanted Noonan to help them decide how to spend it. A lot of the Mellon money, Noonan knew, could be directed into Nature Conservancy projects.

As Noonan prepared to leave the conservancy, he asked Morine to come up with the deal of a conservationist's lifetime, something huge that could be done with Mellon money. Morine responded with the Rivers of the Deep South.

The bulk of the wetlands in the eastern United States was along the coast of Louisiana, the tip of Florida, and the southern edge of Georgia. From the Okefenokee Swamp, a giant Georgia marsh half the size of Rhode Island, to the Everglades, literally a "sea of grass" that covered most of the lower part of Florida, the wetlands were home to some of the most diverse—and some of the most threatened—types of wildlife in North America.

But the major rivers that fed and drained those wetlands were still subject to the whims of private development—and if the rivers were polluted, choked, diverted, or dammed, the wetlands would slowly die. Given the history of wetlands management in the South, especially Florida, Morine and Noonan knew the threat was very real.

So Morine mapped off vast tracts of private land along five major southern rivers—the Pearl, the Tensaw, the Choctawhatchee, the Apalachicola, and the Suwannee. They were the lifeblood for the eastern half of the Gulf of Mexico; the flood plains they formed and the swamps they drained nurtured some of the nation's most significant remaining wetlands. Morine proposed to buy up all the land and resell it to a group of state governments. The potential benefits were tremendous: if several different states could be convinced to treat a group of rivers and swamps as a single ecosystem, one that crossed and superseded state lines, it would put even the federal government to shame and teach the nation an important lesson in ecology.

It was, even for a disciple of Pat Noonan, a project of massive scale, a complex deal that would take a cash grant of $3 million a year and use it to buy $90 million worth of land in just five years. The final package would involve 450,000 acres of swampland and riverfront.

The deal was set up just the way Noonan liked to do business: the first $3 million of foundation money would be used to make a down payment on a $9 million purchase. The conservancy would quickly turn around and sell the land to state wilderness or recreation agencies, providing no-interest interim financing, then recoup the initial investment and do it again some-where else. Each time, the cash down payment would be leveraged 3–1; each time, the money would be rolled over twice. The Mellon Foundation would put up a total of $15 million, and get six times its money's worth in land preservation.

The way Morine saw it, selling the land to state agencies wouldn't be any problem. The Nature Conservancy's tax incentives would convince property owners to sell cheap—and under a well-established and successful program to encourage state nature preserves, the federal Land and Water Conservation Fund would put up half the money. Morine and Noonan had done dozens of similar deals before, on a much smaller scale; once the initial grant money came through, the process was so simple it was almost routine.

And indeed, on November 4, 1980, the Mellon Foundation made the largest single grant in the history of land conservation. A letter came to the new Nature Conservancy president, William D. Blair, Jr., approving the release of $15 million from the Richard King Mellon Land Preservation Fund to support the Rivers of the Deep South program. A check for $3 million was attached to the letter.

And then Jim Watt had pulled the plug.

The interior secretary, in a broad cost-cutting sweep, abolished the Land and Water Conservation Fund. For the indefinite future, the federal govern-ment would no longer offer matching funds for the purchase of environ-mentally sensitive or significant state land. And for the indefinite future, Morine had no idea how he could continue the Rivers of the Deep South program, or what to do with a $3 million check that was looking increasingly worthless.

Morine wasn't just worried about the five rivers. Watt's newest and most violent blow to conservation seriously threatened The Nature Conservancy in general. So many of TNC's projects relied on the federal matching funds program: the states that joined the efforts never had all the money themselves.

The Mellon grant was more than just a single chunk of cash, too. Noonan believed that Mellon could potentially take the lead in carrying private con-servation efforts through the next decade—but the foundation trustees were still wary, and they wanted to see results. In fact, the Mellon general counsel wanted to take a trip to the South in a few weeks to see what his $3 million was buying.

So Morine started looking for help—and he found it in the nation's poorest state, Mississippi.

Charlie Deaton was the special counsel to the Mississippi governor and a former member of the state legislature. As the chairman of the Appropri-ations Committee, he'd helped Morine pull off a deal several years earlier involving a land purchase in the state, and the two men had stayed in touch. Deaton had recently joined The Nature Conservancy board; when Morine called, he came right to the phone.

Deaton understood the dilemma at once. The St. Regis Paper Company was ready to sell seventeen thousand acres of land along the Pearl River—a perfect start for the Rivers of the Deep South program. But under the firm rules Pat Noonan had established at The Nature Conservancy, Morine couldn't just spend the grant money on a single piece of land—he needed to have another buyer lined up, a government agency that would set the land aside as wilderness and pay back the purchase price. Morine had to spend the Mellon money over and over again.

Times were tight in Mississippi, but good personal connections bought a lot of influence in the governor's office, and the thought of upstaging the U.S. Interior Department appealed to the political instincts of quite a few local politicians. Besides, the powerful paper company wanted the deal to work out—selling land to The Nature Conservancy was always good public relations. By the time the Mellon representatives arrived to meet with the governor on the banks of the Pearl River, Deaton had lined up the money.

In the Age of Reagan, that was all David Morine needed to turn his dream into a wildly successful program that would preserve almost half a million acres of land.

56

POLITICAL POISON

July 10, 1981
Sacramento, California

At first, he would later say, all he could think about was poison, raining down from the sky.

At night, when he left the governor's office and went home to his spartan, $400-a-month apartment, Jerry Brown would lie on the floor on a mattress that served as a bed and think about the hundreds of thousands of people living their peaceful lives in the Santa Clara Valley. And he'd think about helicopters, flying low over the rooftops, dumping poison on their heads. It wasn't right, he told his advisers; fruit flies or no fruit flies, he just couldn't accept it.

And for twelve long months, as the tiny, voracious agricultural pest called the Mediterranean fruit fly whipped California into a political frenzy, Governor Brown had held his ground. One by one, the most powerful politicians, business leaders, and newspapers in the state lined up against him. Day by day, fly sightings rose in the Santa Clara Valley, on the edge of some of California's most fertile farmland, and the threat to the largest single industry in the state grew. Week by week, the polls showed Brown's popularity falling. Almost everywhere he turned, he was hearing the same demand:

Forget your righteous ecological purity. Forget the environmental votes. Think about the billions of dollars and thousands of jobs at stake—and start doing the only thing that will work, before the flies spread any further. Soak the whole area with pesticide. Spray it from the air.

And at last, trapped by the conflict between jobs and the environment and backed into a corner by the Reagan White House, Jerry Brown could resist no more. On July 10, a year into the crisis, he called down the poison rain. The decision would shatter his political career.

*   *   *

The Mediterranean fruit fly was a tiny yellow bug that didn't live very long and couldn't fly very far. But it had a huge appetite for at least two hundred types of fruit—like oranges, apples, and apricots—and it reproduced madly. A single female fly could lay as many as a thousand eggs in a lifetime of a few months, burrowing into hundreds of pieces of fruit and leaving a few dozen offspring in every one. The larvae hatched quickly and began to feed on the pulp of the ripening fruit; within days, they turned it into worthless mush.

The Medflies, as they soon became known, were notorious hitchhikers. The larvae spread around the globe inside pieces of healthy-looking fruit, only to emerge and start a new infestation hundreds, sometimes thousands of miles away. No simple inspection could reveal their presence. Even fairly powerful insecticides would not always kill them. In the winter, the flies hibernated, wrapped in tough cocoons that resisted almost any sort of chemical poison. The only sure way to get rid of the pests was to kill them on the wing; the preferred agent of death was a chemical called malathion.

Malathion was part of a class of man-made chemicals known as organophosphates. Some were extremely dangerous: the deadly nerve gases developed by the Nazis in World War Two, for example, had chemical structures very similar to that of malathion. But in chemistry, a few atoms could make a huge difference, and the companies that made malathion insisted that it had very little in common with its awful, deadly cousins. According to the manufacturers, and a lot of other scientists, malathion would easily kill mosquitoes, gnats, and fruit flies—but in the kind of doses that were used to control insects, it wouldn't do any harm to human beings.

Not everybody shared that position. As early as 1962, Rachel Carson sounded the malathion alarm. In *Silent Spring*, Carson explained that compounds like this particular organophosphate might seem harmless to people who were exposed to a small amount, on one or two isolated occasions. But over time, the stuff could accumulate in the human body—and more important, it could interact in the body with a wide range of other fairly common pesticides to create a potent chemical time bomb. People didn't even have to be exposed to the different chemicals at the same time; breathing, eating, or even absorbing small amounts through the skin several weeks apart could cause a toxic reaction a hundred times more severe than that of any one of the chemicals by itself.

Malathion alone, even in comparatively small doses, could be dangerous, especially to pregnant women and children, critics warned. The pesticide worked the same way the Nazi gases did—it disrupted nerve impulses. Over the long term, some studies suggested, even small amounts could create abnormal brain waves in otherwise healthy adults.

Since the summer of 1980, when a handful of Medflies were found in a backyard garden on the southern edge of the San Francisco Bay, almost everyone who had anything to do with the state's gigantic agricultural industry had been in a state of panic. Nobody knew exactly where the bugs had come from—they had probably hidden in a contaminated produce shipment from another country—but farmers knew exactly what the Medfly could do. In 1910, when a few flies first appeared in Hawaii, the tropical islands were lush with all manner of fruits, and Hawaiian fruit farmers were prospering. In a few short years, the flies had destroyed almost everything; only pineapples, which had skins too thick for the bugs to penetrate, survived as a viable export. For most of the century, Hawaiians had paid to import fruits that once grew abundantly on their islands.

To California farmers, and the thousands of people who depended on them, the Medfly threat was very serious business. The area where the first flies were found was just a few miles away from the edge of the fertile San Joaquin Valley, which produced more than 80 percent of the tomatoes, avocados, nectarines, apricots, grapes, plums, and lemons in the United States. Not far to the south, the orange groves exported so much of their juicy fruit that even the state of Florida would often rely on shipments from California to tide it over through the chilly winter.

All told, California's agricultural products were worth almost $15 billion a year. By early 1981, some experts were saying that at least $1 billion of that, maybe more, was threatened by the Medfly infestation. If the bugs weren't eradicated right away, the situation would only get worse.

For twelve months, Brown did everything he could think of to kill the bugs without badly threatening the environment. His agricultural experts released thousands of sterile male flies, hoping they would mate with the females and prevent reproduction. Crews from the California Conservation Corps went through the Santa Clara Valley stripping down trees and gardens wherever flies had been spotted, and more than five hundred National Guard troops carted off and destroyed every last flower and leaf that could possibly be hiding the pests. Roadblocks along the highways stopped almost 300,000 cars and trucks heading into and out of the valley, and agricultural inspectors confiscated produce from 12,000 of them. The governor even let state officials spray a few parts of the valley with malathion—as long as they sprayed from the ground, where the impact could be limited to targeted areas, and kept away from humans.

But the flies kept spreading. By late spring, infestations were found in several hundred gardens, all of them small, all of them private, all of them within the confines of Santa Clara County. Still, the alarm was out—the newspapers and television stations were reporting on the infestation regularly—and by early summer, the first flies showed up in a commercial farm on the edge of the San Joaquin Valley.

The reaction spread far beyond California. The flies traveled in fruit, so several countries, including Japan, that were important markets for California produce, threatened to quarantine all imports unless they were frozen or fumigated—processes that would destroy most of the fresh California fruit. Five other states, including Texas and Florida, followed suit. The immediate costs were well over $100 million. The powerful agribusiness industry was starting to go crazy.

Brown didn't know why all the ecologically sound programs—the sterile flies, the roadblocks, the selective tree-strippings, and the ground spraying—weren't working against the Medfly. His advisers didn't know either—and they couldn't agree on what the next step should be. Some, like B. T. Collins, Brown's former chief of staff who was part of the governor's most trusted inner circle, insisted that the pesticide was harmless, and argued for immediate aerial spraying. The state's largest industry was on the line, Collins said, and so was the governor's political future. If Brown ever wanted to be president, he had to be willing to make a tough decision, to save a billion-dollar business and prevent economic disaster. To prove his point, Collins, a tough-talking veteran who had lost a leg in the Vietnam War, went before the press and drank a tall glass of water laced with the same concentration of malathion that would be sprayed over the residential areas of infested Santa Clara. He showed no immediate symptoms.

The leaders of California's biggest environmental groups urged Brown to hold a steady course. The governor's eradication program wasn't perfect, they agreed, but it was slowly having an effect. The flies weren't spreading as fast as they had in other places, like Hawaii, and most of them could probably be contained. If a few escaped into the San Joaquin Valley, they wouldn't do much damage.

The trick, environmental activists said, was to convince the people who imported California produce that the Medfly threat was more hype than reality. There were risks to that strategy, but the alternative would set a horrible precedent: if Jerry Brown, the most prominent environmentalist in elected office in the United States, was willing to spray poison on several thousand square miles of residential neighborhoods, the cause of pesticide control would lose a tremendous amount of credibility, and years of hard environmental work would be ruined.

For twelve months, Brown took the political heat, stuck with his pledge not to spray, and kept his promises to the environmental community. But the pressure to spray kept building. Brown wanted to run for the United States Senate, and the powerful industrial interests who could make or break his campaign financing were demanding action. Even his wealthy liberal backers, who generally supported environmental causes, were worried about the fruit harvest and the effect of the situation on the state's economy. It wasn't a game anymore, they told him; this ecological, appropriate technology stuff was all well and good, but right now, somebody had to save the crops. And if the organic gurus whom the governor liked couldn't come up with a solution that worked, it was time to turn things over to the people who could.

As the Medfly infestation turned into a full-scale crisis, Jerry Brown got more and more dizzy. Maybe, he told himself, he should have started aerial spraying right away. Maybe he should start it now. Maybe he shouldn't ever spray at all.

The truth was, he didn't know what to do. He couldn't make up his mind.

Then all of a sudden, the federal government forced Brown into action. Early in July, the agribusiness interests found a sympathetic ear in Washington: John Block, President Reagan's secretary of agriculture, announced that he would place an embargo on all California produce unless the governor agreed to start aerial spraying. Essentially, Block was threatening to declare economic war on California. In the worst possibly case, the Medflies might damage $1 billion worth of fruit; a total embargo would wipe out a $15 billion industry, roughly 20 percent of the state's economy.

It was hard to believe Block would go through with his threat. The entire nation would suffer if he insisted on enforcing the embargo. Food prices would soar. Consumers would be furious. But California would be hit the hardest—and this time, Brown decided, he couldn't afford to call the bluff. Not when he wasn't sure he could offer a better solution. Not with an election just sixteen months away. If the alternative was a federal quarantine, Brown agreed to do what most of the state seemed to want. He would send up the helicopters, and spray malathion over every backyard in the Santa Clara Valley.

As he stood before the television cameras to announce his decision, Brown resigned himself to the anger and opposition that would come from his environmental allies. He told his advisers not to worry about his political future: the Medfly mess would blow over. These things always did.

But Brown made a crucial political error. By waiting so long to spray, he lost the support of agriculture and business. By deciding to spray in the end, he lost the support of environmentalists. And by giving up his principles, and changing his mind under pressure, he lost his reputation for integrity. In sixteen months, Brown would give up the governor's office to run for the United States Senate, suffer an embarrassing upset at the hands of a little-known San Diego mayor named Pete Wilson and disappear for almost a decade from the American political scene.

The Medfly was a watershed event. It marked one of the first major environmental showdowns of the Age of Reagan, a high-profile clash over a tough, complicated issue that embodied some of the most pressing policy debates of the day. And the environmental champion collapsed.

57

THE SLEAZE
ALSO RISES

February 25, 1982
Washington, D.C.

All afternoon, Lois Gibbs had a case of nerves. She'd attended hundreds of public meetings since the early days of Love Canal, appeared on dozens of stages, and spoken to thousands of people, but this was different. For the first time, she was trying to raise a substantial amount of money to fund her own political venture, an organization called the Citizens Clearinghouse for Hazardous Waste. It was designed to give local activists around the country something the Love Canal Homeowners Association never had—expert advice on everything from chemistry to community organizing. The fund-raising event would be an important test of how far the grassroots toxics movement had come in the past years. It would show how seriously the Washington community took the issue—and whether Gibbs's crazy idea had any chance of success.

There was no question about the need for the work she was doing. Over the past few months, building on the contacts she'd made at Love Canal, she'd turned her tiny office into a central switchboard for more than a hundred antitoxics groups around the country. More calls came in every day. It was too much to handle alone anymore. With any luck, she hoped, a hundred people would show up for the event. At $50 a person, she could raise $5,000, enough to hire another staff person and keep the office afloat for a few more months.

Gibbs shouldn't have worried. The timing was perfect for fund-raising: a few days earlier, CBS aired a two-hour docudrama called *Lois Gibbs and Love Canal*. Newspapers and magazines covered the made-for-TV movie's release, and Gibbs's antitoxics campaign was the cause of the month. Besides, Ralph

Nader, the world-famous consumer advocate, agreed to host the party at his office and give the keynote speech.

By the time Nader began his talk, the biggest problem on Gibbs's mind was finding a place for everyone to sit. More than 450 people showed up. The food and drinks ran out immediately. The back of the room was jammed with visitors forced to stand through the speech. By the end of the evening, Gibbs had collected $25,000, enough to fund her organization for a full year. And the message was out to the politicians and the news media: the grassroots toxic-waste movement was alive and well, with a solid presence in the nation's capital.

Gibbs had her work cut out for her. Three days earlier, Anne Gorsuch had announced her choice for the second most important post in the Environmental Protection Agency. The new assistant administrator, who would oversee the $1.6 billion Superfund program and administer business compliance with toxic-waste-disposal laws, was a thirty-three-year-old business executive named Rita Lavelle.

Lavelle had no experience cleaning up toxic-waste problems—but she knew plenty about keeping them hidden. Before accepting the $67,000-a-year EPA position, Lavelle had done public relations for the Aerojet Liquid Rocket Company. Its parent company—Aerojet-General Corporation—was the third worst polluter in California, according to the EPA.

The long list of accusations that kept Lavelle's former employer mired in lawsuits included dumping twenty thousand gallons a day of hazardous waste into unlined ponds and swamps. When reporters and concerned citizens asked company officials difficult questions about the dump sites, questions the company would rather not answer, they were sent to Rita Lavelle. Her job was to minimize the damage and make the company look as good as possible.

Lavelle made Gibbs suspicious—an administrator whose background was in public relations, not public health, didn't bode well for the future of Superfund. There were dozens of sites that needed some of the federal cleanup money immediately, and Gibbs feared that without constant pressure, many of them might never see a penny of it. Besides, Lavelle seemed to have at least a potential conflict of interest—her former employer was breaking the laws she was supposed to enforce. But as Gibbs would soon find out, Lavelle's background was only the tip of the iceberg.

From the day she took over the EPA, Gorsuch set out to clean house. One of the tasks Reagan and Watt had given her was to rid the regulatory agency of liberal Carter-era staffers who zealously enforced the rules. Three weeks into the job, she unveiled a restructuring plan which eliminated, for all practical purposes, the entire EPA enforcement office. A staff of more than two thousand scientists, hazardous-waste specialists, lawyers, and others who had enforced the nation's pollution laws were transferred into other programs, leaving only a skeleton crew behind to do the job.

As a final precaution, William Sullivan, the new head of enforcement, warned the heads of EPA regional offices that "every case you do refer" to us for enforcement will "be a black mark against you." The dramatic results were apparent in the first year: in 1980, 313 cases were referred. In 1981, only 59.

Since Gorsuch didn't trust any of the existing staff, she came to rely on a lawyer and old acquaintance named James W. Sanderson as her closest adviser. Gorsuch and Sanderson had formed a casual friendship years earlier in Colorado, when Sanderson had worked on several cases with James Watt and the Mountain States Legal Foundation, cases that captured the fervor of the "crazies." Sanderson had gone on to serve in the Denver office of the EPA as regional counsel.

Gorsuch gave Sanderson a part-time job as an EPA adviser—and while he gave Gorsuch legal advice, he continued to represent private clients. At least one of his clients, a major chemical-waste company, took advantage of one of Gorsuch's more unusual rulings.

Years earlier, the Carter administration had imposed a ban on the disposal of many liquid chemicals in hazardous-waste landfills. But on February 25, the same day Gibbs was holding her fund-raiser, Gorsuch suddenly lifted the ban. As it turned out, the suspension would only last three weeks—but that was long enough for Chemical Waste Management.

Most companies never knew about the suspension until it was over. Of those that did, few had a chance to mobilize operations in time to legally dump their liquid waste. Chemical Waste Management, Inc., however, found time to dump fifteen thousand drums of solvents into the Lowry landfill in Denver, Colorado. At the time, Chem Waste was represented by James W. Sanderson.

With Congress still reeling from the Reagan landslide, and Republicans in control of the Senate, Gorsuch would be able to get away with slashing EPA staff, gutting regulations, and reducing enforcement. But while the toxic-waste flow was rising, the sleaze in her office was reaching high tide—and that would come back to haunt her.

58

HIGHBALL EXPRESS

September 28, 1982
Livingston, Louisiana

The Illinois Central Gulf freight train rolled out of Baton Rouge a few hours before dawn, pulling 101 cars on a short run to the main rail line in Hammond, where it was scheduled to turn north for McComb, Mississippi. The trip was about as routine an assignment as a freight engineer could get—not much more than a hundred miles of track, a few hours in the engine cab. Edward Peyton Robertson had run trains like this one hundreds of times over the years; so had his brakeman, Russell Reeves.

Running a freight train wasn't anywhere near as difficult as running a jetliner; most of the time, it was relatively simple. The Federal Railroad Administration didn't even have rules aginst drinking before work, the way the Federal Aviation Administration did. Engineers weren't supposed to be drunk, but they didn't have to stay completely sober, either. Sometimes, some of the trainmen pushed the limit a bit; most of the time, nobody knew about it. When somebody noticed an infraction, it was rarely reported.

None of the crew members in the Baton Rouge railroad yard had anything unusual to report about the morning train to Hammond. Robertson and Reeves climbed into the locomotive without any visible problems. A third person got into the cab, too, a shipping clerk named Janet Byrd; anyone who might have seen her chose to look the other way. Company rules forbade unauthorized passengers on board freight trains, but the friends of crew members hitched rides now and then, and none of the yard workers snitched.

Byrd was friendly with several of the engineers. Every now and then, she convinced one of them to let her drive an engine around the freight yard. She'd spent much of the evening with Robertson and Reeves, who were staying in Baton Rouge on a layover, waiting for their next assignment. When

287

the motel bar closed, she drove them to a convenience store, where they bought a bottle of whiskey. She went back to their room while they had a few more drinks; when the dispatcher called with their orders, she drove them back to the roundhouse and agreed to join them for the trip to McComb.

The two men were still drinking, she would later recall, as the train left the yard and rumbled down the tracks. A federal investigator would conclude that Robertson had consumed between fourteen and sixteen ounces of liquor that night; his union would insist he was sober. But somewhere along the thirty-mile ride between Baton Rouge and Livingston, Robertson and Reeves both fell asleep, and Janet Byrd took over the controls.

If everything had worked perfectly, the way it normally did, Byrd might have managed to get the freight safely to its destination. But around five A.M., as the train was passing through Livingston, an air hose coupler between the locomotive and the first car malfunctioned, and the brakes on the train automatically locked. An experienced engineer would have disengaged the brakes and allowed the train to coast to a stop; Byrd did just the opposite. She engaged another brake, slowing the front cars rapidly and causing the rear cars to jackknife. Immediately, forty-two cars, some of them tankers carrying volatile chemicals, skidded off the rails and slammed into each other. The force of the impact caused several tanks to explode, shattering windows in the nearby houses, jolting residents out of bed, and knocking out most of the town's electricity.

Robertson woke up as the locomotive ground to a halt. When he realized something was wrong, he tried to throw his drink out the window, which was closed. The liquor splashed back in the cab.

Police and firefighters arrived on the scene to find a hot, roaring blaze, with thick black smoke pouring from mangled tankers filled with an unidentified chemical cargo. Several intact tank cars lay on the ground nearby; nobody knew what was in them, either, or when they were likely to go. The fire was far too hot to even begin fighting it; the authorities hastily evacuated 2,700 residents, and watched as the blaze burned out of control.

For thousands of people across the South, the train wreck would become a chemical Three Mile Island, a disaster that brought the potential dangers of hazardous materials home to anyone who lived near a refinery, a factory, a highway, or a rail line.

The fire continued to burn, day after day. Hoses were useless—several tanks contained sodium metals, which exploded on contact with water. Besides, the heat was so intense that even crews in special firefighting suits couldn't get within range. Huge explosions continued to rock the peaceful town. On October 1, a tanker full of chemicals burst into a gigantic fireball that was visible from Baton Rouge. It shattered the windows of hundreds of houses and destroyed twenty buildings. Eventually, fire crews would have to use dynamite to blow up the rest of the cars so they could begin to attack the blaze.

On October 12, more than two weeks after the accident, Livingston residents were finally allowed to return to their homes, although the fire would still smolder for some time. The authorities assured everyone that they weren't in any danger—they just shouldn't eat any vegetables from their gardens or let their kids play in the dirt, and everything inside and outside their homes should be carefully and thoroughly washed. Aside from that, the situation was fully under control.

Like the official statements after the accident at Three Mile Island, the words of the chemical companies and the Louisiana politicians just didn't ring terribly true. It made the neighbors of chemical plants and waste sites all over the South wonder: When was another unexpected mistake going to send people running from their bedrooms in the middle of the night? What risks were they really taking? And what else were the authorities covering up?

As the Livingston townspeople washed down their houses, cleanup crews dug up the highly contaminated soil around the crash site, and loaded it, along with the remaining chemicals from the leaking tankers, into a convoy of trucks. Then the trucks headed off for a dump site, in the town of Willow Springs.

59

A RARE VICTORY

October 22, 1982
Sacramento, California

Huey Johnson, the director of California's Department of Natural Resources, knew his days as a state official were numbered. Governor Jerry Brown was giving up his office to run for the United States Senate, so a new governor would soon take over—and neither of the major candidates was likely to let Johnson keep running the powerful agency. By now, almost every powerful politician and special interest group in the state was mad at him: the conservatives and the labor unions hated his stubborn refusal to build dams, and the liberals were up in arms over his suggestion that California limit immigration as a way to slow its explosive population growth.

And yet, no matter where he wound up next, Johnson would always be able to look back at October 22 with a wicked sort of pride. A three-judge panel at the federal court of appeals in San Francisco had just issued its ruling on *California* v. *Block,* the lawsuit Johnson filed back in 1979 over the objections of practically every environmental group in the country. Although California hadn't won on every point, the impact of the decision was clear and unequivocal. The appellate judges agreed with the federal district court, and with Huey Johnson: the U.S. Forest Service couldn't open any more wilderness areas to logging or mineral development without doing individual, site-specific environmental impact statements. That was going to take years.

The appeals court decision was particularly satisfying. When the district court ruled in favor of Johnson's position a year ago, the Forest Service had a chance to drop the case. California would have gained the protection of a few million acres of wilderness, but elsewhere in the country, the RARE II procedures would have continued. An individual district court judge couldn't change federal law.

290

A federal court of appeals decision, on the other hand, was a binding national precedent. Now that the Forest Service had foolishly appealed the case—and lost—*California* v. *Block* was a lot more than a local lawsuit. It was a profound change in national wilderness policy. As much as twenty million acres of land, from Alaska to Florida, would be cut off from development, at least temporarily. When local activists moved to take advantage of the situation—and many did—some of wilderness would be saved forever.

The lawsuit Johnson had authorized from a phone booth, with a legal brief his lawyer had snuck into a pile of papers awaiting the attorney general's signature, had turned into one of the most important court cases in the history of environmental law. Every time he thought about it, Johnson had to smile: they were wrong, every one of them, from the chairman of the Congressional Public Lands Committee to the executive director of the Wilderness Society. They were wrong, and Huey Johnson was right—and for once, everyone had to admit it.

60

MRS. CLEAN

January 24, 1983
Lake Charles, Louisiana

Browning-Ferris Industries had always tried to keep a low profile out at Willow Springs. When Ruth Shepard stumbled onto the landfill in 1977, the company would barely admit that the place existed; years later, the narrow back road leading to the site was still poorly marked. High-level company executives didn't make a practice of flying out from Houston to visit Willow Springs—and they certainly didn't try to get publicity.

This time, though, when a local environmental group decided to hold a rally at the dump site, Browning-Ferris sent a corporate vice president along to give the activists a tour of the site. There was no point in trying to hide; everyone knew that the press would be out in full force. It wasn't often that a celebrity like Lois Gibbs came to town.

Gibbs was starting to take it all in stride. Reporters, camera crews, corporate public-relations teams—everywhere she went, it seemed, she made front-page news. If that sort of publicity could help people like Ruth Shepard and Shirley Goldsmith expose waste dumps and build local organizations in places like Willow Springs, Gibbs was always ready to oblige.

Goldsmith was thirty years older than Lois Gibbs when she traded the life of a homemaker for a career fighting chemical waste. A Michigan native, she'd moved to Louisiana with her husband in the 1950s and bought a house on the outskirts of Lake Charles. She raised two kids, joined the United Jewish Appeal and the Calcasieu Junior League, and spent a lot of time in her garden.

For years, she even put up with the foul air that blew across from the oil refineries on the other side of the lake. When the wind came out from the

292

east, she often woke up in the middle of the night with burning eyes and a raspy throat; even the solid brick walls of her house couldn't keep out the smell. A few times, she'd called the company and complained, and once she even wrote to the governor, but she never pursued the matter. It seemed pointless—the refineries were the economic lifeblood of the entire region, and they weren't about to go away.

Then, in October 1982, she read the newspaper reports of the Livingston train derailment. Day after day, the papers described the deadly poisons burning outside the town, detailing how they could cause cancer and make the area unsafe for farming. And she realized that the state was shipping the leftover toxic waste to a dump site in Willow Springs—just a few miles from Goldsmith's house.

For weeks, huge trucks, filled with chemicals and contaminated soil, rolled through town on their way to the Browning-Ferris dump site. Tanker after tanker swerved through the narrow streets like a fleet of toxic time bombs. Goldsmith started getting worried.

In November, Goldsmith's orthodontist died of cancer. He was a young, healthy man with a wife and six kids; he didn't even smoke. When the preacher at his funeral talked about the will of God, Goldsmith almost stood up in her seat and screamed. God didn't kill her orthodontist, she wanted to shout; the chemical companies did. The minute the funeral ended, she went home and called Mike Tritico.

Tritico was something of a local character, a Lake Charles native who had studied chemistry at San Francisco State University, taken odd jobs all over the country, and eventually moved back to his hometown to devote his life to cleaning up the air and water. He was a constant presence at public hearings, testifying about the health hazards of everything the chemical companies wanted to do. He got his name in the local papers a lot, but he never managed to build a serious organization.

Tritico had also recently been working with Ruth Shepard and the High Hopes Road Committee, and had tried repeatedly to get Goldsmith involved. Goldsmith had always insisted she didn't have the time. She told him she'd just changed her mind.

Shirley Goldsmith may have been a reluctant environmentalist, but she was a first-rate organizer. Within hours after the orthodontist's funeral, her front porch was crowded with friends and acquaintances, many of them still dressed in the somber clothes they wore to the morning's funeral. Tritico gave them a brief pep talk, and they agreed to form an organization. They called it the Calcasieu League for Environmental Action Now—for short, it was CLEAN.

Within days, Goldsmith made contact with another legendary organizer, Willie Fontenot, the citizen access specialist at the attorney general's office. Then she did what dozens of other small-town activists had been doing all over the country: she dialed the Citizens Clearinghouse for Hazardous Waste and asked for Lois Gibbs.

 Gibbs's appearance at Willow Springs two months later attracted national media attention and made front-page news all across southern Louisiana. Suddenly, the Willow Springs landfill was a hot political issue—and CLEAN was signing up new members as fast as Goldsmith could write down their names.

61

THE BATTLE OF BALD
MOUNTAIN

February 1983
Grants Pass, Oregon

The letter that brought the Earth First! gang to Oregon had no return address. The writer didn't even sign his name. All Mike Roselle knew was that the mystery correspondent worked as a soil scientist for the U.S. Forest Service, had a family to support, and didn't want to lose his job. But the story he told was enough to convince Roselle, Dave Foreman, and Bart Koehler to drop everything they were doing and head for the small logging town of Grants Pass, where they would make one of the most dramatic environmental stands of the decade.

Over the past few months, the soil scientist wrote, he had learned of a plan that outraged him: the most important virgin wilderness area in the Pacific Northwest, perhaps in the entire nation, was facing extinction. And nobody in the government or the mainstream environmental movement seemed able to stop it.

The Siskiyou Mountains straddled the border between California and Oregon, in the cool, wet, and largely untamed region where the Cascades met the Coastal Range on the edge of the Pacific Ocean. It was a rugged piece of land—the hills were steep and rocky, and much of the year, the moisture-laden ocean winds brought a constant foggy rain. But the climate was perfect for conifer forests, and since the Pliocene epoch, it had been home to a wide variety of pine, redwood, cedar, and fir trees.

The little corner of Oregon wilderness contained one of the oldest forests in North America—some of the giant redwoods that soared more than two hundred feet above the hillsides were alive when Julius Caesar was building the Roman Empire, and quite a few of the trees that lived in the thick wilderness were direct descendants of prehistoric species. It was also, quite possibly, the most diverse conifer forest on Earth: more than twenty-two different cone-bearing trees and fifty different hardwoods had been found in the Siskiyous, and some of the last of the endangered northern spotted owls made their nests in the old-growth trees.

In 1936, Bob Marshall, the recreation director of the Forest Service, recommended that the entire region be set aside as roadless wilderness, and for many years it remained that way. But eventually, the interests of the biologists, naturalists, and preservationists were frustrated by an interest far more powerful: the lumber industry.

Southwestern Oregon was logging country. Since the first American settlers pushed into the uncharted wilds of the Pacific Northwest more than a hundred years ago, the area had been known for the quality, and quantity, of its timber. Pine, fir, and hardwood stands seemed to stretch forever; the redwoods, with their soft and beautiful lumber, were so massive that the biggest saws were useless, and lumberjacks sometimes had to resort to dynamite. Abundant streams and rivers flowing through the area provided easy ways to transport logs to the mill. Over the years, several generations of loggers lived off the abundance. They carved out thousands of miles of roads, cut down huge numbers of trees, and provided a fast-growing nation with the raw materials for millions of houses, schools, churches, and factories. They also built cities and towns of their own, and established an entire regional economy based almost entirely on lumber.

In theory, the people who lived in southern Oregon liked wilderness fine—the area was full of hunters, fishers, campers, hikers, and nature-lovers. But when the cause of wilderness preservation clashed with the needs of the lumber industry, the prevailing attitude changed—without logging, without the mills, without the trucks hauling new trees in and finished boards out, there wouldn't be very many jobs.

So Oregon politicians weren't much for saving old forests—not at the expense of the lumber industry. In 1964, at the urging of environmentalists, Congress set aside 77,000 acres of the Siskiyous as a roadless area, the Kalmiopsis Wilderness. But all further efforts to expand the protected area were unsuccessful. In 1972, after the first Roadless Area study, the Forest Service recommended that everything except the national wilderness area be opened for logging. By 1978, when the Oregon Wilderness Council, among other groups, tried to get some of the Siskiyou region included in the RARE II wilderness bill, only about 325,000 acres of roadless area remained. The effort to save that remaining area was unsuccessful: At one point, Oregon senator Mark Hatfield announced that "not one more acre of wilderness will be added to the Kalmiopsis."

In 1979, the Agriculture Department determined that the area just north of the Kalmiopsis Wilderness would be opened up to logging. In the early 1980s, the Forest Service moved quickly to implement that decision. Timber sales were held for vast stretches of the virgin forest, and lumber companies snapped them up.

The only problem was getting there. Modern logging crews carried heavy equipment, and the less distance the logs had to be hauled from the trucks to the mill, the more time the crews could spend cutting. So the lumber companies, with Forest Service approval, launched an ambitious plan to build some seventy miles of logging roads through the northern part of the National Forest, starting with the Silver Creek watershed below Bald Mountain.

The letter from the soil scientist reached Roselle in Jackson, Wyoming, just as the campaign to save Little Granite Creek was coming to a stunningly successful close.

To the surprise of everyone, particularly Roselle, the Round River Rendezvous in July 1981 had attracted tremendous media attention. The hastily arranged roadside demonstration against Getty Oil's drilling roads made headlines in the local press, and one paper carried a page-one photo of several hundred demonstrators waving "GETTY GO HOME" placards. Enough of the protesters spilled into the highway to block Getty's surveyors and construction crews from reaching the project area, stopping work on the new road, at least temporarily.

Roselle, Foreman, and the Earth First!ers, joined by a few locals, had vowed to block roads all summer, and to continue pulling up stakes, vandalizing construction equipment, and doing whatever else it took to ensure that the project didn't go forward. It was a risky promise: neither Roselle nor Foreman had ever organized a civil-disobedience action before, and both were fairly new to the idea of ecological sabotage. They had no idea what they would do if they were forced to make good on the threats—no idea how long a blockade would hold out, or how many of the newly militant locals would hang on, or how long they and their friends would wind up spending in jail.

But as it turned out, none of that was necessary. Two days after the rally, with newspaper reporters and TV crews from all over the West descending on Jackson to examine this new, radical wilderness-preservation crusade, and with a lot of good, conservative Wyoming cowboys and ranchers talking about how much they agreed with those long-haired kids, the governor, Ed Herschler, announced he would fight the well. He filed a new legal appeal, and by the end of the week, the Agriculture Department granted a temporary injunction halting the road construction while the case was heard. A few weeks later, the Interior Department's Board of Land Appeals vacated Getty's drilling permit and ordered a new environmental impact statement that would examine the option of preserving the area as a roadless wilderness.

Suddenly, Getty Oil lost its interest in pursuing the exploratory well at Little Granite Creek. The cost of preparing a new EIS would be steep, and the delay considerable. Besides, the threat of more Earth First!-type protests, the further damage to expensive equipment, and the potential for an ongoing, high-profile environmental controversy made the whole thing more trouble than it was worth. When Congress began discussing a bill to designate the Gros Ventres as a national wilderness, Getty and the other oil companies barely put up a fight.

Roselle was thrilled. Legions of well-paid lobbyists for powerful national environmental groups like the Wilderness Society and the Sierra Club had been unable to get the Gros Ventres designated as a roadless area, even under a supposedly friendly, Democratic administration. And yet, Roselle realized, a new, not-terribly-organized group called Earth First!, with the help of one dedicated and creative environmental lawyer, had pulled it off fairly easily, despite the openly hostile Republican administration of President Ronald Reagan and Interior Secretary James Watt.

The more he thought about it, the more Roselle was convinced: the Gros Ventre campaign proved that the established political wisdom of the national environmental movement was absolutely, totally wrong. By working together, speaking with one voice and pushing for modest, "realistic" goals, the national organizations had lost millions of square miles of wilderness to commercial development. In Jackson, established local environmental groups were prepared to do the same, compromising on the Little Granite Creek well to save another wilderness area at Cache Creek.

Like Huey Johnson in California, though, Roselle and Wolke had refused to go along. They denounced the compromise, and when the local groups balked, they stormed into meetings and demanded to be heard. That had an immediate impact on the political debate. It guaranteed that the preservation of Cache Creek would be seen as the "moderate" alternative, and would not be compromised any further.

The second thing Roselle decided was that Little Granite Creek had shown the value of "ecotage" and civil disobedience as tactics of delay. Oil exploration—like road construction, mining, logging, and most of the other activities that threatened wilderness areas—was an expensive prospect, and every day that work was halted, the costs escalated. If the potential delays increased costs enough, the project might become too risky to continue. Meanwhile, anything that slowed down construction brought more time for legal and political intervention at other levels. Once the road was built, all the lawsuits in the world couldn't save Little Granite Creek; by slowing it down, Earth First! had made the wilderness preservation possible.

On top of all that, he thought, it never hurt to bring the news media right into the wilderness area where the battle was being fought. When television brought Vietnam into America's living rooms, it made the horrors of war more real to the people at home; if those same people could see what the oil drillers, loggers, miners, and road builders were doing to America's wilderness, maybe it would create the same sort of outrage. The Kalmiopsis Wilderness in Oregon seemed like a fine place to try his theory out.

*   *   *

The letter had been mailed from a Forest Service office in Galice, a tiny Rogue River town about twenty miles west of Grants Pass, on the northern edge of the Siskiyou National Wilderness. The Earth First! activists made the trip to Grants Pass in Foreman's van, and the day they arrived, Roselle and Koehler made their way up the winding mountain road to the modest office where, by all available evidence, their unknown informant was employed.

The chief ranger for the Galice district was a tall, imposing man named Bill Butler. When a couple of tough-looking cowboys in western boots, wide-brimmed hats, and plaid shirts strolled through the door, he didn't bat an eye. "Something I can do for you?" he asked.

"Sure," Roselle told him, speaking loudly enough for anyone else in the office to hear. "We're a bit concerned about the logging you're planning in the Kalmiopsis."

Butler gave the visitors a puzzled look. "And just what organization do you represent?"

"Earth First!," said Roselle.

The ranger shook his head. "Sorry. Never heard of it. So what's your problem?"

"Well," Koehler broke in, "we feel the same about this area as Aldo Leopold did. We don't want the Bald Mountain logging road, and we're going to do whatever it takes to stop it. We just thought we'd come by and tell you that."

Ranger Butler was singularly unimpressed, but among the rest of the office staff, the arrival of the Earth First! cowboys created quite a stir. When the chief ranger went back to work, half a dozen employees peered out from their cubicles to take a look at the strange and unexpected visitors. After a few minutes, a slender, middle-aged man emerged from a back office, looking, Roselle figured, like the world's greatest yuppie bureaucrat. For a minute or two, he stood somewhat awkwardly in the lobby, staring at the pair as if they were intruders from outer space. Then Roselle, who had decided he was getting bored, asked the guy if he knew where to find a decent bar in the area.

"Yeah," the Forest Service employee said. "There's one right down the road."

Roselle nodded and turned to leave, but the yuppie-looking guy stopped him. "Are you from Earth First!?" he asked. Roselle nodded.

"Then," the forester said, "I think maybe I'll go down there with you."

A few minutes later, in the comfort and privacy of a nearly empty roadside tavern called the Wonderbar, a senior soil scientist working for the Forest Service in the Galice Regional Office of the Siskiyou National Forest looked up from his beer and told Roselle and Koehler a truly incredible tale.

The soils in the Siskiyou Forest, the scientist explained, were among the most unusual in the world; that's why the vegetation was so extraordinary, and the ecology so incredibly complex. When the lumber companies asked for a permit to build the Bald Mountain Road, the Forest Service had been forced to do an environmental impact statement; he had been assigned to prepare a detailed soil survey for inclusion in the final report.

After months of work, the scientist had reached a clear and unequivocal conclusion: the soils of the Kalmiopsis Mountains, including the Bald Mountain region, were so fragile that extensive road building, or clear-cut logging, would threaten the stability of the entire forest ecosystem. Any serious environmental study, the scientist argued, should examine alternatives to road-building and clear-cutting.

Although the scientist didn't know it, the study was precisely the sort of ammunition the small Round River Chapter of the Sierra Club needed. The chapter was fighting the Bald Mountain Road, but the odds were not good, and the national organization was reluctant to make any insignificant commitment of resources to what seemed to be a hopeless cause. The scientist figured that as soon as his report became public, as part of the final EIS, the case against logging would be so clear even the Reagan administration wouldn't be able to ignore it.

The scientist's boss in Galice had nothing but praise for the soil study. In fact, he said, it was so important the scientist ought to include his original draft, with all his original research notes, in the package of material that was being put together for the authors of the EIS. The scientist readily agreed.

But a few months later, when the EIS came out, the entire soil report had been condensed into a single paragraph. The conclusion—that no disturbance of any sort was possible without serious consequences—was nowhere to be found.

Suddenly curious, the scientist made some calls—to the Forest Service office in Grants Pass, then the regional office in Portland, then, finally, to the headquarters in Washington, D.C. Nobody had any record of his report. It was gone. The original draft, the research notes, everything had disappeared. There was no record of anything he had written, anywhere. As far as the official record was concerned, his carefully documented reservations about soil disturbance just didn't exist. The most important old-growth conifer-forest ecosystem in the entire United States was about to be destroyed, and apparently, there was nothing a regional Forest Service employee could do about it.

And that's when the mild-mannered soil scientist decided to write to Earth First!

62

GOOD NIGHT, IRENE

February 25, 1983
Arlington, Virginia

From the window of her high-rise apartment, Rita Lavelle could see the crowd of protesters gathered on the street below. Reporters and camera crews were showing up, too: demonstrations were a rare event at the fashionable Crystal City apartment complex. Besides, anything involving Lavelle was big news these days.

As the subject of all the fuss retreated behind her closed curtains, the protesters took up a taunting refrain, sung over and over, to the tune of "Good Night Irene": "Rita come out, Rita come out ... We'll see you in the jail." The demonstration organizer stood at the front of the crowd, her head tilted up toward Lavelle's apartment. In the chill February air, Lois Gibbs sang with gusto.

Life was changing fast for Rita Lavelle. A few months before, she had held one of the most influential and prestigious environmental jobs in Washington. Now she was out of work, hounded by reporters and protesters, and facing a criminal indictment, maybe even a jail term.

She wasn't alone. Almost every day, more high-level EPA officials were losing their jobs. The agency President Reagan had entrusted to Anne Gorsuch was in serious trouble, and Gorsuch was trying desperately to survive the scandal.

Ironically, though, the criminal charges that threatened to bring down the entire EPA administration were relatively minor, compared to what the agency was doing with full legal impunity almost every single day.

*   *   *

The scandal that drove Lavelle from her EPA job arose from a statement she made to a congressional committee investigating her former employer, Aerojet-General Corporation. Aerojet had dumped some toxic waste under questionable circumstances at a site in California, and Lavelle tried to convince the committee that she wasn't involved. But she lied under oath about the date of the incident, and the committee members caught her.

Lavelle wasn't the first person to mislead Congress on a detail of that nature, and if she had apologized and accepted a reprimand, she might have survived with her career intact. But before she was done testifying, she made an even bigger mistake: she lied about her attempts to get rid of one of her employees, Hugh Kaufman.

In many ways, Kaufman was a bureaucrat's bureaucrat. Clean-shaven, short-haired, and studious, he earned a master's degree in engineering administration and served for four years as an Air Force officer before joining the EPA. He advanced through the ranks under both Republican and Democratic administrations, rising to the position of assistant to the director of the toxic-waste management program.

By 1976, long before Love Canal became news, Kaufman and his coworkers had identified hundreds of sites where toxic wastes were threatening the environment. Some of the other civil servants were happy to keep quiet and wait for new orders, but Kaufman insisted on spreading the word. He sent information to Congress. He spoke to the press. He appeared at public meetings and on television talk shows. Whenever anyone would listen, he issued his warning: a toxic bomb was about to explode.

When Congress started to pay attention, Kaufman helped draft the Resource Conservation and Recovery Act, which gave the EPA broad new powers over chemical waste. But even after President Gerald Ford signed the bill into law, Kaufman kept up the pressure: the EPA, he insisted, just wasn't doing its job. The regulators weren't enforcing the law. The waste manufacturers and dumpers were getting away with murder.

The Carter administration found Kaufman annoying, particularly when he went on a television program and announced that the president was ducking the toxic-waste issue. Still, Carter's top environmental advisers were reluctant to crack down on someone environmentalists increasingly saw as an ally. Kaufman's comments in the news media had attracted a lot of attention. People like Willie Fontenot and Shirley Goldsmith in Louisiana realized he was a rare and valuable asset, a senior government employee who actually seemed to be on the activists' side. Kaufman was becoming the Lois Gibbs of the EPA—whenever grassroots organizations or small-town-newspaper reporters needed information, they'd call Kaufman's office, and when he wasn't in his office, they'd call him at home. He always took the calls; he always tried to help. With his sharp political instincts and inside expertise, he was often invaluable.

Kaufman was used to a little pressure from the top, but until 1981, he always managed to diffuse it. When Rita Lavelle arrived, the situation changed. All of a sudden, Kaufman's mail was mysteriously commandeered, opened, and destroyed. His supervisors ordered him not to talk to the press, and tried to discourage him from talking to Congress or providing technical assistance to communities with toxic-waste problems. When he resisted, Lavelle did everything she could to get him fired—EPA officials even spied on Kaufman and accused him of meeting a woman in a motel room while on agency business. It turned out he was on vacation, and the woman was his wife.

In July 1982, Kaufman filed a complaint with the Labor Department, accusing the EPA of harassment and illegal spying. In December, the department ruled in his favor and ordered Lavelle to refrain from activities that curtailed his free-speech or privacy rights. In the process of investigating the case, the department collected evidence suggesting that Lavelle was trying to retaliate against Kaufman for blowing the whistle on EPA wrongdoing, and was trumping up charges in an effort to get rid of him.

But early in 1983, Lavelle told a congressional committee that she had never tried to fire Kaufman—and when the committee members examined the Labor Department evidence, they charged her with perjury. On February 4, under pressure from the White House, Lavelle submitted her resignation. She was later tried and sentenced to six months in jail.

Gorsuch had mounting legal troubles, too. They began in earnest the previous November, when the Congressional Public Works Committee, investigating EPA enforcement of Superfund, demanded to see a number of documents from the agency's internal files. Gorsuch, under orders from President Reagan, refused to hand over the records, insisting that the president and his staff had "executive privilege."

The move set off a political and legal furor. Congress and the White House traded angry charges, the Justice Department and congressional lawyers struggled to resolve the immensely complicated constitutional issues, and the Washington press corps splashed it all over the front pages. Then one day a funny thing happened: someone in the EPA building took a thick stack of the documents in question and sent them through a paper shredder.

Suddenly, the battle took a new turn. The White House could make a relatively plausible case for refusing to honor a congressional subpoena, but destroying records that were part of a pending legal case was clearly a crime. The FBI launched an investigation. Gorsuch insisted she knew nothing about the incident, but even Republicans in Congress were outraged. Before long, there were six congressional subcommittees investigating the EPA. The press dubbed the whole affair "Sewergate."

Gorsuch made a desperate effort to control the damage. She began pointing fingers, steering the blame away from herself and making her top appointees take the rap instead. Over the course of a few weeks, ten senior EPA officials were fired, paralyzing much of the agency and leaving the staff in disarray.

On February 22, with the EPA coming apart at the seams, Gorsuch suddenly flew to Missouri, to announce personally a decision that environmentalists had demanded—and Gorsuch had delayed—for the past several months. In a dramatic statement, she authorized the purchase of all 2,400 homes in the town of Times Beach, which had been rendered uninhabitable by dioxin contamination. Gorsuch attended a well-orchestrated ceremony, then met with the news media in a local schoolhouse to describe her evacuation and relocation program.

But Times Beach residents were barred from the meeting, and Gorsuch refused to take any questions. The minute her presentation was over, she left for the airport and caught the next flight back to Washington. Like most of what she had done recently, it reeked of a publicity stunt—and it wasn't enough to save her from a scandal that was fast becoming a serious political liability for the White House. Early in March, she would follow Rita Lavelle, and submit her resignation.

Environmentalists were thrilled to see two of their worst enemies forced out of office. Whenever possible, they used the scandals to focus public attention on the environmental failures of the Reagan administration. But while the press and Congress were obsessed with criminal indictments and FBI investigations, some activists insisted the most serious charges had never been aired: on the worst environmental offenses, they argued, Anne Gorsuch got away clean.

From the beginning, Gorsuch refused to abide by the spirit of the legislation that established the EPA. The agency was charged with enforcing the public interest in environmental protection. One of its prime directives was to control pollution and assist the victims. Helping businesses cut costs or make profits was never in its charter—other federal agencies, like the Department of Commerce, had that responsibility.

But Gorsuch did everything possible to undermine environmental regulations, to cripple their enforcement, and to shield big businesses from public scrutiny. Congress appropriated money for the EPA's traditional operations, but Gorsuch refused to spend it. She ignored existing environmental laws and blocked the implementation of new regulations. Instead, she enacted tough barriers to prevent citizen groups and pollution victims from learning what was going on.

Congresswoman Barbara Mikulski, a Maryland Democrat, summed up the situation in a hearing on the agency's failure to implement the Resource Conservation and Recovery Act. Mikulski's home district had a serious toxic-waste problem, and with all her seniority and political clout, she couldn't get the EPA to respond. She told her colleagues on the committee that she couldn't even find out what chemicals were in the ground and how dangerous they might be.

Lois Gibbs, on hand to testify, offered Mikulski the assistance of the Citizens Clearinghouse for Hazardous Waste, the small organization she had founded a year earlier. The Clearinghouse, Gibbs explained, did a lot more than hold demonstrations. Her staff was quite familiar with the kind of situation Mikulski was facing—all over the country, citizen groups had similar problems. The Clearinghouse, Gibbs told the congresswoman, could line up expert assistance, conduct tests, and help identify the culprits.

"Ms. Gibbs," Mikulski answered, "I accept your offer. Yet it is really a bitter situation here. I worked all my life to become a member of Congress. . . . Here we are, big wheels, often more self-important than we really are, and I can't get from Anne Gorsuch and her cronies . . . the help that I need. I have to come to a citizens group, that exists on voluntary contributions and bake sales."

Months later, even as she sang her cheerful taunts under Rita Lavelle's apartment window, Gibbs knew the situation was not about to change.

63

A HECK
OF A PROBLEM

June 22, 1983
Washington, D.C.

The bright lights were unnerving; the room was too hot. The members of the Congressional Subcommittee on Environment, Energy and Natural Resources all looked very serious—and they were all looking right at Herbert Rigmaiden. He shifted uncomfortably as the hearing came to order. The witness was still a little dazed from his trip; he'd never been on an airplane before. Besides, he never felt comfortable in his suit. At home in Louisiana, he only pulled it out for funerals.

But Rigmaiden knew exactly what he had to say, and he wasn't a bit reluctant to say it. Lois Gibbs had arranged for him to testify at the hearing; Shirley Goldsmith booked his flight and lined up his hotel room. CLEAN paid all the expenses. All Rigmaiden had to do was tell the truth—to explain what happened to people like him, who lived near the Willow Springs waste dump.

The chairman, Congressman Mike Synar of Oklahoma, concluded taking the roll, and Rigmaiden began talking. He told the committee how his cattle bloated and died, how his niece suffered crippling illnesses after being born healthy, how other relatives had died, how his water had all gone bad, and how the landfill owner, Browning-Ferris Industries, and local politicians kept denying anything was wrong. Congressman Larry Craig of Idaho asked him a question: "Is Willow Springs a licensed landfill, do you know, monitored by county or city government?"

"I think it is monitored by the company themselves," Rigmaiden responded. "Then we have some experts out of Houston who came in, and they did some monitoring. They seem to think we have a heck of a problem."

"It sounds like you have a heck of a problem," agreed Craig.

"It [the toxic waste] is already in the fifty-foot sands," said Rigmaiden. "If

306

it is in the fifty-foot sands, then it has got to be in the hundred-foot sands. I use one deep well, three hundred fifty feet deep. That is the contaminated well. You gentlemen have to remember that every time you throw a beefsteak or hamburger up to your face, you are eating that meat which comes off of that contaminated water underneath because I have no other way to water cattle."

Congressman Craig smiled grimly. "I appreciate that. I am a cattleman myself."

Congressman Synar joined the questioning. "Dr. Stanley Smith," he noted, "who is the pathologist at West Calcasieu Community Hospital in Sulphur, had the following observations about your situation: 'There's enough pathology on the farm to keep a team of scientists busy for years. I don't see how anybody could go in and talk to those people and come away with any conclusion other than they've been poisoned.'

"Smith also points out that one of your neighbors stopped drinking the water in his well when benzene, which we all know is a carcinogen, was found in their children's blood. That benzene was found in five or six of the children. Is that correct?"

"Yes, sir, that is correct," Rigmaiden replied.

"All right," Synar continued. "What I find hard to believe is that the federal government would continue to license the dumping of hazardous waste in that area. I think that this situation that you have pointed out to us today shows how weak the EPA interim regulations program has been. Mr. Rigmaiden, after all these years of complaining about this problem and the lack of action taken by government, why don't you tell me very simply how much faith you have in government to protect you and other people?"

"Our [local] government—not from Washington, D.C.—is not worth one plug nickel," said Rigmaiden plainly. "But I want to make this clear. We have got some good senators and some good representatives down there, but the problem is this. The Browning-Ferris people are not poor. That is a billion-dollar company. Browning-Ferris has paid all those local people off. That is the problem that I believe we have."

64

WILD BY LAW

July 1, 1983
Grants Pass, Oregon

The Casa del Rio was crowded, even for a Friday afternoon. Since Mike Roselle and the Earth First! crew had arrived a few months ago, the only Mexican restaurant in town had been doing a huge business. The radical environmentalists from Wyoming were living in a trailer; they didn't have a proper office, so they'd moved into the Casa bar and set up shop at a big table near the phone booth in the corner. By midafternoon, you could count on five or six of them to settle in for a few hours of political discussion, over at least a few pitchers of beer.

But this wasn't an ordinary afternoon. At least a dozen new people—out-of-towners, mostly—had come in with Roselle, and before long, more than twenty of them were packed into the small bar. As always, they were drinking and laughing, but beneath the party spirit, the atmosphere was unusually serious.

The latest group of Kalmiopsis protesters, three men and three women, all from California, had just gotten out of jail—and for the first time since the protests began, their release had been neither easy nor routine.

The Josephine County authorities were running out of patience. At least once a week, a couple of deputy sheriffs had to drive up to Galice and round up another gang of Earth First!ers, who were sitting on the ground, blocking the path of the road-construction equipment. Since Roselle and Foreman were arrested blocking the first bulldozer's path in April, the deputies had collared more than forty Earth First! activists, in groups of two, four, and increasingly, six or more.

The Grants Pass jail was designed for only about twenty people, and most of the cells were already full. As the blockades continued, the judges began to release demonstrators immediately, as soon as they had been booked. Everyone who agreed to plead guilty was given a light sentence, usually a fine and probation with no jail time. So a growing number of activists were starting to show up at the Bald Mountain blockades repeatedly, ignoring court orders to stay out of area. The courts were getting as crowded as the jails—and the blockades showed no sign of letting up.

The Earth First! blockades had put the Kalmiopsis on the map. The Bald Mountain Road controversy was big news all over Oregon, and the papers in California were starting to pick it up, too. Earth First! had hit the big time: from as far away as San Francisco, environmental activists were climbing in cars and buses and heading for Grants Pass, Oregon. A lot of the newcomers were young and idealistic, hippies and college students, the same ones who were part of the antinuclear movement.

Like the antinuclear blockades at Seabrook, the demonstrators were initially let off with a lecture by a judge. But after ten weeks of demonstrations, Roselle realized, the judges were starting to get tough. The most recent group of protesters had to put up several hundred dollars' bail to win their release; the next time, Roselle feared, some poor kid from Berkeley could be looking at a six-month sentence for trying to save a forest he'd never even seen.

From now on, Roselle decided, the blockaders would have to get serious; they'd need tight planning, organizational structure, legal strategy—all the things that he and Foreman had always disliked about environmental groups. Saving the wilderness wasn't just fun and games anymore.

However, the hippies from California weren't the only ones who noticed the news reports on the Bald Mountain Road blockades. With all the media attention, a lot of mainstream environmentalists saw the stories, too, and some of them started to see the Kalmiopsis wilderness in a whole new light.

Since March, the phones at the offices of the Oregon Natural Resources Council had been ringing off the hook. Hundreds of people who couldn't imagine sitting in front of a bulldozer but wanted to do something to help called, and Andy Kerr knew just what to tell them. With a little bit of money, he explained, the ONRC could go back to court, and now that the state of California had won its case, a suit against logging in the Kalmiopsis had a good chance of winning, too.

Day after day, the checks poured in. By the end of May, Kerr was looking for lawyers, and on June 30, attorneys Neil Kagan and James Arneson marched into federal court, cited *California* v. *Block,* and asked for an immediate injunction halting all work on the Bald Mountain Road. Judge James Redden agreed to hear their argument the next day.

Mike Roselle knew all about Andy Kerr's lawsuit, but that didn't stop his blockades. Over the past few months, he'd helped the Oregon Natural Resources Council line up a group of coplaintiffs, people who would have firm legal standing, mostly southern Oregon residents who spent a lot of time in the Kalmiopsis wilderness. As a sign of gratitude, Kerr insisted that the first name on the suit—the one that would go down in the lawbooks if the case ever made legal history—was not ONRC, but Earth First!

Still, Roselle thought the court injunction was a long shot, and he couldn't spend a lot of time thinking about it. The demonstrations were keeping him occupied, and his main legal concern was keeping blockaders out of jail by raising bail.

It was late in the afternoon, and over the Casa del Rio barroom din, Roselle was deep in a heavy discussion about the future of the Bald Mountain blockades, when somebody reminded him that Kerr and the lawyers were supposed to have gone to court earlier that day. Sure, Roselle said, a bit distracted. Might as well find out what happened. A local activist named Kevin Everhart was dispatched to the pay phone to place a call to Eugene.

And two minutes later, Everhart was running across the bar, knocking over tables and screaming out the news: the injunction took effect two hours ago. After months of lawbreaking, the Bald Mountain Road had been stopped, by law.

65

WATT'S WRONG

October 9, 1983
Santa Ynez, California

An hour's drive north of Los Angeles, in the mountains where Ronald Reagan, Bo Derek, Michael Jackson, and other members of the Hollywood elite owned their sprawling ranch estates, Interior Secretary James G. Watt and his wife Leilani arrived on horseback at a cow pasture where the elite of the Washington press corps had assembled for a Sunday-afternoon announcement.

The news had already reached most of the reporters who had trudged up to the remote mountaintop where Watt was vacationing. The secretary of the interior, by far the most controversial member of Reagan's controversial Cabinet, had decided to resign.

Watt told the makeshift press conference that he had delivered his resignation letter to the president about an hour ago. "My usefulness," the letter said, "has come to an end."

The environmentalists had lost one of their most bitter enemies. In some ways, it was a mixed blessing.

Watt had been everything environmentalists feared, and more. His decisions had been horrendous to environmental causes. First, he had placed an indefinite and absolute ban on initiating the acquisition of any new national parkland, a move that had stirred up anger across political and ideological boundaries. It was no secret that the national park system was deteriorating, largely from overuse and from encroaching development. An obvious solution to both of these problems was to expand the size of parks by buying the land surrounding them.

Then Watt moved to open all one billion acres of offshore coastal waters to oil drilling. His other offenses were numerous. He tried to completely scrap RARE II and open up every single acre of public land outside the national park system to eventual mineral development. He suggested that private companies, like Walt Disney, could be given concessions to run the national parks. His single most dramatic attempt to open public lands for private exploitation was his push to grant coal leases: during his first two years in office, the Interior Department processed about forty thousand energy and mineral leases, almost as many as were processed in the entire previous decade. Many of the leases went against the advice of the General Accounting Office, which argued that Watt was about to glut the coal market; existing leases covered enough coal deposits to fuel the nation for twenty-five years.

Watt's moves set off a tremendous wave of environmental outrage and activism. Friends of the Earth and the Sierra Club announced a petition drive to demand that Congress replace the interior secretary; by the end of 1981, the two groups had collected a million signatures. Watt's offshore-oil leasing plan spurred David Brower and Jerry Mander to resurrect their old tactic of the full-page newspaper ad. A broadside in the *San Francisco Chronicle* warned Californians,

AGAINST COASTAL DRILLING?
YOU'D BETTER SAY SO NOW.

So many coupons from the ads arrived in the offices of congressional representatives and senators that Congress soon imposed a moratorium on offshore leasing, overruling Watt's initiative. In 1982, the House of Representatives voted 340–58 to reject Watt's plan to open all federal lands to leasing.

Ultimately, though, it wasn't Watt's environmental policies but his notorious insensitivity to people that cost him his job. Through almost three years of stirring up the anger and outrage of environmentalists, President Reagan stuck behind his interior secretary. But when Watt made a statement offending women, Jews, blacks, and the disabled, all in one sentence, nobody in the administration could do anything more to save him.

The occasion was a speech to a business group on September 21, 1983; the statement, apparently, was Watt's idea of a joke. A coal-leasing advisory commission he had just appointed, Watt explained, was full of the sort of diversity liberals loved: "We have every kind of mixture you can have," he said sarcastically. "I have a black, I have a woman, I have two Jews and a cripple. And we have talent."

A lot of people didn't find it funny.

After delivering his resignation announcement, Watt admitted that the statement, and the furor surrounding it, had "accelerated" his decision to resign. He didn't explain that Reagan, facing an election the following year, couldn't afford to alienate that many constituents.

Environmentalists all over the nation would celebrate Watt's demise. But a few of them had to admit that Watt had been good for the environmental business. During his tenure, the membership of Friends of the Earth had risen by 50 percent, and the Sierra Club's membership had doubled, from 180,000 to 360,000 people. All those members meant more money, for more staff, more lobbyists, and more campaigns. And it had meant a lot more attention to environmental issues, at every level of government, in every corner of the country.

And now, they wouldn't have James Watt to kick around anymore.

PART 9

MOTHER NATURE BATS LAST

What noise or shout was that? It tore the sky.

—*Milton*, Samson Agonistes

Nobody wanted to live near a nuclear power plant. Nobody wanted a toxic landfill in the neighborhood. Most people had sympathy for the victims of Love Canal and the neighbors of Three Mile Island, and quite a few were angry at the politicians and businesses who were responsible.

But for millions of Americans, environmental disasters had always seemed like something that happened somewhere else. Smokestacks and tailpipes sent air pollution away on the breeze. Landfills covered up trash. Rivers washed sewage and chemicals out of sight.

Then all of a sudden, halfway through the 1980s, there was nowhere left to hide.

At vacation spots along the East Coast, the tide was bringing in old syringes, used bandages, and other medical waste. From Long Island, a barge filled with industrial garbage was wandering the world, looking for a place to dump the refuse that New York's overflowing landfills just couldn't hold.

In Antarctica, a conservative British scientist was ready to go public with the evidence he had gathered so painstakingly over the past few years: the ozone layer, a shield of gas that protected the Earth from harmful radiation, was vanishing at a rapid rate.

In the jungles of South America, a maverick biologist was prepared to announce that some of the most important ecological systems on Earth were facing extinction. The entire planet would feel the impacts, and the United States was largely responsible.

And in Washington, D.C., one of the nation's most respected scientists was about to drop a political bombshell: the widespread use of fossil fuels,

317

he would tell Congress, was creating a huge global crisis, one that could spell the end of life as anyone in the United States knew it.

Suddenly, the American backyard was a whole lot bigger. The U.S. environmental movement started shifting in a global direction. International issues like rain forest preservation, global warming, and ocean ecology took center stage, and activists tried to demonstrate how domestic policies contributed to ecological problems thousands of miles away.

66

THE FLOATING FURNACE

March 16, 1984
Lake Charles, Louisiana

After years of high-powered Washington lobbying, the fate of an ambitious plan to burn toxic waste in the Gulf of Mexico came down to an obscure Louisiana zoning law. When all the shouting was over, Calcasieu Parish had earned a place on the national environmental map, and a network of local activists had proven a powerful concept: if everybody fought to keep his or her own backyard clean, then the toxic-waste dumpers would have no place to go.

At-Sea Incineration arrived in Lake Charles with a project that seemed unstoppable. The plan, officials of the New Jersey company insisted, was the answer to all of Louisiana's toxic-waste problems: instead of dumping poisonous chemicals in dump sites like Willow Springs, where they could wind up contaminating water supplies, At-Sea was prepared to load the waste onto a ship, carry it out two hundred miles offshore, and burn it in high-temperature incinerators. The process, the company insisted, would reduce most of the dangerous material to a few harmless by-products.

The floating furnace called *Vulcanus II* would carry the latest in navigation equipment, and its smokestacks would be fitted with some of the most sensitive emission monitors in the world. The incineration process would destroy more than 95 percent of the low-level hazardous waste, and 99.9999 percent of the most highly toxic material. The instant the emission levels passed those strict benchmarks, the sensors would automatically shut the furnaces down. A federal monitor would be on hand at all times to make sure the *Vulcanus II* crew didn't cut any corners.

A lawyer with high-level connections at the Environmental Protection

Agency had pushed through a special permit. The Coast Guard had signed off on the idea. Even Congress was going along. The only thing standing between the *Vulcanus II* and the open sea was the Calcasieu Parish Police Jury, which had to issue a routine zoning variance to allow chemical-waste trucks onto the Lake Charles loading dock.

Ocean incineration wasn't a new idea. Since the late 1960s, European nations had been burning their toxic waste at sea. But the the process was much more expensive than landfill disposal, and as long as the United States had plenty of space for waste dumps, it didn't seem very appealing.

By 1984, however, the hazardous-waste disposal problem was getting out of control. The nation generated huge amounts of waste—millions of tons a year. Superfund regulations called for hundreds of tons more to be removed from sites where contamination was threatening nearby residents, and the government expected to spend more than $20 billion in the process. But ultimately, the residue dug up from the Superfund sites wouldn't disappear— it had to be shipped, and buried, somewhere else.

For years, the waste-disposal industry purchased land in remote rural places like Willow Springs, where laws were easy and enforcement was lax— and where the residents had neither the sophistication nor the resources to do anything about it. But people like Shirley Goldsmith were starting to get in the way.

Across the "toxic-waste belt" of the rural South, a network of small-town activists was coming together, creating a political force that was turning into the chemical industry's worst nightmare. Most of the leaders were women. Most had no previous political organizing experience. But most of them at some point had talked to Lois Gibbs at the Citizens Clearinghouse for Hazardous Waste, or to Willie Fontenot in the Louisiana attorney general's office— and after a while, they all started talking to each other. They stayed in touch constantly, trading stories, tracking chemical companies, sharing strategies, and passing along the latest news. They drove hundreds of miles to join each others' rallies. They formed delegations to meet with public officials. By the mid-1980s, there were more than a hundred grassroots organizations fighting toxic waste in Louisiana alone—and when they all got angry about something, they could stir up a glorious fuss.

It was stunning, what Gibbs and Fontenot had started.

Gibbs and her growing network of allies heard the same constant complaints, from politicians, corporate officials, and even some environmental leaders: attacking a local chemical plant drove jobs out of the community. If the waste wasn't dumped in one place, it would have to be dumped in another. Fighting toxics on a town-by-town basis was naive, simplistic, and shortsighted. Underneath it all, Gibbs was starting to hear a broader message: the men who ran the government, industry, and organizations didn't think a bunch of women who hadn't even gone to college had any business making public policy.

But after the smoke screens had blown away, Gibbs knew the solution to the toxics problem was really pretty simple: the chemical industry had to stop producing such a huge volume of waste. In theory, Congress could stick manufacturers and users of hazardous chemicals with stiff taxes and tight regulations. In practice, local activists could make it so difficult, time-consuming, embarrassing, and expensive to dispose of toxic waste anywhere in the country that the companies would have to start reducing the waste stream anyway.

The chemical industry wasn't interested in that sort of simple solution. The industrial engineers kept looking for sophisticated, high-tech disposal methods—and At-Sea Incineration was exactly the sort of approach they liked. It would be relatively inexpensive; the potential capacity was almost unlimited. And nobody would have to worry about a local toxic-waste dump. The incinerator ships wouldn't even be tossing anything dangerous overboard—the only remnants of the waste would emerge as smoke and ash. The smoke would drift over the water far from human population centers, and the ash would be scattered into the vast depths of the ocean.

Shirley Goldsmith and the members of CLEAN didn't see it quite the same way. For starters, they pointed out, the trucks filled with chemical waste would drive through the center of Lake Charles and discharge their cargo along a prime fishing area. A traffic accident, a drunk driver, a leaky hose, a bad storm—all kinds of factors could cause an accident that would turn her hometown into the next Livingston, or the next Times Beach. Once the ship was loaded, the deadly cargo would pass through the rich waters of the Gulf Coast, a region prone to sudden, brutal storms that could put even the biggest, best-equipped vessels in jeopardy. The coast was crowded with ships—everything from giant oil tankers to small fishing boats worked the waters off Louisiana, and in bad weather, collisions were always a possibility. Federal officials freely acknowledged that an accident would be devastating. A toxic spill near the shore, an EPA report stated, would "destroy many organisms, and contaminate the area for a long time." But the agency insisted the chance of a mishap was so remote that it wasn't a valid reason to interfere with the project.

Goldsmith wasn't interested in scientific statistics about probability and risk. She knew that *people* would be operating the equipment—and common sense told her that at some point, they were bound to screw something up.

At-Sea Incineration had no trouble winning a federal permit. The company's lawyer was James Sanderson, who also happened to have a part-time job advising EPA administrator Anne Gorsuch. In fact, Gorsuch reversed the agency's normal procedures in the At-Sea case. Instead of formulating consistent, national regulations for ocean incineration of toxic waste, a process that could have taken years, she insisted that the matter be handled on a case-by-case basis—and when Sanderson's client filed an application, it was quickly approved.

But tactics that worked in Washington didn't always apply in southern Louisiana.

By the time At-Sea was ready to apply for its zoning permit, CLEAN had established a serious presence in Calcasieu Parish. After Lois Gibbs's visit, the Willow Springs dump site had become big news, and the local papers were constantly calling Goldsmith for comment. Dozens of people who had never imagined calling themselves environmentalists were joining the organization.

Louisiana politicians were starting to get the message. The toxic crusaders had hit a nerve, and in a part of the country known for populist uprisings, elected officials would ignore it at their peril. When Goldsmith began complaining about At-Sea Incineration, John B. Breaux, the congressman from Lake Charles, took immediate notice. Breaux happened to chair the House Subcommittee on Fisheries and Wildlife Conservation and the Environment, and in December 1983, he called a hearing on the ocean-burning proposal. Among those he called to testify were Shirley Goldsmith and Jacques Cousteau.

The little-known Louisiana activist and the famous oceanographer made remarkably similar points and used remarkably similar language.

"Calcasieu Parish is a rain barrel," Goldsmith told the panel. "Please do not ask us to add one more drop of unproven technology to our barrel. . . .

"At almost every presentation, [representatives of At-Sea Incineration] have changed their information. . . . They represented at their first presentation to us that one of the safety features they were so proud of would be their fleet of trucks. These shiny stainless steel trucks looked good enough to contain milk. They would be radio-controlled and have the very latest up-to-date equipment.

"Later on, when questioned about the trucks, we are told they will not have their own trucks, but instead will contract with various trucking firms to handle their waste. Now, who will supervise and regulate each truck?

"We were told not to worry; their ship was so maneuverable it could outrun a hurricane. Last week, they said that was wrong. Now they are advised [in the event of a hurricane] to fill the ship with waste to make it heavy and ride [the hurricane] out in open water. Please imagine the many hundreds of shrimp boats, oil-related vessels and boats of all description coming in to safe harbor while [the *Vulcanus II* is] trying to get out to sea. Have you seen what the sea looks like in 125-mile-an-hour winds?"

Cousteau said he understood the problems of toxic-waste disposal in landfills, and the need for alternatives. But incineration at sea, he said, combined "the risk of accidents at sea, plus accidents in the harbor, plus transportation.

"Someone here mentioned storms," Cousteau noted. "Well, I know about that pretty well, and not only are storms dangerous for the vessels. I assure you that carrying on a delicate operation on a ship with a moderate sea is not easy; people are losing more than 50 percent of their intelligence and capacity to work at sea, and the controllers that would be sent over there would probably be seasick, and not do their job effectively."

The congressional hearing did little to change federal policy, but it did wonders for CLEAN's local zoning campaign. Three months later, the Calcasieu Police Jury found itself in the middle of one of the most heated political battles in parish history. With hundreds of Calcasieu voters crowding into the hall, and reporters taking down every word, the police jury had little choice: it rejected the zoning change.

At-Sea would spend another year wandering from New Jersey to California, looking for a port town that was willing to take the risk of hosting a toxic-waste ship. But the word was out on the toxic network, and everywhere the company went, controversy followed. After Shirley Goldsmith and her neighbors had kicked the *Vulcanus II* out of their back yard, activists in dozens of other communities took up the cause and did the same thing. With nowhere to go, At-Sea filed for bankruptcy, and ocean incineration quietly dropped off the political horizon.

Two months later, Browning-Ferris announced it was closing down the Willow Springs dump site.

67

THE SOUTER FILES

The Clamshell Alliance lawsuit was moving through the federal courts with the speed of a glacier. Rennie Cushing had to wonder if any of the plaintiffs would still be alive when it finally went to trial. The organization was essentially defunct; some of the members had moved out of New Hampshire, and a few had dropped out of politics altogether. But Cushing was still around, working for a consumer group, fighting electric rate hikes caused by the Seabrook power plant, and watching the case with growing fascination. The Clamshell's ACLU lawyers kept coming up with amazing new information.

The Greater Newburyport Clamshell Alliance had sued the state of New Hampshire and the Public Service Company in 1981, charging that the use of an undercover police informant in the organization violated the civil rights of the alliance members. The state and the company kept winning delays, and nobody could even guess when the Clamshell members would get their day in court. In the meantime, though, the legal team kept digging for evidence and finding what Cushing considered political gems.

There was, for example, the sworn deposition of Richard J. Campbell.

Campbell was an executive officer of the New Hampshire State Police. Under questioning, Officer Campbell admitted exactly what Cushing had suspected all along: James Nims wasn't the only undercover cop to infiltrate the Clamshell Alliance. In fact, the police had placed spies in the organization before it was even two months old. Since 1976, every Clamshell demonstration had been monitored by police informants. At least four different investigators had been assigned to pose as antinuclear activists over the past eight years, and almost every important Clamshell decision was in the hands of the authorities hours after it happened.

324

The most interesting bit of information, though, was buried deep in the eighty-four-page deposition transcript. Campbell testified that he always kept the state attorney general informed of any information he got from undercover informants, particularly in the days before a major demonstration.

If that was true—and if Campbell's predecessor had followed the same policy back in 1977—then David Souter, who was now a New Hampshire Supreme Court Justice, must have known exactly what the Clamshell Alliance was doing long before that fateful weekend when Cushing and almost two thousand other people had been locked up in the National Guard armories.

And if he knew there were undercover cops in the Clamshell Alliance, then Justice Souter had lied about it, under oath.

Cushing began putting everything he knew about Souter into a file. He realized it was probably a waste of time: even if he could prove Souter had lied, the conservative state legislature wasn't going to impeach him. And the shy, intellectual justice wasn't about to give up his seat to pursue higher office. The way Cushing figured, David Souter would be on the New Hampshire Supreme Court for the rest of his life.

68

DEBT FOR NATURE

October 4, 1984
New York City

Thomas E. Lovejoy probably knew more about tropical rain forest ecology than anyone else in America. And that wasn't much at all.

For almost fifteen years, Lovejoy had studied the Amazon Basin, the world's last great wilderness. He started back in his days as a doctoral student at Yale in the late 1960s, and he never really stopped. Since 1974, as the World Wildlife Fund's chief rain forest biologist, he had spent hundreds of hours crawling around the floor of the jungle and climbing its lush green canopy. He had identified, cataloged, and tracked thousands of species of birds, insects, and other animals and compiled thick files of material on the astonishing diversity of rain forest life.

What Lovejoy knew was that the tropical rain forest contained some of the most important information human beings could ever have a chance to learn. Under its canopies, along its shadowy floors, and under its rivers and streams lay the fruits of billions of years of evolution. Fires, volcanoes, floods, predators, and countless diseases had swept through the rain forests, wiping out anything that wasn't tough enough or adaptable enough to survive. The remainder—the intricate web of plants and animals that inhabited the jungle, largely untouched by the ravages of civilization—held fantastic clues to the mysteries of evolution, adaptation, and survival.

And if something didn't change pretty soon, Lovejoy worried, none of it would matter. Before long, there wouldn't be any rain forest left to study.

Humans were moving rapidly into the vast tropical wilderness, hacking away at its edges with chain saws, machetes, and bulldozers, plowing roads through its interior, cutting down its hardwood trees for sale as lumber, and burning its undergrowth to make room for ranches and farms. The existing balance was crumbling: hundreds of species were becoming extinct every single month.

Lovejoy didn't turn to an obscure scientific journal to bring these facts to the public's attention. He used the op-ed page of *The New York Times*. His article was read by millions and would help turn an obscure crisis taking place far beyond the United States borders into a central focus of the nation's environmental movement.

As Lovejoy explained, most of the South American rain forest was in the country of Brazil, a poverty-stricken nation with a rapidly expanding population. The country owed billions and billions of dollars to banks in the United States, and the interest payments alone were taking a big bite out of its national budget. You couldn't expect a desperately poor nation, with millions of starving mouths to feed, to set aside large amounts of its most valuable resource—rain forest land—as a nature preserve. Global ecology meant little to the hungry, homeless, and sick that packed Brazil's teeming slums. And it sounded hypocritical for the United States, which had already mowed down virtually all of its own native forest in the name of expansion and economic development, to make the request.

The rain forest also contained a wealth of resources that were worth money on the global market: exotic hardwood trees, precious minerals, and all manner of fruits, nuts, and other foods. Lovejoy thought the United States could offer Brazil a deal: forgive a portion of the debt in exchange for preserving a part of the wilderness.

Lovejoy wasn't exactly sure how the deal would work: After all, private banks, not the government, held much of the debt, and the banks wanted to get at least part of their money back. Still, a lot of the loans were in danger of default already. Maybe some form of government tax breaks would encourage the banks to write off a part of their outstanding debt.

Lovejoy's ideas filled only six paragraphs on the *Times* op-ed page, but his point was compelling. "What is at stake here," he wrote, "is more than the preservation of exotic species for the amusement of tourists. Proper management of tropical landscapes is critical to the survival of the variety of life on earth."

To a biologist, the problem was obvious: acre for acre, the Amazonian forest was far and away the most diverse ecological system on the planet, and even conservative estimates claimed tropical deforestation was causing about five thousand species to go extinct every year. To most people, the importance of "biodiversity"—the need to preserve all those obscure types of insects and flowers—was a bit harder to fathom. But over the next few years, photographs and television footage of a jungle most Americans would never actually visit caught the nation's imagination.

Before long, environmentalists in the United States were leading the crusade for rain forest preservation, demanding policy changes at home to save an endangered wilderness thousands of miles away. It had a distinct advantage over some other wilderness battles, one that even brought a few conservative business people into the fold: preserving a forest in Brazil wouldn't cost many United States jobs.

69

THE SKY IS FALLING

October 1984
Antarctica

The South Pole was a wonderful place for an atmospheric research lab, if you could handle the weather. The air was about as clean as it got on planet Earth: the nearest factories and power plants were thousands of miles away. The British Antarctic Survey had been going to the South Pole every summer since the late 1950s, using the remote outpost to study the "trace gases," the obscure but important elements that made up a tiny but critical part of the atmosphere. At the South Pole, a scientist could actually measure the concentration of a gas like ozone, without worrying about interference from somebody's dirty smokestack.

In 1982, Joe Farman had seen something very strange in the ozone readings he was picking up in Antarctica. But the fifty-year-old British researcher was not an alarmist, and he didn't want to jump to conclusions; the implications were just too scary. In 1983, he saw it again.

And when the same figures appeared once more, for the third straight year, even the conservative Farman was convinced it was time to make the information public: there was a giant hole in the ozone layer. Miles above Antarctica, part of the sky was disappearing.

By the time Farman's conclusions appeared in the April 1985 issue of the scientific journal *Nature,* word of his discovery was making headlines around the globe. Scientists had been monitoring ozone levels since 1973, when Rowland and Molina discovered that chlorofluorocarbons, the common industrial chemical, destroyed atmospheric ozone, but all of the measurements had been sporadic and unreliable. Farman's data was meticulous and consistent. There was no way to avoid the impact of his findings: unless the

329

industrial nations of the world took dramatic action, quickly, the invisible shield that protected the Earth from harmful ultraviolet rays would soon be destroyed.

Within a few years, ominous newspaper accounts warned, cancer rates would start to rise. Then plants and animals would start to die, fried by the unfiltered sunlight. Eventually, humans would be unable to venture outside for more than a few moments without risking third-degree burns.

It was enough to make an environmentalist out of just about anyone.

70

A WATERY GRAVE

July 11, 1985
Auckland, New Zealand

The telex went out a little after one A.M., New Zealand time, flashing the word to Greenpeace offices around the world:

> URGENT. APPROXIMATELY TWO HOURS AGO, RAINBOW WARRIOR SUNK BY TWO
> EXPLOSIONS IN AUCKLAND HARBOUR, NEW ZEALAND. SABOTAGE SUSPECTED.
> VERY LITTLE NEWS FORTHCOMING AT PRESENT. ONE CREW MEMBER MISSING.
> PLEASE DO NOT, REPEAT NOT, CALL AUCKLAND OFFICE, AS TELEPHONES ARE
> JAMMED. WILL HAVE MORE INFO IN AN HOUR OR SO.

By dawn, the headlines in hundreds of major cities were repeating the tale, in all its graphic horror. The phones at the Auckland office were indeed jammed. Every reporter on Earth seemed to want an interview.

Greenpeace, which practiced and preached a strict code of nonviolence, had suffered a brutally violent assault. The act would outrage much of the civilized world.

Just a few hours earlier, the members of the *Rainbow Warrior* crew were celebrating Steve Sawyer's twenty-ninth birthday and planning their next expedition, back to the Polynesian island of Moruroa, where they would continue their campaign of harassing the French government over its nuclear testing program. The *Warrior* was in top shape: the flagship of the Greenpeace fleet had just undergone a $130,000 renovation job, and sported new sails, new radar equipment, a rebuilt bridge, and overhauled engines. Sawyer, the veteran ship's manager who was now a member of the Greenpeace International board of directors, was proud of the work, and excited about the

331

twenty-thousand-mile voyage that would be the rebuilt *Warrior*'s first major cruise. From Florida, where the work was done, the ship sailed to Honolulu, where it picked up Sawyer, who would direct the campaign, and a Dutch photographer named Fernando Pereira, who was going to capture the operations on film.

From Hawaii, the *Warrior* sailed west to the tiny island of Rongelap, part of a string of volcanic atolls in the Marshall Islands, where Greenpeace was planning a rescue mission known as Operation Exodus.

The residents of Rongelap were suffering the lingering effects of radioactive fallout from twelve years of open-air U.S. atomic bomb testing at nearby Bikini Atoll. Shortly after the first blast, the rates of miscarriage and stillbirth among island women had doubled and after three decades had never returned to normal. Cancer, birth defects, and other health problems seemed abnormally high. In 1984, the Rongalese leaders asked the Marshall Islands government to relocate them, but the tiny nation didn't have the money, so it passed the request on to the United States, which still had a United Nations mandate to help administer the islands. The U.S. government told the Rongalese the radiation levels weren't high enough to cause any health problems, and refused to underwrite the move. So a Rongalese senator contacted Greenpeace.

The Rongalese wanted the *Rainbow Warrior* to ferry the entire population to another, safer island 120 miles away; Greenpeace was happy to oblige. Not only would the mission have tremendous humanitarian value, but it would also almost certainly generate international publicity and help focus attention on the plight of those living with the deadly legacy of open-air nuclear tests.

On May 29, the *Rainbow Warrior* cast off from Rongelap for the last time, carrying its final load of pigs, chickens, canoes, and islanders. After dropping the happy Rongalese off at Mejato, one hundred miles away, the *Warrior* set a course for New Zealand, where it would take on new supplies and prepare for the voyage to Moruroa.

By the evening of July 10, all seven members of the Greenpeace International board were in Auckland to see the *Warrior* off. The group had announced its plans long before—the *Warrior* would lead a six-ship "peace flotilla" to Moruroa, where it would stage an extended, and presumably high-profile, protest against continued French atomic testing. The seven directors planned to spend the evening celebrating with Sawyer, then sleep aboard the ship; at the last minute, they all decided to retire to a nearby beach house instead.

At 11:38 P.M., only a skeleton crew was on board when the first of a pair of bombs exploded underneath the *Rainbow Warrior*'s hull. The explosive was placed with expert precision: it blew a hole the size of a car through the only part of the ship that didn't have a protective double hull. Water began pouring in, and within seconds, the *Warrior* began listing.

The captain, Pete Willcox, was in the mess cabin having a drink with several others when he heard the blast. He quickly ordered everyone to evacuate, and in minutes, the entire crew was safely on the dock.

All except for Fernando Pereira, who had dashed below decks to retrieve his cameras. While he was below the waterline, a second bomb went off. The rush of water pouring through the hull cut off his escape route; he was dead before anyone knew he was missing.

David McTaggert, the veteran Greenpeace leader who had skippered the first mission to Moruroa fourteen years ago, heard the news in London, where he was attending a meeting of the International Whaling Commission. At first he told himself the French government was probably responsible. Then he decided the idea was ridiculous: even the French couldn't be that stupid.

But two months later, the French minister of defense, Charles Hernu, abruptly resigned, and the director of the French intelligence agency, Admiral Pierre Lacoste, was fired. For a day or two, it looked as if President François Mitterrand might have to resign, too, and the entire government might fall— all over the sinking of the *Rainbow Warrior*.

The French government finally had to admit what many environmentalists suspected: the General Directorate for External Security, the French equiv- alent of the CIA, had been responsible for the bombing. A team of French spies, including an undercover agent who infiltrated the Auckland Green- peace office, had followed the movements of the *Rainbow Warrior* for weeks. When the ship tied up in the harbor, an explosives expert had snuck alongside in a rubber dinghy, placed the bombs under the hull, and fled. All of it was done under orders from Paris.

The bombing had destroyed the *Rainbow Warrior* forever; the shattered hull was towed out to sea and scuttled. But the protests at Moruroa went on—and with all the media coverage, Greenpeace was fast becoming an international celebrity. In the offices of Greenpeace USA, letters of support, accolades from the press, and thousands and thousands of dollars in checks just kept pouring in.

Like so many other tragedies, the bombing would do the environmental movement a tremendous amount of good.

71

THE END
OF THE ROAD

September 11, 1985
Washington, D.C.

The Westway opponents were up early, working the phones from a few borrowed desks in the offices of New Jersey congressman Frank Guarini. It was the day Marcy Benstock had been waiting for for much longer than she liked to remember: in a few hours, the United States Congress would take up debate and vote on an amendment to cut off all federal funding for the highway project.

After twelve years of nonstop, often solo fighting, Benstock's crusade had become a national environmental campaign. Groups like the Sierra Club, Friends of the Earth, and the New York Public Interest Research Group had taken up the cause. Recently, the National Taxpayers Union joined the team, creating the same sort of coalition—progressive environmentalists and conservative fiscal watchdogs—that had defeated the SST back in 1971.

As in so many other environmental battles, it was a lawsuit filed under the National Environmental Policy Act that gave the opposition a chance to grow. In 1979, Benstock had convinced a young lawyer named Al Butzel to help her appeal the project's air-quality permit; although that effort failed, Butzel discovered that the Westway environmental impact statement virtually ignored the impact the project would have on the Hudson River's striped bass.

For reasons nobody really understood, millions of tiny young bass, born in freshwater spawning grounds a hundred miles upriver, migrated south to the small strip of land along Lower Manhattan. There, in the protected salty waters, they grew from less than two inches to a foot or more in length before swimming out of the mouth of the river to begin the next stage of their life cycle in the Atlantic Ocean. The striped bass from the Hudson were becoming increasingly important to the entire East Coast. The only other major eastern breeding ground, the Chesapeake Bay, was so badly polluted and so heavily developed that its bass population was in a state of rapid, perhaps irreversible decline. The Hudson was polluted, too—PCB levels were still high enough that adult striped bass living upriver were unsafe for humans to eat. But the young fish in New York Harbor were surviving, and as long as they did, there was hope for the future of the species.

Local politicians scoffed at the issue and insisted that a few little fish couldn't stop a major highway project. The federal courts disagreed. In 1982, Judge Thomas Griesa ruled that the Westway EIS was scandalously flawed. Every permit for Westway was immediately revoked until a new, adequate EIS was prepared, taking into account the true impacts on the striped bass population. The delay lasted more than two years.

The lawsuit also gave Benstock a chance to get the real facts about Westway out in the open. From the start, the major New York papers had ignored all the problems she uncovered. With the exception of the weekly *Village Voice,* every big paper in town had blacked out most of her arguments and joined the chorus of Westway promoters.

Benstock was a bit confused by the obvious press bias, especially at *The New York Times.* She'd always thought of the *Times* as one of the city's treasures, the authoritative, objective national paper of record. She understood that the editors of the *Times* might disagree with her—that was what editorial pages were for. But the *Times* news reports kept leaving out important facts (or ignoring the story altogether), and Benstock, like a lot of Westway critics, kept wondering if something unusual was going on.

Something was—and on August 19, less than a month before the congressional debate, *The New York Times* confirmed it. In a terse, two-paragraph statement, the paper announced that one of its star editorial columnists, Pulitzer Prize–winner Sydney Schanberg, author of the best-selling book *The Killing Fields,* would no longer be writing for the op-ed page. His twice-weekly urban affairs column was canceled, effective immediately; within a few days, Schanberg refused a new assignment and resigned.

The move startled the journalistic world. For as long as anyone could remember, *The New York Times* had given its op-ed page columnists a virtual lifetime tenure. Canceling a column was a radical, possibly unprecedented act, and forcing out such a respected journalist for no apparent reason went against everything the *Times* seemed to stand for.

But nothing ever stayed secret for long in a newsroom, and reporters at rival papers like *The Los Angeles Times* and *The Washington Post* began telling the inside story. Schanberg had been doing what nobody else at the paper would do: he'd written a series of columns that criticized Westway. His July 27, 1985, piece had been the last straw—Schanberg blasted *The New York Times* for ignoring the Westway "scandal," and suggested that the *Star-Ledger,* a paper in Newark, New Jersey, was doing a better job on the story.

Months later, Schanberg's colleague, Tom Wicker, would appear before a journalists' association in San Francisco and provide a more blunt explanation. "I can write whatever I want about the president of the United States, whether the publisher of the *Times* agrees with me or not," Wicker said. "It's different when you attack the pet project of some close friends of the publisher's wife, and the publisher has to hear complaints about you every morning at the breakfast table."

These days, Marcy Benstock took nothing for granted. She was in Washington almost every day, sleeping at the houses of friends, using a desk and phone that the Environmental Policy Institute had loaned her, and racing back to New York every few days to keep the pressure up on the home front. All day long, she made phone calls, typed up lengthy, detailed fact sheets, and ran off copies. Late at night, she roamed the halls of Congress with her newest ally, Jill Lovelock of the National Taxpayers Union, slipping her latest missives under the doors of each of the 435 members.

Like the SST, Westway had strong labor union support. AFL-CIO lobbyists worked the floor of the House as the vote neared, cornering traditional liberal allies and warning them how important this was to their union members back home. Mayor Ed Koch wrote a letter to all of his former colleagues in the House, asking them to approve Westway's funding as a personal favor to him. The chairman of the Public Works Committee, Congressman James Howard of New Jersey, strongly opposed the funding cutoff, and made it clear that anyone who wanted pork-barrel projects from his panel in the future would do well not to cross him.

The opposition was remarkably nonpartisan. Leading the charge against Westway was a veteran Massachusetts Republican, Silvio Conte, the ranking minority member of the Appropriations Committee. Conte was a congressman of the old school, a blustery fighter who managed to stay friendly with his worst political foes. He had the respect and admiration of almost everyone in the House, and kept close relationships with the leaders of both parties. On economic issues, he generally sided with the Republican administration; on environmental issues, he was far more likely to vote with the liberal Democrats.

Marcy Benstock sat in the crowded visitors' gallery and watched the action on the floor below. Technically, the issue at hand was an amendment to a highway appropriations bill; if it was approved, the bill would go through without Westway, and the giant project would be doomed. If the members rejected the amendment, Westway would be funded along with all the other highway projects under way around the country.

The debate was the stuff of Benstock's dreams. For the first time ever, a major policy-making body discussed the merits of the case; all the lies, the cover-ups, the misinformation was shot down, and the real issues were becoming clear. The Westway supporters did their best, but the opposition was winning the debate. The way the evidence was shaping up, Westway was an economic and environmental nightmare. The builders were prepared to destroy an entire ecosystem, create a vast new artificial landscape by dumping sand and gravel into a river, spend unimaginable sums of money to dig a tunnel through the landfill, and then give away the real estate above it to friends of the mayor and governor who had no solid proof that it would ever be successfully developed to benefit the people of New York.

Congressman Conte had the final word, and he took full advantage of his pulpit. "We are spending millions of dollars to clear up the Chesapeake Bay habitat, which along with the Hudson River accounts for 90 percent of the striped bass along the Atlantic Coast," he said. "How silly we would look today to spend millions of dollars to save the bass while we permit New York State to waste over $1 billion in federal money for a landfill that would destroy the habitat of the fish along the Hudson River. It is important that New York, and the Federal Highway Administration, understand that congressional intent does not permit the construction of landfills such as this, which are primarily for real estate development instead of transportation, with federal highway money.

"I know that many of the members have heard from our former colleague and now mayor of New York, Ed Koch," Conte continued. "Ed Koch opposed this project in 1977. Ed Koch was right in 1977. The project has not changed at all. It is still an environmental and economic fiasco.

"Ed, I hope you are watching this on C-SPAN. Shame on you, Ed Koch. Shame on you. Shame on you for trying to destroy our striped bass. Shame on you for trying to bail out the developers in New York, these greedy developers. Vote for the amendment, and return some sanity to this bill."

As the members began to vote, and the totals began to show up on the big scoreboard, Marcy Benstock realized she had no idea what the outcome was going to be. All these months, she'd never bothered to count votes, never bothered to assess her chances. She just kept up the fight, hoping something she did would work. Her nerves were about to snap as the balance shifted back and forth, and the totals in the yes and no columns piled up.

The electronic votes were counted quickly, and the final result was absolutely clear: 287 ayes, 132 noes, and 15 abstentions. The amendment was approved. Westway was history.

Up in the visitors' gallery, a bone-weary forty-three-year-old woman sat back in a daze. It was over. The fight was all over. Marcy Benstock didn't know whether to laugh or to cry.

72

BROWER'S BABY

September 21, 1986
San Francisco

For the second time in seventy-four years, David Brower was ready to give up.

He'd fought the Axis forces in the Italian Alps, fought the Bureau of Reclamation at the Grand Canyon and Dinosaur Monument, fought the oil companies, the mining companies, the ranchers, the nuclear power industry, and at least half a dozen United States presidents. He'd just fought off bladder cancer, surviving an operation that was risky even for men half his age. He'd won more than his share, and lost a few heartbreakers. He almost never walked away.

But for the second time in more than half a century of environmental activism, his own organization was rejecting him. And he knew he had to throw in the towel. After a bitter two-year struggle for the soul of Friends of the Earth, Brower was resigning from the board of directors.

"It just got hopeless," he told reporters who had been following the story. "I thought I might as well not burden them any further."

The story of Friends of the Earth was a metaphor for much of what was going wrong and right with the environmental movement in the 1980s. It was also a tribute to a steadfast veteran who was unwilling to shift his principles to fit the political mood of the day, who cared more about causes than organizations, who would rather fight for everything and lose than shake hands and meet halfway. At seventy-four, the patriarch of what for most of his life was often a conservative movement seemed to embody the spirit of a slogan crafted by the radicals at Earth First!—"No compromise in defense of Mother Earth."

* * *

Brower liked to say that any environmental organization with a balanced budget and money in the bank wasn't doing enough work. That wasn't a problem at Friends of the Earth: the organization Brower founded back in 1969, when he was forced to leave his Sierra Club job, had never operated in the black. Brower had too much passion to be a careful, prudent manager. When someone with a unique talent, like Amory Lovins, showed up, Brower put him on staff; when an important battle occurred, he sent the organization to the front lines. He worried about how to pay for it later.

Much of the time, Brower did figure out how to pay for his projects. When the annual membership dues didn't cover the bills, he raised funds any way he could, through personal appeals, special campaigns, and foundation grants. When that didn't bring in enough, he borrowed.

In 1979, Brower had stepped down as executive director, although he remained chairman of the board. But five years later, the organization was racked by a financial crisis that threatened to tear it apart. Friends of the Earth was $550,000 in debt, mostly to some of its members. The budget was a mess: revenues from a declining membership base couldn't possibly cover the costs of a substantial staff, offices in San Francisco and Washington, D.C., and a host of projects around the world. In 1985, the staff voted to unionize; the new chief executive officer, Rafe Pomerance, announced his plans to resign.

In some ways, the crisis had been a long time coming—and it reflected the changes the environmental movement had undergone in the past fifteen years.

When Brower started Friends of the Earth, the board of directors was largely a token body, created to meet the legal requirements for a nonprofit organization. The operation belonged to Brower; the directors who came on board in the first few years were people who had supported his initiatives at the Sierra Club and wanted to help him continue his crusades. Friends of the Earth policy was David Brower's policy; the group's priorities were Brower's priorities.

When Brower officially retired as executive director, things changed a bit—but not really all that much. For all practical purposes, Brower still wanted to call the shots. Then all of a sudden, a new group of managers was supposed to take over, and Brower was supposed to step back and stay out of the day-to-day decisions of running the organization. It never quite worked out: Brower wasn't the type to fade gently into the background. He still considered Friends of the Earth his baby, and he couldn't quite let it go.

The financial crisis was in part the result of a changing attitude among the environmental organizations that had come of age in the 1960s and early 1970s. The new generation of directors and managers were of a different sort than Brower—they were as much professionals as activists, people with skills and backgrounds in management and finance, people who couldn't tolerate the idea of running at a perpetual deficit and keeping a major organization afloat year-to-year on little more than the founder's faith and credit. Business was business, the argument went, and no matter how important the cause, Friends of the Earth couldn't keep living beyond its means.

The way Brower always saw it, Friends of the Earth was supposed to be everything the Sierra Club wasn't. It was supposed to take risks that the more established, sedate conservationists wouldn't. It was supposed to be a group that clung to the spirit of the days when volunteers joined up to fight for the cause, and worked their way into staff positions when the money was around to pay them. It wasn't supposed to be a corporation, where the staff got hired out of business schools and tried to act professional. It wasn't supposed to worry about winning respect through compromise. It certainly wasn't supposed to become a part of the Washington, D.C., establishment.

But early in 1986, over the strong objections of Brower, Friends of the Earth closed down its San Francisco office and moved to Washington. The staff was cut from more than fifty to thirteen full-time positions. A lot of Brower's favorite programs were eliminated; Amory Lovins and the soft-energy project were gone.

The board of directors approved the move to Washington by a vote of 8–7, after furious lobbying by both sides. Supporters, including the new executive director, Karl F. Wendelowski, who held a masters degree in business administration from MIT's Sloan School of Management, argued that the consolidation would save $12,000 a month. Others said it was designed primarily to put three thousand miles between the FOE staff and David Brower, who just couldn't keep his fingers out of the operation.

Either way, Brower insisted on putting up a fight. In April, without consulting the board or the management staff, he quietly took a copy of the entire membership mailing list and sent out, at his own expense, a letter denouncing the Washington move and warning that the future of the organization was in jeopardy. He reminded the members that board elections were in May, and urged them to oust all the directors who had supported the move to D.C. and to replace them with a slate Brower had put together. He also asked for contributions—to a separate foundation called the Earth Island Institute that he had set up and controlled—to help pay for the campaign. More than $20,000 came in.

Board members railed at the unauthorized mailing, insisting that Brower had no right to use the membership list for a private campaign, and no right to raise money from FOE members for his own personal crusade. But there was nothing anyone could do; the mailing had gone out, and the elections had to take place on schedule. All the board could do was present its side of the story—in the FOE newsletter, *Not Man Apart,* in mailings, and in the mainstream press—and leave it in the hands of the members.

The turnout for the board elections was unprecedented. But when the votes were counted, Brower's slate had lost, by a margin of about 3 percent. The anti-Brower faction was in full control.

There was nothing more David Brower could do at Friends of the Earth, no more room for him or his style of politics. It was time to move on, to turn his little Earth Island Institute into a new organization. Time to get out of the infighting, and get back to the real battles again.

73

THE BANKERS' BURDEN

September 29, 1986
Washington, D.C.

As dignitaries from all over the globe climbed out of limousines in front of the World Bank headquarters, two young men climbed the side of an eleven-story building across the street. When the urban mountaineers reached the top, they unfurled a forty-by-twenty-foot blue and white banner, with a blunt message for the national news media and the international delegates to the bank's annual conference:

"WORLD BANK DESTROYS TROPICAL RAINFORESTS"

Bank officials weren't at all happy. Rain forest destruction was starting to become a hot issue, and they didn't want to be the bad guys. Spokesmen insisted that the bank was doing all it could to protect all forms of life on Earth. But the climbers and their associates, representing the newly formed Rainforest Action Network, passed out fliers to the contrary. "World Bank loans," the literature proclaimed, "support projects responsible for the destruction of 100 acres of rainforest every minute."

The numbers the Rainforest Action Network used were rough estimates. The World Bank was one of the most secretive publicly funded institutions in the Western world, the equivalent of a military intelligence or national security agency. But its overall role in Third World development was no secret at all, and neither were the devastating effects of some of its decisions.

The bank was a great target. Randy Hayes would use it for all it was worth.

The founder of the Rainforest Action Network always had a bit of the entrepreneurial spirit. He got it from his father, Ace Hayes, a man who spent his life following the self-imposed rule that no job should ever last more than five years. He moved from business to business, sometimes working for other people, mostly working for himself. From backwater towns in West Virginia to the swamps in central Florida, the young Hayes grew up watching his father do everything from racing stock cars to running a garbage company, with a few restaurants and a private delivery service thrown in along the way.

Hayes wasn't a terribly political kid, but he loved a good time—and when he enrolled in college, at Bowling Green State, it didn't take him long to figure out where the fun was. The campus hippies were always having a blast. Before long, he was hanging out with the longhairs—and soon, he was heavily involved in antiwar politics. By his senior year, he was also deeply involved in environmental issues.

After graduation, Hayes moved to San Francisco and began looking for something to occupy his ecological energy. In the fall of 1973, an acquaintance invited him along on a trip to the Hopi Indian reservation in northern Arizona. He met a few very old and very traditional Hopis, men who were already great-grandfathers by the time Peabody Coal Company drove its dump trucks onto Black Mesa in 1970. The visit changed his life.

For the next ten years, Hayes divided his time between San Francisco, working odd jobs to support a masters degree at the state university, and the deserts of New Mexico. He loved helping the Hopi elders—he'd run errands for them, drive them places, play secretary at meetings. He spent hours hanging around their hogans—traditional Hopi mud huts—listening to the tales of the Hopi world in years past and how it had changed. Indigenous people from around the world would show up at the Hopi reservation; some of the people Hayes met were aborigines from Hawaii, Central America, and Australia. All of these people spoke of the destruction of their traditional homeland, land the white man called rain forests.

"How can I help?" he asked one day with sympathetic earnestness.

After a long silence, one of the Indians answered. "We don't need your help," he said. "Go fix your own community's problems."

Hayes went back to San Francisco and hustled up a grant to pay his way to Costa Rica, where he decided he was going to study the tropical rain forest. He knew forest destruction was an issue in the United States; he thought it might be something he could help "fix" in his own community. So he spent three weeks wandering around the jungle, trying to figure out what all the fuss was about. By the time he found his way out, he was weak with hunger and dysentery. He'd also fallen in love with the tropical wilderness—and like Tom Lovejoy, he'd seen firsthand how close it was to extinction.

Hayes was a lot more political than Lovejoy. He realized the issues surrounding rain forest destruction were complicated, but the closer he looked, the more he concluded that the trail of the bulldozers led back to the United States.

The World Bank was funneling loans from U.S. banks to Third World countries that couldn't possibly afford to pay them back. To cover the interest, countries like Costa Rica and Brazil were opening up the forests for mining and ranching. To survive in countries where all the money was going to pay off the foreign banks, some peasants on the edges of the forests were chopping down trees and planting crops. In the meantime, giant ranches, owned in many cases by United States businesses, were burning down the rain forest to make way for cattle-grazing land. The cattle were feeding the insatiable American desire for beef.

One night in September 1985, Hayes sat down in a San Francisco bar with his friend Mike Roselle. They'd stayed in touch ever since Hayes passed out the homebrew and filmed the Earth First! action at the Glen Canyon Dam, and whenever Roselle was in town, they'd get together for a beer or seven. That night, they talked about rain forests. The issue was about to explode, the two men agreed: with the right organizing strategy, a group in the United States could have a big impact. It could bring attention to the role U.S. banks, businesses, and institutions were playing in allowing the forests to die—and it could teach people how much was really at stake in those mysterious jungles almost nobody had ever seen. The rain forests seemed to appeal to a broad cross-section of society; a preservation group could raise money from places a lot of environmental organizations would never be able to touch. And Randy Hayes needed a job.

With a bit of press-type and a hand-drawn logo, Roselle and Hayes created some official stationery, and the next day, the Rainforest Action Network was in business. Within two years, it would have a sizable staff, a comfortable office, and a healthy base of donors. All of the contributions came from people who worried about endangered tropical species; it's unlikely all of them understood how much of their money was going toward attacks on the World Bank.

The World Bank operated, officially anyway, under the auspices of the United Nations. Along with the International Monetary Fund, it was established after World War Two to help underdeveloped nations get access to capital. The idea was simple: The IMF would give Third World countries a line of credit, to guarantee they could pay for imports of Western goods, like buses and tractors. The World Bank would raise money from Western governments—mainly the United States—and loan it out for infrastructure development projects, like dams and highways.

Before long, though, the role of the World Bank was largely delegated to private Western bankers—and the two U.N. agencies became, in effect, their collection agent, setting up shop in Third World capitals and making sure that every available penny of natural resource wealth went to pay off the loans. For U.S. banks, it was an extremely lucrative proposition: as long as the country had oil or minerals in the ground, or valuable land to be sold, and as long as the IMF made sure none of the money ever went for food, health care, or other domestic needs until the bankers got their due, the debt payments were virtually guaranteed. Loan officers pushed credit as far as the developing countries would accept it, often far beyond the level that the country's gross national product could sustain. After a while, the government would be forced to take out more loans just to pay the interest—and eventually, they would have to exploit every last scrap of their natural resources to service the expanding debt.

In Central and South America, where the rain forests were vanishing at an alarming rate, the World Bank cast an overwhelming shadow. Brazil, for example, was desperately trying to get out of its hole; the Western banks were desperately trying to get their money back. So instead of following Lovejoy's plan, the World Bank was pouring even more money into the country, underwriting the development of the nation's last valuable resource: the Amazon rain forest.

Randy Hayes had heard about debt-for-nature swaps, and he understood the appeal. The banks might be happy to settle some of the most dubious outstanding loans for a small percentage of the actual debt, if they could be guaranteed immediate payment. The U.S. government could offer to buy out some of Brazil's loans at a few cents on the dollar, in exchange for a promise that the rain forest would be saved.

But he had a major problem with that sort of plan. He didn't think a lot of the debt was legitimate; the banks, after all, made some foolish loans, and that was the bankers' fault, Hayes figured. The impoverished nations shouldn't have to repay all those bad loans—let the World Bank work out how to cover the loss.

In the meantime, he'd keep up the cry: World Bank Destroys Tropical Rainforests.

74

BLOOD ON THE SPIKE

May 8, 1987
Cloverdale, California

Summer came early to the Russian River valley, a narrow strip of lowland wedged in the mountains of northern California; by late April, temperatures were well into the nineties, and the heat wave was breaking every record on the books. A few minutes after five A.M., with the air already starting to feel warm, George Alexander gave his wife a last, long hug, crawled out of bed, and threw on his clothes. Thank God it's Friday, he told himself as he stumbled out the door; just one more day, and this job is history.

Alexander could hear Ricky Phillips's pickup truck approaching from several blocks away. Phillips pulled up in front of the small, rented house, and Alexander climbed in. The trip to the Louisiana Pacific lumber mill took about twenty minutes; most mornings, the two workers passed the time with a bit of idle talk, punctuated by long stretches of silence. Alexander and Phillips had become good friends in the year or so since they began riding to work together, and they didn't feel the need to make conversation.

But this morning, Alexander was so agitated he couldn't stop talking for a minute. Over and over, he repeated his complaints: The mill was falling apart. The company was too cheap to buy any new equipment, or even to replace the gear that was breaking down. The saws were old and full of cracks. The logs were all full of steel—old nails, and telephone wire, and pieces of barbed-wire fence, and God knows what else—but management didn't see any reason to pay for a metal detector.

For three months, Alexander told his friend, he had brought his concerns to the foreman and the plant manager. He explained what was wrong, and even told the bosses how to fix it. When nothing happened, he went back to his job, quietly. Alexander wasn't a troublemaker, and he knew $9.19 an hour was good pay for a twenty-three-year-old kid with only a high-school education. Besides, he had a wife to think about—a pregnant wife. In six more months, he'd have a kid.

But the situation kept getting worse, and Alexander was running out of patience. The day before, he gave the foreman an ultimatum: if the mill didn't start to shape up—tomorrow—there would be one less worker showing up on Monday morning.

It's crazy, Alexander said as they pulled into the sawmill parking lot. One of these days, somebody's going to get hurt.

Alexander slipped a plastic face shield over the top of his hard hat and walked across the floor of the sprawling mill. In a few hours, he knew, the place would be a hothouse. The guys up on the catwalks would be sweating as they worked the machinery that guided the big logs into the giant saws. But down on the floor, Alexander would be cool. When you worked three feet from the head rig, heat was the least of your problems: a fifty-two-foot saw blade made a hell of a fan.

The head rig was a band saw, a steel belt that spun around on two pulleys like a giant, upright bicycle chain. The blades were strips of tempered steel, fifty-two feet long and about eleven inches wide, with sharp teeth cut into one side. The blades were welded into a loop, and stretched tight around a pair of huge metal cylinders, which spun around at nine thousand revolutions a minute.

All day long, massive tree trunks came down a metal conveyor, driven by chains and rollers into the edge of the band saw, which could slice through the biggest logs in a matter of seconds. Alexander's job was to watch the logs coming out of the band saw, and decide where to send them next. A solid log that had been cut cleanly and had no visible defects would be cut into boards. Logs with problems, like big knots, or termite holes, would be diverted to a recut saw, where the faulty parts could be pared away.

Almost every day, the blade would hit some steel: when you cut down a lot of two-hundred-year-old trees, chances were good that a few of them once had a No Trespassing poster nailed to the trunk, or a barbed-wire fence wrapped around it. Over the past few years, however, lumber mill workers had been increasingly concerned about a different kind of nail—new ones, often eight inches long, that were intentionally pounded into tree trunks in an effort to stop logging.

"Tree-spiking" was one of the most controversial practices promoted by radical groups like Earth First!. Supporters argued that a few big nails did little harm to a living tree—but if loggers tried to cut it down, the hidden spikes could destroy chain saws and mill equipment. If the authorities were notified that a section of forest had been spiked, the potential danger to workers would force them to call off the logging, advocates sugested; if nothing else, they argued, a spiked forest was less valuable to lumber mills, which wouldn't want to risk damaging their saws.

But there was little evidence that spiking was significantly reducing the number of trees that were cut in the Pacific Northwest. The lumber companies complained about what they called ecological "terrorism," but they didn't stop logging. They didn't run into many serious problems, either: normally, a well-maintained band saw at a good mill could cut through almost anything.

Band saws wore out quickly. When Alexander started the job a year earlier, the head rig would shut down about every two hours, and a team of technicians would change the blade. The used blades were examined for cracks; if they were sound, the edges would be sharpened and the blades would be put back into use. Cracked blades were repaired, and after a while, discarded.

But new blades were expensive—they ran as much as $2,000—and these days, Alexander was convinced, the company didn't want to spend the money. Louisiana Pacific was building a new mill, Alexander had heard, a state-of-the-art facility with computerized controls and high-speed conveyors that could cut far more logs, in far less time, with far less staff. Word had it the old mill was going to be torn down.

The Cloverdale mill was running two nine-hour shifts; the night crew came on late in the afternoon, and the plant shut down a little after midnight. Alexander barely knew the guy who worked the head rig at night—they'd see each other for a few minutes at shift change, maybe crack a couple of jokes—so he was a little surprised to find a note from the night saw operator taped to his work station. But the night man had some bad news: the mill had run out of blades. The last one was on the saw.

"It's not worth a shit," the note said. "Good luck."

Alexander shook his head. One more day, he reminded himself. Just one more day.

The logs coming into the mill had been smaller than usual over the past few weeks. For the moment, Louisiana Pacific wasn't cutting a lot of old-growth; the loggers were working their way through a stand of younger trees in an area that had been clear-cut about seventy-five years ago. It wasn't a particularly important wilderness area; even Earth First! hadn't made any public fuss about it.

On the other hand, some of the people who lived near the site were distinctly unhappy. The logging equipment was making a mess of the narrow county road that linked the remote, hilly region and the nearby town of Elk. Besides, the operation was noisy. In March, Mendocino County supervisor Norman de Vall contacted Louisiana Pacific officials and advised them to expect some opposition; the company hadn't paid much attention.

The mountain folks near the logging tract tended to be loners, and some of their habits were a little odd. Over the past month, Mendocino County authorities had received several reports of strange animal mutilations in the area. Louisiana Pacific employees told of finding a beheaded dog and several dead pigs and sheep strewn on top of their construction equipment when they arrived for work one morning. But the incident didn't get much press attention, and the company downplayed its importance.

The chief saw operator on the day shift liked to push his crew as hard as he could, but he knew about the saw blades, too, and he was taking it a little easy. The logs were moving through the head rig more slowly than usual, and everyone was watching carefully for signs of metal. But around seven-thirty A.M., an eleven-inch nail slipped through, buried in the trunk of a medium-sized redwood. It was easy to miss: The nail had been driven deep into the butt end of the log.

The tree had been spiked after it was cut down, and there had been no public announcement, no effort to inform the authorities and thus undermine the logging. It definitely wasn't the Earth First! style.

At 7:50 A.M., the band saw struck the nail head-on. The blade shattered instantly. George Alexander didn't even have a chance to duck.

Ricky Phillips was on the catwalk overhead when he heard the sickening sound of metal striking metal. He realized immediately that something was wrong; everyone in the mill seemed to be frozen, in a state of shock. He leaned over the railing and looked down at the head rig.

Within a split second, Phillips had torn his T-shirt off and was racing down the ladder. By the time he reached his friend, Alexander was lying in a pool of blood, screaming in pain as he struggled desperately to free himself from a twenty-foot section of saw blade that had wrapped itself tightly around his body.

Alexander was a mess. A piece of the blade had struck him in the face, ripping through the plastic shield, knocking out all of his upper teeth, and severing his jugular vein. Bits of shrapnel had torn holes in his chest and arms, and he seemed to be bleeding from everywhere.

Phillips jammed the shirt into one of the biggest wounds and forced Alexander to stay still while a welder cut the steel coils away from his body. It took half an hour for the ambulance crew to get him to the nearest hospital, and another hour to stabilize him and load him onto a helicopter bound for San Francisco.

By then, word was already spreading through the top ranks of the timber industry, and soon, it would be in all the newspapers: tree spiking had claimed its first casualty.

75

DAY OF THE DOLPHIN

August 1987
San Francisco

Sam LaBudde strolled into the office of the Rainforest Action Network and announced himself to the receptionist. He'd been reading about the destruction of the forests, he explained, and he thought it was just awful. He'd come by to talk about a job. Was the executive director available?

The receptionist sighed as she looked at the scruffy figure in front of her desk. People like that wandered in off the streets all the time; a lot of them wanted jobs. The Rainforest Action Network was getting a fair amount of publicity; it was also growing fast. Randy Hayes had a dozen people working for him now, and his annual budget was more than $1 million. By activist standards, the RAN offices were almost plush—big glass windows, nice chairs and desks, personal computers, even a comfortable sofa by the front door.

The man standing in the office had never met Randy Hayes, and he was sure Hayes had never heard of him. But he wasn't just another nut off the street. LaBudde was a biologist with a long history of political activism, and he was looking to find a full-time job working on environmental issues. He'd tried the local Greenpeace office, but there weren't any policy jobs there; he figured he'd stop in at the Rainforest Action Network. Hayes sounded like a good person, he told the receptionist. He thought they might have a little talk.

The receptionist rang Hayes's assistant on the intercom and passed on the word. Hayes was on the phone, she told the visitor. There was no way of knowing when he might get free. LaBudde thanked her, took a seat on the couch, and said he would wait.

He sat there quite a while. Hayes often spent most of his day on the phone—working out strategies, conducting press interviews, and raising money. The rain forest cause had taken off; Hayes was constantly in demand, constantly busy. He didn't always have time for casual visitors who wanted to chat.

After a few minutes of waiting, LaBudde started flipping through the magazines on the table in front of him. The first one that caught his interest was the *Earth Island Journal,* a quarterly publication put out by David Brower's Earth Island Institute. One article explained how the intelligent, peaceful mammals were getting butchered by the thousands on the high seas, at the hands of fishermen who were out to catch tuna. The fishermen didn't have any interest in the dolphins—there wasn't any market for dolphin meat. But the creatures got caught up in the mile-long tuna nets, after the coordinated assaults of helicopters, speedboats, and trawlers herded everything in sight toward the underwater mesh. The easiest way to untangle the dolphins and free up the gear was to kill them and cut them up.

LaBudde was aghast. Suddenly, he had lost all interest in tropical rain forests.

The slender thirty-one-year-old thanked the receptionist again and walked out the door. He'd checked the address on the magazine and discovered that Earth Island Institute was just across the street. He figured he'd try his luck there.

Like Randy Hayes, David Brower was far too busy to meet with everyone who walked in off the street. But two of the Earth Island staff, David Phillips and Todd Steiner, did their best to answer LaBudde's questions.

Why, LaBudde wanted to know, was there so little public awareness of the dolphin slaughter? Why did people keep buying tuna fish when the fishing fleets killed so many of these gentle creatures, for no good reason at all? Why wasn't Congress doing anything to save the dolphins from potential extinction?

Like whales, the Earth Island staffers knew, dolphins had been a concern of environmentalists for more than a decade. In 1978, an activist from Hawaii named Dexter Cate witnessed the massacre of more than 1,300 dolphins at the hands of Japanese fishermen, and launched a personal crusade to halt the killings. The Japanese fishing industry, he learned, blamed dolphins for the decline in squid and yellowtail fish along the coast of Japan, and the government actually paid a bounty for every dolphin killed. The dead animals were ground up and sold for pig food and plant fertilizer. Early in 1980, Cate took a small boat out to a secluded Japanese island where a fishing fleet was holding a catch of some 200 dolphins in underwater nets. He untied the mooring lines and set the captive creatures free. The act cost him three months in a Japanese prison, but helped bring international attention to the random slaughter of the rapidly vanishing creatures.

But these days, Phillips and Steiner told their visitor, the most serious threat to the dolphins came from tuna fishing boats—and so far, the newspapers and politicians were only marginally interested in the story. The problem was getting hard evidence. Most of the information Earth Island could provide was a string of dry numbers about declining populations, data that meant a lot to a biologist but that didn't exactly inflame the passions of the person on the street. Witnesses who had ridden on the fishing boats provided some horrible tales of dolphin killings, but the fishermen denied it all. And nobody had any solid proof.

LaBudde considered the problem. He didn't see why it would be so hard to get the evidence—all someone had to do, he suggested, was sign on for a stint on one of the boats and sneak a video camera aboard. When the dolphins were pulled in for the kill, the camera could record the carnage, and the tape could be smuggled home for everyone to see. LaBudde said he'd be happy to do the job. He just needed a camera and a ticket to Mexico, where the closest fishing fleet pulled in to port.

The Earth Island Institute staffers thanked LaBudde for his interest, and promised to take it up with the boss. When LaBudde checked back again in a week, they had some unpleasant news: Earth Island couldn't afford to send someone that nobody really knew to Mexico, with an expensive piece of video equipment, for a job that might or might not come to pass. They wished him the best of luck, though.

Then Phillips and Steiner went back to work. Nice idea, they told each other. Too bad the guy didn't have a chance.

76

HATS AND
SUNGLASSES

September 15, 1987
Montreal, Canada

The scientific issue had always been simple: since the day Joe Farman discovered the ozone hole over Antarctica, scientists agreed that a widely used group of industrial chemicals called chlorofluorocarbons was destroying the Earth's protective ozone layer. To stop the process, use of the CFCs, as they were known, had to be rapidly phased out.

Politically, the problem was a lot more complicated.

The destructive chemicals came from thousands of different sources scattered over dozens of countries. Some of the industries employed large numbers of people and made products that generated sizable profits. The chemicals couldn't simply be eliminated overnight. The problem required a far-reaching international accord, but the questions were a diplomatic nightmare: Who would phase out what, and by when? Who would bear the economic burden? Who would monitor whom, to be sure agreements were kept?

The task of hammering out a workable treaty to limit the use of CFCs fell to the United Nations Environmental Program. UNEP, born in the optimistic days that followed the 1972 Stockholm environmental conference, had never lived up to the hopes of its founders; it lacked the money, power, and respect to force bitterly divided parties to settle their differences. But after fifteen years, UNEP had finally come into its own: at the agency's urging, representatives from forty-three nations had come to Montreal to work out a solution to the ozone problem, and by September 1987, they were close to a deal.

Except for the United States.

The United States delegates came to the Montreal conference with plenty at stake. U.S. companies produced a third of the world's CFCs, more than any other nation, and the Reagan administration was reluctant to crack down

353

on a major industry. In the early stages of the negotiations, Interior Secretary Donald Hodel announced his personal suggestion: if the ozone disappeared, he proposed, Americans could start wearing hats, sunglasses, and extra suntan lotion.

The battle came down to what seemed like an obscure issue—the number of countries that would have to approve the treaty before it went into effect. The original draft stated that 60 percent of the participating nations would have to ratify the document; delegates argued over other issues, but most assumed the ratification process was set. Then on September 9, just one week before the final treaty, the U.S. negotiator, Lee Thomas, demanded that the approval rate be raised to 90 percent.

The move caught the other delegations by surprise, but the reasoning was actually fairly obvious. In the interest of saving the planet, the United States was willing to accept some reductions in CFC emissions—but only if all the other major countries did, too. If another nation refused to abide by the deal, that country's industries would have a competitive advantage over their counterparts in the United States, potentially hurting corporate profits. That, the U.S. delegation seemed to be saying, was more important than the ozone layer—short-term profits for American companies were more important than the long-term survival of life on Earth.

The remaining delegates were startled. Very few international agreements ever had 90 percent support, and the U.S. position could undermine the entire treaty. But the United States never really intended to win the 90 percent battle. The demand was a bargaining ploy, a way to force the ratification numbers just a little bit higher. And it succeeded—without the United States, the treaty would be meaningless, so the others had to accept a compromise on American terms. After a week of tense discussions that teetered more than once on collapse, the negotiators settled on 67 percent.

With that hurdle surmounted, the specific terms were simple: twenty-six nations agreed to freeze production and consumption of CFCs at 1986 levels by 1990, reduce them another 20 percent by 1994, and reduce them another 30 percent by 1999. It was a remarkable accomplishment for the United Nations; it was a symbol of a new level of international cooperation on environmental issues. It was also a victory for the United States negotiators, who managed to use their powerful leverage to make sure that U.S. industry was protected. Ironically, the United States was in a great bargaining position for the worst of all possible reasons: it was the largest polluter in the world.

Perhaps more alarming, the attitude of the Reagan administration at the Montreal convention pointed to a fundamental failure of the U.S. environmental movement, one that presented a profound political challenge. On the local level—in cities like New York and towns like Lake Charles—environmentalists were winning landmark battles. In the international sphere, from saving rain forests to saving whales, U.S. environmental groups were taking the lead. United States consumers were starting to force big businesses to adopt ecologically sound practices and offer less-damaging products.

But when it came to the most important office in the land, environmentalists couldn't seem to make any headway. No matter how bad, the environmental record of a United States president never seemed to make much of a difference at the polls.

77

WES JACKSON'S LUNCH

October 1987
Salina, Kansas

Days started early at the Land Institute. Wes Jackson was up with the dawn, and if his students knew what was good for them, they were up, too. Transforming American agriculture wasn't a job for the lazy. After a long morning working in the patches of grass that formed the institute's genetic laboratories, the crew worked up a healthy appetite.

Lunch was normally a potluck meal of vegetables and grains, grown on the institute's few acres of traditionally cultivated land. But on an otherwise normal October day, Patty Boehner, a young intern from Nebraska, had prepared a special treat. She carried it proudly out of the communal kitchen, and set in down in front of the crew. It looked just like corn bread, except it wasn't made out of corn.

Boehner's steaming loaf was the first tangible evidence that Jackson's ambitious project might have a chance of success. The bread was baked with the seeds from a hybrid strain of eastern gama grass, fresh from the Land Institute's experimental plots.

After a few bites, the students began smiling and talking about how good the gama bread tasted. Thom Leonard, a former baker who ran the institute's seed bank, said he could eat it every day. Jackson wasn't so sure: for the moment, he decided, he'd stick to corn and wheat. But the new grain was certainly edible—and that was a major accomplishment.

The gama grass Boehner had baked into bread wasn't anywhere near ready to present to the farming industry. It was a frail strain that needed constant care and attention. The seeds had a tendency to shatter before they could be harvested. Years of careful breeding would be required to make it

356

into something that could be grown commercially. It might take even longer to teach the world outside of the Land Institute kitchen to appreciate the rather unusual flavor.

But Jackson had always said that his edible, domestic prairie was at least fifty years away. Gama-grass bread for lunch after only a decade of work wasn't a bad start.

78

THE SCAM OF
THE CENTURY

November 3, 1987
Phoenix

In a small Phoenix café, across the street from the copper-clad walls of the Phelps-Dodge mining company headquarters, Stewart Udall steeled himself for what he thought might be the last, best thing he could ever do for the American West. For a man well beyond retirement age, Udall was in remarkably good health. He still had the energy, he decided, for one final assault on an environmentally disastrous law that seemed to have the life of Dracula.

Udall was an elder statesman of the environmental movement, a former congressman from Arizona who served as secretary of the interior under the administrations of Presidents Kennedy and Johnson. He hadn't always pleased everyone—Jack Loeffler would never forgive him for allowing the mining of Black Mesa—but in retrospect, even his opponents agreed he had been one of the better people ever to hold the nation's top environmental job. The brother of Congressman Morris Udall, who chaired the powerful House Interior Committee, Stew Udall was respected in Washington, popular with the press, and friendly with most of the nation's major environmental leaders. And yet, for twenty years, he hadn't been able to make the slightest headway on what he once called "the most important piece of unfinished business on the nation's natural resource agenda": repealing the General Mining Law of 1872.

Udall's lunch companion was a longtime Sierra Club member named Phil Hocker. Hocker was something of a rarity in the mainstream environmental movement—he shared Udall's obsession with the obsolete, century-old mining law. His Sierra Club colleagues never made it a priority; neither did the Wilderness Society, the Audubon Society, or any of the other major wilderness lobbying groups. In fact, when Hocker met the former interior secretary by chance at a conference in Jackson Hole in 1985, he didn't realize anyone of Udall's stature was still interested in the issue; it never got much press attention.

The situation never ceased to amaze Hocker: every significant environmental law written before 1960 had been modified, ratified, or repealed in the past two decades—all except the General Mining Law. It was easily the most abused and outdated federal law on the books. In fact, it was hard to believe the bill was still the law of the land.

The basic principle behind the mining law was simple: anyone who discovered "valuable minerals" on public land had an automatic right to mine them. A miner would file a claim on a piece of land, and that claim secured rights to the minerals indefinitely, as long as a minimal amount of work was done on the claim each year. The miner paid no rent for the property, and no royalties on any minerals discovered. In fact, if any minerals turned up on the claim, the miner could immediately purchase the land, and all its mineral rights, for a maximum of $5 an acre—about what empty western land was worth in 1872.

The law seemed eminently reasonable in the second half of the nineteenth century, when Congress was eager to encourage settlement and economic development in the West. Offering strong incentives to search for so-called "hardrock" minerals—gemstones, gold, silver, copper, and the like—seemed like a good way to help accomplish the goal.

By 1987, however, the law had become a mind-boggling absurdity. At $5 an acre, it had to be the greatest real estate bargain in the world—and the people who took advantage of it weren't just finding gold with their shovels. For example, congressional investigators would learn that a man named Anthony Perchetti bought $500 worth of public land on a mining claim in 1986 and 1988; he did nothing substantive to develop the claim for hardrock mining, but he held on to the land. In 1989, the Department of Energy would buy it back from him for $250,000. As of October 1987, the General Accounting Office found that 265 patent applications were pending for more than eighty thousand acres of public land. Investigators visited twelve of these sites and concluded that if all the claims were approved, the government would receive about $16,000—for land appraised at between $14.4 million and $47.1 million.

But to Hocker and Udall, the giveaway of public assets was probably the least of the law's problems. The mining act never required miners to clean up any of the mess that their operations inevitably left behind. Nothing could interfere with the sweeping rights granted under the mining law; not even the National Environmental Policy Act of 1970 could force miners to consider the environmental impacts of their projects.

By the 1980s, these were not small messes. Mining was generating twice as much hazardous waste in the United States as all other industrial and public activities combined. Giant strip mines, deadly toxic-waste pools, poisoned streams—all were protected, in the name of an economic development policy more than a century old. No national law regulated the chemicals seeping into the aquifers from active or abandoned mines. By the 1980s, the major beneficiaries of those loopholes weren't small-time wildcat miners, they were giant mining corporations, which were able to abandon contaminated sites and leave millions of dollars' worth of cleanup bills behind, to be paid by the federal government.

The 125-year accumulation of toxic mining waste scattered around the country was staggering—fifty billion tons, by some estimates. The EPA identified a site in Colorado where one stretch of a river contaminated by mining waste would cost the taxpayers several hundred million dollars and take more than a decade to clean up. In Montana, a 120-mile stretch of toxic sites from Missoula to Butte made up the largest Superfund site in the nation.

Since the days of Cecil Garland, grassroots groups in small towns had taken up the cause in every state in the West. Occasionally, they won a local campaign; more often, they failed. Garland's Upper Blackfoot River was a classic example—after all his work, the Montana legislature finally allocated $400,000 to clean up the Mike Horse Mine, but by the time the money wound its way through the state bureaucracy, none of it was actually spent cleaning the river. Years later, when Robert Redford arrived at the Upper Blackfoot to film *A River Runs Through It,* he found the water so filthy that he used another location.

A magazine called *The High Country News,* started by Ed and Betsy Marston in Paonia, Colorado, helped spread the word of grassroots mining battles, and on a smaller scale, a network of activists similar to the toxic crusaders in the South sprung up across the West. But the mining foes had no Love Canal to gain public attention and no Lois Gibbs to generate support and publicity. More important, perhaps, the mining companies always had an ace in the hole—the General Mining Law of 1872.

Udall had written the issue off as a lost cause years earlier. But Phil Hocker was getting him excited again—the more they talked about it, the more Udall began to think the time was right to try again. The environmental movement had come a long way since he left office in 1968. Even without the major Washington lobbying groups, a campaign to repeal the General Mining Law might be able to stir up quite a fuss. The mining companies had been getting away with the scam of the century. It couldn't go on forever.

79

H E A T W A V E

June 23, 1988
Washington, D.C.

It was turning into another hot summer, one more for the books. Six of the past eight years, the summer temperatures had broken records, and two days into the 1989 season, the trend seemed to be continuing. Air conditioners were already running day and night in North American cities, and kids were popping fire hydrants open for instant relief. In suburbs, the cool corridors of shopping malls were crowded with people who had no intention of buying anything. In the country, farmers were running short of water.

Everywhere, people talked about the heat wave.

The United States Senate was talking about it, too. In fact, some of the leading scientists in the nation had come to the sweltering Capitol to offer a frightening theory. The string of brutal summers wasn't a fluke: the world was heating up. The process scientists called the "greenhouse effect" threatened to bring on a global catastrophe—and to a large extent, the United States was responsible.

Most weather patterns were hard to explain, and almost impossible to predict. But the greenhouse effect was simple.

The glass roof of a greenhouse allows sunlight—in scientific terms, short-wave energy—to pass through. But inside the structure, some of that energy turns into heat, which travels in long waves. Heat can't pass through glass the way light can, so it gets trapped inside, warming up the greenhouse air to tropical temperatures even in the dead of winter.

Glass wasn't the only substance that let in light and trapped heat. Carbon dioxide did it, too.

Technically, carbon dioxide wasn't a pollutant—it was the same gas people

361

released from their lungs every time they exhaled. But it was produced when almost anything burned—wood, coal, paper, gas, or oil—so it was by far the most common industrial emission. The smokestack scrubbers on factories and the emission control devices on cars captured other noxious gases, but they did nothing to contain carbon dioxide. A 1988 Mustang released as much carbon dioxide as an original Model T Ford.

Up in the sky, carbon dioxide acted like glass. A certain amount was critical. Without it, all the heat would escape from the atmosphere, and the Earth would become a frozen wasteland. But a little too much could make the planet roast like the inside of a car with its windows rolled up on a sunny day.

The members of the Senate Subcommittee on Energy Regulation and Conservation had what seemed like a simple question: how much carbon dioxide was too much, and how much was in the atmosphere? The implications were staggering. If the levels were getting high enough, the increased temperatures could melt the polar ice caps, causing the oceans to rise by several feet and flooding coastal cities all over the globe. The greenhouse effect could turn America's fertile grain belt into desert. It could render tropical areas uninhabitable, and transform the chilly Arctic tundra of Canada and the Soviet Union into the breadbasket of the world—at least, for a few years, until even higher temperatures made any large-scale agriculture impossible.

Senator Tim Wirth of Colorado, who chaired the committee, was convinced that the problem might be serious—and equally convinced that the White House wasn't paying attention. As the sun beat down on Washington, he convened a hearing that he hoped would provide some evidence—credible evidence, that even the president couldn't ignore. He invited the best climatologists in the world.

Dr. James Hansen was the star witness. The forty-seven-year-old held one of the most distinguished positions in American science—director of NASA's Goddard Institute for Space Studies. It was a remarkable achievement for someone in his field.

Just a few years earlier, climatology—the study of trends in temperature, precipitation, winds, ocean currents, and other weather phenomena—was considered a crude science. Researchers with hand-held calculators interpreted piecemeal data collected by hot-air balloons and airplanes. But climatology had been changing dramatically. Advanced dating techniques were coaxing detailed historical pictures of the Earth's climate from long-buried sediments. Satellite photographs captured tiny annual shifts in the ice and snow cover on inaccessible polar regions. Powerful computers analyzed the data at speeds that once seemed impossible.

Predicting weather patterns was still immensely difficult. There were far too many variables involved. Some climatologists liked to explain their work by asking people to imagine throwing a stick into the middle of a river—and figuring out exactly where it would be ten minutes later. Analyzing the speed and direction of the floating object would be a formidable task by itself—and the slightest change in the current, or the tides, or the wind, or even a passing boat could make all the other calculations useless. Turn the river into the entire Earth's atmosphere, and the stick into a few thousand constantly changing factors, and the nature of the challenge would become apparent.

But scientists like Hansen were starting to develop ways to chart some broad, overall trends with a reasonable degree of accuracy—and the latest evidence was making Hansen increasingly nervous.

Climatologists had known for years that the sharp temperature differential between the equator and the poles was a critical factor in regional weather—the interaction between the cold polar air and warm tropical air created the prevailing winds that brought normal seasonal patterns of rain, snow, sun, and storms. The more pronounced the temperature difference, the stronger the prevailing winds, and the more predictable the pattern.

The greenhouse effect, Hansen feared, would not only warm up the Earth, it would also reduce the temperature gradient between the equator and the poles, disrupting one of the most fundamental weather systems on the planet. At that point, all bets were off. Rain forests could become deserts. Farmland could become swamp. Some rivers might dry up, and others might overflow. Nobody could predict which regions would get the droughts and which would get the floods. Nobody could be sure exactly what would happen.

Of course, nobody even knew if the apparent global warming of the past few years was a significant trend, a random natural event, or a meaningless statistical anomaly. And if it was a trend, nobody could prove why it was occurring—not for certain. Not scientifically.

Virtually everyone in the scientific community agreed that high enough levels of carbon dioxide in the atmosphere would create a greenhouse effect. Virtually everyone agreed that the levels of carbon dioxide in the atmosphere were increasing. And everyone agreed that the weather had been getting unusually hot. But in climatology, absolute proof was still an elusive concept—if the temperature rose to 110 degrees for fifty days in a row, it could still be construed as a statistical anomaly instead of a pattern. Researchers had found evidence of a global warming trend as early as the late 1800s, but much of the scientific community—especially the government scientists—continued to insist that the evidence was still inconclusive. The connection to increased carbon dioxide emissions, they argued, was entirely a matter of speculation.

There was another issue, too. Reducing carbon dioxide emissions would require some major changes in the life-styles and business practices of the major industrial nations, starting with the United States. Almost every form of energy except nuclear, solar, and hydro power involved burning fuel. The greenhouse gas couldn't be filtered out or cleaned in a smokestack or tail pipe—the only way to reduce it was to cut back on energy consumption. In the era of Ronald Reagan and George Bush, that was something nobody in official Washington liked to talk about.

Jim Hansen was a cautious, careful researcher who always insisted on the highest standards of evidence. But at a certain point, he realized, planetary science was a matter of instinct—and at a certain point, the risks were too great to accept. The industrial nations, led by the United States, were playing Russian roulette with the planet, and Hansen was sick of the game.

He stated his opinion unequivocally to the senators, reporters, and visitors packed into the tense, sweaty room. "Global warming," he said, "has reached a level such that we can ascribe with a high degree of confidence a cause and effect relationship between the greenhouse effect and observed warming. It is already happening now."

As Hansen cited study after study, and pointed to chart after chart, the reality began to sink in. His testimony would make front-page headlines across the heat-stricken nation.

No one could prove for certain that global warming had begun, but Hansen proved that his guess was as good as anyone's—and probably a whole lot better. He raised the definitive question: if any remotely credible evidence suggested that the entire future of the planet was being threatened by practices that could still be changed, what was the point in arguing? Why even take the risk?

The Bush administration would take the exact opposite stance: as long as nobody could prove for certain that anything was wrong, why make any changes? In fact, in May 1989, Bush's Office of Management and Budget would attempt to alter Hansen's testimony before another congressional committee, to block him from saying that scientific evidence proved human activities were the main cause of global warming.

And once again, in what was becoming a completely predictable pattern, the American public was left with a no-win choice: either jobs would evaporate, modern conveniences would be regulated out of existence, and life in the United States would get a lot less pleasant, or else at some point in the future, the planet would face ecological ruin.

Way up in the Rocky Mountains, in a place called Snowmass, Colorado, scientist Amory Lovins had another alternative. David Brower's energy whiz kid was living in a high-altitude think tank of his own creation, a stone, glass, and wood structure that ran entirely on solar energy. With simple technology, Lovins and his staff at the Rocky Mountain Institute could stay warm even if the temperature outside dropped to forty below zero, and they never had to burn a bit of fuel.

Year after year, he offered a program that defied the doomsayers on both sides of the old energy debate: with a bit more intelligent planning, the United States could live even better on a fraction of the oil, coal, gas, and nuclear energy it currently used. Government agencies from around the world, and big private corporations in the United States, were paying him thousands of dollars a day to explain his ideas to their engineers. Bits and pieces of his strategy were appearing in projects around the country; newspapers and magazines quoted him regularly.

But his basic message had one essential problem—it would eliminate the need for a large percentage of the private centralized energy business. A nation living better, for less money, with little environmental impact would have no need for hundreds of big utilities, oil refineries, and nuclear power plants. And almost every politician in the United States had a wealthy, powerful constituent making money selling energy.

Of course, bringing houses, factories, farms, offices, shops, trains, buses, and countless other things up to the Amory Lovins standards would cost a lot of money. The price would almost certainly be lower than what the nation was paying for wasted, unnecessary energy—but political leaders would have to figure out who was going to put up the cash, and that wasn't a popular prospect.

So the world kept getting warmer—and the most attractive alternative to the global energy problem kept getting blown away in all the hot air.

PART 10

SHOWTIME

It was the failures who had always won, but by the time they won they had come to be called successes. This is the final paradox, which men call evolution.

—*Loren Eiseley*

In the late 1980s, tragedy, disaster, and fear did what science, law, and politics never could: they put environmental protection at the top of the national agenda. Politicians and major corporations lined up to proclaim their support for the cause. Environmentally safe products became a big business.

On one level, the attention was everything a generation of activists had dreamed of. Organizations that had been ignored for years were suddenly on the front pages of national newspapers. Politicians with bad environmental records were facing sharp scrutiny. Companies that had always dismissed environmental criticism started changing their ways. Consumers who had always looked for the cheapest and most convenient products began shopping around for organic produce and recycled toilet paper, and taking their purchases home in reusable bags. Communities that had never spent money on recycling or waste treatment scrambled to set up model programs. Even religious leaders began speaking out on the importance of preserving the things of this earth.

But environmentalism had also become a fad. People with no real concern for the natural world were wrapping themselves in a green flag to raise money, make profits, or win elections. And a lot of them were getting away with it.

At the same time, some of the toughest, most important issues still weren't getting addressed—and some of the most serious problems were only getting worse. And all over the country, people kept fighting the same old battle. One side argued that environmental protection was destroying jobs. The other side claimed that economic growth was wrecking the environment. Both sides were right—and as long as the debate was framed on the same old obsolete terms, both sides were destined to lose.

80

SNUFF FILMS

January 1, 1988
Off the Costa Rican coast

The *Maria Luisa* pitched gently in the warm Pacific breeze. The new year had brought good news, and the captain and crew were in high spirits—the fishing boat just received formal permission to work the territorial waters of Costa Rica. The Costa Rican government had finally agreed to stop worrying about saving dolphins, and let the tuna fishermen get back to business.

As far as the crew of the *Maria Luisa* was concerned, the decision was long overdue: the fishing had been terrible for the past few months. Unless the captain could find a healthy school of yellowfin tuna pretty soon, the supplies would be gone, the boat would be coming home empty, and everyone would be out of work for another year. But the Costa Rican coastline looked promising. The Central American nation was stingy about granting fishing privileges, and few tuna boats had been allowed in the area. If all went as usual, the hunt would be easy—all the crew had to do was look for a school of dolphin, diving in and out of the water. Where there were dolphins, there were almost always tuna.

Suddenly, there was action in the water. The fishermen dashed to the supply lockers for the nets and ropes. Sam LaBudde dashed back to his bunk and snatched the video camera hidden underneath. The newest member of the crew slid into a secluded position as the nets hit the water. In the rush of excitement, nobody looked for him.

Within minutes, LaBudde knew his long months at sea had been worth the effort. He squeezed the recording switch, and focused the camera on an adult male dolphin, struggling for freedom in the *Maria Luisa*'s nets. It managed to pull its snout free, but the rest of its body was still tangled in the plastic mesh. As a giant mechanical winch pulled the net out of the water and hauled it toward the boat, the dolphin began bucking and twisting, trying desperately to escape. As the camera rolled, the dolphin's dorsal fin became snared in the netting. The animal continued to thrash, and the fin snapped off, spewing blood as it fell into the water.

The dolphin continued to fight as the net carried it aboard. The crew methodically released it from the netting, then tossed it casually into a chute that led to a powerful grinding machine. In seconds, the dolphin had been chopped to bits.

Over and over, the scene continued. As LaBudde kept his finger on the camera trigger, the *Maria Luisa* crew slaughtered some two hundred rare Costa Rican spinner dolphins. The endangered mammals went through the grinder with abandon, and the bloody mash was thrown overboard. Shark feed, the sailors called it. Left on deck was the day's catch—about a dozen yellowfin tuna.

LaBudde wrapped the videotape in waterproof plastic and shoved it into the secret bin by his locker. He washed the blood off his hands and arms, and joined the rest of the crew for dinner. If he could survive just a few more weeks, he told himself, the *Maria Luisa* would put ashore. Then he could get the hell off of this stinking ship of death.

81

OF MICE AND MEN

April 12, 1988
Washington, D.C.

Fortune magazine would hail it as one of the hottest new products of the year. It came in one basic color—white, with red eyes—and fit easily in a shoebox. The manufacturer figured it would sell for somewhere around $50. E. I. du Pont, the giant chemical company, called it one of the most important technological breakthroughs of the decade. The *Wall Street Journal* called it a milestone.

The United States Patent and Trademark Office called it a work of human invention, a product, in the words of a landmark Supreme Court case, "not of nature's handiwork."

Jeremy Rifkin called it a disaster of epic proportions.

Most people called it a mouse.

After years of legal and political battles, the bureaucratic agency that oversees patent rights took a step that the strongest supporters and critics of genetic engineering had always predicted: it ruled that Harvard University had the right to patent an animal. Donald Quigg, the head of the Patent and Trademark Office, tried to make sure nobody blew the issue out of proportion: "The agency," his spokesman insisted, "will not patent human beings."

The ruling would raise profound moral and ethical questions, energize the movement to restrict biotechnology, and bring some strange bedfellows into the environmental cause.

The 1980 court decision that allowed patents on bacteria attracted considerable attention in scientific and business circles. The 1988 patent office ruling attracted considerable attention almost everywhere in the civilized world. Granting a private institution the exclusive right to sell microscopic bugs was unusual; granting the exclusive right to sell a patented mouse was

372

astonishing. The patent didn't just apply to an individual mouse, either—Harvard owned the rights to every one of its new creature's offspring, for at least the next seventeen years.

The mouse was the work of Philip Leder, a Harvard Medical School researcher, and Timothy Stewart, who worked for the private firm Genentech. The two had spliced a gene that gave animals a prediction for cancer into a laboratory mouse; the result was a small furry creature, unique in the animal world, that provided the perfect guinea pig for cancer research. Du Pont, which had donated $6 million to Harvard several years earlier, had the exclusive marketing rights.

Genetic engineering had blossomed into a hot political issue, in large part because of Jeremy Rifkin and a strawberry patch in Brentwood, California. In 1983, scientists at the University of California perfected what they described as a major new tool for American agriculture—a genetically engineered bacterium that would prevent frost from forming on fragile types of fruit. The researchers applied to the Environmental Protection Agency for permission to test the product outdoors; when the EPA agreed, Brentwood residents rebelled—and Rifkin launched a nationwide assault. For five years, Rifkin's Foundation on Economic Trends kept the permit tied up in court; when a frustrated researcher decided to try the product out on the roof of the lab, Rifkin found out and exposed the violation. In the wake of the public uproar, the lab paid a stiff fine.

By the time the courts finally allowed the tests to proceed, the issue was national news. Earth First! activists vowed to disrupt any further tests; cities from Berkeley to Cambridge enacted laws limiting genetic-engineering work; Congress began holding hearings on several bills that would change the patent laws and regulate the biotechnology industry. Everyone from the Sierra Club to the Catholic Church was getting in on the action.

82

THE COLOR RED

April 13, 1988
Washington, D.C.

The lights went out in the Senate hearing room. A hush fell as the video deck clicked on and the television monitor began displaying shot after sickening shot of dead and dying dolphins, in full bloody color. It was almost too much to take; the members of the Commerce, Science and Transportation Subcommittee were visibly relieved when the tape was over.

When the lights came on, the chairman called the next witness, the man who could explain firsthand what the horror film was about. Sam LaBudde collected his thoughts and began talking.

The fishing fleets, LaBudde told the committee, often worked in teams, with helicopters dropping small explosive devices into the water and speedboats helping herd the schools of tuna toward the nets. The dolphins, he explained, were simply innocent bystanders, but they were "completely terrorized, deafened, and disoriented by the effect of this bombing on their extremely sensitive hearing and sonar." They fled toward the ships and the nets, where they became hopelessly entangled. No matter how hard they fought, or how loud they shrieked, they were, LaBudde testified, "fated to slow and sometimes excruciating deaths."

The matter before the committee was the reauthorization of the Marine Mammal Protection Act of 1972, a measure designed in large part to protect ocean mammals like dolphins from injury and death at the hands of tuna-fishing operations. Even then, biologists had warned that several species of dolphins were fast becoming endangered, subject to random slaughter at the hands of fishing fleets. But the experts and lobbyists fought over numbers, and the bill was watered down. The legislation was delayed until 1976, when

374

it finally became federal policy to halt the devastation of marine mammals at the hands of United States fishing fleets.

Starting in 1976, official estimates of incidental dolphin kills dropped off significantly. But in 1981, the Reagan administration changed the official target of zero dolphin deaths to an allowable limit of 20,500 dolphin kills a year. Already, more than one million dolphins had been legally killed since the passage of the Marine Mammal Protection Act, and the administration was resisting any effort to tighten the regulations.

In the early 1970s, food- and fishing-industry lobbyists had used their political muscle in Congress with considerable success, and as recently as 1987, some environmentalists feared a repeat performance. But the situation had just changed, dramatically. Over the previous three months, LaBudde's film had set off a political furor. Since the day he arrived back in San Francisco with his precious videotape, the organized environmental community had snapped to attention. Copies of the tape circulated around the country; letters began pouring in to Congress. Defenders of the tuna-fishing fleet quickly shifted political gears and began backing away.

But perhaps the most important thing that happened had nothing directly to do with Congress or the marine mammal bill. Three days before LaBudde's Senate appearance, the Sea Shepherd Society, the Marine Mammal Fund, Earth Island Institute, and Greenpeace launched a coordinated national boycott, urging the consumers of the United States not to buy canned tuna until the industry agreed to stop killing dolphins.

Americans always seemed to have a strong emotional response to dolphins. From *Flipper* to Jacques Cousteau's nature programs, the creatures were romantic heroes of the television screen; playful dolphins performed for children at zoos and theme parks; legends of dolphins rescuing sailors were established in popular mythology. The pictures of bloody, mutilated dolphins, butchered for no reason by callous fishermen, brought the cause out of the narrow world of determined activists and into the mainstream of American society. The horror was as close as the television set, as immediate as the evening news.

The effect on tuna sales wasn't quick or dramatic: boycotts always took time to get rolling. On the surface, the effect on the tuna industry was minimal. But behind closed doors, some powerful business executives were sweating blood.

83

ON THE ROCKS

March 24, 1989
Valdez, Alaska

The *Exxon Valdez* was the fanciest ship in the fleet, the pride of the largest oil company in the world. The $125 million supertanker had just about every gadget and system known to modern nautical science. With sophisticated radar, satellite navigation systems, electronic depth-finders, and automated, gyroscopic controls, it practically ran itself. Most of the time, the four officers who took turns on bridge had very little to worry about. Even the trip in and out of the port of Valdez was becoming routine.

Valdez was nestled at the end of a long, narrow estuary that jutted inland from the vast Prince William Sound. The sound was an ecological wonderland, one of Alaska's leading tourist attractions and the center of some of its biggest fishing fleets. It was also one of the busiest tanker routes in the world; the port of Valdez was the terminus for the Alaska oil pipeline.

The shipping lanes were wide enough to handle the traffic with ease. The deepwater channel was ten miles across, leaving plenty of room for even the largest supertankers. But the waters outside the channel were treacherous—hundreds of rocky islands dotted the surface, and thousands of uncharted reefs lay hidden below.

From the earliest days of the battle over the Alaska pipeline, a few environmentalists had raised questions about the possibility of an oil spill in the pristine, sensitive sound. But like the nuclear power industry, the oil companies insisted that the risks involved in the venture were minor, particularly compared to the rewards. Company officials insisted that every possible step would be taken to avoid environmental damage. The government agreed to help.

The Coast Guard, which patrolled Prince William Sound, promised to install a state-of-the-art radar tracking system to monitor every ship coming in and out of the area. In 1972, Interior Secretary Rogers Morton vowed that all tankers would have special safety equipment, and all of them would be built with double hulls. Just in case some accident did occur, the consortium of pipeline companies known as Alyeska promised that a full crew of cleanup and containment experts would be on alert twenty-four hours a day, every day of the year. The crew would be able to reach the site of any spill and begin taking action within five hours.

The Coast Guard insisted that no ship would be allowed to enter the sound unless the captain had been fully certified to navigate those waters. The oil companies promised that only their most trusted, experienced officers would command oil tankers on the Valdez route.

Captain Joseph Hazelwood seemed like a perfect candidate for the job: as old-timers would say, he had the sea in his veins. Exxon had recruited him as one of the top graduates of the tough, prestigious New York Maritime Academy, and he quickly demonstrated an uncanny skill at handling the company's ships. In 1978, at age thirty-two, he became Exxon's youngest tanker captain. A decade later, he was commanding the *Valdez*. In 1987 and 1988, Exxon singled him out for its coveted "safety and service" award; his Coast Guard license gave him "unlimited pilotage," the highest possible rating for a skipper in Prince William Sound.

About nine P.M. on Thursday, March 23, the *Exxon Valdez* pulled out of the Alyeska oil terminal and eased into the narrow estuary that led out to Prince William Sound. It rode low in the Arctic water, its storage tanks heavy with 51 million gallons of North Slope crude. Following Coast Guard regulations, a local port pilot, Ed Murphy, was on board for the short passage through the twisting harbor waterway known as the Valdez Narrows. A launch followed behind to ferry him back to shore.

At 10:58, as the ship cleared the narrows, Murphy handed the bridge over to Captain Hazelwood. He would later recall feeling slightly nervous about leaving the *Valdez* under Hazelwood's command: he could smell alcohol on the captain's breath. But the veteran skipper seemed perfectly alert and well in control of his faculties. Besides, Murphy knew that Hazelwood was an outstanding seaman and that he'd sailed this route dozens of times before.

What Murphy didn't know was that Hazelwood had a history of drinking problems. Twice in the past five years, he'd been convicted of driving under the influence of alcohol near his home on Long Island, New York. But apparently, nobody reported the incidents to the Coast Guard. The authorities who issue licenses to drive motor vehicles had no formal process for passing on that sort of information to the authorities who issue licenses to pilot oil tankers. In fact, in 1986, a court ordered Hazelwood to enroll in a drunk-driving program—but granted a time extension on the grounds that he was a sea captain, and was often away from home.

Exxon shipping officials, on the other hand, were well aware that their star skipper had trouble with alcohol. In 1985, at the urging of his boss, Hazelwood took some time off and checked into a hospital for treatment. Company policy encouraged troubled employees to come forward and seek help, so Hazelwood wasn't penalized. Shortly after he completed the twenty-eight day rehabilitation program, he was reinstated as a captain.

Over the next two years, as Hazelwood commanded an East Coast Exxon tanker, supervisors kept an eye on him, paying a visit every few months to evaluate his progress. He was still officially under observation when he was transferred to the *Valdez* in 1987. By then, he had started drinking again, and although he was far from discreet, none of his superiors seemed to have noticed.

On the afternoon before the *Valdez* set sail, Hazelwood went ashore and spent several hours in a local saloon, drinking straight vodka with a member of the crew. Nobody at the bar found his presence unusual: alcoholic beverages were strictly forbidden on board oil tankers, so the vast majority of the sailors who came into port took advantage of the opportunity to put a few down before heading out to sea.

When Hazelwood returned to the tanker, port security guards noticed nothing unusual. He navigated the long, narrow, sloping gangplank without missing a step.

March was often a stormy month in Prince William Sound. But on Thursday night, the sea was perfectly calm, the skies clear, the visibility excellent. A few miles into the sound, the ship's radar picked up a cluster of icebergs in the outbound shipping lane, dead ahead. That was entirely normal—icebergs often drifted into the sound in the spring. Hazelwood discussed the situation with his third mate, a junior officer named Gregory T. Cousins, who normally served watch under the captain's direct supervision. Cousins wasn't certified to pilot a tanker through the sound, but around eleven-thirty, Hazelwood left a set of clear, specific orders, handed over the bridge and went below to his private quarters.

Hazelwood later insisted he thought the latest regulations allowed junior officers to take the bridge a few miles out of port, if the weather conditions were good. Under normal circumstances, the second mate, a seasoned, fully certified officer, would have been available, but Exxon had recently cut the size of its tanker crews to save money, and the second mate had been working long hours to compensate. He was in his bunk, exhausted and fast asleep.

At 11:38, the *Exxon Valdez* radioed Coast Guard traffic control and asked permission to move into the inbound lanes to avoid the ice. The entire channel was empty, so the duty officer granted the request. It was a simple, routine maneuver, the sort of thing tanker captains did all the time in Prince William Sound.

But for some reason, the *Valdez* kept veering off course, heading for Bligh Reef, a well-known hazard that lay about five miles beyond the channel markers. Nobody in the Coast Guard radar station noticed any problems; the duty officer would later say that the ship had vanished from the screen. Other officials would testify that tanker paths were rarely monitored when traffic in the sound was light.

Just before midnight, Cousins noticed that an island near the reef was looming too close off the bow. Nobody would ever be able to reconstruct exactly how the tanker had gone so far off course, but apparently it was a combination of minor mistakes. Cousins hadn't noticed that the automatic pilot was on, interfering with manual controls. The helmsman, who had been promoted from a food server and room steward just a year earlier due to high crew turnover, may have turned the wheel the wrong way. A bow lookout might have noticed the problem earlier, but thanks, perhaps, to the staff cuts, none was on duty at that hour.

Cousins ordered the rudder turned hard to the right, but by then it was too late. Just after midnight, he called below and warned Hazelwood that the vessel was in serious trouble. He was still on the phone when the *Valdez* hit a string of submerged rocks. With its tremendous momentum, the tanker kept moving forward, shaking and twisting as the rocks tore into the steel hull. A few minutes later, it smashed into Bligh Reef and came to a grinding halt.

At 12:28, Hazelwood notified the Coast Guard that the tanker had run aground, and was starting to leak oil.

Thursday night was the start of a long Easter weekend for Alyeska employees, and by the time the terminal superintendent learned of the spill, a good percentage of his cleanup crew had left town. Round-the-clock operations had been scrapped back in 1980, in a round of corporate budget cuts. There were other problems, too. The main barge that carried the cleanup gear was under repair, and the equipment had all been removed. Only one of the employees who showed up at the dock in the middle of the night knew how to run a forklift, so the reloading process went slowly. By the time the containment operation was up and running some fourteen hours after the accident, it would be much too late.

Oil was gushing out of the grounded tanker at a frightening rate, bursting to the surface in three-foot geysers. Almost two million gallons an hour were escaping from a series of huge gashes in the ship's steel skin. For all its fancy gear, the *Exxon Valdez* lacked what may have been the single most important safety system available: a double hull. The oil companies had managed to block federal regulations requiring the extra layer of steel, arguing that the cost would be excessive. In the case of the *Exxon Valdez,* it might have been a few million dollars—about what the company was losing every hour that the gooey black hemorrhage continued.

Ultimately, Exxon would spend more than a billion dollars trying to undo the damage. Some of that would come from the public treasury: the company would write off a sizable part of the loss as an income tax deduction.

As the oil slick spread rapidly across the sound, the extent of the ecological tragedy became more and more alarming. The timing couldn't have been worse. In just days, the second-largest salmon run in the world was expected to begin. As many as fifty million young Alaska salmon would be making their way down the hundreds of freshwater streams that emptied into the sound. With all that oil in the water, the fishermen couldn't place their nets, but that was the least of the problem. The heavy tar in the unrefined oil was trapping some of the more volatile petroleum products, preventing evaporation and causing the toxic material to dissolve into the water. The effect could wipe out much of the microscopic algae and plankton that formed the base of the local food chain. The salmon—and all the rest of the marine life—could be virtually wiped out.

The geography couldn't have been much worse, either. The sound was enclosed on three sides, so instead of drifting out to sea, all the oil drifted into shore.

Of course, the vast numbers of birds and mammals that swam or dove for food in the sound would quickly be soaked with oil, and in many cases, that would be a death sentence. The oil destroyed the insulating ability of feathers and fur, leaving the oil-soaked creatures to freeze in the icy water. As the oil hit the beaches, the damage would spread to other species.

Under tremendous political pressure, Exxon vowed to clean up every last drop of the spilled oil, but within days the task had become almost hopeless. The spill stretched for miles in every direction, and the winds and tides were spreading it farther by the hour.

At first, the company tried to set the oil on fire, hoping to burn most of it off the surface of the water. But the project didn't start until almost two days after the spill, and by then, the weather was changing. Gale-force winds and choppy seas made burning impossible. Any thought of containment was ridiculous, and chemical dispersal agents proved largely ineffective.

Even loading the remaining oil from the *Exxon Valdez* hold into another tanker proved difficult. The process had to be stopped when a leaky hose began forming another oil slick a few hundred yards from the wreck.

Months later, when the totals started to arrive, the damage would be found staggering. More than a thousand miles of beaches and coastline would be fouled. More than 200,000 birds and at least 1,000 otters would be killed. And the long-term impacts had only begun.

*   *   *

At Three Mile Island, Pennsylvania, Livingston, Louisiana, and Prince William Sound, Alaska, the same basic pattern applied: when the job becomes routine, people get complacent, and accidents happen. When big accidents happen, everything seems to go wrong at the same time, and every little mishap interacts with the others in ways that nobody could ever have predicted. No system of backups, controls, and safety monitors can prepare for that possibility. The oil spill would reinforce a fundamental message of the environmental movement: nothing that human beings do is ever completely foolproof. That's a fact of life, and no amount of money or technology will ever change it.

The accident at Prince William Sound also showed the folly of terms like "containment" and "restoration." Once eleven million gallons of oil got out of the ship's tanks, there was nothing anyone could do to recover it. Ecologically, the damage was so far-reaching, there was no conceivable way to repair more than a fraction of it. Physically, the mess was so enormous and the contamination so profound that even $1 billion in Exxon resources couldn't make more than a dent in it. In many cases, the best the company cleanup crews could do was to try to sop up the sticky black tar with big paper towels. When that didn't work, some crews just blasted the oil off the rocks and sand with high-powered hoses, sending it right back into the sound.

The pictures, descriptions, and video footage of the devastated wasteland that was once among the world's most stunning natural resources sent shock waves across the nation. Like the Santa Barbara oil spill twenty years earlier, it spurred extensive legislation, some of which might help make the odds of another tragic accident a little bit lower.

Calls to "Boycott Exxon" sent consumers scurrying across the street, to the Chevron and Mobil stations—but the boycott had no effect on overall gasoline consumption.

Within a few days after the accident, the shipping lanes were open in Prince William Sound, and oil from the Alaska pipeline was flowing freely from the terminal at Valdez. The supply of crude was barely interrupted. It's unlikely a single major refinery came even close to running short.

But on Wall Street, oil prices rose sharply—and even before the impacts of any supply reduction could possibly be felt, consumers were paying more at the gas pumps. Within three days of the accident, the wholesale price of unleaded regular shot up almost two cents a gallon—and in some cases, the retail price rose by more than twice that amount.

Even by oil industry standards, it was quite a spectacular windfall.

84

THE $6 BILLION MISTAKE

May 19, 1989
Seabrook, New Hampshire

Very few demonstrators showed up to mark the event. After thirteen years of drama the final act was almost routine: the Nuclear Regulatory Commission approved a low-power license for Seabrook Unit One by unanimous vote. Soon, the reactor would heat up, and the $6 billion power plant would start to generate electricity.

The owners of the New Hampshire nuke didn't emerge victorious, and neither did the national proponents of nuclear power. Cost overruns had driven the Public Service Company into bankruptcy. Soaring electric rates had spurred the conservative state to rebellion. The second Seabrook reactor unit had been canceled.

After all the angry environmental protests, the future of nuclear power had come down in large part to money. In the battle of the bottom line, the reactors invariably lost.

In Columbus, Ohio, Harvey Wasserman took the news of Seabrook in stride. He'd recently moved back home to take over the family business. Some days, he worried about mail-order shoe sales as much as nuclear power.

Looking back, Wasserman agreed the antinuclear movement had lost the battle of Seabrook. But by almost any standard, he argued, it won the national war. When Sam Lovejoy climbed the tower in Montague, Massachusetts, the nuclear industry was talking about building a thousand plants in the United States. Fifteen years later, only ninety-eight were finished. Not a single new reactor had been ordered in more than a decade.

And despite hundreds of tense confrontations at plant sites around the United States, nobody had ever been killed in an antinuclear protest, and very few had been seriously hurt. By that standard, the strict discipline of the activists' nonviolence code had been a remarkable success.

In Concord, New Hampshire, Rennie Cushing was still on the case. When the Clamshell Alliance disintegrated, most of its members went back to school, started careers, or found another cause. Cushing just shifted gears. Unlike many of his former colleagues, the New Hampshire native had no problem taking the antinuclear campaign into a different forum. Before long, he was running the Campaign for Ratepayers' Rights, a fairly traditional consumer group that worked to keep Public Service Company's customers from paying the full cost of the $6 billion nuclear mistake.

And he was still watching David Souter.

In 1984, Cushing sat in the hearing room of the New Hampshire Supreme Court as Bob Backus, the lawyer for the ratepayers' group, prepared to deliver an oral argument against a Seabrook rate hike. The state Public Utilities Commission had agreed to let the Public Service Company pass much of the plant's cost onto its customers, and Cushing's group had appealed. To his astonishment, just as the argument began, Justice Souter stood up and left the room.

The court later noted that Souter had recused himself from the case. He gave no explanation, but under New Hampshire law, none was necessary: Supreme Court justices had the sole discretion to decline participation in cases that might pose a conflict of interest. As far as Cushing could tell, Souter was following the strictest possible interpretation of the law—the only apparent conflict was the fact that Souter had worked many years ago for a private firm that represented PSCO on unrelated cases.

Without Souter, the five-member court split, 2–2. That meant Cushing's appeal was denied.

A year later, Cushing and Backus were back at the Supreme Court, this time arguing a case with serious, lasting implications for utility regulation in New Hampshire. PSCO wanted to sell $525 million worth of "junk bonds"— unsecured corporate notes—to finance the completion of the Seabrook plant, and wanted to charge the ratepayers to guarantee repayment on the bonds. The proposal contradicted every legal precedent in New Hampshire history. Like most states, New Hampshire only allowed utilities to charge ratepayers for finished projects and safe, reasonable investments. When the Public Utilities Commission approved the plan anyway, Cushing and Backus took it to court.

On January 31, 1986, the New Hampshire Supreme Court issued a ruling upholding the junk-bond deal and overturning more than one hundred years of precedent. The landmark decision split the court, 3–2. When Backus read the majority opinion, he knew at once who had written it—the language, style, and argument were vintage David Souter. Virtually every other lawyer and legal scholar who reviewed the case would later agree.

But in a highly unusual, perhaps unprecedented move, one of the most important rulings ever issued by the New Hampshire Supreme Court remained officially unsigned. For some reason, Souter, who had mysteriously recused himself from the last Seabrook case, didn't put his name on the opinion.

A year later, when President Bush startled the nation by naming Souter to the U.S. Supreme Court, reporters from all over the country would call Bob Backus to ask about the reclusive New Hampshire jurist. Backus would tell them the same story, over and over: Souter had written the majority opinion overturning a century of legal precedent to save a nuclear power plant—and in a radical departure from traditional practice, he never put his name on it. As far as Backus knew, none of the reporters ever pursued the story.

Cushing would go much further. As the Senate prepared to consider the nomination, he would send all his files to the staff of the Judiciary Committee—the information about Souter's bizarre actions at Seabrook in 1977, the police informants in the Clamshell Alliance, and the depositions suggesting that the justice had lied under oath. But none of the senators would ever ask Souter about any of Cushing's charges. Souter was confirmed easily; nothing from the Clamshell Alliance files ever saw the light of day.

85

THE EMPIRE
STRIKES BACK

May 31, 1989
Tucson, Arizona

Dave Foreman was fast asleep when four armed men showed up at his door. The neighbor's dog liked to bark at all hours, so Foreman had taken to wearing earplugs to bed; he never heard the loud knocking, or the sound of his wife Nancy ambling out of the kitchen and down the hall, wondering aloud just who in the world was paying a visit to their quiet suburban neighborhood at seven o'clock on a Wednesday morning. He didn't hear Nancy's startled gasp as the men, clad in full body armor and brandishing pistols, burst into the modest brick house and raced toward the bedroom. He didn't hear them shout out their identification: "FBI!"

Foreman didn't hear a thing until the federal agents were standing over his bed, pointing their .357 magnums at his face and ordering him to stand up and put his hands behind his back. The agents dragged the stark naked Foreman to his feet, handcuffed him, and read him his rights. They let him pull on a pair of shorts before marching him out to the car.

Foreman was halfway to the federal detention center in Phoenix, 120 miles from home, before he managed to get the agents to explain what the early-morning raid was about. According to the United States government, Dave Foreman had bankrolled a clandestine, sophisticated plot to blow up simultaneously the electrical supply lines to three major nuclear reactors, cutting off the power to the cooling systems and potentially triggering a series of devastating accidents that would leave tens of thousands dead and render huge urban areas uninhabitable for centuries.

The crime was conspiracy to destroy a government energy facility. The maximum penalty was five years. Foreman was forty-three; five years in a federal prison sounded like a very long time. Once the shock wore off, though, he settled down. The founders of Earth First! had always assumed that the government would come after them sooner or later. In a strange way, it was almost a compliment: Earth First! had obviously made the government angry—angry enough to justify a full-scale campaign to put the group's most prominent spokesman out of commission for a while.

Maybe for quite a while.

The FBI's timing was ironic. After almost a decade at the forefront of the radical wing of the environmental movement, Foreman had recently announced he was retiring from any leadership role in Earth First! He wasn't even an active member anymore. The group was losing its sense of purpose, he told his friends. It was getting too caught up in issues that had nothing to do with wilderness.

By 1989, a lot of Earth First! members spent as much time discussing animal rights, feminism, paganism, labor unions, and Native Americans as they did saving the forests and deserts. Earth First! was starting to look like the Clamshell Alliance. Gatherings were bogged down in endless debates over process. A new wave of activists tried to make the group toe a "politically correct" line. It wasn't what Foreman had in mind when this whole thing began—and it wasn't much fun anymore.

Foreman was a reluctant radical. He always said he was forced into ecological warfare by the clear and present danger to the natural world, and if the crisis could be resolved, he would just as soon go back to his nice, southwestern Republican redneck life. Foreman's Earth First! was never meant to be a broad coalition of revolutionaries carrying the banner of social transformation. Earth First! was about saving wilderness, about keeping people and progress from ruining the rest of the planet. Maybe some people would get hurt along the way—a few loggers might lose their jobs, or get cut by a broken band saw that hit a twenty-penny nail in the trunk of an old-growth redwood tree. Nobody wanted that to happen, but Foreman wasn't going to go into mourning if it did. As far as he was concerned, the lives of the men who cut down trees were no more important than the lives of the trees they cut, or the owls that lived in them, or the fish that spawned in the shade of their branches. There were times when Foreman was ready to argue, not entirely tongue in cheek, that famine and plague were just nature's way of stabilizing a biological system grown way beyond its carrying capacity.

It's no wonder Dave Foreman made the FBI nervous. Anyone who argued that human beings weren't the most important creatures on the plane was playing with political fire. More important, perhaps, the Earth First! message was spreading. Acts of "ecotage" were cropping up all over the country, many of them spurred by stories of Foreman's antics. His 1985 book *Ecodefense: A Field Guide to Monkeywrenching* was a best-seller in some parts of the country, and it taught thousands of would-be ecoteurs the tricks of the trade. After years of routine condemnations, some of the more mainstream environmental groups were even starting to acknowledge the value of Earth First! in the movement, if only because it made them look reasonable.

Anyone who knew Foreman would realize that a plot to set off a triple meltdown in a string of nuclear power plants was completely out of character. A meltdown would be an environmental catastrophe, reaching up and down through every level of the Earth's ecosystem. Human casualties would be the least of the problem. But the charges could generate a lot of bad publicity for the radical environmentalists. If the government could get a conviction, Foreman and the cause he represented would be badly discredited.

Dave Foreman was obviously an important symbol—the FBI had gone to tremendous lengths to set up his arrest.

Peg Millett wasn't thinking about the FBI when she met a wiry, bearded man named Mike Tait at Earth First!'s July 1988 Round River Rendezvous in Washington State. Millett, a friendly, outspoken woman who worked for Planned Parenthood in Prescott, Arizona, had been involved with Earth First! for years. She always made new friends at the rendezvous; that was one of the reasons she kept attending them.

Tait told Millett he was a dyslexic Vietnam vet recovering from a battle with alcoholism. He seemed emotionally fragile, in need of support. She spent several nights talking with him, and when he showed up a few months later in Prescott, saying he was working as a carpenter, she started taking him around to local bars and introducing him to her friends.

One of the people he met was Mark Davis, a thirty-eight-year-old martial artist and woodworker with an intense personality and a passion for wilderness. Davis and Tait hit it off right away, and before long, they were spending a lot of time together, working out on the punching bag in Davis's makeshift gym, eating lunch at a local sandwich shop and cruising the funky dance clubs in the rough-and-tumble town. They often talked about environmental politics.

Before long, Davis and Millett told Tait their biggest secret: the two were serious monkeywrenchers. They'd already sabotaged the chair lift at a ski resort that was under construction on sacred Native American land, and they had some other plans for the future. Tait made a confession of his own: he was an ardent tree-spiker, and was ready to escalate the struggle. He would love to join the Prescott monkeywrench gang.

If Davis and Millett had any doubts about their new friend, they were erased soon afterward, when Tait helped Davis break into an Arizona Public Service Company storage yard on the outskirts of town and steal some thick steel plates, the kind the power company used to hold together its giant electrical transmission towers out in the desert. Davis wanted to know how long it would take for a blowtorch to cut through the plates; that would give him some idea how much time he would need to sever the legs of one of the towers. If all went according to plan, Davis, Tait, Millett, and another friend, named Marc Baker, would head into the desert late in May and topple the transmission facilities, cutting off the power to the Central Arizona Project pumps.

Tait seemed entirely committed to the project—at one point, he even tried to convince Davis to use dynamite instead of a blowtorch, explaining that he knew a network of Vietnam vets with access to the explosives. He seemed happy with his life in Prescott, too—for the past eight months, he'd been dating a friend of Millett's, and the relationship was looking pretty serious.

None of Mike Tait's new friends had any reason to believe he was actually a high-ranking agent in the Phoenix office of the FBI.

Shortly after sundown on May 30, 1989, some fifty federal agents—on horseback, on foot, and in a pair of military-style assault helicopters—converged in the Arizona desert, near the tiny town of Wenden. At 8:15, one of the agents fired a series of red phosphorus flares into the moonless night sky, signaling the members of an FBI SWAT team, dressed in black jumpsuits and equipped with infrared night-vision goggles and semiautomatic weapons, to move in for the bust.

This small army of law-enforcement officers surrounded the four suspects, who were crouched beneath a Central Arizona Project transmission tower. Davis and Baker tried to run, but they couldn't move very quickly: Davis was wearing a welder's mask, and both men had strapped wooden planks to their shoes to avoid leaving footprints. They were apprehended easily, and taken into custody.

Somehow, Millett managed to escape arrest, elude a dragnet of bloodhounds and an airborne search team, and make her way back to Prescott. She was picked up the next day at the Planned Parenthood office where she worked.

Mike Tait simply disappeared.

Tait's real name was Michael Fain. He was a veteran FBI operative, the highest-ranking agent in the Phoenix office, and an expert at undercover work. For more than two years, Fain had been involved in an FBI investigation into the downing of several major power lines in central Arizona and the sabotage of a chair-lift pylon at the Fairfield Snow Bowl.

By the time Davis and Baker were busted in the desert, the investigation had become the largest operation the Phoenix bureau had ever undertaken. Fain spent a year undercover, often wired with a recorder, and collected more than a thousand hours of taped conversations. Several phone taps, personally authorized by Attorney General Edwin Meese, filled hundreds of additional hours of tape.

Long before the spectacular nighttime bust, the FBI had collected enough evidence to make a pretty solid case against Davis, Millett, and Baker. If the power-line and ski-lift vandals were all the government wanted, the investigation could have ended months earlier.

But Fain continued his charade, encouraging the other three to go through with the Central Arizona Project caper. In fact, his encouragement went even further. He urged his coconspirators to branch out beyond Arizona, beyond the hated CAP, and strike directly at the heart of a far more deadly environmental plague: the nuclear power and weapons industry.

Fain, Millett, and Davis began discussing a plan that was far more ambitious and radical than anything the monkeywrenchers of Earth First! had ever attempted. The ecoteurs would simultaneously knock out the power supplies of three major nuclear installations—the Palo Verde power plant in Arizona, the Diablo Canyon power plant in central California, and the Rocky Flats nuclear weapons facililty near Denver, Colorado. When the lights went out, the pumps that ran the cooling systems would shut down, and backup generators would have to kick in. The generators were probably old, and badly maintained; some of them might not work right away. The resulting chaos, the theory went, would demonstrate just how vulnerable these technological nightmares were to natural disasters, human error, or a deliberate terrorist attack. It would highlight the awful risk of continuing to operate plants that could poison hundreds of square miles of land and kill millions of people if something as simple as a backup generator should fail at the wrong time.

Fain promised to contact some people he knew in California and Colorado who would be willing to help. And he suggested that they might be able to raise a little extra money for the action, by contacting Dave Foreman.

Davis barely knew Foreman. They'd met once or twice, in passing, but they didn't travel in the same circles. Millett and Foreman had become acquainted during the Earth First! rendezvous, but she wasn't exactly a close friend, either. Still, Davis had good connections in the Arizona environmental community; he made a couple of calls, and on March 29, he and Fain made a trip to Tucson, where Foreman gave them a grand total of $580. A few weeks later, they talked him into forking over another $100.

Fain reported all of this to his contacts in the FBI. He made it clear that he didn't see Foreman as a major kingpin in the conspiracy; he didn't think Foreman was particularly violent or dangerous, and he didn't think Earth First! was a serious threat to society. At one point, he told another agent that Foreman's group was "low-budget, and I really don't look for them to be doin' a lot of hurtin' of other people." With the tape recorder on his body inadvertently running, he explained that Foreman "isn't the guy we need to pop, I mean, in terms of the actual perpetrator. This is the guy we need to pop to send a message."

When the handcuffed Dave Foreman arrived in Phoenix to be fingerprinted, booked, and put into a federal holding cell, United States Attorney

Stephen McNamee was ecstatic. He called a press conference immediately, and announced that a major terrorist ring had been broken. It was, he proclaimed, "a significant development for law enforcement." Bail was set at $50,000.

Foreman demanded his right to make a phone call, and dialed a number in Jackson, Wyoming. Gerry Spence, the famous, flamboyant cowboy lawyer came on the line. He had only one question for his prospective client: "Will this slow you down, or make you less active?"

Foreman said no, and Spence booked a seat on the next flight to Phoenix.

86

THE COLOR OF MONEY

August 1989
Rochester, N.Y.

The national news media took little notice of the announcement. Only trade journals like *Advertising Age* gave it much attention. New car models got limitless hype; new computers were always news. Plastic bags were a very different story.

But while none of the reporters were looking, Mobil Chemical, a branch of the giant oil company, introduced something truly remarkable to the great American market: biodegradable Hefty garbage bags.

At first glance, the new bags were just like the old green ones that had been around for years. The cardboard box told a different story, though. It carried the word "degradable" in a prominent position, where no super-market shopper could miss it. Company chemists knew the label wasn't precisely accurate, not in a scientific sense, but the marketing experts weren't concerned about details. A few small competitors were making "environ-mentally sound" garbage bags, and they were selling like low-fat cheesebur-gers. Mobil didn't want to miss any of the action.

The "degradable" bags, it turned out, were something of a gimmick. A special resin coating made the plastic sensitive to sunlight; after a few days of direct exposure, it would break down into tiny fragments. The fragments were still plastic, of course, but they were harder to see. If the bag wound up buried in a landfill, like most garbage did, it would never get enough sunlight to make it disintegrate anyway.

But for millions of consumers, any product that claimed to be environ-mentally safe was suddenly becoming the first item off the store shelf. A "green consumer" wave was sweeping the nation. In almost every city and town, shoppers were searching supermarket aisles for household cleaning supplies, beauty aids, and even food that carried some sort of ecological label. A deodorant that wouldn't hurt the ozone could sell for a good bit more than the old-fashioned competition, and shopkeepers wouldn't be able to keep it in stock. Recycled paper towels, biodegradable soap, organic chickens, fruits grown without pesticides . . . in the course of a few short years, environmental concerns had given rise to a whole new line of consumer products—and spurred an industry potentially worth many billions of dollars.

Ironically, one of the most important factors in the rise of the "green consumer" was a growing national crisis brought on in large part by the same relentless consumerism: Garbage.

Garbage had been a low-level problem for decades, but it didn't attract much national attention until the summer of 1987, when a barge loaded with three thousand tons of Long Island, New York, trash captured the morbid fascination of millions as it circled the globe for months in search of a receptive port. Three countries and six thousand miles later, the scow came back to its point of departure, where local authorities had to face an ugly question that was instantly on everybody's mind: where is it all going to go?

A year later, the nation watched with disgust as television cameras showed a tide of used hypodermic needles and other hospital waste washing up on the popular beaches of New York and New Jersey. The land couldn't hold any more; the sea was sending it back. In a blisteringly hot summer, with global warming in the headlines and the fear of blood-borne disease stamped firmly on the public consciousness, the images of "Needle Beach" had an impact that rattled the nation. The whole world seemed to be swimming in some kind of deadly swamp—a chemical leak at a Union Carbide plant in India had killed thousands in their sleep; a nuclear reactor in the Soviet Union had contaminated crops all over Europe; the ozone hole was letting cancerous rays bombard the planet; the air and the water was heating up; oil was destroying the Alaskan wilderness; dolphins were getting slaughtered on the evening news.

The politicians couldn't seem to do much of anything about it—and to a growing number of disenchanted voters, they were all starting to sound the same. It was easy to feel powerless at the polls; the supermarket was a different story.

In December 1988, the Council on Economic Priorities published a slim, pocket-sized paperback entitled *Shopping for a Better World*. The staff of the nonprofit group analyzed the environmental, social, and political records of more than 130 companies that produced major supermarket products, and compiled a scorecard for each one. To the surprise of almost everyone, particularly the authors, the book was an instant success. An initial press run of 150,000 sold out in months, and before long, half a million copies were on the streets.

Consumers couldn't seem to get enough information on how to vote with their money and how to make a difference in their everyday lives. When a tiny publishing company in Berkeley, California, introduced an inexpensive paperback called *50 Simple Ways to Save the World,* it became a national best-seller.

For environmental groups that understood how to use it, the wave of consumer interest was a natural political opportunity. The garbage barge and the needles on the beach had created an opening for a radical-sounding but entirely reasonable message: no form of waste disposal will solve the problem; the only way to clean up the landfills and oceans is to produce a lot less trash. Lois Gibbs had been making that point for years. In 1989, she organized a campaign to boycott McDonald's hamburgers on the grounds that the giant chain wrapped all of its sandwiches in Styrofoam—a source not only of garbage but of considerable toxic waste. The "Ronald McToxic" campaign had an almost immediate effect. Early in 1990, company president Edward Rensi announced that the fast-food chain would switch to paper wrappers. The plastic shells, he insisted, were just as environmentally sound—but "our customers don't feel good about it, so we're changing."

Lois Gibbs and the Council on Economic Priorities weren't the only ones who noticed what was going on in the marketplace. Hundreds of small entrepreneurs and big business executives saw it, too, and they started to respond with a barrage of new products and services. As a few activists tried to point out, "green" shopping wasn't always a black-and-white decision.

There were, for example, those biodegradable Hefty bags.

At first, the trash bags were a tremendous hit—they offered consumers the best of both worlds, a chance to continue wrapping household garbage in a convenient, lightweight disposable bag, and the satisfaction of knowing the plastic wrapper wouldn't clog the local landfill for the next hundred years. But the closer the experts examined the matter, the worse Mobil's claim began to look. Among other things, a self-proclaimed "garbologist" from the University of Arizona reported that his landfill excavations had turned up thirty-year-old newspapers—still in good enough shape to read. The message undermined everything Mobil was trying to promote; if old newspapers never died, then degradable plastic wasn't worth the extra nickel.

When several environmental groups, and eight state attorneys general, began discussing legal action, Mobil quickly backed down and agreed to pull the "degradable" label off the new Hefty bags. Company spokesman Allen Gray summed up the oil industry's position nicely: "Nothing degrades in a landfill," he told reporters. "Degradability isn't a solution to the waste problem—only a diversion."

87

SHOWDOWN AT PINEY CORRAL

October 13, 1989
Twin Falls, Idaho

Sunrise was a few minutes away when Ranger Don Oman pulled his truck up to the Piney Cabin Corral. Even in the pitch dark, he could hear the cows—hundreds of them, stamping and lowing in the chilly morning air. He didn't bother to guess the exact number: as soon as it was light, he'd take a formal count. In the meantime, he was happy to wait where he was; he was expecting trouble, and his armed escort still hadn't arrived.

Rancher Mike Poulton had been there for hours. He didn't expect much company—just a couple more cowboys, coming to help sort out the herds. It was an annual ritual. All summer long, local ranchers let their cattle loose to graze on the vast federal lands of the Sawtooth National Forest. When the grass started to turn brown, and the night air got cold, cowboys would drive the animals toward Piney Cabin, where the ranchers would pick out their brands and prepare the herds for winter. Everybody knew that, in theory, forest rangers monitored the process, to make sure the private cattle ranchers weren't overgrazing the public land; everybody also knew that, in practice, senior Forest Service officials told the rangers to leave the cowboys alone. It had been that way for generations.

When he saw the unfamiliar truck, Poulton put down his work and walked over to see who had business this far from the beaten track, this early in the morning. "Ranger Don Oman, Forest Service," the visitor said, shaking Poulton's hand. "Mike Poulton," the cowboy responded, moving to within an inch or two of Oman's face. "And just what the hell are you doing here?"

When Oman explained that he was conducting a cattle count, Poulton flew into a rage. "You're messing with our livelihoods," the angry cowboy screamed. "I'm warning you—don't get in our way."

"I won't be in your way at all," Oman continued, trying to keep calm. "I'm just here to count cows."

And that, Oman suspected, was exactly what Poulton was afraid of.

Since the age of thirteen, Don Oman had wanted to be a forest ranger. Back in Montana, where he grew up, he'd read a book called *Wild Animals of the Rockies: Adventures of a Forest Ranger,* with a hero named Ranger Bill Rush—a brave, honorable man who caught poachers and saved wildlife starved out by cows or left to die by thoughtless hunters. It was the kind of job a boy could dream about.

Seven years later, after completing a degree in forestry, Oman got his first job with the Forest Service. And in 1986, with a personnel record full of flattering commendations, he was assigned to the job of district ranger for the Twin Falls region of the Sawtooth National Forest, five hundred square miles of high plains east of Boise.

National forests weren't like national parks. Although many were open to recreational hikers, hunters, and boaters, they were mainly used for logging, grazing, and mining. In fact, much of the 191 million acres of national forest wasn't even forest. On the high plains of Montana, Wyoming, Idaho, and eastern Oregon, forest rangers patrolled through miles of wild grasses and sagebrush, not stands of Douglas fir. And on those rangelands, the Forest Service issued permits to ranchers, who bought the right to graze a specified number of cattle there. And when it came to enforcing the permits in the Twin Falls region, Ranger Don Oman was the law.

Don Oman had no problem with grazing on Forest Service land—he knew it was a valid, legal use of land set aside for such purposes. He wasn't a troublemaker, either. Soft-spoken, almost professorial in manner, Oman was a devout churchgoer, a Sunday-school teacher, and a devoted father and family man. But he knew the basic charter of the Forest Service: the land shouldn't be grazed, or logged, or hunted faster than it could restore itself. A ranger's primary job was to make sure the land was preserved for future generations—and on the 320,000 acres of the Sawtooth National Forest, that hadn't happened in years.

By 1989, people familiar with the Sawtooth didn't refer to it as high plains. They called it high desert. The cattle had chewed and trampled much of the life out of the land.

Oman had seen some bad grazing practices before, but nothing like what he saw the day he started his job in the Sawtooth. Grasses were chewed down to the root, and inedible weeds had taken over. In the places most heavily grazed, erosion had formed dry, lifeless gullies and ravines. Worst off were the riparian systems, the sensitive areas surrounding streams and rivers.

Biologists measured the well-being of an area by the condition of its riparian systems, and every riparian system Oman came across in the Sawtooth was severely damaged. Ranchers, in violation of their permits, had allowed their herds to trample freely along the riverbanks. As the cattle kicked dirt into streambeds and flattened the banks, the waterways became wider, shallower, warmer, and slower. Water evaporated in the hot sun. In some cases, damaged streambanks allowed water to seep outwards into the surrounding area like a ruptured blood vessel. Other streams disappeared entirely, leaving behind shallow, muddy bowls.

In the damaged streams and rivers, wildlife was dying. Some fish asphyxiated in the mud-choked waters. Others, notably trout, were very sensitive to changes in water temperatures, and began dying in the warm, shallow streams. Large animals had trouble finding enough fresh water on their travels over large stretches of plains. After a few months on the job, Oman knew he'd have to crack down on the illegal grazing practices, before the land was literally mauled to death by too many cows.

The single worst part of the district was an area called the Goose Creek Allotment, where five ranchers known as the Wild Rose Grazing Association had permits to run their cattle. Oman first visited the site in November, four weeks after all the cows should have been rounded up and taken off the land for the winter. The previous ranger had given Wild Rose a two-week permit extension, something Oman considered astounding; the regular grazing-season practices alone had apparently been unacceptable. But even after that extension ended, the Goose Creek Allotment was full of cows. Oman contacted the ranchers, who told him that they'd never had to worry about seasonal deadlines before; they just left all their fences open, and waited until the weather was cold enough that the cows would leave the high country of the open range and return to the warmer, low-lying ranches on their own.

Oman announced that the old methods had just ended. The ranchers were stunned. When he began demonstrating that he was serious, they began gearing up for a fight. In the spring of 1989, after three years on the job, he filed the first enforcement action against a rancher in the history of the Sawtooth Forest; it was a relatively mild sanction against a truly flagrant scofflaw, but the message went out loud and clear: Don Oman was trouble. The ranchers began to prepare for the modern equivalent of an old-fashioned range war.

The ranchers who worked this area had been known to threaten forest rangers in the past. At one point, a cattleman had even warned some of Oman's colleagues that he "wasn't above shooting a man out of the saddle." One of the Wild Rose cowboys had recently demanded that Oman climb out of his truck and settle a dispute with a fistfight.

When he began to suspect that the Wild Rose ranchers were grazing more cattle than permitted on the Goose Creek Allotment, he considered conducting a full-scale roundup—sending a Forest Service crew out to capture every single beast on that part of the range. But he was trying to avoid confrontations, so he decided to take a much milder step. He'd wait until the cowboys were doing the roundup themselves and just show up to count heads.

But even that, he feared, could trigger a violent response—and out on the range, Oman would be badly outnumbered. So he took what seemed like the only prudent step: he arranged for adequate backup. And on the morning of October 13, as Mike Poulton's manner became increasingly belligerent, the ranger hoped that his troops weren't far behind.

But as Oman and Poulton argued, four more federal trucks were working their way up the dirt road that led to Piney Cabin Corral. Two of the trucks carried armed federal agents, and another had a special agent from the Targhee National Forest who was also packing a gun. They'd followed Oman closely out of town, but had been forced to drop back when they pulled off the paved highway and his oversized truck started kicking up so much dust that it blinded anyone less than a few hundred yards away. In the confusion, they'd missed an unmarked turn, and lost a few minutes circling back. They arrived just as Poulton's diatribe was degenerating into a string of obscenities; when he saw the first agent walk toward him, pistol prominently displayed in a police-sytle ammunition belt, the cowboy backed off.

In fact, once the tension of that encounter was over, the entire count went smoothly. The ranchers were cool, but polite; Oman's team members did their best to stay out of the way and avoid delaying anyone's work. It was all over by sundown.

The numbers convinced Oman that he'd been absolutely right about the Goose Creek Allotment. One rancher, for example, held a permit for grazing 122 mature cows; Oman's team counted 115, well within the limit. But they also counted 127 calves that were less than a year old. If the rancher had actually brought in his entire herd, then his cattle were reproducing at a rate that defied all the known laws of livestock biology. Perhaps somebody had tipped the ranchers off to the surprise count; perhaps a few hundred cows had been hiding somewhere off in the hills, and the cowboys just couldn't find them.

Either way, Oman wasn't about to press his luck; he left without issuing a single citation. But he left behind a lot of angry ranchers who were already plotting their next move.

88

DIRTY JOB

February, 1990
Sebastopol, California

George Alexander shoveled sawdust out behind the lumberyard. It was chilly and damp in February; in a few months, it would be boiling hot. Either way, the job was rotten. And after all he'd been through, eight dollars an hour was an insult.

Three years after the mill accident, the scars on Alexander's face and body had healed. But underneath, the man who became a pawn in the lumber industry war against tree-spiking was feeling pretty sore.

At first, the men from Louisiana Pacific had been about as gracious as bosses could be. When the band saw exploded, the company made sure he was getting the best medical care money could buy. Through the long weeks he spent in the San Francisco hospital, while the surgeons tried to put his face back together and repair his neck and the muscles in his arms and legs, Louisiana Pacific took care of his rent and made sure his wife and their newborn child had plenty of food on the table. The company executives even came to visit once he was well enough to sit up and talk.

But he didn't like the way they were talking. The company saw the accident that almost cost Alexander's life as a great public relations tool: the Earth First! types were making a lot of headway with their campaigns to save the redwood trees, but the press, the politicians and the public would lose sympathy quickly if the group could be linked with an act that maimed a nice young millworker with a nice young family to support. All Alexander had to do was join an industry team on a national speaking tour, and show off his scars, and tell all the reporters how close the radical tree-spikers had come to taking his life.

"You know," Alexander finally told the corporate executives, "I don't have any love for Earth First!, and I don't have any sympathy for people who spike trees.

"But I don't have much sympathy either for people who force their employees to work with old, defective equipment just to save a few dollars. I'm not really sure who to blame." The executives went away.

After a while, the doctors pronounced Alexander fit to go home. As soon as his body stopped aching and he was able to walk, he showed up at the sawmill to ask for his job back. And suddenly, the bosses weren't such nice guys anymore.

No, the manager said, Alexander couldn't go back to work on the floor. No, there wasn't another job for him that paid the same sort of salary. No, he didn't have seniority anymore—after all, he'd been out of work a long time. No, there wasn't much chance of a job like his old one opening up very soon—the economy was bad, and the whole industry was cutting back. None of the other mills would be hiring, either.

Of course, the manager said, Alexander could always shovel sawdust, for eight dollars an hour, out back in the yard.

89

NOT GUILTY

March 22, 1990
Anchorage, Alaska

The defendant showed no emotion as the jury foreman prepared to deliver a verdict in what had to be the most celebrated drunk-driving trial in history. From his calm, impassioned expression, Joseph Hazelwood looked almost resigned to whatever fate the court had to offer. His life was already in ruins. On a chilly Alaska night just short of a year ago, in the dark waters of Prince William Sound, the obscure sea captain made a mistake that turned him into one of America's most wanted criminals.

Hazelwood wasn't a lawyer, and he'd never been trained in public relations. When the *Exxon Valdez* ran aground on a reef, he didn't think about lawsuits or spin control. He did what good ship captains have always done: he took responsibility. Like almost everything that happened that day, it came back to haunt him.

A senior Exxon shipping official testified that Hazelwood placed a call over the ship's radio just a few minutes after his *Valdez* plowed into the rocks and informed the company that he had been in command and should be held accountable. A Coast Guard blood test showed the captain had been drinking, and even Hazelwood agreed he had left the bridge while the giant tanker, loaded to the brim with oil, plowed at full speed through the dangerous, rocky waters.

For a while, he even seemed to be a fugitive from justice—shortly after he turned the stricken vessel over to a salvage team, he left Valdez and flew home to New York. He didn't realize that state authorities had issued a warrant for his arrest. Alaska police conducted a well-publicized manhunt for several days before anyone had the sense to make a call to Long Island.

Meanwhile, every newspaper, magazine, and television station in the world seemed to be after him. When news of his drinking problem surfaced, it was all over the headlines. Soon, reporters were showing up in front of his modest suburban house picking through his garbage and, in one case, rifling his mail. He shaved off his beard in a desperate attempt to change his appearance, but it made little difference. He was a marked man—"the architect," one prosecutor put it, "of an American tragedy."

When news of the Coast Guard blood tests came out, Exxon instantly dismissed Hazelwood and stopped giving him legal support. The Coast Guard revoked his captain's license. More than a hundred individuals and organizations filed lawsuits demanding he compensate them for damages. When the police arrived at his Long Island house and hauled him back to Alaska for trial, bail was set at $1 million. The way one judge put it, Hazelwood was responsible for the worst environmental disaster since the bombing of Hiroshima.

But after seven weeks of testimony, a jury of six men and six women from the state where the disaster occurred reached a very different conclusion. On the three main charges—criminal mischief, piloting a vessel while intoxicated, and reckless endangerment—the panel found Hazelwood innocent. He was guilty only of negligent discharge of oil, a misdemeanor which carried a maximum sentence of ninety days in jail and a $1,000 fine.

The way the jurors explained it, Hazelwood was just a convenient scapegoat. He might have made an error in judgment, like most people do at some point in their lives, and he might have been a little careless on the job. But there were supposed to be all sorts of monitors, backup systems, and safety procedures in place to prevent one human being from causing such a horrible tragedy—and none of them had worked. The Coast Guard and the oil companies had made commitments that they couldn't or wouldn't keep. The federal government had promised regulations that were never enacted or enforced. Exxon and the pipeline consortium had been cutting corners to save money at the expense of safety standards. None of those things were Captain Hazelwood's fault.

Hazelwood wasn't responsible for approving the Alaska pipeline or allowing oil exploration along the North Slope, either. And he wasn't responsible for a national energy policy that continued to promote expanded fossil fuel production and ignore conservation, or a national economic policy that put cheap gasoline and oil company profits ahead of environmental protection, or a national political failure to develop alternatives to the private automobile.

He wasn't responsible for the fact that government and industry continued to pretend that fancy technology could somehow eliminate the human factor from the environmental equation.

Although his family and friends broke into cheers, the former star skipper

90

BUILDING BRIDGES

April 10, 1990
Arcata, California

All day long, the telephone was ringing off the hook. CBS News, the *San Francisco Chronicle,* Associated Press, *The New York Times*—it seemed like every reporter in the country wanted an interview. The Humboldt County headquarters for Redwood Summer was starting to feel like the White House press room. Mike Roselle looked over at Judi Bari and smiled. Anything that gets this much attention can't be such a bad idea, he thought to himself. Particularly when Earth First! was trying to launch the biggest wilderness campaign in history.

All day, he took the same question, and gave the same answer. Yes, he said, the reports were true. One of Earth First!'s most visible leaders had given up his most famous tactic. Mike Roselle wasn't spiking trees anymore.

Yes, Roselle agreed, the organization had always insisted on "no compromise in defense of Mother Earth." Yes, he was making this move in an effort to build connections to the lumber mill workers. If somebody wanted to call it a compromise, fine. Under the circumstances, Roselle could live with that.

Without really trying, Roselle had become one of the most important figures in the fastest-growing social movement in the United States of America. He had discovered he was a born organizer, a person who could generate ideas, develop strategies, and direct campaigns almost effortlessly. He was also a natural politician: no matter how heated the debate, he managed to bring the opponents together—and more often than not, convince them to do things his way.

But above all, he was willing to change his mind. For ten years, Roselle's

403

life had been in an uproar. The events around him moved so quickly he could barely keep up. Change was the only constant. So when Judi Bari started making a case for renouncing tree-spiking, Roselle listened. When she made a good enough case, he agreed to go along.

Roselle knew a radical idea when he heard one, and what Bari was doing was about as as radical as anything he could imagine. She was trying to build a new chapter of Earth First!—one made up of organized workers in the timber industry. The chapter was both an environmental action group and a union local, affiliated with the Industrial Workers of the World, the legendary Wobblies who had long held down the left flank of the labor movement. Bari called it IWW–Earth First Local 1; its logo was the old Wobbly black cat, brandishing a new monkeywrench. You didn't get much wilder than that.

Judi Bari was a child of the 1950s. She dated football players at a middle-class Baltimore high school, enrolled at the University of Maryland, and expected to graduate in four years and start a family. Then she discovered the Vietnam War, Karl Marx, and Chairman Mao; after three years of college, she dropped out to join the proletariat. Bari landed a job in a grocery-store bakery, and quickly got fired for writing an antiwar slogan on the icing of a cake. After the union filed a grievance, Bari was reinstated; soon, she was a devoted labor activist.

In the early 1980s, Bari moved to Mendocino county and got married. The marriage broke up after a couple of years, leaving her with two young daughters to support. She went to work as a carpenter, and soon was earning $12 an hour as a crew boss.

In 1988, she helped build a vacation home for a wealthy executive, who wanted his walls fashioned from the finest old-growth redwood. When Bari asked the contractor where the wood had come from, he told her to treat it with respect—those trees, he said, were more than a thousand years old.

Bari had never been comfortable with all of the clear-cutting she was seeing in Mendocino, but this time, something in her Marxist consciousness snapped. She realized she was using the destruction of an ancient forest, an irreplaceable public resource, to serve the fancy of a man so rich he could afford to build a house that he would use only a few days a year.

As quickly as she had become a union advocate, Bari became a devoted environmentalist. She saw the two groups as natural allies, with a common political enemy. The split between environmentalists and loggers, she decided, wasn't a natural state of affairs. There were powerful forces at work here, forces that had a lot to gain from the conflict. Expose those forces, and you could start to break down the whole corrupt system that exploited the working class and plundered the natural world for the private profits of the few.

*   *   *

Bari had her work cut out for her. By 1988, the hills of the Pacific Northwest were a war zone, and none of the combatants showed much interest in negotiating a truce. In every town, the lines were sharply drawn. Since the Earth First! crew arrived in Oregon five years earlier, the middle ground had been shrinking.

The ancient redwood and pine forests were everybody's last stand. For three generations, the tough, independent people of southern Oregon and northern California had built their lives on the logging trade. Now the decent jobs were drying up; the mills were laying off workers by the hundreds. Since 1982, thirteen thousand jobs were lost in the timber industry; before long, some people feared, entire communities—an entire way of life—could be wiped out.

The way a lot of mill workers saw it, the problem was simple: all the best lumber was suddenly off-limits. The environmentalists had used the courts and the political system to restrict logging in more and more of the national forests; now even the private land wasn't safe. Not since the government took an interest in those owls.

For three generations, environmentalists had fought to save the thick, deep, primeval forests that held the oldest, biggest living things on Earth. By some measures, they were fairly successful. More than four million acres of old-growth forest had been set aside for preservation in national parks and wilderness areas. But they lost far more along the way. About 90 percent of the ancient forests had been cut down since the first white settlers arrived in the Northwest 150 years ago.

Outside of the protected areas, just three million acres were still intact, scattered across dozens of public and private stands in California, Oregon, and Washington. For environmentalists, that forestland was more than just a place of natural beauty: it was home to thousands of different plants and animals—and at least one endangered species.

The northern spotted owl was a shy, reclusive predator that lived in the branches of tall redwood trees, far from the noise and interference of human civilization. For years, environmentalists had warned that the owls were losing the last of their habitat, and the population was shrinking; in 1988, the U.S. Fish and Wildlife Service agreed. Federal biologists decided that the owls were threatened by continued old-growth logging; only a few thousand nesting pairs remained, the scientists reported, and unless steps were taken to save them, the entire species could become extinct.

Under the Endangered Species Act, that was a mandate. Federal and state officials were required to adopt immediate plans to identify and save the remaining habitat of the spotted owl. Anywhere that the elusive birds were nesting was off-limits—to developers, road-builders, and, most important, loggers.

To the timber industry, the Fish and Wildlife ruling was a bombshell. With the price of logs at an all-time high, those three million acres of old-growth represented tens of millions of dollars—and for a company like Pacific Lumber, that revenue was absolutely critical.

For 125 years, Pacific Lumber was a stable, locally owned operation, a mid-sized company that took a fairly conservative, long-term approach to timber management. Palco, as the company was known, owned the largest tracts of private old-growth in the Northwest, but wasn't rushing to cut it all down—the firm had a policy of "sustainable" logging, which meant it harvested lumber only as fast as new trees could grow to replace it.

Then in 1985, Maxxam Corporation, a giant Texas conglomerate, seized Palco in a leveraged buyout deal. To finance the purchase, Maxxam issued high-interest junk bonds. The payments on the bonds were massive, dwarfing Palco's normal cash-flow, but the corporate financiers in Texas had a plan that would stop the flow of red ink and make the merger profitable. The conglomerate planned to "liquidate" Palco's most valuable asset: the last of the old-growth timber.

Selling the logs would be easy. The U.S. market was healthy, but more important, the Japanese economy was soaring, and Japan was desperate for lumber. Of course, shipping freshly cut logs to Japan didn't help employment in the United States. Tree-cutting provided only a small fraction of the timber industry jobs; most of the work came after the trees were cut, in the mills, pulp factories, and distribution networks that turned the logs into finished products and brought them to the market. But shipping the whole logs suited the Texas executives just fine: with the heavy debt burden, Palco had to cut back its workforce anyway.

Bari began working the Palco mills, inviting the employees to join her new IWW local. At first, she didn't talk much about the environment—her arguments were based on traditional labor issues. In its mad rush to cut more logs with fewer people, she said, Palco was risking its workers' safety. The mills were becoming sweatshops. Salaries were too low, and benefits were awful. Meanwhile, the fat cats in Texas and the investment bankers on Wall Street were making a killing. Slowly, the message began catching on—at Palco's main plant in the town of Scotia, workers began putting out an underground newsletter, challenging the company's handouts. The official Palco employee newsletter was called *Timberline;* the IWW activists called their version *Timber Lyin'.*

In the meantime, the timber industry cranked up a full-scale public relations campaign to promote continued logging. Bumper stickers began appearing urging people to "save a job, kill an owl." Roadside posters described lumberjacks as an endangered species. A sixteen-page color brochure from the Southern Oregon Timber Industries Association proclaimed the battle as "East Coast environmental groups against freckle-faced loggers."

In Washington, Senator Hatfield pushed through a bill halting all environmental appeals against Forest Service timber leases.

The backlash against environmentalists had an ugly side, too. In the summer of 1989, a logging truck ran Judi Bari's car off the road, leaving Bari and her two young daughters with concussions, whiplash, and glass cuts.

It was time for a dramatic move. On March 4, 1990, opportunity knocked, in the person of a mill worker named Gene Lawhorn.

Bari met Lawhorn at an environmental law conference while she was in the midst of organizing the Earth First! Redwood Summer project. Redwood Summer was the most ambitious campaign Earth First! had ever attempted. It was based on the model of one of the most dramatic, successful political organizing efforts in modern U.S. history—Freedom Summer, the 1964 civil rights campaign that brought thousands of college students from across the nation to register black voters in the Deep South. The way Roselle and Bari envisioned it, Redwood Summer could be a watershed event in the environmental movement, with college students and other sympathizers showing up by the busload to join a series of rallies, marches, and civil disobedience actions to save the old-growth forests.

The prospect of a few thousand college students invading the hills of northern California in the middle of the logging season had industry officials up in arms—and a lot of local residents were starting to join them. Tensions were high; both sides were braced for confrontation. The ghost of Freedom Summer—and the three young civil rights workers who lost their lives to racial violence—hung heavy in the air.

When Bari was invited to speak at the environmental conference, the sponsors told her she'd be sitting on a panel with a mill worker. It made her a bit nervous—she knew anyone who agreed to appear with her in public was either an industry plant, or was risking his job. But Lawhorn seemed to have no fear of his employers. He said he supported Redwood Summer, believed in what Bari was doing, and wanted to get loggers and environmentalists together.

But he had one serious problem, and wanted Bari to confront it right then and there. Timber workers were terrified by tree-spiking; you could argue all day about the companies' responsibilities, he said, but the jobs they had were already dangerous, and the spikes made the situation worse. Nobody wanted to be the next George Alexander.

The only way Bari's alliance would ever work on any sort of scale, Lawhorn told the audience, was for Earth First! to renounce tree-spiking. Now.

He turned to his copanelist, and in a pause that seemed to last forever, Judi Bari made a decision. "In that case," she said, leaning toward the microphone, "I hereby renounce tree-spiking." The room erupted in applause.

Nothing Earth First! had ever done attracted as much media interest as the statement Roselle and Bari issued a few days later. At the time, Roselle was surprised—tree-spiking was only a small part of Earth First! politics, and he didn't see why a change in position was such a big deal. But as time passed, he realized why Bari had set off such a furor. The entire timber industry strategy relied on keeping the loggers and mill workers at war with the environmentalists.

Just months after helping Earth First! make an important.connection with lumber mill workers, Bari had an unusual accident that would never be fully explained. A crude bomb exploded under the seat of her car, leaving her badly maimed and very nearly taking her life. Police claimed that Bari might have planted the bomb herself; she and her friends were all carefully investigated, and ultimately cleared. No charges were ever filed. As far as Bari's lawyers can tell, no lumber company official was ever considered a suspect.

91

"DEAR MR. O'REILLY..."

April 12, 1990
Washington, D.C.

Anthony J. O'Reilly, the flamboyant multimillionaire chairman of H. J. Heinz, Inc., strode into a rented conference room at the Marriott Hotel to confirm, with a smile, the success of a consumer boycott aimed at one of his biggest products.

O'Reilly shook hands with Sam LaBudde and looked out with obvious surprise at the sea of reporters who had arrived from all over the country for the hastily called press conference. More than forty camera crews were on hand; dozens of newspaper writers were holding notebooks and tape recorders. "What are we doing here," O'Reilly whispered to one of his executives, "signing an arms control agreement?"

The news wasn't quite that big, but it was still a major event. Heinz, the Pittsburgh food-processing giant, owned the nation's largest tuna canning company, which sold its wares under the name of Starkist. And from that moment on, O'Reilly announced, Starkist would stop buying tuna from fishing boats that participated in the killing of dolphins.

For Heinz, it was a terrific public relations coup, a chance to stake a solid claim to the growing market for products prepared with at least some degree of sensitivity to the natural environment. It was also a chance to deflect the growing criticism leveled at tuna processors by a wide spectrum of people who had seen the graphic images of death captured on Sam LaBudde's videotape.

And it was a way for O'Reilly, a fifty-four-year-old Irishman who owned a twenty-eight-room mansion, to avoid facing an incessant barrage of emotional postcards from the friends and acquaintances of a fifteen-year-old high school student in Cape Elizabeth, Maine.

*   *   *

Joel Rubin learned about the dolphin killers in his freshman biology class. Dr. Paul Hackett, who taught science to most of the three hundred students at Cape Elizabeth High School, thought anyone old enough to learn about the natural world was old enough to understand what human beings were doing to disrupt it. When Hackett read about LaBudde's video, he contacted the Earth Island Institute, which was happy to send him a copy. Earth Island had made saving the dolphins its biggest priority; with the advice of Herb Gunther, a protégé of Jerry Mander at the Public Media Center, a public-interest ad agency in San Francisco, the institute had begun running full-page boycott ads urging people to write to the chairman of H. J. Heinz to demand an end to the slaughter.

Early in the spring semester, Hackett showed the tape to his classes. Almost everyone who saw the bloody footage was upset. Rubin was outraged.

Cape Elizabeth wasn't the sort of town that fostered radical politics. An old New England community, it moved to the slower rhythms of a time when everybody in town knew everybody else, and all of them worked hard to earn an honest living. Once Rubin set his mind to something, he didn't like to give up, and the day he saw the LaBudde film, he set his mind to stopping the slaughter of the dolphins.

Rubin hadn't seen the Earth Island ads, so he didn't know where to write to O'Reilly. But with Dr. Hackett's help, Rubin learned that Heinz was the nation's largest tuna processor, and he tracked down the home addresses of the three top Heinz executives. Then he began writing postcards. The messages were all simple—"Please," one said, "use your authority to stop the useless killing of these gentle, intelligent creatures. After all, they have done you no harm"—and he used them over and over again. He lined up his friends and neighbors, too; all they had to do was copy down the message— or write one of their own—and the address, and sign their names on the bottom line.

At the O'Reilly residence, the emotional, handwritten appeals started filling up the mailbox.

While Joel Rubin was writing his postcards, another effort to contact O'Reilly was happening on a very different level. A fashion model named Ani Moss had been staying in a San Diego hotel in June 1989 when LaBudde showed his film to an International Whaling Commission meeting. Moss loved dolphins, and she happened to catch the film. It drove her to tears, and when it was over, she introduced herself to LaBudde. When he explained that Earth Island was focusing its efforts on a boycott—and particularly, on Heinz—she agreed to help.

As it turned out, her husband, Jerry Moss, was a recording industry mogul who had founded A&M Records; he had heard O'Reilly speak and thought the man sounded reasonable. For months, he tried to set up a meeting; in

December, O'Reilly agreed. Moss made his case over lunch at Heinz corporate headquarters. O'Reilly was impressed by his visitor's low-key approach, and promised to get back to him.

But O'Reilly never called back, and by April 1990 Moss was ready to give up. Earth Island had announced that April 14 would be National Dolphin Day, featuring a series of events aimed at Heinz. Out of the blue, a Heinz representative contacted Moss April 3, and after a meeting, they called Earth Island. Several late-night negotiating sessions led to a deal: Heinz would adopt a safe dolphin plan, and Earth Island would endorse it fully. The announcement would come two days before National Dolphin Day, April 12.

By April, Joel Rubin had learned that Earth Island was the center of national dolphin activity. When his parents decided to take the family on a spring vacation to Hawaii, he begged them to stop overnight in California so he could visit the Earth Island office and talk to the people who worked there. When they agreed, he ran to the phone to make an appointment. Brower and his colleagues were thrilled to hear from the energetic high school student, and were happy to set up a meeting. The only day Rubin could do it was April 12.

Joel Rubin had no idea why the entire office seemed to be in such a frenzy when he showed up for his appointment. The phones were ringing off the hook; everyone seemed to be dashing around like crazy. Brower was caught in some important event, and couldn't make the meeting. David Phillips, the executive director, was in Washington for a press conference. When the entire remaining staff filed into the conference room for a meeting, Rubin followed along, and quietly took a seat in the back.

The meeting started off with an important announcement. Just minutes ago, a staff member said, Heinz had agreed to stop patronizing the dolphin killers. Phillips was still tied up at the press conference, but a *New York Times* reporter had just called to pass along a great story. The chairman of Heinz had mentioned some kid in New England who had been writing all these postcards. Heinz executives had received hundreds. "Listen to the stuff this kid was saying," the staffer continued, and began reading from his notes:

"Dear Mr. O'Reilly: Please use your authority to stop the useless killing of these gentle, intelligent creatures. . . ."

Joel Rubin smiled. "After all," he said to himself, "they have done you no harm."

92

TWENTY YEARS AND COUNTING

April 22, 1990
Washington, D.C.

All over the country, the weather was perfect. A warm sun and gentle breezes brought perfect spring temperatures to almost every city in North America. It was a great day for a fair, a parade, a rally on the Washington Mall or concert in Central Park or a lakeside festival in Chicago or a nature walk in southern California. It was a great day for Earth Day.

From the giant stage at the steps of the Capitol, Dennis Hayes looked out over a crowd that had to be close to 300,000 strong. The mall was a sea of people, stretching for more than a mile, all the way down to the Washington Monument. Reports were already coming in from other parts of the country, where the turnout was every bit as spectacular: 200,000 in Boston; 100,000 in Chicago; at least half a million in New York; fifty thousand in San Francisco, the only place in the country where it was raining.

The news from the rest of the world was good, too. All told, Hayes figured, somewhere around 200 million people in 136 countries were celebrating the twentieth anniversary of the event that helped spark the modern environmental movement.

Earth Day 1990 had turned out to be the largest grassroots demonstration in history. He was glad he'd decided to do it.

Boston, Massachusetts

The cherry blossoms and magnolias were in full bloom along the Charles River as a crowd four times as large as organizers had predicted arrived at

412

the Esplanade bandshell for a concert celebrating "music for the Earth." Flanked by representatives of some of the most established religious groups in Boston, Andras Corben Arthen, codirector of the pagan EarthSpirit Community, began a convocation ceremony that would celebrate the planting of a young oak tree.

"Blessed be this tree whose branches reach out to the heavens and whose roots embrace the heart of the Earth," Arthen intoned, pouring a pitcher of water into the ground. "May all who find comfort in its shade, who eat of its fruit, and who are inspired by its beauty be reminded of their own rootedness in the Earth, and their connection with all of nature."

New York City

At ten o'clock in the morning, the air in Times Square was actually clean. No traffic was allowed within several blocks of the area; Sixth Avenue was closed all the way from Forty-second Street to Central Park for an environmental exposition that featured everything from giant sequoia seedlings to composted manure. Volunteers hung burlap sacks on every corner to collect garbage that would be sorted and recycled the next day.

As Mayor David Dinkins took the stage, a strange hush fell over the rapidly swelling crowd. New York seemed to be a city transformed. No fights, no rioting, nobody trying to heckle the mayor. No trash in the streets. No exhaust fumes.

"Today," the mayor announced with a smile, "we are all green."

A few blocks away, the Roman Catholic archbishop of New York, John Cardinal O'Connor, sounded an unusual note in his Earth Day homily from the altar at St. Patrick's Cathedral.

"The Earth exists for the human person, and not vice versa," he proclaimed. Rather than focus on "snails and whales," he said, good Catholics should be concerned about "the sacredness of the human person."

Earth Day, he told his congregation, should not be "a pagan Easter," or "an attack on the establishment, left over from the Vietnam War." And it certainly shouldn't be "a political charade designed to promote nontruths," like the notion that overpopulation was a cause of the world's problems.

"I do not think," he concluded, "that the total number of people in the world is an ecological and environmental problem."

Chicago, Illinois

After a week of cold, wintry weather, the morning broke clear and warm on the shores of Lake Michigan. The Lincoln Park playing fields were packed with people who seemed eager to take advantage of the first real day of spring. After an opening ceremony led by a group of Native Americans, the crowd danced to the music of popular singer Michelle Shocked and laughed at the humor of comedian Aaron Freeman. In between, they stood quietly and listened as keynote speaker Lester Brown, of Washington's Worldwatch Institute, delivered some sobering news.

Since the first Earth Day, Brown said, the population of the world had grown by 1.6 billion people—an increase of more than 50 percent. In the meantime, the rich topsoil that farmers all over the globe depended on to grow the crops that could feed all those people was disappearing at the rate of 24 billion tons a year.

"This decade is a decade of reckoning," he warned. "If we don't reverse present trends, there is a very real possibility that environmental degradation will lead to economic decline by the end of the century."

Islamorada, Florida

Like Richard Nixon two decades ago, President Bush had declined to participate in the Washington Earth Day events. Bush may have vowed to be the "environmental president," but right now, he was on vacation, enjoying a fishing trip in the Florida Keys.

Early in the morning, he took a break from his leisure activities to present a citation to a volunteer group called "Reef Relief," which installed buoys to which boats could tie up just off the shore of the Keys, to avoid dropping their anchors onto the only living coral reefs in coastal waters of the United States. Shortly afterward, he held a brief press conference, and dropped an environmental bombshell.

A long-awaited White House plan for new offshore oil drilling leases, the president told reporters, would probably not include any of the sensitive areas along the Florida coast. But he pointedly ignored the other major area where new drilling had once again been proposed, after years of congressional restrictions: off the coast of California.

As the president dashed off to his waiting boat, reporters pressed his aides for more details, and quickly discovered the not-so-subtle implication of the president's remarks. If Bush had his way, the California coast would be the nation's next major domestic oil field.

Washington, D.C.

Denis Hayes had thought long and hard about what he was about to say. Twenty years of history didn't fit into a few neat little sound bites. And yet, he knew, the words he chose were immensely important. Hayes was the person who organized the first Earth Day, and he was the person who decided, after talking to dozens of old friends and associates, to try to pull it off again twenty years later. The world had gone around a few times since the brash young graduate student walked into the offices of Senator Gaylord Nelson looking for a low-level job with the Earth Day operation and wound up running the show.

The movement that grew out of the early 1970s had an astonishing record of accomplishments. But the problems he identified back then were still very real, and some of them were just getting worse. In retrospect, he decided, twenty years wasn't much time to change the world. In reality, he knew, another twenty years might be too late.

"Let the historians record," he began, "that on Earth Day, 1990, the people heard the cry of the Earth, and came to heal her. . . .

"Twenty years ago, on Earth Day 1970, I delivered the following lines on the mall in Washington D.C.:

" 'Industry has turned the environmental problem over to its public relations departments. It would appear that things are already fine, and will soon be perfect. But the people of America are still coughing. And our eyes are still running, and our lungs are still blackening, and our property corroding, and we're getting angry. We're getting angry at half-truths, angry at semitruths, and angry at outright lies.'

"The lies of 1970," he explained, "seem pale before the lies of 1990.

"Twenty years ago, Earth Day was a protest movement. We no longer have time to protest. The most important problems facing our generation will be won or lost in the next ten years. We cannot protest our losses. We have to win.

"This week, I've been asked hundreds of times, 'What should people do?'

"The answer is to look inside your own moral compass, and follow it. Don't let others define what you are. Don't let advertisers mold you. Don't let zealots ensnare you. Don't let conventional wisdom trap you.

"Look deep inside yourself and ask yourself what's right. Whether you are buying a car or casting a ballot, choosing a job or planning a family, weigh carefully the consequences of your choice.

"Remember, you are part of something larger."

Santa Monica, California

News traveled fast in the Electronic Age. Less than an hour after President Bush had spoken to reporters in Florida, stories were out on the national wires, and journalists on the West Coast were asking local politicians for a response. California assemblyman Tom Hayden heard the word just as he was preparing to address some 35,000 people at the Santa Monica Pier. With the gentle roar of the Pacific surf echoing behind him, Hayden interrupted his prepared remarks and led the crowd in a loud and lengthy chant: "No Drilling!"

Fifty miles north, in the hills above Santa Barbara, Bud Bottoms was blissfully unaware of what the president had said. The man who fought to Get Oil Out after the oil spill twenty-one years ago wasn't going to rallies much anymore.

Bottoms still cared about environmental issues, he told his friends, but he was tired of politics, and since the offshore drilling had stopped many years ago, he didn't seem to have much inspiration anymore. Besides, he was busy with a new career. He carved statues of dolphins. Everyone seemed to love them.

PART 11

GIANTS AND THE EARTH

There was a time when meadow, grove, and
stream,

The earth, and every common sight,

To me did seem

Apparelled in celestial light,

The glory and the freshness of a dream.

It is not now as it hath been of yore;—

Turn wheresoe'er I may,

By night or day,

The things which I have seen I now can see no

more.

—*William Wordsworth*

By the time Denis Hayes organized the second big Earth Day, millions of American consumers had gotten a powerful message: bigger wasn't always better. Cars and computers had gotten much smaller. Communications had effectively shrunken the globe.

And the environmental movement had become a behemoth. In 1980, fewer than 5 million Americans belonged to any of the nation's major environmental groups. A decade later, more than 25 million were active, or at least dues-paying, members of dozens of organizations ranging from the cautious and conservative National Wildlife Federation to the unruly and unpredictable Earth First!

Those members meant serious money. Door-to-door canvassers, direct-mail solicitations, telemarketing appeals, and slick media ads raised tens of millions of dollars a year, which paid for lawyers, lobbyists, and campaign organizers. It also meant bigger, more diverse staffs, with broader interests and agendas and bigger management problems—and sometimes, ironically, it meant slower, less-effective political action.

As Harold Gilliam, the veteran environmental activist and columnist for the *San Francisco Chronicle,* would write on the Sierra Club's hundredth anniversary:

"Looking back on its first 100 years of monumental achievements, the [club] is confronted with the agonies of growth that afflict any organization, from a corporation to an empire, when its size becomes a handicap.

"It's been a long haul for the club, expanding its purpose from saving Yosemite to saving the planet, and along the way something got lost. Until the 1960s, the club leadership consisted principally of companions of the trail—Californians, mountain-lovers who had known each other for decades and shared views on how to accomplish their conservation goals. . . .

"With the explosive nationwide membership increase that accompanied the rise of environmentalism, the club has acquired both locally and nationally a diversity of leaders with different backgrounds, adversarial temperaments and widely varying points of view on strategy. An increasing proportion of time and energy has necessarily been devoted to reconciling differences, to internal organization, to the corporate-type structure that requires a large bureaucracy devoted to operating the machinery.

"Another danger . . . is that the club has become too cumbersome to act decisively, too involved with the government establishment, too prone to compromise environmental goals to get some legislation. . . ."

And as environmentalists elected the first outwardly sympathetic president since Jimmy Carter, the challenges that faced major national groups in the late 1970s—and caused some of the most dramatic splits in the movement—would inevitably arise again. This time, though, the critics would have a particularly sharp question to ask the leaders, many of whom had been around during the Carter years:

Have you learned the lessons of history—or are we doomed to repeat it?

93

THE LONE RANGER

August 24, 1990
Twin Falls, Idaho

The headlines called him everything from a Nazi storm trooper to a latter-day Lone Ranger. He was featured in *People* magazine and the Sunday *New York Times*. Over the past few months, Don Oman, the soft-spoken forest ranger who dared to count cows, had suddenly become national news.

But the biggest story of all never made the front pages. The cattle industry had demanded that Oman be fired for the crime of enforcing the law—and the people who ran the Forest Service had secretly agreed to go along. An internal investigation by the Agriculture Department's inspector general confirmed the whole scheme; it even revealed that an aide to one of Idaho's senators had been present at the meeting where the plan was hatched. There were allegations that the secretary of agriculture was also involved.

And as Oman sat in his office and read the 313-page inspector general's report, he realized that nobody in Washington was going to do anything about it.

Oman's surprise cattle-count back in October 1989 hadn't turned up any violations, but it stirred up a huge political furor. Nobody had ever done anything like that in the Sawtooth National Forest. Within a few days, the Idaho Cattle Association had cranked up a media campaign, and the papers were filled with indignant comments from ranchers who had used the public land with impunity for more than a century. The *Western Livestock Journal* called Oman's action a "Gestapo cattle count," reporting that "a disputed number of armed Forest Service agents swooped down on a cow camp in southern Idaho Oct. 13." The journal said that "an airplane was used to assure that all cattle were counted," and complained that "all were intimidated by the behavior of the ranger and of the special agents on the scene. . . . The 30 people in the camp that morning included a number of women and children."

The way Oman remembered it, none of the cowboys had been the least bit intimidated, and the armed federal agents had spent most of the day leaning against fenceposts and dozing in the sun. The women and children had been so friendly that they offered to cook lunch for Oman's whole crew. A tiny, single-engine spotter plane had circled the range once or twice before the pilot decided there were so many trees, canyons, and shadows that he couldn't see any cows from the air anyway, and gave up. But the Idaho Cattle Association sold the same sort of account to several local newspapers, and within a few weeks, the Forest Service office was flooded with angry letters.

By November 15, 1989, when the cattle association held its annual convention in Idaho Falls, the campaign against Don Oman was in full swing—and Forest Service officials were signing on. Ray Hall, a senior Forest Service staffer from Ogden, Utah, met with several association members at the convention to discuss the cattle count and Oman's future; John Hatch, an aide to Senator Steven D. Symms, attended the meeting. Stan Tixier, the regional forester who oversaw all operations in the Rocky Mountain region, was kept informed of the details of the discussion and the agreement that emerged.

The deal was outlined in detail in a letter the cattle association's lawyer sent to Tixier on December 5. "As you know," the letter stated, "recent actions by the District Ranger on the Twin Falls Ranger District have caused a tremendous uproar within the local and national livestock grazing communities. . . . This [is] directly attributed to the presence, management style and policies of the Twin Falls District Ranger, Mr. Donald Oman.

"The Forest Service [has] admitted that there may be an irreconcilable conflict between the [ranchers] and the Twin Falls Ranger in question. Therefore, the Forest Service has committed to take action to alleviate this problem before the beginning of the next livestock grazing season.

"In addition, the Forest Service promised that any revision or negotiation of all livestock grazing agreements, grazing permit renewals, allotment management plans etc. will be conducted through the Forest Supervisors office, without the assistance of Twin Falls District Ranger [Donald Oman]."

In exchange, the letter said, the members of the Idaho Cattle Association would back off on its requests for a congressional investigation, and would "discontinue issuing press or media statements about the Piney Corral incident and encourage the same restraint from other outside groups."

Almost immediately, Oman's superiors began offering him transfers to other jobs, outside the Sawtooth National Forest. Several different positions came up in the discussions, but they all had the same basic characteristics. None were positions that carried the responsibility of a district ranger's job—and none had anything to do with livestock management. Oman politely declined the offers, saying he was happy where he was. Besides, his kids were still in school, and he wasn't ready to move to another part of the country.

Then the transfer talk started getting serious. Oman's boss told him that he wasn't communicating well with the local ranchers, that he carried too much "baggage." The message was crystal clear: Forest Service management didn't want Don Oman to be counting any more cows.

The formal policies that he had been following all along—the ones that justified his enforcement of grazing regulations—suddenly seemed to be changing, too. Shortly after the infamous cattle count, Ray Hall had sent out a written statement outlining and clarifying Forest Service policy on grazing permits, and it backed up everything Oman had done at Piney Cabin Corral. The plan, Oman was told, was to release the statement to the press, in an effort to counter some of the misinformation the ranchers had been putting out. But at 5:39 P.M. on November 16, the day the meeting took place at the Cattleman's Association convention, Oman received a terse message by electronic mail: "Ray [Hall] requests that under no circumstances should [the policy statement] be released to the public at this time. Negotiations are continuing on this issue." A note attached to the message added that "Bert called today from Idaho Cattle Assoc. meeting to reiterate this."

The crossfire was getting too heavy, and coming in from all sides. In January 1990, Oman fired back a salvo of his own. He filed a formal complaint under the federal "whistleblower" program, charging that Forest Service officials and cattle industry representatives had conspired to get rid of him.

Before long, word of the battle spread beyond Idaho. *The New York Times* sent a reporter to Twin Falls, and his story told more than a million readers how "a handful of cattlemen have squared off against a stubborn ranger in a battle over land, water and a way of life as old as the mythology of the American West." The slick, scandal-hungry *People* turned Oman into a tabloid hero, with a lengthy feature headlined "The Lone Ranger Rides Again." Environmental publications like *High Country News* and *Audubon* magazine followed Oman around the range and reported on his struggle to keep the cows and the cattlemen under control.

But Oman's fame had a price. Death threats came over the phone almost as often as calls from the news media. One local rancher told the *Times* that he wanted to slit Oman's throat. For the first time since he arrived in Twin Falls, Oman started to lock all his doors and windows at night. When he left home, he carried a gun.

While the newspapers and magazines were quoting Oman's charges, countering with the ranchers' responses and portraying the whole thing as a modern range war where it was hard to tell the bad guys from the good, the Inspector General's Office in the Agriculture Department was slowly investigating the whistleblower complaint. The process took seven months, and the final results were couched in enough bureaucratic language, but the bottom line was stunning:

"This investigation," the August 24 report stated, "has established that Mr. Oman's allegation of an agreement between regional [Forest Service] management and cattle industry interests to transfer him from his current position as District Ranger is in fact true."

There were even suggestions that the scandal reached the highest levels of the Department of Agriculture, which oversaw the Forest Service. A rancher named W. B. Whiteley, who was among Oman's most vocal critics, admitted to an investigator that he was trying to get Oman transferred by any means possible, and said he had "a personal relationship with the secretary of agriculture going back to 1957."

The Inspector General's Office stopped short of directly implicating Agriculture Secretary Clayton Yeutter or Senator Symms, saying there was no conclusive evidence that either was directly involved in an attempt to get Oman transferred. But the investigators didn't pursue the point very far— even if the secretary and the senator had played a role, the report noted, their actions would not have violated any law. Senators and Cabinet members had a legal right to get involved in almost anything the government did, including internal Forest Service personnel matters. And if a few Idaho ranchers wanted to contact a couple of powerful friends in Washington and ask them to help get a troublesome ranger fired, that was perfectly legal, too.

The report made clear that everything Oman had done in his tenure at the Sawtooth National Forest was completely in line with official Forest Service policy. It acknowledged that powerful private interests had tried to get him fired for doing his job too well, and that his superiors had gone along. In short, it said, the cattle industry was still calling the shots on the public range— and any ranger who dared to interfere was risking his career.

But it also concluded that nobody had broken any laws—as long as Oman remained on the job, none of his superiors could be cited for firing him or forcing his transfer. The report wound up on a shelf; not one person involved in the conspiracy to get rid of Oman received so much as a written reprimand. Oman had fought himself into a standoff; he had his job, but no official support. The ranchers had to put up with him, but could keep on doing almost everything they'd always done.

As far as the Agriculture Department was concerned, the case was closed. As far as the news media were concerned, the story of legally sanctioned internal corruption that subverted well-established government policy was a lot less sexy than a "range war"; if Oman wasn't getting shot or fired, there apparently wasn't much news anymore out on the high plains of Idaho.

And in the Sawtooth National Forest, a few hundred square miles of remote and starkly beautiful land owned by the American people slowly continued to decay.

94

THE HUMAN FACTOR

August 13, 1991
Prescott, Arizona

In a crowded federal courtroom high in the central Arizona mountains, five criminal defendants hugged each other and wept. A few feet away, two FBI agents stared forward, the expressionless faces they had worn for most of the two-month trial finally showing distinct signs of fatigue. In the back of the room, one of the lawyers on the prosecution team sat all alone, watching as the world-famous defense counsel, Gerry Spence, shook hands with Assistant U.S. Attorney Roslyn Moore-Silver and pleasantly said good-bye.

One of most important political trials of the new decade had just abruptly ended—and contrary to all obvious indications, the government had won.

After eight weeks of electrifying testimony that revealed the ugly, sordid details of a federal sting operation designed primarily to set up the founder of Earth First! on what were obviously false charges, the environmental activists had thrown in the towel. In a move that surprised and shocked even his closest allies, Dave Foreman had agreed to plead guilty to a crime that even the government knew he didn't commit. The best-known misanthrope of the modern environmental movement had sold a piece of his political soul to save four other people whom he barely knew—and whom, for the most part, he totally despised.

The news of Foreman's guilty plea flashed to news desks on five continents, and made headlines all over the world. In almost every case, the stories did just what the government had wanted all along: they reported that the notorious Dave Foreman had admitted to a violent felony crime. Leading media outlets like *The New York Times*, *USA Today*, the *Chicago Tribune*, and United Press International put out details of the plea bargain to millions of readers without mentioning what any reasonable person in the Prescott courtroom should have known: something was very wrong with this picture.

From the start, nobody ever seriously suggested that Dave Foreman was involved with the monkeywrenching operation that damaged part of a chair-lift apparatus at the Fairfield Snow Bowl ski resort near Flagstaff, Arizona, in October 1987. The U.S. Attorney's office had charged Foreman with a different crime—conspiracy to damage high-voltage power lines that led to a nuclear power plant. Foreman had given a few hundred dollars to one of the other activists, although it wasn't clear whether he had any idea what the money was going for. But his primary role in the conspiracy, the trial had made clear, was writing a book called *Ecodefense: A Field Guide to Monkeywrenching,* which the government contended helped encourage the four other defendants to attempt to destroy the power lines.

The trial got under way in June, before a fairly conservative jury drawn from the Prescott area, about a hundred miles northwest of Phoenix. Local motels quickly filled up, as legions of reporters arrived to cover the story and caravans of Earth First!ers arrived to watch and lend support. From the start, the testimony was riveting. FBI officials admitted that they had infiltrated Earth First! for more than three years and had known in advance about several "monkeywrenching" actions—including, apparently, the Fairfield Snow Bowl incident—but did nothing to stop the property destruction. Testimony also showed that two of the prosecution's top witnesses—Ron Frazier, a paid FBI informer, and undercover agent Michael Fain—had consistently encouraged the others to commit crimes. Frazier admitted that he taught defendant Mark Davis how to operate the cutting torch he allegedly used at the Fairfield Snow Bowl. He'd also urged the others to use explosives, something they were reluctant to do. Fain, who joined the group under the alias Mike Tait, had convinced them to approach Foreman and ask for money.

That, of course, seemed to make a strong case for entrapment—the government can't, by law, entice people into committing crimes and then arrest them for doing it. At the same time, the credibility of Frazier, whose allegations were central to the case, began to fall apart. Prosecutor Roslyn Moore-Silver filed a legal motion asking Judge Robert Broomfield to bar all information about Frazier's background from the trial; in the motion, she acknowledged that her star witness had been a heavy drug user who sold LSD for more than twenty years. And that was just the beginning: Moore-Silver's motion stated that Frazier had fired a gun at another man in an outburst of violence, and that he had been linked to unsubstantiated allegations of child abuse and even abuse of a sheepdog.

When he took the stand, Frazier insisted he went to the FBI as a good citizen, concerned that his environmentally minded friend Mark Davis was drifting toward violence. But he also acknowledged that he was angry over the fact that his onetime lover, Ilse Asplund, had left him for Davis. And he said he thought Davis was trying to control his brain through telepathic signals.

Foreman, by the accounts of most legal observers, had very little chance of getting convicted. But his codefendants, especially Davis, were in much more serious trouble. Not only were they caught in the act of attacking the utility tower, but the prosecution had strong evidence linking them to the ski resort case. If the entrapment defense failed—and it might—Davis could easily be facing twenty years. Midway through the trial, the three offered to plead guilty to reduced charges, in exchange for a promise of lighter sentences. Prosecutors almost always accepted those sorts of pleas, but this time, the federal authorities refused: the only way the government would deal, they explained, was if Foreman were part of the package.

Foreman wouldn't have to spend any time in prison; he'd just get a few years of probation. In fact, he could plead guilty to the snow bowl caper, even though everyone knew he wasn't involved, since the crime was less serious and the penalty even lighter. But the message was simple: Dave Foreman, innocent or not, would have to accept a felony conviction, allowing the government to portray him forever as a criminal and use the label to damage everything he had worked for. Or else three other people might have to spend most of their remaining lives behind bars.

It was, we finally decided, an offer he couldn't refuse.

But ironically, as Foreman's codefendants thanked him and prepared for jail sentences that would range from one to six years, Roslyn Moore-Silver looked as angry and bitter as she had throughout the trial. Perhaps she realized, as journalist Mike Lacey would later write, that "the government has prevailed, but the dignity implied by the rule of law was cheapened in the play."

95

UNCLE SAP

September 13, 1991
Washington, D.C.

The sponsor of the 1991 mining-law reform bill wasn't what you'd normally call a radical environmentalist, and his legislation was decidedly modest. But the way the western mining industry and its allies were talking, you could see the end of the world reflected in the pages of S. 433.

Senator Dale Bumpers, the genteel country lawyer from Arkansas, had sided with the Reagan administration on its early, crucial budget initiatives, and had consistently supported federal subsidies for the giant tobacco industry. For all his conservative southern gentility, though, Bumpers had a cranky, independent side; he didn't like fast-talking hustlers, and he knew a scam when he saw one. And even by the pork-barrel standards of the United States Congress, he knew the General Mining Law of 1872 was a scam of monumental proportions. When Stew Udall and Phil Hocker were looking for someone to champion their campaign to repeal the archaic measure, Bumpers was happy to oblige.

It made perfect sense. The government was losing hundreds of millions of dollars a year on the deal, and Bumpers was always looking for ways to save the taxpayers money. Besides, the law gave tremendous benefits to hard-rock miners, people who dug for gold and silver way out on the western range; the men and women who carved coal out of the Ozark Mountains in Dale Bumpers's home state didn't get that sort of advantage.

The Bumpers bill that would overturn more than a hundred years of western mining policy had worked its way through the labyrinthine system of congressional committees, and along the way, Bumpers had accepted some compromises. But the essence of the bill hadn't changed. It called for miners who staked claims on public lands to pay regular, annual royalties, and would

428

force them to file plans with the interior secretary. Most important, perhaps, the bill would require hard-rock miners on public lands to clean up any environmental mess they created, and restore the land to some semblance of its original condition.

Grass-roots activists in dozens of western communities had fought to save mountains, streams, deserts, and forests from the destruction that came with mining operations, but few had won more than token victories, and many had lost altogether. As long as the old federal mining law was on the books, the miners would have the upper hand. Ultimately, the battle had to be fought far from the remote mining sites, in the marble hallways of Capitol Hill.

Udall and Hocker were experienced Washington hands, and they'd done a stunning job of generating publicity for their cause. *The New York Times,* the *Washington Post,* half a dozen other big-city dailies, and several major national magazines had published lengthy features on the issue, pointing out some of the most blatant abuses. National environmental groups like the Wilderness Society, the Natural Resources Defense Council, and the Sierra Club were publicly promoting the Bumpers bill. A poll conducted by the National Plains Resource Council showed that even in conservative Montana, people supported mining-law reform by a margin of 12–1.

But the General Mining Law had survived since the days of Ulysses S. Grant, and it wasn't about to die easily. Like grazing, mining on public lands was a tremendous cash cow, and like the ranchers, the mining industry was a powerful, entrenched force in the politics of the western United States. The people who controlled that industry were veterans at playing the Washington lobbying game.

When the Bumpers bill was first introduced, along with a companion bill introduced in the House of Representatives by Congressman Nick Joe Rahall, the mining lobby sprung into action. Within weeks, newspaper editors from Los Angeles to Billings, Montana, were receiving copies of a slick, expensive study concluding that repeal of the mining law would cost as many as thirty thousand jobs. Each editor got a breakdown of how many jobs would be lost in his or her state—one thousand in California, for example, and five thousand in Idaho and Montana. The study received prominent coverage, and once again, the few environmentalists who even cared were forced into a defensive posture.

In the vast rural stretches of the Rocky Mountain states, mining was among the only sources of local employment; as Cecil Garland had learned twenty years earlier, that could be a serious problem. For the most part, the areas where mining went on weren't places of stunning natural beauty, either; unlike the rain forests of South America, you couldn't feature bright-colored local flora and fauna on posters and T-shirts. For the majority of environmental activists and supporters, who lived in the suburbs and cities, the whole mining issue seemed fairly abstract and remote.

On the final day of debate, Senator Bumpers presented his case to the packed chamber with the well-honed skills of a trial lawyer who had faced a hundred juries. His facts were impressive, his sources impeccable. But his emotional speech acknowledged a political problem: "I think [the mining law] is so bizarre and such a colossal scam that nobody believes it.

"This is the way it worked in 1872, and this is the way it works today," he said. "You can go out to any state, particularly in the West, and put four stakes in the ground after you survey twenty acres, and you can take that twenty-acre claim down to the courthouse and file it and that twenty acres is yours for use as long as you put in one hundred dollars' worth of work a year on that mining claim.

"Now, last year, between four billion and six billion dollars' worth of minerals were taken off federal lands. Do you want to know the sequel to that? Uncle Sap did not get one penny in royalties. Not one thin dime.

"Go back a moment. Let us assume that this person who has convinced the government to give him the deed to this land because he says it has hard-rock minerals under it, let's assume he would rather sell it to a developer who wants to put a ski resort on it. There is not one single prohibition in the law today that will prevent him from doing just that."

In Phoenix, Arizona, Bumpers noted, a gravel-mining operation picked up 19 acres of public land in 1987 for $47, then sold the parcel for $3.8 million. In Colorado, a prime 160-acre tract went for $400 in 1983; eight years later, most of the land had been sold off at $11,000 an acre. "A miner in Aspen, Colorado, staked a claim to ten acres of Forest Service land next to a downhill ski run. He can buy the land for $2.50 an acre, and that's not bad, where a quarter-acre residential lot sells for $776,000."

But the cheap land was only part of the scandal. Even when a legitimate miner was finished with a site, he could usually walk away and take no responsibility for the environmental damage left behind.

"If you get permission to mine land in Arizona and New Mexico, where federal lands are not covered by state environmental laws," Bumpers explained, "you can wreak havoc and leave it, abandon it for the taxpayers to clean up. I promise you, we have billions of dollars' worth of those sites right now that have been abandoned. You see them all over the West. The rape, ruin, and run boys have left it for us to pick up the tab."

But when the crucial vote went down on the Bumpers bill, most of the news media that had so recently been so excited about these royal scams didn't seem to be paying attention. In the days following the Senate debate, not one major national newspaper reported Bumpers remarks—nor the fact that his bill was defeated by a single vote, 47–46.

And not one major newspaper noted that among those who voted to defeat the bill—and whose vote could have changed the outcome of the entire mining-law reform campaign—was Senator Al Gore.

96

ENVIRONMENTAL
JUSTICE

October 26, 1991
Washington, D.C.

Michael Fischer, the affable fifty-one-year-old former bureaucrat who ran the Sierra Club, had spoken at hundreds of community forums, national conventions, congressional hearings, and press conferences over the years, but he'd never been to a meeting like this one before. Sitting in front of him, in a cavernous ballroom at the Washington Court Hotel, were more than five hundred environmental activists, representing organizations in all fifty states—and none of them were white.

The Reverend Benjamin Chavis, Jr., the veteran civil-rights leader and executive director of the United Church of Christ Commission on Racial Justice, was polite and friendly as he introduced Fischer, calling for "a consensus of understanding" and "mutual respect." But after three days of emotional meetings, the delegates to the first National People of Color Environmental Summit were finally getting a chance to confront the white men who led some of the country's biggest environmental organizations, and everybody could feel the tension in the air.

Already, one of the other panelists had taken the Sierra Club to task. Pat Bryant, who ran the Gulf Coast Tenants Association in New Orleans, complained that for most of the past decade, the club had been missing in action while black communities along the Mississippi River were fighting the chemical industry. "We could not go up against some of the world's biggest chemical corporations alone," he said. "But when we reached out to the Sierra Club, only one Sierra Club member could understand us. The rest could not understand how the sons and the daughters of sharecroppers could be talking to them about coalition building."

In Washington, Bryant complained, the big environmental groups were willing to compromise with their congressional friends on legislation that was costing black southerners their lives. "For example," he said, "there is this concept of acceptable risk," a federal toxic-waste policy that allowed chemical companies to reduce their emissions to a lower level, without eliminating toxic pollution altogether. Some environmental lobbyists had been willing to go along with the concept, because the alternative—a radical overhaul of the way thousands of major corporations did business every day—had little support in Congress. Regulations that reduced toxic waste by a moderate amount were better than not reducing it at all, the lobbyists argued; in the game of national politics, they had to take what they could get.

"But we have had to accept the risks, because we are poor," Bryant explained. "If you want to see what acceptable risk means, just come down and we'll show you."

Michael Gelobter, an assistant environmental commissioner for the city of New York, drove the point home even further. "The environmental movement has, contrary to popular belief, created more jobs than it has eliminated. But for whom have those jobs been created? Who works in the Sierra Club? You are even less diverse, in many ways, than the corporations you fight."

Michael Fischer knew it was pointless to argue. His staff, his board of directors, his whole operation was, like most big environmental groups, overwhelmingly white. His members were overwhelmingly white, too, mostly upper-middle-class people who had the financial freedom to worry about the fate of a wilderness area they would probably never see. And in the halls of Congress, where groups like the Sierra Club cut deals that changed people's lives, the people in the trenches were invisible. The Sierra Club was making the same mistake at home that international rain forest preservationists were making in the jungles of Malaysia and Brazil.

When the delegates at the People of Color conference talked about a concept called "environmental justice," which brought the basic principles of civil rights into the politics of ecology, they were giving people like Fischer a dramatic challenge: the environmental movement had to change the way it worked—and its leaders had to change the way they thought.

After four years at the helm of the Sierra Club, Fischer was feeling some frustrations of his own. By some standards, the organization John Muir had founded with a few hiking friends a century ago had become a tremendous success: 625,000 members strong, with a staff of 350 and an annual budget of $42 million, Fischer's Sierra Club was now a major player in American politics. But as some environmentalists had always argued, growth was a mixed blessing—and in the case of political organizations, Fischer had come to believe, those critics had a point. With size came power, money, and influence, but so did bureaucracy, compromise, and stagnation. The club couldn't move quickly anymore; it couldn't change direction the minute a new issue emerged. It couldn't take as many risks, do things that might offend important supporters, big donors, or friendly politicians. It couldn't risk looking radical or unreasonable.

"We know that we have been conspicuously missing from the battles for environmental justice all too often," he told the audience, "and we regret that fact sincerely. We are here to reach across the table and build the bridge of partnership with all of you.

"Beyond the fact of it just being right," he noted, "we must be practical. We in the environmental movement know that it is in our enlightened self-interest to be fully involved in seeking environmental justice, or we risk becoming irrelevant."

The first National People of Color conference had its roots in a chemical crime that took place almost ten years earlier, in a remote corner of North Carolina. Warren County was a long way from anywhere, a stretch of tiny towns and spit farms that had never attracted much political attention until the federal and state authorities decided it was the best place to get rid of a horrible toxic mess.

Between June and August of 1978, a New York truck driver and would-be entrepreneur named Robert Burns and his sons had sprayed 31,000 gallons of contaminated oil on the sandy roadsides of rural highways along the North Carolina–Virginia border, in an effort to avoid the cost of legal disposal. The oil was laden with PCB, one of the most toxic chemicals ever invented by American industry.

In June 1979, after state officials discovered the "midnight dumping," EPA administrator Doug Costle ordered the state to scrape up every bit of the oil-soaked soil—roughly fifty thousand tons—and bury it in a secure landfill. North Carolina didn't have a toxic disposal site that met EPA specifications, so state officials began a frantic search for a place to build one. They settled on a wheat field in Afton, a tiny town in Warren County.

A small, predominantly black group called Concerned Citizens About PCBs began meeting in the Coley Springs Baptist Church to oppose the dumping, with the Reverend Luther Brown leading the crusade. Over and over, members wrote letters of protest to public officials, but their efforts made little headway. As the dump was about to open, the meetings got larger and louder, and more and more white residents joined the group. All of the members agreed: Warren County had been chosen because it was poor, politically powerless, and largely black. The state was dumping on a community that politicians figured was unable to fight back.

That was a miscalculation. Early in September, Luther Brown called the Reverend Leon White, head of the United Church of Christ Commission on Racial Justice in Raleigh. White called two other ministers, Reverend Chavis, a prominent national civil rights leader in New York, and the Reverend Joseph Lowery, head of the Southern Christian Leadership Conference in Atlanta.

Lowery sent a staff organizer to Afton to teach the residents how to stage mass protest marches. Then he called Congressman Walter Fauntroy.

And by the time the trucks started showing up at the entrance to the landfill, civil rights leaders from all over the country had descended on Warren County, bringing with them dozens of reporters from national newspapers and TV networks. Fauntroy was among more than five hundred people who sat in front of the trucks and got arrested, generating extensive media coverage. By the time the state police cleared away the last protester, and the last of the toxic-waste trucks spilled its load into the landfill, the tiny community had become the center of considerable national attention.

Slowly, the message started to spread from Warren County, North Carolina. All over the country, blacks, especially rural blacks, were the major victims of toxic pollution; the overwhelming majority of the nation's most contaminated and least well monitored dump sites were in low-income black communities. But for the most part, the environmental movement, including the antitoxics organizations, was overwhelmingly white. It was one of the most disturbing flaws in environmental politics—and for the most part, neither the news media nor the major environmental organizations paid much attention to it.

In 1979, Robert Bullard, a professor of sociology, began to document the problem when his wife, Linda, an environmental lawyer, took on a case involving a toxic landfill that Browning-Ferris Industries, the giant garbage company, wanted to build near a middle-class black neighborhood in Houston. Linda Bullard wanted to argue that BFI and local officials had chosen the neighborhood in part because the residents were mostly black; she asked her husband to do a study on the siting of landfills and waste dumps in the Houston region.

Robert Bullard was startled by his findings. Over the past fifty years, all five city-owned landfills had been built in black neighborhoods. So had six of the eight city-owned garbage incinerators, and three of the four private dumps. Blacks made up only a quarter of Houston's population; it was, the young sociologist had to admit, more than a random statistical pattern.

What bothered Bullard the most was that the pattern cut across socioeconomic lines. Comparatively wealthy black neighborhoods had to put up with toxic-waste sites, too—and even the poorest white neighborhoods didn't. He began looking at other cities in the South, and over and over, the same pattern emerged: garbage, whether it was leftover chicken bones, eggshells, and yard waste or the deadly by-products of the chemical industry, was disposed of far too often in places where African-Americans lived. He compiled his research into a book, *Dumping in Dixie,* which shattered one of the most common assumptions of both sociologists and environmental activists: in the South, toxic waste wasn't a matter of social class; it was a race thing.

By 1987, Benjamin Chavis was running the Commission on Racial Justice, and he set in motion a study that took Bullard's work nationwide. *Toxic Waste and Race in the United States* made national news; it spurred a growing number of civil rights activists to take on a phenomenon that Chavis called "environmental racism."

The People of Color conference was more than just the outgrowth of an emerging concern with the racial elements of toxic-waste policy. It represented the start of a potentially profound change in the way two social movements defined themselves and established their priorities.

As numerous conference speakers pointed out, people of color were hardly newcomers to environmental activism. In black, Hispanic, and Native American communities, people had been organizing around local environmental problems since long before the first Earth Day; in fact, conference organizers noted, on the day Martin Luther King, Jr., was shot, he had come to Memphis to support black sanitation workers concerned about environmental safety on the job.

But for the past twenty years, many minority leaders in the United States had taken the same basic approach to environmental issues that Third World leaders took in underdeveloped countries. Preserving the natural world was less important than promoting economic development. Often, white professionals in the environmental movement would find themselves fighting blue-collar unions and people of color over laws that big business claimed would destroy industrial jobs. It happened in San Francisco in 1986, where environmentalists wanted to limit high-rise office development, and labor unions and black community leaders joined developers to oppose the plan. It happened in the Midwest in 1984, where automakers said that acid-rain controls would shut down factories and the National Conference of Black Mayors sided with the Reagan administration to oppose the restrictions. It happened in Washington in 1978, when the NAACP issued a policy paper denouncing Jimmy Carter's energy-conservation efforts as barriers to black economic advancement.

That sort of thinking drove Carl Anthony crazy. Anthony was an architect and planner from Berkeley, California, who had decided long ago that the exploitation of Third World people and the destruction of the global environment were part of the same basic problem—and that more of the same old-fashioned industrial development was the worst possible solution. At the University of California, where he often taught and spoke, the soft-spoken planner didn't look or act the least bit like a revolutionary; clean-shaven and short-haired, dressed in the traditional tweed coat, Anthony could have passed for a conservative professor of business management, or a nuclear engineer.

He wasn't known for self-promotion. Even the environmental reporters at the major local papers tended to ignore him, and he never made national news. But Anthony was doing something profoundly important. He was challenging the basic assumptions of both the environmental movement and the civil rights movement, and offering a clear, logical, and workable alternative. Anthony and his allies called it "sustainable development."

The concept amounted to modern economic and social heresy. Its supporters suggested that the answer to unemployment and poverty was not faster economic growth; if anything, the global economy needed to slow down, to shrink to a level where it wasn't using up resources faster than they could be replenished. In the process, social justice could be achieved by shifting existing resources away from the endless wasteful uses, like big, private cars and disposable plastic containers, that made life so convenient in the developed world, and into more productive activities in places that lagged behind.

David Brower recognized the genius of Anthony's work, the same way he'd recognized the genius of Amory Lovins, and brought him on board with the Earth Island Institute; by 1991, Anthony was the institute's president.

Anthony led a workshop at the People of Color conference, laying out his thesis in the usual calm, understated tone that belied the significance of what he was telling the delegates. "The global ecosystem," he explained, "can no longer support patterns of economic growth which have become the dominant force for social change since the Industrial Revolution."

Anthony outlined the political dilemma in simple terms: "Liberals and progressives . . . argue that without economic growth, the poor both within the United States and in underdeveloped countries will have severely restricted opportunities for achieving a better way of life or even meeting basic human needs. From this perspective, the politics of sustainability is incompatible with the politics of social justice."

But in the modern era, he argued, growth "causes significant problems of pollution, traffic, congestion, unstable prices, housing shortages, structural unemployment, and worker impoverishment, in addition to depletion of land, air, water, and biological resources on which our future survival depends." And he pointed out that "the negative consequences of growth are felt much more acutely in poor communities and communities of color."

He concluded with a warning: "Communities of color have yet to engage in the policy debate about sustainability." And if that didn't change—if the same old battles continued along the same old lines—then in the long run, the same communities were going to pay the price.

The conference put environmental racism on the political map. Every major newspaper in the country covered it, many with lengthy front-page pieces that described the dramatic new alliance between the environmental and civil rights movements. The challenges were profound, the tensions deep, but everyone who participated agreed that in one weekend, environmental activism took a giant step forward.

Still, for everyone who hadn't attended—the tens of millions of people who relied on the media for news of the event—one of the most important elements of the conference was never explained. Most of the stories described the same old arguments and reported the same old rhetorical responses; not one major news article mentioned sustainable development. Not one quoted Carl Anthony.

97

THE EYES OF THE WORLD

June 12, 1992
Rio de Janeiro, Brazil

For eleven days, the United Nations Conference on the Environment and Development—the "Earth Summit"—dominated newspapers, magazines, and broadcast news shows all over the planet. Eight thousand reporters roamed a few square miles of Brazil's legendary semitropical resort, scrambling for scraps of information. More than 100 heads of state and 35,000 other delegates, observers, and unofficial visitors milled around luxury hotel lobbies, colorful pavilions, and a giant, brand-new conference center on the outskirts of the slums of Rio.

The whole world was watching—and after months of hesitation, doubletalk, criticism, and controversy, even the president of the United States had finally agreed to show up and speak. It would be the single biggest media event of the whole gigantic show, a chance to make a statement to an audience that probably numbered in the billions. For the Rainforest Action Network, it was the stuff that dreams were made of.

Randy Hayes couldn't resist the potential publicity for his cause. He'd prepared a creative—if legally risky—plan to crash the Bush speech and unfurl a banner calling on the president to "lead or get out of the way." But with the speech only an hour away, a nasty glitch had emerged.

Rio was inundated with political statements, many of them painted on big pieces of paper or cloth. After almost two weeks, fresh supplies were at a premium. Hayes had wangled a piece of canvas from a colleague, who had promised that it had only been used once; the other side was blank, and Hayes could fill it with anything he wanted. When he opened the sheet, however, he realized somebody had made a terrible mistake. There wasn't a square inch of empty space anywhere.

Too late to go back to the pavilion where the political groups were based and try to score another one. Too late to paint out the old slogans, let the coating dry, and paint in his new ones. Too late, maybe, to tell the world what U.S. rain forest activists thought of President Bush. He began walking away, across the wide stretch of park that separated the conference center from the waterfront, where a small fleet of visiting ships had docked. And as he idly gazed at the vessels, Hayes noticed a familiar logo—a bright-colored rainbow flag, with the word *Greenpeace* in big white letters. He dropped his worthless canvas cargo and began to run as fast as he could toward the berth of the *Rainbow Warrior*.

Sweating and panting like the winner of a tropical marathon, Hayes convinced the tough-looking gangplank guard to let him on deck. When the captain realized who the visitor was, he told Hayes to relax. If the head of the Rainforest Action Network needed a banner to confront George Bush, Greenpeace was happy to help. He led Hayes down several stairwells and deep into the prow of the boat—where, to Hayes's astonishment, the *Rainbow Warrior,* recommissioned after the 1985 bombing, operated a fully equipped banner shop.

Friendly crew members pulled out a big, fresh canvas, already equipped with grommet holes for ropes and loops for a wood frame. They showed Hayes a wide selection of colorful, quick-drying paints, various different stencils for lettering, and rapidly prepared a clean, bright poster. In minutes, the banner was dry, folded, and tucked under his arm, and Hayes was on his way.

The United Nations security forces were a bit less accommodating.

As the crowd assembled for Bush's speech, Hayes and a friend slipped into the main lobby. They waited until several hundred reporters were on hand, then ducked under the rope barricade that kept unauthorized people away from the official auditorium entrance. "We have a statement to make to the press," Hayes announced; his voice was a bit hoarse from shouting slogans all week, but loud enough to catch the attention of a few nearby news crews. Immediately, the press corps began to converge on the two protesters in a dense, noisy pack.

For ten minutes, Hayes had center stage. He unfurled his banner, made a long speech describing how Bush's policies were promoting rain forest destruction and took a few questions, while the United Nations security officers struggled to break a path through the crowd. Then the last reporter moved out of the way, and a team of eight armed guards dragged Hayes and his partner out of the lobby and into a small interrogation room on the edge of the conference center.

The two protesters tried to be polite and cheerful, explaining that they never intended to hurt anyone, but the U.N. authorities weren't interested. After a brief discussion, Hayes and his partner were handed over to the

Brazilian national police. "I want to make an example of these people," one official said as the two were taken away in handcuffs. A Peruvian journalist who saw them leave the building whispered a warning: "Sorry guys—you're fucked."

For the next eight hours, the two were handcuffed to chairs in a tiny corrugated-tin shack in back of the giant center, as a series of cops shouted angry questions. The prisoners couldn't mount the slightest defense: the cops spoke almost no English, and neither American spoke much Portuguese. There was no water, no food, no chance for the two Americans to relieve themselves. Hayes began to visualize a long, nasty stretch in a very unpleasant place.

Then the day shift ended for the Brazilian police, and the night shift arrived—and for the two Americans in the detention shack, the whole world started to change. The night police captain spoke enough English to ask what Hayes and his partner were in trouble for; Hayes managed to point to his crumpled banner, and the captain unfolded it on the floor. His partner knew just enough Portuguese to translate the slogan; it was all the captain needed to hear.

At the snap of his fingers, half a dozen officers arrived to remove the prisoners' handcuffs and give them an official escort back to the conference center. "I don't see the problem," he told Hayes as they left the makeshift jail. "What you say about Bush, it sounds good to me."

Almost twenty years after the United Nations held its first major environmental conference in Stockholm, tensions between the North and the South had changed very little. The northern, industrialized nations wanted to maintain their affluent life-styles, built on tremendous environmental devastation, while insisting that the valuable natural resources of the undeveloped South be preserved in the name of global ecology. The southern, impoverished nations wanted money—to feed people, build decent housing, provide modern medical care, and develop productive technology, so the people of the South could someday be just as fat and happy as those of the North. Just as in Stockholm, those essential conflicts defined much of the official debate in Rio de Janeiro.

This time, though, there was another, more visible conflict: the United States against the Rest of the World.

Twenty years after the first Earth Day put activists from the United States in the vanguard of the global environmental struggle, and just fourteen months after Earth Day organizer Denis Hayes had once again orchestrated the largest worldwide environmental demonstration in history, Americans found themselves in a strange position in Rio. On environmental issues, the United States government was completely isolated.

George Bush, who as U.N. ambassador had shunned the 1972 Stockholm conference, provoked worldwide condemnation all spring when he steadfastly insisted he wouldn't attend the Earth Summit. Instead, he named EPA administrator William Reilly to head the U.S. delegation— then undermined Reilly's credibility and authority by forcing him to reverse course on one of the most critical summit issues, the treaty on "biodiversity."

The biodiversity pact addressed what scientists and environmental leaders worldwide agreed was a terrifying problem: the vast majority of the world's plant and animal species—the global "gene pool"—lived in rain forests and other relatively pristine areas, mostly in the Third World. Those areas were being destroyed at a stunning rate—developers cut down an acre of rain forest every minute. At stake wasn't just natural wilderness and physical beauty. To pure scientists, the flora and fauna of the world's remote regions held some of the basic secrets to life itself; to medical researchers, those undiscovered species held the potential codes for medicines that could cure cancer, AIDS, and countless other diseases.

The biodiversity treaty had two central thrusts. It would slow, and eventually stop, the destruction of irreplaceable habitat for the great mass of flowers, shrubs, trees, and creatures representing most of Earth's biological diversity. And to help compensate the impoverished nations that were host to this biological treasure, it would require businesses that found something of value in those ancient mountains and jungles to give the host countries a percentage of the profits.

That concept infuriated the powerful U.S. pharmaceutical industry. Drug companies spent millions of dollars researching and developing new products, some of which inevitably had their roots in places other than the companies' private gardens. Merck and Company, for example, made a popular glaucoma drug out of extracts from a shrub found only in the Amazon; paying Brazil a share of the profits could cost a fortune. The rapidly growing biotechnology industry was even more alarmed. Most new forms of chemical and biological products were based on genetic information from existing species.

Bush appeared to see the issue in the same sort of simplistic political terms that had guided his public career. He'd always supported lofty foreign policy ventures, but with an election year approaching, the national economy was in free-fall—and that meant the only relevant issue was American economic growth and American jobs. If a major industry said the Rio treaties would threaten business prospects at home, then Bush would hold the line: until the drug companies were happy, the United States would not sign a biodiversity treaty.

In reality, Bush was making a major mistake. Almost every credible economist in the world had long since come around to a different way of thinking. Only a few old-fashioned diehards still tried to argue that saving jobs and preserving the environment were conflicting goals; at Rio, most world leaders were saying exactly the opposite.

Reilly understood that fact, and privately urged the president to accept the biodiversity treaty. The U.S. allies in Rio, including Britain and Canada, wanted to work for consensus. If Bush was unhappy with some of the treaty's language, Reilly noted in a confidential memo, it wouldn't be hard to fix the problem.

Hard-liners in the administration were still determined to block any deal. But Reilly insisted that some compromise version of the treaty could be signed, and at his urging, key provisons of the documents were substantially watered down. After the other delegates finally approved a treaty far less important than the original plan, Bush still refused to sign it.

Oddly enough, Bush had some unexpected allies. Most of the indigenous people attending the conference opposed the treaty, too. Their argument was simple, and followed the line they had taken with environmental activists for several years. The treaty required businesses who used products from the rain forests to pay royalties to the governments that controlled them. The people who lived there were left entirely out of the bargain.

There was a larger issue, too, but in all the thousands of pages of position papers, press releases, fliers, and news articles on the treaty, it was almost completely ignored. The biodiversity treaty was based on the fundamental assumption that human beings ought to be taking the existing global gene pool and molding and mutating it for their own benefit and profit—that people should be creating new species in the lab, and patenting those creatures as if they were machines.

The implications of that assumption were staggering. But in the big, high-profile, media-driven politics of the Rio Earth Summit, complex ethical issues never had a chance.

And yet, for Randy Hayes, and the vast majority of the other ten thousand activists who attended the Earth Summit as unofficial guests, the event was a huge success. On one level, it marked the official end of the Cold War era. Instead of two East-West blocs coming together to plot military confrontation, a global coalition had agreed on some fundamental principles of ecological cooperation. The United States had forced the delegates to eliminate many of the most effective elements of a new treaty on global warming, but at least a treaty existed. And by the end of the conference, the United Nations had established a new council on sustainable development, with a mandate to find more ecologically sound ways to bring prosperity to the underdeveloped world.

Besides, as Hayes reminded his colleagues, the international conference had given environmentalists from the United States a chance to challenge, and embarrass, George Bush on what was supposed to be his strongest political turf—foreign policy.

Only months later would some of the Rio participants figure out the lesson that Jack Loeffler and a few other pioneers took home from the Stockholm conference. Big, global affairs can build the groundwork for lasting shifts in consciousness. But the battle to save the Earth will be won and lost not by presidents, princes, and prime ministers, but by ordinary people, fighting grassroots battles to protect their own backyards.

THE PRICE OF JOBS

October 7, 1992
Wallace, Louisiana

Only about twenty-five people showed up at the Friends of Charity Hall to celebrate Wilfred Greene's victory over what would have been the world's largest rayon factory. It was among the most dramatic and unusual success stories in the modern environmental movement; activists, journalists and politicians all over the country were taking notes. But in Wallace, it was Friday night, and on Friday nights, just about everyone in town went to the high-school football game.

Nathalie Walker, the Sierra Club lawyer from New Orleans, was a little embarrassed that she had scheduled the victory party for a weekend night. The football conflict had never occurred to her. New Orleans was only fifteen miles from Wallace, but to an educated white professional in the big city, the place was worlds away.

Greene didn't seem a bit disappointed by the turnout. The crowds had been around when he needed them; over the past few months, his weekly meetings had been packed. The local newspapers had been calling him constantly, and now reporters from papers like *The New York Times* and the *Atlanta Constitution* were checking in for comments. For the most part, the seventy-year-old retired school principal was thrilled with the outcome of his three-year battle against one of the largest chemical companies in the world. He also knew that some of his neighbors didn't share his enthusiasms.

"I'm wishing and praying that the people in this community will understand our position," he told the small but boisterous group as Nathalie Walker handed him a testimonial plaque. "We can't conceive of jobs at the cost of our lives."

*   *   *

When Formosa Plastics, the industrial giant out of Taiwan, announced plans to build a $700 million rayon factory in a deeply depressed region along the Mississippi River, almost everyone assumed the deal was done. Louisiana officials went out of their way to attract chemical companies to the state, offering lucrative tax incentives, the promise of cheap and plentiful labor, and some of the most relaxed environmental standards in the country. Formosa was offering jobs—at least one thousand permanent, full-time jobs—and for a community like Wallace, that sounded like an economic miracle.

Wallace was tucked along the western bank of the Mississippi in the last undeveloped piece of waterfront between New Orleans and Baton Rouge, a stretch known as "cancer alley." All but a handful of the town's residents were black, the descendants of slaves who had worked the vast sugarcane plantations that once were the economic lifeblood of southern Louisiana. Across the river, where the interstate highway ran, the plantations had long since given way to a strip of oil refineries and chemical factories. But the roads that connected Wallace with the rest of the world were poor and badly maintained, and the postwar industrial boom had passed the community by. The old slave quarters still stood, alongside the historic Underground Railroad station, the antebellum graveyard, and the dilapidated wood-frame buildings that served as homes, stores, and churches. On the outskirts of Wallace, the last functioning sugar plantation in Louisiana continued to operate, providing a decent source of income for a few local farmers. But the majority of the residents of Wallace and the surrounding area were either too old to work or too young to leave.

Wilfred Greene had the chance to leave once, back in the 1950s, after he borrowed $2 from his father to pay for the entrance exam at Xavier University and then $95 more to pay for the first year's tuition. By the time he'd earned a master's degree in education, Greene could have found work almost anywhere. Instead, he came back to his hometown, to teach. He moved into the house his parents had built, on land his great-grandfather bought in 1874. Back then, the place was considered worthless—just an empty, weed-choked lot five thousand feet long, with sixty-four feet of frontage along the Mississippi River—and nobody except a few black plantation workers like Greene's great-grandfather had any interest in it. But in the summer of 1989, the Formosa Plastics Company suddenly wanted Greene's land very badly.

Formosa had just purchased a 1,740-acre former plantation site a few hundred yards downriver from Greene's house; that was enough space for even the gigantic factory Formosa officials had in mind. But there was a major problem: the rayon plant needed vast supplies of raw materials. Among other things, it would use 1,800 tons of hardwood a day to make pulp, wood that would have to be brought to the factory by boat. And along the old plantation shoreline, the Mississippi was too shallow to accommodate river barges.

Dredging was a waste of time; the sand deposits along that stretch built up faster than anyone could reasonably haul them away.

But where Wilfred Greene and his neighbors lived, the river was comparatively deep. With access to that one small strip of waterfront, the supply problem would disappear and Formosa could start to build.

When company representatives showed up with cash offers that ran as high as $50,000, most of Greene's neighbors sold out quickly. But Greene, whose land was right in the middle of the deep-water strip, told company lawyers it wasn't for sale. And by themselves, the strips of frontage on either side of Greene were too small for a commercial shipping port.

Greene was attached to the land. It was part of his family history, something he could leave to his children. He didn't want to leave Wallace, either. He'd been a teacher and a school principal there for most of his adult life, and he felt a strong commitment to the community. He'd also seen a frightening new corporate trend happening all up and down "cancer alley." Having poisoned the land around them so badly that it was unsafe, big chemical companies had discovered an alternative to costly cleanups and lawsuits: They were buying the polluted towns, lock, stock, and barrel, moving the residents out, and fencing off the contaminated property. In the past few years, Greene had seen places like Morrisonville, Sunrise, and Reveilletown vanish off of the map, their once-stable black communities scattered to the winds. Extended families who had lived near each other for generations were broken up forever. A few thousand dollars from the chemical companies couldn't make up for that.

And no matter how many jobs it was offering, Greene had learned enough about this chemical company and its proposal to realize that the rayon factory would not be an asset to the Wallace community.

Formosa had a long history of environmental problems. Most recently, in October 1990, the Environmental Protection Agency fined Formosa a record $8.3 million for releasing so much chemical waste near its Point Comfort, Texas, plant that it might as well be operating an unregulated toxic dump site. After an appeal, Formosa agreed to pay a reduced fine of $3.375 million, the highest ever collected by the EPA.

The plant in Wallace would discharge sixteen billion gallons of wastewater a year into the Mississippi. It would use millions of gallons of toxic chemicals to transform southern hardwood forests into rayon fibers. Company officials said it would be a "state of the art" technological facility.

Greene knew from the start that very few Wallace residents would have the formal education and training to get jobs operating Formosa's high-tech chemical-engineering equipment. And since the state and local government had offered the company $400 million in tax reductions to attract the plant, he suspected that there wouldn't be much tax money left to improve local services. If any benefits did trickle down, he was convinced that the community would be mortgaging its health, its safety, and its future in the name of a few immediate jobs for a few job-hungry people. Like the offer on the house, it seemed to be a rotten deal.

When the St. John the Baptist Parish Policy Police Jury began to hold hearings on the zoning permits for the plant, Greene began showing up to ask questions—and more often than not, the local elected officials had no credible answers. So he rounded up a few neighbors, held a few meetings in the Wallace firehouse, and put together an organization to oppose the new plant. But the permits kept moving forward, and Formosa began pursuing ways to build a port without using Greene's land; after a few months, the lanky, soft-spoken schoolteacher began to think he was in over his head.

Late in 1989, a woman named Audrey Evans showed up at one of the police jury hearings. Evans had grown up across the river, in La Place; she went off to college and graduate school in Washington, D.C., and came back to New Orleans to take a job as community outreach coordinator with the Environmental Law Clinic at Tulane University. The Louisiana newspapers weren't paying much attention to the growing battle in Wallace, but Evans had read a story about it in a Washington weekly called the *City Pages* just before she left, and when she settled into her new job, she decided to check it out.

By the time Evans arrived, the situation in Wallace was getting increasingly ugly. Opponents of the plant would get into shouting matches with supporters at public meetings, and sometimes parish officials had to call the police. The meeting she attended was no exception—but before the mayhem broke out, a tall, slender man who was obviously pushing seventy stood up to speak. In a clear, articulate voice, the man asked a simple question: Did any of the jurors have a potential financial interest in the outcome of their decision on Formosa's local zoning permits, and would those interests present a conflict?

The officials refused to entertain the question, but Evans tracked down the elderly speaker and asked a question of her own: Did the Formosa opponents need any extra help? Wilfred Greene said he thought that was a fine idea.

Before long, the fledgling crew in Wallace was plugged into a growing network of grassroots activists who were giving the chemical industry headaches all over the Deep South. Organizations from the Louisiana Environmental Action Network to Greenpeace joined the fray—and as word of the battle spread, a few national activists began to discover its true implications. In Wallace, black community leaders were refusing to accept the idea that economic development required environmental compromise; in Wallace, environmental protection was becoming a civil rights issue.

By the spring of 1991, the Sierra Club Legal Defense Fund had opened an office in New Orleans. One of the first things its managing attorney did was drive up to Wallace and talk to Wilfred Greene.

Nathalie Walker was an expert on laws like the National Environmental

Policy Act and the Endangered Species Act, and she realized right away that Formosa Plastics had some serious legal problems. The company was asking for so many different federal permits—wastewater-discharge permits, air-quality permits, toxic-chemical-transportation permits, wetlands-encroachment permits, and so forth—that the very act of approving its construction amounted to a major environmental activity. And under NEPA, that meant it required an environmental impact statement. The local EPA office had figured that out, too. For the first time in history, the agency ordered a private company, which owned private land, under what would normally be state jurisdiction, to prepare a detailed federal EIS before putting a single brick in the ground.

In the process of preparing the EIS, Formosa's consultants stumbled onto a serious problem. The plant engineers were counting on using extensive amounts of wood from regional hardwood forests—but cutting down all those trees could threaten some of the last remaining habitat of the Louisiana black bear. The information was buried in obscure language in the first draft of the document, and Formosa tried to hide it from the public, but Nathalie Walker knew where to look. She filed a formal demand under the Freedom of Information Act for the draft report, and when she realized what it showed, she quickly filed a petition with the Interior Department requesting that the bears be listed as endangered.

For a few moments, Walker was afraid that the Wallace community would rebel against the endangered-species strategy, that the Sierra Club would get painted again as an elitist organization that worried more about bears and owls and snail darters than human families living in towns where there weren't any jobs. But she and Audrey Evans had spent a tremendous amount of time in Wallace, working with Wilfred Greene, going to meetings at the firehouse, and teaching local people how to write press releases, testify at hearings, and demand information from the government. Greene, the old school principal, knew how much his neighbors didn't know, and was always happy to have new teachers in town, and he could tell that Walker was a pro. When she explained what the Endangered Species Act was about, and how the rape of the forest habitat and the rape of a small community were part of the same brutal process, where the losers never had a chance, the growing crowds at Greene's weekly meetings had nothing but applause.

Walker took a short break in May 1992, to speak at an American Bar Association conference in Virginia, where she met a reporter from the *National Law Journal* named Marcia Coyle. Coyle was involved in a ground-breaking project, a detailed report on the role of racism in environmental policy. When the series appeared on September 21, 1992, it shocked the legal and political world of Washington, D.C., and reverberated all over the country. Coyle's report on Wallace, Louisiana, was a central part of the story.

The executives at Formosa Plastics knew a lost cause when they saw one. The official announcement came a few days later after Coyle's stinging article; the announcement cited undue regulatory burdens and a hostile business climate, red tape, and legal delays, but everyone at Wilfred Greene's party knew what really happened.

In Wallace, Louisiana, the community fought back.

99

THE OZONE MAN

November 3, 1992
Little Rock, Arkansas

For political insiders, the suspension had already ended an hour or two after the election-day sun rose over the East Coast. By ten A.M., campaign staffers in Washington were calling friends in California, where the polls hadn't even opened, to say the verdict was in. The early exit polls confirmed what most observers had predicted for weeks: for the first time in twelve years, the United States was electing a Democratic president. George Bush was losing almost everywhere, from New Hampshire to Georgia. States that had been considered solid Republican strongholds for more than a decade were rejecting the incumbent president in favor of a forty-six-year-old Arkansas governor who had no foreign policy background, no military record, and until about thirteen months before, very little name recognition outside of his home state.

William Jefferson Clinton was making history, shifting control of the country into the hands of a generation born and raised after the Second World War. His running mate, Senator Al Gore, was making history, too: for the first time ever, a member of a successful American presidential ticket had campaigned first and foremost as an environmentalist.

Albert Arnold Gore, Jr., was not a radical child of the sixties. A senator's son born to wealth and privilege, he grew up in Washington, D.C., worked hard in an exclusive private school, wore his hair short, was captain of his high-school football team, and for the most part stayed away from rebellion and protest. He graduated with honors from Harvard, married his high-school sweetheart, and when his draft notice came in 1969, he enlisted in the Army and served a tour of duty in Vietnam.

For a brief moment, Gore considered avoiding the draft the way many of his friends had done, by moving to Canada. His parents, both bitterly opposed to the war, said they'd support his decision; his mother even offered to go to Canada with him. But even at twenty-one, he understood political reality: Senator Al Gore, Sr., a generally liberal, antiwar Democrat from generally conservative, prowar Tennessee, was locked in a heated reelection battle—and news that his son had fled the country to avoid the draft would be a political death sentence. Instead, the Gore campaign filmed an emotional television ad showing father and son shaking hands as young Al headed off for basic training. "Son," the elder Gore announced for the cameras, "always love your country."

It didn't work. Al Gore, Sr., who stood on principle against the popular mood, lost his senate seat by 46,000 votes. Al Gore, Jr., never forgot that lesson.

When he returned from a fairly uneventful year of service as a reporter for an Army newspaper based in Saigon, Gore took an entry-level job with the *Nashville Tennessean* and began writing small-time local stories about pigeon thieves and hamburger-eating contests. He stuck with the job, patiently learning the craft of journalism, and after three years, he was promoted to the Nashville City Hall beat. His persistence was a powerful asset: a lengthy series he wrote on a City Council bribery scandal sent several leading officials to prison. After seven years, he was becoming one of Tennessee's top investigative reporters.

All along, he insisted that he had no desire to pursue a political career of his own. He told friends that the memory of his father's crushing defeat, and the conduct of the Nixon administration in Vietnam, had destroyed his appetite for politics. His personal interests tended more to the spiritual: while he was writing for the *Tennessean,* he took night classes at Vanderbilt Divinity School.

But slowly, between the Watergate scandals and his own City Hall reporting, Gore began to realize that American politics was ripe for change. A smart, ambitious individual with a bit of patience could have quite an impact—and make quite a name for himself. He dropped his divinity studies and enrolled in law school. He didn't finish his legal education, either. In 1976, two years before he was scheduled to graduate, Gore learned that the incumbent congressman from Nashville had unexpectedly decided to retire. Within days, Gore announced he would run for the seat. He made an appealing candidate—handsome, charming, and articulate. His family name didn't hurt, either: Al senior had represented the same heavily Democratic congressional district between 1938 and 1952 before moving on to the Senate, and was still immensely popular in that part of the state. Young Al emerged at the top of a scrappy field of Democratic primary hopefuls, and won the general election going away.

Congressman Al Gore, Jr., proved right away that he was a very different brand of politician than his father had been. The senior Gore was an old-fashioned firebrand populist who rarely accepted compromise or checked with the latest polls before taking controversial positions. He was also an old-fashioned Washington insider: even when Congress wasn't in session, he tended to stay in the nation's capital, concentrating his attentions on the movers and shakers of domestic and foreign policy instead of returning to his home state to work on constituent service. His son seemed determined not to repeat either practice. He made frequent trips home, sometimes spending three weekends a month in Tennessee to meet with community groups. He also kept a careful finger in the air to monitor the winds of political change.

Gore used his journalistic skills and his natural instincts to tremendous professional advantage. He recognized hot new issues long before other politicians did, tracked down every last scrap of information available on the issue, and studied the subject until he could talk like an expert. By the time his colleagues stumbled onto the new political turf, Gore had already found the high ground and staked out a strategic position. His goal, savvy observers noted, was almost always the same: to generate the most publicity and get in the least trouble.

The issues Gore chose tended toward Mom, God, and the Flag. He went after insurance companies that sold bogus policies to senior citizens. He pushed legislation setting strict nutritional standards for infant formula. After a group of high-school girls told him that they were convinced nuclear war was inevitable in their lifetimes, he turned his attention to arms control, coming up with a novel proposal to modify ballistic missiles that even hawks like Henry Kissinger came to accept as prudent policy.

In 1984, at the age of thirty-six, Al Gore won a seat in the United States Senate. And more and more, as his national profile grew and his thoughts turned toward the White House, he began talking about the environment.

Years later, Gore would proudly assert that he'd been concerned about the fate of the Earth from his childhood, when he spent his summers on a rural spread the family owned outside of Carthage, Tennessee. But his early political record didn't reflect much in the way of vibrant environmental enthusiasm—particularly not when it appeared to conflict with local economic considerations. As a congressman and a senator, Gore sometimes infuriated Tennessee environmentalists; among other things, he supported to the bitter end two of the most environmentally destructive projects in his state—the Clinch River nuclear breeder reactor and the Tellico Dam.

On October 12, 1979, shortly after Congress had exempted the dam from the Endangered Species Act, he wrote a letter to a concerned citizen that outlined his position: "I consistently supported the completion of the Tellico Dam.... It was unfortunate that the controversy over the snail darter was used to delay completion of the dam after it was virtually finished. I am glad that Congress has now ended this controversy once and for all."

Outside of his own backyard, Gore was a bit more ecologically conscious, although he rarely clashed directly with big business. Early in his congressional career, he developed an abiding interest in the threat to the ozone layer; his extensive research taught him almost as much as some of the scientists who appeared before his committee to testify on the subject, and the press attention he gathered helped turn the problem into a national issue. (It also later earned him the nickname "Ozone Man.") But Gore consistently treated ozone destruction as a global issue, something that required a vast, international effort—he rarely attacked the American companies that continued to make money from the industrial activities that created the problem. He was one of the first members of Congress to call for hearings on the toxic contamination at Love Canal, but he also supported an amendment to the bill that would have given businesses at lot more leeway in sticking the government with the cleanup costs.

In 1986, the League of Conservation Voters gave Gore a very middling 67 percent rating on its national voting scorecard. That was fairly consistent with his historical record. His lifetime rating from the league—a mainstream organization that no credible observer could possibly call radical—was just 77 percent, lower than that of many Republicans.

In 1987, a number of wealthy, conservative-checkbook Democrats approached Gore and suggested he run for president. The campaign financiers were convinced that a traditional northern liberal like Walter Mondale, who had suffered a brutal defeat in 1984, would never defeat the popular Republican incumbent. Disappointed that more established luminaries like Senator Sam Nunn of Georgia had decided not to enter the race, they saw Gore as a reasonable alternative—a bright, young southerner whose record was moderate enough to appeal to a broad national audience.

The thought had already occurred to Al Gore. For several years, he'd been dreaming of becoming the youngest president in American history, the baby-boomers' John F. Kennedy. But in one of his rare political mistakes, Gore had decided in 1985 to sign on with a high-profile crusade that undermined two of his critical national assets: his fund-raising ability and his generational appeal. With his wife, Tipper, he'd launched a crusade against obscenity in popular music.

Tipper Gore was a high-profile leader in the national campaign against lewd and violent lyrics, the founder of the Parents Music Resource Center, which demanded federal standards for records and tapes that could be sold to young children. She took up the cause when she listened to her eleven-year-old daughter's new Prince album and heard the word "masturbating." Her efforts began to attract serious press attention when her husband, a member of the Senate Commerce Committee, arranged for a hearing on the issue.

More than a few observers said that the hearing was among the boldest, most unabashed attempts at publicity seeking in the history of a notoriously media-conscious body. Among those summoned to testify were rock stars Frank Zappa and John Denver; at one point, a committee consultant read aloud, for the record, a series of the most offensive rock lyrics Tipper Gore's group could find. The press coverage was sensational; almost overnight, the young senator from Tennessee became a national symbol of old-fashioned family values.

Tipper Gore began a promotional tour for her new book, *Raising PG Kids in an X-Rated Society,* in 1987, the same month Al Gore began his presidential campaign. But along the road to the White House, the clean-cut image backfired. No baby-boomer candidate running a generational campaign could get away with bashing rock 'n' roll. To his natural constituency, Gore was widely perceived as an uptight prude. Perhaps even worse, he had alienated the wealthy, powerful Hollywood entertainment industry, which traditionally offered millions of dollars, and immeasurable free publicity, to promising Democratic candidates.

When he realized how much damage he'd done, Gore set up a private meeting with a few top recording-industry executives, and brought his wife along. Tipper Gore acknowledged that she'd gone too far, and promised to back off. The senator apologized for his role in the hearings and vowed never to support government censorship over the content of musical lyrics. In the following years Tipper Gore went out of her way to make amends—between 1988 and 1992, she testified, made public statements, and otherwise helped industry executives defeat censorship regulations in twenty-two different states. In 1990, Al Gore began to see the payoff: Hollywood financiers gave almost $65,000 to his Senate reelection campaign.

By then, he had dropped dirty music and shifted his attention to another political crusade: preserving the global environment.

The way Al Gore later told it, his conversion to devout environmentalism had a deeply spiritual dimension. It started one day in April 1990, when his son Albert was struck by a car after a Baltimore Orioles baseball game and was very nearly killed. Gore held Albert in his arms as the paramedics arrived and took him to the hospital, and spent much of the next few weeks sleeping on couches in the waiting room outside the intensive care unit. It was there, with his son clinging to life, that he began to write the book that he called *Earth in the Balance.* It compared Albert's struggle with death to the fate of the planet, and put Gore on record as an advocate of progressive environmental policy. It also became a national best-seller, and directed the political spotlight onto Gore once again.

This time, in a passage sounding almost confessional, he acknowledged his past sins: "I have become very impatient with my own tendency to put a finger to the political winds and proceed cautiously," he wrote. "... The integrity of the environment is not just another issue to be used in political games for popularity, votes or attention. And the time has long since come to take more political risks—and endure much more political criticism—by proposing tougher, more effective solutions and fighting hard for their enactment."

But overall, his book was everything a longtime Gore observer might have expected: articulate, carefully researched, full of sweeping policy ideas and inspirational rhetoric, but lacking in specific proposals that would directly offend any powerful American business interests—or any significant block of voters. Gore presented the global environmental crisis in microscopic detail, with extensive charts, graphs, and figures. Then he framed his solutions in macrocosmic terms, calling primarily for a new, somewhat abstract social awareness. "Unless we find a way to dramatically change our civilization and our way of thinking about the relationship between humankind and our earth," he wrote, "our children will inherit a wasteland." The major villain in his book was "society"; the only discussion of big business was a glowing passage on corporate environmental responsibility.

Gore discussed at some length the controversy over the endangered spotted owl in the Pacific Northwest, insisting that the issue shouldn't be seen as just a struggle over the future of an obscure type of bird. The owl, he wrote, was actually a "keystone species," whose health was a metaphor for the entire regional ecosystem. The senator's language echoed much of what Zygmunt Plater had said more than ten years earlier, when he fought to save the snail darter back in Tennessee—but not once in *Earth in the Balance* was there a single mention of the Tellico Dam. And while he insisted that the time had come "for the elimination of those public expenditures ... that encourage and subsidize environmentally destructive economic activity," the book didn't mention Senator Gore's decisive vote in 1991 to block the repeal of the General Mining Law of 1872.

By the spring of 1992, however, Gore had established himself as what the *New Republic* called "the most prominent environmental activist in the U.S. Congress." Although he had ruled himself out as a presidential candidate shortly after his son's injury, Gore's appearance at the Earth Summit in Rio de Janeiro, and his attacks on George Bush, made him an increasingly appealing choice for the number two spot on the Democratic ticket. When Bill Clinton chose Gore as his running mate, the president of the League of Conservation Voters, former Arizona governor Bruce Babbitt, boasted that "Senator Al Gore's environmental record is second to none in the U.S. Senate."

Gore immediately picked up the environmental mantle. When President Bush attacked him as "the Ozone Man," he wore the label with pride. And

EPILOGUE

THE GOOD FIGHT

December 1992
San Francisco

Every good (and bad) loser in town came to Huey Johnson's sixtieth birthday party.

Outside the trendy new cafe tucked into an old industrial district, the parking lot was full of foreign cars. In the crowded main room, at least two hundred Friends of Huey were sipping cabernet, munching on whole-wheat pizza, and hugging long-lost comrades from ancient wars.

At cocktail parties from coast to coast, other prominent environmentalists were busy discussing the possibility of jobs in the new administration. At this party, nobody was suffering those delusions. The people who celebrated the start of Huey Johnson's seventh decade had all voted for Clinton and Gore, and most of them were hopeful about the new administration, but nobody was on the short list for a high-level Washington job.

In a crowded corner, David Brower, who had built and lost two major environmental organizations and was working on his third, was surrounded by jostling fans. "I'm doing fine, I guess," he kept telling well wishers, "considering that I'm eighty years old." After a few minutes, a journalist managed to squeeze his way forward and ask the world's greatest living environmentalist a quick question. "What do I think about the election?" Brower responded. "Well, I suppose it could have been worse. But of course, my candidate didn't make the final round."

As if on cue, Jerry Brown strolled in the door, dressed in a windbreaker, slacks, and running shoes, working the crowd like a political addict.

By most normal standards, Brown's upstart 1992 presidential campaign was a bust; he'd never really come even close to beating Clinton, and he'd alienated the entire power structure of the Democratic party. The national media, after a brief respite, still treated him like a silly joke.

But once again, after all these years, Brown had touched a sensitive nerve in the body politic. In a race in which he never had an official chance, he'd outlasted all the other Democratic primary challengers, won over millions of disgruntled voters, and created a whole new style of national populist campaigning. He traveled cheap, refused to take big contributions, slept in the homes of supporters, raised money with a low-budget high-tech 800 number—and in a primary campaign in which the front-running Democrat talked incessantly about economic growth, Jerry Brown often talked about the environment.

When the issue came up, Brown was brutal. Ecology wasn't a matter of political debate, it was a matter of scientific reality. The biggest problem wasn't saving industrial jobs in cities, it was getting rid of industrial lobbyists in Washington. When a few malcontents tried to ask Brown about problems like the Medfly, which helped bring on his long political exile, the former governor of California found some amazing new ways to duck the question.

As the lights went down and the crowd grew quiet, the head of Patagonia Corporation, Yvon Chouinard, picked up a microphone and thanked everyone for coming. The successful entrepreneur who had sold environmental consciousness to millions of consumers, at great profit to himself, didn't try to pretend:

Huey Johnson, he said, was a rare and wonderful person, a true believer who would never sacrifice principle for practicality. "I could never do that," he said. "I couldn't keep on losing all the time."

After a few more speeches, Jerry Brown took the stage. Huey Johnson, he told the crowd, had taught him a great political lesson. "When it comes to the environment," Brown said, "you can't back down, you can't do what works instead of what's right.

"That's what Huey told me fifteen years ago. And I was too stupid to listen."

NOTES

A Note on Sources:
   This book is a work of journalism; we didn't make up anything. Our research took more than three years. We interviewed more than 250 people, and read more than 50 books and probably a thousand newspaper and magazine articles. Thanks to the Freedom of Information Act and state public records laws, we extracted hundreds of pages of documents from government agencies. We traveled extensively.

   It would be impossible to list all our sources, and even if we could they would probably fill another book. Many of the people we interviewed work for federal or state governments, or for private businesses that are involved in environmental controversies; others were involved in illegal activities. Often, to preserve their jobs or their freedom, they spoke only on the condition that we would keep their names confidential. In one case (and only one case), we used pseudonyms: the eco-saboteur known as the Fox, who to our knowledge has never before spoken to journalists, insisted his real identity, and that of one of his "partners in crime," not be revealed.

   We've been in the newspaper business long enough to know that everything published isn't necessarily true. When we've cited published sources like *The New York Times, The Washington Post, Time,* and *Newsweek,* we have almost always confirmed the information with at least one other source.

   The notes below provide the major sources for all the factual statements in our book. We've torn out a good bit of our hair and a lot of our souls trying to make sure everything was accurate; we thank whatever gods may be for the parts we managed to get right.

Naturally, all opinions, conclusions, and random observations are entirely the responsibility of the authors.

—MARC MOWREY AND TIM REDMOND

PART ONE: EARTH DAY: TAKING IT TO THE STREETS

ONE: BLACK TIDE (pp. 15–19)
Interviews with Bud Bottoms, 3/23/90, 1/15/91, and 1/24/91. Details on spill drawn in part from Robert Easton, *Black Tide: The Santa Barbara Oil Spill and Its Consequences* (New York: Delacorte Press, 1972), and James Ridgeway, *The Politics of Ecology* (New York: E. P. Dutton, 1970). A series of articles by Robert Sollen in the *Santa Barbara News Press* published in January and February 1969 also proved valuable, as did "The Spill 20 Years After," a three-part supplement in the *Santa Barbara News Press,* 1/28/89 to 1/30/89. Bottoms allowed us to review the Get Oil Out archives, from which we drew extensive information. The California Coastal Commission's *Coastal Access Guide* provided background on Santa Barbara coastal geography.

TWO: THE NIGHT OF THE FOX (pp. 20–23)
Interviews with the Fox (real name withheld), 11/7/89, 1/3/90, 5/2/91; interview with Dick Norman (real name withheld), 1/4/90. Additional info: Patricia Tennison, "Sly Fox Still on the Prowl," *Chicago Tribune,* 9/21/83; "Con Ed Stages Fox Hunt," *Daily Courier-News,* 3/30/85; "The Fox," *Newsweek,* 10/5/70; "The Fox Strikes Again," *Newsweek,* 1/11/71.

THREE: CIVIL WAR (pp. 24–28)
Interview with David Brower, 4/7/91. *David R. Brower: Environmental Activist, Publicist, and Prophet* (Berkeley, Calif: Sierra Club History Series, University of California Regional Oral History Project, 1980). Interviews conducted by Susan Schrepfer, 1974–1978. Material used with the permission of Brower and the Bancroft Library. See also: John McPhee, *Encounters with the Archdruid* (New York: Farrar, Straus & Giroux, 1971); David Brower, *For Earth's Sake* (Layton, Utah: Gibbs-Smith, 1990); "Outside of the hotel . . ." *San Francisco Chronicle,* May 3, 1969.

FOUR: THE SENATOR AND THE TEACH-IN (pp. 29–30)
Interview with Gaylord Nelson, 1/19/90. Nelson also provided copies of personal records and correspondence from his Earth Day archives, including several speeches and articles. An August 29, 1963, letter from Nelson to President Kennedy describes his environmental agenda and passion in great detail. Background on Nelson's political carrer comes in part from Michael Barone and Grant Ujifusa, *The Almanac of American Politics 1978* (Washington, D.C.: The National Journal, 1978).

FIVE: THE SIEGE OF BLACK MESA (pp. 31–36)
Interviews with Jack Loeffler: 1/14/90, 2/6/90, 11/13/90, 3/12/91, 8/8/91; interview with Stewart Udall, 11/14/90; interview with Joe Brecher helped clarify legal issues, 8/16/91; interview with Alvin Josephy, 1/13/89. Other background: Jack Loeffler, *Headed Upstream: Interviews with Iconoclasts* (Tucson, Ariz.: Harbinger House, 1989). Background info about Hopis and Navajos, also details of Peabody ar-

rangement: Alvin M. Josephy, "Murder of the Southwest," *Clear Creek,* 1971. Info on power plants in part from: Melissa Savage, "Black Mesa Mainline: Tracks on the Earth," *Clear Creek,* No. 13. Information on lease deal: Mark Miller, Judith Miller, and Jonathan Moreno, "The Navajo Mineral Swindle: Wheeling and Dealing on the Reservation," *USA Today,* May 1981. Information on Central Arizona Project: Lloyd Linsford, "The Central Arizona Project: A Little Closer to God," *Clear Creek,* 1971.

SIX: TWO TONS OF GADGETS (pp. 37–38)
The text of Walter Reuther's Earth Day speech was published in *Earth Day: The Beginning* (New York: Arno Press, 1970), p. 162. Biographical background on Reuther: Frank Coumier, *Reuther* (Englewood Cliffs, N.J.: Prentice-Hall, 1970), and a *New York Times* obituary published 5/12/70.

SEVEN: EARTH DAY (pp. 39–43)
Interviews with Denis Hayes, 10/3/89, 2/10/90; Gaylord Nelson interview, op. cit. Among the more than fifty newspaper and magazine articles from 1970 that provided us with information on Earth Day events, the most useful included "Earth Day," *The New Yorker,* May 2, 1970; "A Memento Mori to the Earth," *Time,* May 4, 1970; and Steve Cotton, "Earth Day: What Happened," *Audubon,* July 1970. The text of Hayes's speech was published in *Earth Day: The Beginning,* op. cit.

PART TWO: THERE OUGHT TO BE A LAW

EIGHT: A LEG TO STAND ON (pp. 49–56)
Interview with Jim Moorman, 4/15/91; interview with David Sive, 5/30/91. Our best source of background material on environmental law was Tom Turner, *Wild by Law: The Sierra Club Legal Defense Fund and the Places It Has Saved* (San Francisco: Sierra Club Books, 1990). See also Sierra Club v. Morton, 2 ELR 20192, particularly dissent of Justice Douglas; "Should Trees Have Standing," 45 S Cal. L. Rev. 450 (1972); Lynton K. Caldwell, "Is NEPA Working?" *Environment,* December 1989. Alaska pipeline history is recounted in Wilderness Society v. Hickle, 479 f 2nd 842, and Michael D. Lemonick, "SEG Meet, Hears Prudhoe Bay Case History," *Oil and Gas Journal,* 4/13/81; "The Two Alaskas," *Time,* 4/17/89; Ward Sims, "Trans-Alaska Pipeline Flow Going Strong After 10 Years," *Los Angeles Times,* 6/14/87.

NINE: TWISTS OF FATE (pp. 57–59)
Frank Coumier, *Reuther,* op. cit. National Transportation Safety Board records, "Brief of Aviation Accident," file 3-0125, 5/9/70. "But that wasn't all that haunted . . .": Brower interview, op. cit.

TEN: LAY WASTE THE SKY (pp. 60–69)
Interview with William Shurcliff, 1/17/91; interview with Jerry Mander, 4/29/91; Brower interview, op. cit. Hearings of the Subcommittee on Economy and Government, *Congressional Record,* May 12, 1970; *Congressional Record,* Senate, 3/24/71, pp. 7801 et. seq. Background on Senator Proxmire drawn from *The Almanac of American Politics 1988* (Washington, D.C.: The National Journal, 1988). The authors are greatly indebted to Mel Horwitch's excellent account of the SST battle, *Clipped Wings* (Cambridge, Mass.: MIT Press, 1979), as well as Shurcliff, *The SST and Sonic Boom Handbook* (New York: Ballantine Books,

1970) and Tom Turner, *Friends of the Earth: The First 15 Years,* an FOE internal history. "The move infuriated President Johnson...": Stewart Udall interview, op. cit.

ELEVEN: THE MAN IN THE GRAY SUIT (pp. 70–73)
See notes on Chapter Five.

PART THREE: POLITICAL SCIENCE

TWELVE: THE CRACKPOT (pp. 79–81)
Interview with James Lovelock, 12/10/89. James Lovelock, *Nature,* 1972; Stephen H. Schneider, *Global Warming* (San Francisco: Sierra Club Books, 1989); Robert H. Boyle, "Forecast for Disaster," *Sports Illustrated,* 11/17/87.

THIRTEEN: TOO MANY PEOPLE (pp. 82–87)
Loeffler interviews, op. cit.; interview with Barry Commoner, 2/28/91; interview with Paul Ehrlich, 1/10/91; Declaration of the United Nations Conference on the Human Environment; "Stockholm Conference Eco," the collected set of Eco newspapers, 6/6/72–6/16/72. Jack Loeffler, *Headed Upstream,* op. cit.; Paul Ehrlich, *The Population Bomb* (New York: Ballantine Books, 1968); Barry Commoner, *The Closing Circle* (New York: Bantam, 1972); Donella H. Meadows et al., *The Limits to Growth* (New York: Universe Books, 1972); Garrett Hardin, "Sheer Numbers," *E,* Nov/Dec 1990; John Tierney, "Betting on the Planet," *The New York Times,* 12/2/90; Jane E. Brody, "Experts Agree on Overpopulation Peril, but Disagree Sharply on Remedies," *The New York Times,* 6/21/74.

FOURTEEN: GENESIS (pp. 88–90)
Interview with Jeremy Rifkin, 2/20/91; Jeremy Rifkin, *Algeny* (New York: Viking Press, 1983). The story of the Cohen and Boyers discovery drawn in part from: Frederick Golden, "Shaping Life in the Lab"; and "Profiting from Gene Splicing," *Time,* 3/9/81; David Perlman, "On the Cutting Edge," *San Francisco Chronicle,* 10/8/89; James Gleick, "Holdout on Big Science: Stanley Cohen," *The New York Times,* 10/14/86. Watson and Crick background widely available, including from: David Remnick, "Gadfly of the Gene Scene: Jeremy Rifkin," *The Washington Post,* 5/18/84.

FIFTEEN: OUT OF COURT (pp. 91–94)
Interviews with Nelson, Moorman, op. cit. *Congressional Record,* Senate, July 13, 1973.

SIXTEEN: COMMUNITY SERVICE (pp. 95–96)
Interviews with the Fox, op. cit.

SEVENTEEN: A FISHING TRIP (pp. 97–101)
Interview with David Etnier, 1/22/93; interview with Zygmunt Plater, 2/12/93. Background on Little Tennessee Valley drawn in part from: Plater, "Reflected in a River," *Tennessee Law Review,* Vol. 49 (1982); Plater, "Snail Darter as Paradigm," *Journal of Law Reform,* Vol. 194 (Summer 1986); Peter Matthiessen, "The Price of Tellico," *Newsweek,* 12/17/79; Environmental Defense Fund v. Tennessee Valley Authority, 339 f. Supp 806 (1/11/72); EDF v. TVA, 371 f. Supp 1004 (10/25/73); Sequoya v. TVA, 620 f. 2nd 1159 (4/15/80); Hill v. TVA, 549 f 2d 1064 (1/31/77); TVA v. Hill, 437 US 153 (6/15/78).

EIGHTEEN: OUT OF GAS (pp. 102–105)
Text of Nixon's speech, *The New York Times,* 11/9/73. Background on oil production in U.S. drawn in part from: Barry Commoner, *The Poverty of Power* (New York: Alfred A. Knopf, 1976); Morton Mintz and Jerry S. Cohen, *America Inc.* (New York: The Dial Press, 1971). The best case for the role of oil money in the Middle East arms buildup is presented by Jonathan Kwitny, *Endless Enemies: The Making of an Unfriendly World* (New York: Congdon and Weed, 1984). See also "Don't Blame the Oil Companies, Blame the State Department," *Forbes,* 4/15/76.

NINETEEN: KILLER CANS (pp. 106–108)
Interview with Robert Boyle, February 1991. Sharon Roan, *The Ozone Crisis* (New York: John Wiley & Sons, 1989); Robert Boyle, *Forecast for Disaster,* op. cit.; Owen B. Toon and Richard P. Turco, "Polar Stratospheric Clouds and Ozone Depletion," *Scientific American,* June 1991.

TWENTY: POISON POWER (pp. 109–118)
Interview with Harvey Wasserman, 5/22/91. Sam Lovejoy's attack on the Montague tower is detailed in the documentary *Lovejoy's Nuclear War,* by Green Mountain Post Films. Wasserman's *Energy War: Reports from the Front* (Westport, Conn.: Lawrence Hill and Co., 1979) describes the incident, the background, and the trial. Other background on radiation and the nuclear industry comes in part from: Mark Hertsgaard, *Nuclear Inc.: The Men and Money Behind Nuclear Energy* (New York: Pantheon Books, 1983); Ralph Nader and John Abbots, *The Menace of Nuclear Energy* (New York: W. W. Norton, 1979); Richard Rudolph and Scott Ridley, *Power Struggle: The Hundred-Year War over Electricity* (New York: Harper & Row, 1986); John W. Gofman, *Radiation and Human Health* (New York: Pantheon Books, 1983); Mark Green and Robert Massie, Jr., *The Big Business Reader* (New York: The Pilgrim Press, 1980); Anna Gyorgy, *No Nukes: Everybody's Guide to Nuclear Power* (Boston: South End Press, 1979); and Catherine Caufield, *Multiple Exposures: Chronicles of the Radiation Age* (London: Penguin Books, 1989). See also David Ehrenfeld, "The Science of Edward Teller," *California,* August 1985.

PART FOUR: THIS LAND IS OUR LAND

TWENTY-ONE: THE COWS COME HOME (pp. 123–127)
Interviews with Johanna Wald, 5/4/91, 6/7/91, 6/17/91; interview with William Meiners, 5/14/91; interviews with Don Oman, 4/24/91, 5/29/91, 5/30/91, 6/6/91. James Nathan Miller, "The Nibbling Away of the West," *Reader's Digest,* December 1972. Background information about the early American West drawn from: Alvin M. Josephy, Jr., ed., *The American Heritage History of the Great West* (New York: American Heritage, 1965). *High Country News,* the excellent bimonthly newspaper by Ed and Betsy Marston, was enormously helpful, especially issues of 3/12/90, 5/7/90, 9/10/90, and 4/8/91. See also Henry S. Grave, Forester, Robert V. R. Reynolds, "Grazing and Floods: A Study of Conditions in the Manti National Forest, Utah," U.S. Forest Service Bulletin 91, Sept. 15, 1911; Arthur W. Sampson and Leon H. Weyl, "Range Preservation and Its Relation to Erosion Control on Western Grazing Lands," U.S.D.A. Bulletin 675, June 25, 1918. Background on BLM man-

agement of federal land: *Environmental Law Reporter,* 1986 16 ELR 20508; *ELR,* 1986 16 ELR 20096; opinion of Judge Ramirez in Natural Resources Defense Council, Inc. v. Hodel, 618 F.Supp. 848. Grazing problems: James K. Morgan, "Last Stand for the Bighorn," *National Geographic,* Vol. 144, No. 3; 34th Report by the Committee on Government Operation, "Federal Grazing Program: All Is Not Well on the Range," 5/8/86, 99th Congress, 2nd Session; interview with Denzel and Nancy Ferguson, 5/21/91; Denzel and Nancy Ferguson, *Sacred Cows at the Public Trough* (Bend, Ore.: Maverick Publications, 1983); Edwin G. Dimick, *Livestock Pillage of Our Western Public Lands* (Caldwell, Ida.: Edwin G. Dimick, 1990). Additional information: Richard Conniff, "Once the Secret Domain of Miners and Ranchers, the BLM is Going Public," *Smithsonian,* September 1990; Elizabeth Royte, "Showdown in Cattle Country," *The New York Times Magazine,* 12/16/90; N.R.D.C. v. Cecil D. Andrus, 488 F.Supp.802 (4/14/78); U.S. General Accounting Office, "Public Rangelands," GAO/RCED-88-105, June 1988; G.A.O., "Rangeland Management," GAO/RCED-88-80, June 1988; G.A.O., "Rangeland Management," GAO/RCED-91-17, December, 1990; Johanna Wald, David Alberswerth, NRDC and NWF, "Our Ailing Public Rangelands," October 1989. U.S. Department of Interior, Bureau of Land Management, Instruction Memorandum No. 80-487, "Interim Guidance on Grazing Decisions," 4/30/1980; U.S. Department of the Interior, Office of the Solicitor, Memorandum to Director, BLM and Director Office of Budget, re: the McClure rider, 5/14/1980.

TWENTY-TWO: THE OUTCAST (pp. 128–130)
Interview with Cecil Garland, 8/20/91; interviews with Becky Garland, 8/19/91, 8/20/91, 8/28/91. Numerous people in Montana were happy to discuss mining issues, among them: Mark Gerlach, 8/20/91; Joe Azure, 8/20/91; Jim Jensen, 8/19/91; Peter Nielsen, 8/19/91. *The American Heritage History of the Great West,* op. cit. Hearing before the Subcommittee on Mineral Development and Production of the Committee on Energy and Natural Resources, United States Senate, 6/7/89.

TWENTY-THREE: HIGHWAY ROBBERY (pp. 131–136)
Interview with Marcy Benstock, 7/15/91. The most accurate, comprehensive information on Westway comes from more than fifty *Village Voice* articles written between 1979 and 1986 by Joe Conason, who graciously shared his files and the outline of a still-unpublished book that he called "The Westway War." The authors also thank Sydney Schanberg, the former *New York Times* columnist, who wrote more than a dozen hard-hitting opinion pieces on Westway between 1984 and 1985. Other major sources include: Jack Newfield, "The Woman Who Blocked Westway," *The Village Voice,* 8/3/82; Joyce Purnick, "Dedicated Foe Resumes Life Without Westway," *The New York Times,* 9/29/85; Sam Roberts, "The Legacy of Westway: Lessons from Its Demise," *The New York Times,* 10/7/85; Sam Roberts, "The Battle of Westway: A Bitter 10-year Saga of a Vision on Hold," *The New York Times,* 6/4/84; and "Highway in the Hudson a Cheap-Land Bonanza for Real Estate Developers," *Newark Star-Ledger,* 3/17/85. "More than the invisible hand . . .": See U.S. v. National City Lines, 334 US 573.

TWENTY-FOUR: LET'S MAKE A DEAL (pp. 137–141)
Interviews with Pat Noonan, 4/21/91, 4/24/91; interview with Lynn Greenwalt, 7/25/91; interview with David Morine, 7/10/91. Other sources: "Key to a Beautiful America: Renewed Personal Pride," *U.S. News & World Report,* June 13, 1977;

Peter Wood, "Business-Suited Saviors of Nation's Vanishing Wilds," *Smithsonian,* December 1978; "A Perfect Marriage," *Forbes,* March 19, 1979; "A Slew of Environmentalists," *The National Journal,* January 3, 1981; "Whither Goest the Land and Water Conservation Fund," *American Forests,* August 1983; "Reagan Picks Recreation Panel; Commission on American Outdoors," *Travel Weekly,* August 26, 1988; *The Nature Conservancy Annual Report, 1973;* David E. Morine, *Good Dirt: Confessions of a Conservationist* (Chester, Conn.: Globe Pequot Press, 1990).

TWENTY-FIVE: GOOD NEWS, BAD NEWS (pp. 142–144)
Wald interviews, op. cit.; interview with Roger Beers, 6/7/91; interview with Bill Meiners, 5/14/91; Bill Meiners affidavit, NRDC v. Morton, signed 1/31/74; Earl Snadvig affidavit, NRDC v. Morton, signed 2/4/74. NRDC v. Morton, 12/31/74, op. cit. Denzel Ferguson, letter to Lynn Greenwalt, director, U.S. Fish and Wildlife Service, 4/10/76.

TWENTY-SIX: WRONG SIDE UP (pp. 145–149)
Interviews with Wes Jackson, 11/19/90, 4/13/91. Wes Jackson, *New Roots for Agriculture* (Lincoln: University of Nebraska Press, 1980); Jackson, "Toward a Sustainable Agriculture," in *Not Man Apart,* Friends of the Earth, Mid-November/December 1978; Evan Eisenberg, "Back to Eden," *Atlantic Monthly,* November 1989; Jerry Sullivan, "Bringing Back the Prairie," *Audubon,* July 1988; Jon R. Luoma, "Soil Is Not a Factory," *Audubon,* July 1988; Ingolf Vogeler, *The Myth of the Family Farm: Agribusiness Dominance of U.S. Agriculture* (Boulder, Colo.: Westview Press, 1981); Sheldon L. Greene, "Promised Land: A Contemporary Critique of Distribution of Public Land by the United States," *Ecology Law Quarterly,* Vol. 5, No. 4 (1976); Center for Rural Affairs, newsletter, August 1979; "Food or Fuel," *The Progressive,* April 1979; Peter Meyer, "Land Rush: A Survey of America's Land," *Harper's,* January 1979; Roger Burbach and Patricia Flynn, *Agribusiness in the Americas* (London: Monthly Press Review, 1980); Robert Emmet Long, ed., *The Farm Crisis,* The Reference Shelf Series (New York: H. W. Wilson Co., 1987); Wendell Berry, *The Unsettling of America* (San Francisco: Sierra Club Books, 1977); Joan Dye Gussow, *The Feeding Web: Issues in Nutritional Ecology* (Palo Alto, Calif.: Bull Publishing Co., 1978). Tonnage of soil erosion, and priority for USDA from: "Agriculture's Soil Conservation Programs Miss Full Potential in the Fight Against Soil Erosion," GAO/RCED-84-48, 11/28/83; "To Protect Tomorrow's Food Supply, Soil Conservation Needs Priority Attention," GAO report, USCED-77-30, 2/14/77.

PART FIVE: THE MORAL EQUIVALENT OF WAR

TWENTY-SEVEN: MODERATION IS FOR MONKS (pp. 155–158)
The authors have followed Jerry Brown's political career for more than a decade, and interviewed him numerous times. Interview for this book conducted 4/92. Interview with Sim Van Der Ryn, 1/16/91; interview with Huey Johnson, 4/16/91. Description of Brown's press conference comes from Orville Schell, *Brown* (New York: Random House, 1978). Other background sources include Neil R. Pierce, "California's Whirling Dervish on the Face of the Future," *The*

National Journal, 5/14/77; Jerry Gilliam and Richard West, "Brown to Run as Native Son," *Los Angeles Times,* 3/13/76.

TWENTY-EIGHT: THE ROAD NOT TAKEN (pp. 159–162)
Interview with Hunter Lovins, 11/16/90. Amory Lovins, "The Road Not Taken," *Foreign Affairs,* October 1976. Turner, op. cit. Other major sources include: Ed Quillen, "At Home in a High-Altitude Think-Tank," *Country Journal,* 7/86; Amory and Hunter Lovins, "Leading the Soft Energy Revolution," *The Mother Earth News,* July/August 1984; Brad Lemley, "The Soft Path of Amory Lovins," *The Washington Post,* 6/29/86; Julia Rubin, "Measuring Megawatts for Savings," *Los Angeles Times,* 5/27/90.

TWENTY-NINE: A SLOWER, SIMPLER AMERICA (pp. 163–164)
Text of Jimmy Carter's inaugural address: *The New York Times,* 1/21/77. Also James M. Naughton, "Crowd Delighted as Carters Shun Limousine and Walk to White House," and Hedrick Smith, "A Call to the American Spirit," *The New York Times,* 1/21/77.

THIRTY: WAR AND PEACE (pp. 165–166)
Text of Carter's speech: *The New York Times,* 4/19/77. Also Hedrick Smith, "A Rare Call for Sacrifices," *The New York Times,* 4/19/77.

THIRTY-ONE: NO NUKES (pp. 167–176)
Wasserman interview, op. cit. Interview with Rennie Cushing, 7/14/91; Wasserman, *Energy War,* op. cit. Other major sources on Seabrook history include: "Reddy Kilowatt Eyes the New Hampshire Coast," *New Hampshire Times,* June 6, 1973; "Seabrook Station: A Troubled History," special supplement to Essex County Newspapers-Rockingham County Newspapers, 5/8/84; "A Chronology of Seabrook Project," *The Boston Globe,* 5/19/89; "The Seabrook Saga," *The Washington Post,* 3/2/90; Society for the Protection of New Hampshire Forests et al. v. Site Evaluation Committee, 115 N.H. 163 (4/23/75). "On August 1st . . .": Wasserman, op. cit., and "18 People Arrested During Nuke Protest," *The Daily News* (Newburyport, Mass.), 8/2/76. See also Joe Conason, E. J. Kahn III, and Dick Bell, "A Siege at Seabrook," *The Real Paper* (Boston), 5/14/77; "A Power Problem in New Hampshire," *The New York Times,* 5/7/77. Souter's role in demonstration: Sworn deposition of David Souter (taken 6/1/77 and 6/6/77) in the case of Catherine Wolff et. al. v. Meldrim Thomson, Jr., et al., U.S. District Court No. 77-143.

THIRTY-TWO: SOUTER'S CRUSADE (pp. 177–179)
Souter deposition, op. cit.; Wasserman, op. cit. "David Souter wasn't . . .": see Margaret Carlson, "An 18th-Century Man," *Time,* 8/6/90; Richard Lacayo, "A Blank Slate," *Time,* 8/6/90; "In Search of Souter," *U.S. News & World Report,* 8/6/90; "The Quiet Man," *Newsweek,* 8/6/90; Bob Hohler and Peter S. Canellos, "Jurist Reveals Little, Even to His Friends," *The Boston Globe,* 7/26/90.

THIRTY-THREE: TO TELL THE TRUTH (p. 180)
Cushing interview, op. cit.; Souter deposition, op. cit.

PART SIX: THE TOXIC TIME BOMB

THIRTY-FOUR: NO PEACE, NO QUIET (pp. 185–187)
Interviews with Ruth Shepard, 6/20/91, 6/28/92; interviews with Willie Fontenot, 11/27/90, 6/27/91; interview with Mike Tritico, 11/26/90; interview with Wade

Abadie, 7/10/91; interview with Herbert Rigmaiden, 9/20/91; interview with Shirley Goldsmith, 4/3/91; interviews with Lois Gibbs, 2/20/91, 4/2/91; interview with Peggy Frankland and Mary Ellender, 11/25/90; interviews with Les Ann Kirkland, 1/14/91, 11/27/90; interview with Mary Lee Orr, 11/27/90.

THIRTY-FIVE: THE AMERICAN NIGHTMARE (pp. 188–190)
Interviews with Lois Gibbs, op. cit. Lois Gibbs, *Love Canal: My Story* (Albany: State University of New York Press, 1982); Gregg Easterbrook, "Cleaning Up," *Newsweek,* 7/24/89; Michael Brown, *Laying Waste: The Poisoning of America by Toxic Chemicals* (New York: Pantheon, 1980). See also Brown's articles in the *Niagara Gazette,* Summer 1978.

THIRTY-SIX: HIGH HOPES (pp. 191–193)
Interviews with Ruth Shepard, op. cit.; interview with Herbert Rigmaiden, op. cit.; interviews with Willie Fontenot, op. cit. Mark Schleifstein, Jay Koelzer, and Cliff Treyens, "Empire of Waste," a thirty-two-page special in *The Clarion Ledger,* 12/3/80; Mark Schleifstein and James O'Byrne, three-part series, *The Times-Picayune,* 3/24/91–3/26/91; Schleifstein and O'Byrne, four-part series, *The Times-Picayune,* 2/17/91–2/20/91. "Dumping Matter Delayed," *Lake Charles American Press,* 4/17/78; Bill Shearman, "Waste Disposal: Committee Hears Testimony," *Lake Charles American Press,* 6/8/78; Jeff E. Schapiro, "Willow Springs Well: Cancer-Causing Agent Found," *Lake Charles American Press,* 7/14/78.

THIRTY-SEVEN: ANTINUCLEAR MELTDOWN (pp. 194–200)
Wasserman interview, op. cit. Demonstration and Clamshell conflict: Bill Peterson, "Nuclear Protest Recalls Antiwar Drive," *The Washington Post,* 6/26/78; Steve Stallone, "Seabrook in Perspective," *It's About Times,* 11/79; Rory O'Connor, "The Clamshell Struggles Toward the Showdown," *The Real Paper,* 5/13/78; Murray Bookchin, "The Plot Thickens: MUSE and the Demise of the Clamshell Alliance," *It's About Times,* August 1981, Wasserman, op. cit. Political and financial factors: Donald Holt, "The Nuke That Became a Lethal Political Weapon," *Fortune,* 1/15/79; Stacey Jolna, "Embattled Seabrook A-Plant Girds for Fight on Money," *The Washington Post,* 8/16/79; "Sunk Costs," *New England Monthly,* July 1990. PSCO financial records drawn in part from Re: Public Service Company of New Hampshire (66PUR4th 349); Appeal of Conservation Law Foundation (New Hampshire Supreme Court No. 85-252, 1/31/86.)

THIRTY-EIGHT: WOMEN AND CHILDREN FIRST (pp. 201–204)
Interviews with Lois Gibbs, op. cit.; Gibbs, *Love Canal: My Story,* op. cit.; Michael Brown, *Laying Waste,* op. cit. Ralph Nader, Ronald Brownstein, and John Richard, *Who's Poisoning America?* (San Francisco: Sierra Club Books, 1981); Lewis Regenstein, *America the Poisoned* (Washington, D.C.: Acropolis, 1982).

THIRTY-NINE: A FEW SLINGSHOTS (pp. 205–207)
Interviews with Willie Fontenot, op. cit. The history of oil in Louisiana came in part from: George Getschow and Thomas Petzinger, four-part series, *The Wall Street Journal,* 10/22/84–10/26/84; Mark Schleifstein, Jay Koelzer, and Cliff Treyens, "Empire of Waste," a thirty-two page special in *The Clarion Ledger,* 12/3/80; Schleifstein and James O'Byrne, three-part series, *The Times-Picayune,* 3/24/91–3/26/91; Schleifstein and O'Byrne, four-part series, *The Times-Picayune* 2/17/91–2/20/91.

FORTY: LIVE AND LEARN (pp. 208–209)
Cushing interview, op. cit.; Wasserman, op. cit.; Holt, op. cit.

FORTY-ONE: GHOST TOWN (pp. 210–212)
Gibbs interviews, op. cit.; "Carter Signs Cleanup Bill on Upstate Toxic Waste," *The New York Times,* 10/2/80; "Last Days for Superfund," *The Washington Post,* 10/2/80; "Superfund Hangs on Third-Party Liability," *Chemical Week,* 10/1/80; Comprehensive Environmental Response, Compensation, and Liability Act of 1980 (Superfund), legislative history compiled by Wilmer, Cutler & Pickering, including Hazardous and Toxic Waste Disposal Field Hearings: Joint Hearings Before the Subcommittees on Environmental Pollution and Resource Protection of the Senate Committee on Environment and Public Works, 96th Cong., 1st Session., pt.2, 5/18/79, 6/29/79; "Tighter Rules for Hazardous-Waste Disposal," *Business Week,* 10/10/77; Resource Conservation and Recovery Act Reauthorization hearings before the House of Representatives, 3/31/82, 4/21/82, op. cit.; Jonathan Lash, et al., *A Season of Spoils,* op. cit.

PART SEVEN: THE CALL OF THE WILD

FORTY-TWO: THE WILD, THE INNOCENT (pp. 216–220)
Interview with Dave Foreman, 12/10/89; interview with Huey Johnson, op. cit.; interview with Andy Kerr, 5/19/91. Foreman, *Confessions of an Eco-Warrior* (New York: Harmony Books, 1991). Other Foreman background: Christopher Manes, *Green Rage* (Boston: Little, Brown, 1990); Rik Scarce, *Eco-Warriors* (Chicago: The Noble Press, 1990); John Davis, ed., *The Earth First Reader* (Salt Lake City: Gibbs-Smith, 1991); Michael Parfit, "EFirsters Wield a Mean Monkey Wrench," *Smithsonian,* April 1990; "Defending the Earth and Burying the Hatchet," *Whole Earth Review,* 12/22/90. Other RARE II background: Dennis M. Roth, *The Wilderness Movement and the National Forests, 1980–1984,* Forest Service History Series FS-410 (8/88); Catherine Caufield, "The Ancient Forest," *The New Yorker,* 5/14/90; California v. Block, 690 f 2d 753 (10/22/82); Earth First v. Block, 569 f. Supp 413 (7/15/83).
FORTY-THREE: A NUCLEAR ERROR (pp. 221–224)
Details of the TMI accident were compiled from dozens of news accounts and offical records, including testimony before the Report of the President's Commission on the Accident at Three Mile Island (5/30/79) and testimony before the House Task Force on Three Mile Island. Among the best simple capsule summaries we found was Bob Van Scoy, "One Accident's Story," *It's About Times,* March 1980. See also "Nuclear Accident," *Newsweek,* 4/4/79.
FORTY-FOUR: THE LAW OF THE SEA (pp. 225–229)
Interview with Paul Watson, 10/89. Paul Watson, *Sea Shepherd,* as told to Warren Rogers (New York: W. W. Norton, 1982). Other sources include Kenneth Brower, "Environmental Vigilante," *The Atlantic,* Nov. 1980; Eric Schwartz, "Eco-fighters," *Omni,* Feb. 1981; "A Pirate Whaler Meets Its Match," *Newsweek,* 7/30/79; "Paul Watson, Angry Shepherd of the Seas," *The Washington Post,* 8/24/79; *The Earth First Reader,* op. cit.; Michael Brown and John May, *The Greenpeace Story* (Scarborough, Ont.: Prentice-Hall Canada, 1989).
FORTY-FIVE: SO SUE ME (pp. 230–238)
Johnson interview, op. cit. Other background sources include: "A New Flap over State Forest Lands," *San Francisco Chronicle,* 8/5/79; Bryce Nelson, "Carter Opens 35 Million National Forest Acres," *Los Angeles Times,* 4/17/79; Carl Irving, "Carter

OKs Logging State Wild Areas," *San Francisco Examiner,* 5/8/79; Dale Champion, "State Sues for More Wilderness," *San Francisco Chronicle,* 7/27/79.
FORTY-SIX: THE KILLER RABBIT (pp. 236–243)
Background on Frank Moore and Jimmy Carter: Judy Bachrach, "I Love Those People on the Hill," *The Washington Post,* 11/3/77; Martin Schram, "Carter's Week: Managing to Upstage Kennedy Challenge," *The Washington Post,* 11/30/79; "The Banzai Bunny," *Newsweek,* 9/10/79; "Mr. President . . .": Plater interview, op. cit. Endangered Species Act background: Plater, op. cit.; Charles C. Mann and Mark L. Plummer, "The Butterfly Problem," *The Atlantic,* Jan. 1992; Hill v. TVA, 429 F Supp 753, 549 F 2d 1064, 437 U.S. 153 (1978). Sources on congressional Tellico dam fight include: Linda K. Lanier, "Tellico Dam Battle: It's Not Just a Snail Darter," *U.S. News & World Report,* 9/17/79; Ward Sinclair, "Lawmakers Cutting Legal Corners to Save Tellico Dam," *The Washington Post,* 7/17/79; Margot Hornblower, "Panel Junks TVA Dam, Cites Cost, Not Snail Darter," *The Washington Post,* 1/24/79. "CEA Chairman Charles Schultze . . .": Unpublished transcript of Endangered Species Committee hearings, 1/23/79, cited in Plater, op. cit.
FORTY-SEVEN: THE BUG MAKERS (pp. 244–246)
Diamond v. Chakrabarty, 447 U. S. 303. Genentech and Swanson: Philip J. Hilts, "The Rush of Companies into Biotechnology Is Waning," *The Washington Post,* 11/3/81; interview with Jeremy Rifkin, op. cit. Additional Rifkin background in part from: Edward Tivnan, "Jeremy Rifkin Just Says No," *The New York Times Magazine,* 10/16/88. Asilomar information: "The Genetic Alternative," *The Economist,* 4/30/88; Ronald Bailey, "Ministry of Fear," *Forbes,* 6/27/88.
FORTY-EIGHT: OPENING DAY (pp. 247–251)
Interview with Mike Roselle, op. cit.; interview with Randy Hayes, 3/21/91. Data on Glen Canyon dam drawn in part from informational material on display in the Visitor Center, Page, Arizona; see also Eliot Porter, *The Place No One Knew* (San Francisco: Sierra Club Books, 1968); Mark Reisner, *Cadillac Desert* (New York: Viking Penguin, 1986); McPhee, op. cit.

PART EIGHT: THE CENTER CANNOT HOLD

FORTY-NINE: TEN YEARS LATER (pp. 257–258)
Joanne Omang, "Earth Day, A Decade Later," *The Washington Post,* 4/22/80; David Salisbury, "Ten Years Later, Environmental Concern Part of U. S. Life Style," *Christian Science Monitor,* 4/22/80; "A Low-Key Earth Day Observance," *The Washington Post,* 4/23/80; Merrill Shiels, "Fiery Cloud over Earth Day," *Newsweek,* 5/5/80.
FIFTY: ROAD WARRIORS (pp. 259–263)
Joe Conason, "Road to Riches," *The Village Voice,* 4/28/80; Conason, "Westway War," op. cit.; Sam Roberts, "The Legacy of Westway" and "The Battle of Westway," ops. cit.; Benstock interview, op. cit.
FIFTY-ONE: LANDSLIDE (pp. 264–265)
Election results: Edward Walsh, "A Concession with Grace and Class," *The Washington Post,* 11/5/80; David Broder, "Carter Yelds Early in Night," *The Washington Post,* 11/5/80; "Two Third Parties Suffered Setbacks in the Election," *The New York Times,* 11/6/80. Other background: Peter Goldman, "Now for the Hard Part," *Newsweek,* 8/25/80; T. R. Reid and David Broder, "Kennedy Takes Tougher

A-Plant Stance," *The Washington Post*, 2/20/80; Lawrence Mosher, "Talking Clean on the Hustings," *The National Journal*, 11/1/80; E. J. Dionne, "A Shifting Wind Alters Energy and Environment as Political Issues in Presidential Race," *The New York Times*, 10/28/80.

FIFTY-TWO: TREE HUGGERS AND PRAIRIE FAIRIES (pp. 266–268)

Interview with James Watt, 8/31/91; William Turnage quotes from: *The National Journal*, 1/3/81; Russell Peterson quotes from: James Kelley and Gregory H. Wierzynski, "Hearing and Believing: The Senate Begins Surveying Reagan's Cabinet Choices," *Time*, 1/19/81; Watt biographical information from: Senate Confirmation Hearings, *Congressional Record*, Vol. 127, Part 1, pp. 760–811, 1/5/81–2/2/81; Bil Gilbert and Robert Sullivan, "Inside Interior: An Abrupt Turn," *Sports Illustrated*, 9/26/83; *The National Journal*, 11/5/83.

FIFTY-THREE: SECRET SERVICE (pp. 269–271)

Interview with Kevin Lawless, 6/30/91. Details on Macdonald/Nims infiltration are disclosed in the following documents: Transcript of sworn testimony of Donald Bazin, taken in chambers before Judge Louis Wyman, New Hampshire Superior Court, Manchester, 1/22/81; Sworn depositions of New Hampshire State Police Major Richard Campbell, Captain Willard Dodge, and Officer James Nims in Greater Newburyport Clamshell Alliance v. Public Service Company of New Hampshire, No. 83-0066-MA and 87-307D, and 838 F2d 13, 12/29/88. Also see defendants' answer to complaint in 83-0066-MA, filed 6/4/83; Slip opinion in 83-0066-MA, issued 5/25/83.

FIFTY-FOUR: THE RAGGED EDGE (pp. 272–274)

Interviews with Lois Gibbs, op. cit.; Lois Gibbs, *Love Canal: My Story*, op. cit.; Jonathan Lash, Katherine Gillman, and David Sheridan, *A Season of Spoils: The Reagan Administration's Attack on the Environment* (New York: Pantheon Books, 1984). We used this book extensively throughout Part Eight as a source about specific members of the administration, as well as the general federal regulatory framework.

FIFTY-FIVE: THE PRIVATE SECTOR (pp. 275–278)

Interview with David Morine, 7/10/91; interview with Lynn Greenwalt, op. cit. David E. Morine, *Good Dirt: Confessions of a Conservationist* (Chester, Conn.: Globe Pequot Press, 1990). Dyan Zaslowsky and the Wilderness Society, *These American Lands* (New York: Henry Holt, 1986). Additional biographical information: "Hard Covers in Brief," *The Washington Post*, 12/16/90. Information about the Bureau of Outdoor Recreation came in part from: David R. Gergen, "Ah, Wilderness!" *U.S. News & World Report*, 8/31/87. Biographical material on Anne Gorsuch in part from: Joanne Omang, "Denver Lawyer Reagan's Choice to Head EPA," *The Washington Post*, 2/21/81. Additional sources: Bill Gilbert, "Inside Interior," *Sports Illustrated*, 9/26/83; *Environmental Law Review*, 1986 16 ELR 20096; Bil Gilbert, "The Nature Conservancy Game," *Sports Illustrated*, 10/20/86; Donald G. Schueler, *Preserving the Pascagoula*, (Jackson: University Press of Mississippi, 1980).

FIFTY-SIX: POLITICAL POISON (pp. 279–283)

Brown interview, op. cit.; Johnson interview, op. cit.; Van der Ryn interview, op. cit. Background info: K. M. Chrysler, "Bug Bites Farmers and Jerry Brown," *U.S. News & World Report*, 8/31/81; "Too Many Flies and Jerry Brown," *The Economist*,

7/18/81; William A. Henry III, "Jerry Brown's Political Fortunes Are Stung by the Pesky Medfly," *Time,* 9/14/81; Claudia Wallis, "Trying to Thwart the Fruit Fly," *Time,* 7/21/81; "Aerial Spraying of Malathion Backed by Attorney General," *San Jose Mercury News,* 3/12/81.

FIFTY-SEVEN: THE SLEAZE ALSO RISES (pp. 284–286)

Lois Gibbs interviews, op. cit; Lois Gibbs, *Love Canal: My Story,* op. cit.; Jonathan Lash et al., *Season of Spoils,* op. cit. Biographical information on Rita Lavelle came in part from: Al Kamen, "Testimony in Perjury Trial: Lavelle's GOP Campaign Help Detail," *The Washington Post,* 11/19/83; Al Kamen, "Executive Testifies He Warned Lavelle About Statement," *The Washington Post,* 11/22/83. Information about Sanderson and landfill: Howard Kurtz, Mary Thornton, and Cass Peterson, "Gorsuch Adviser's Client Dumped Solvents in '82 After She Lifted Ban," *The Washington Post,* 2/17/83; Mary Thornton and Howard Kurtz, "Justice Department Probe of EPA," *The Washington Post,* 8/12/83.

FIFTY-EIGHT: HIGHBALL EXPRESS (pp. 287–289)

Interviews with Shirley Goldsmith, Peggy Frankland, Willie Fontenot, and Mike Tritico, ops. cit. Report of the National Transportation Safety Board on the Livingston Train Derailment, issued 6/14/83. Other background: Reginald Stuart, "Spilled Chemicals Spread Farther," *The New York Times,* 9/3/82; Stuart, "Derailment Still Keeps 1,500 Away from Town," *The New York Times,* 10/11/82; Douglas B. Feaver, "Investigator Says Clerk Ran Train While Two in Crew Imbibed," *The Washington Post,* 11/15/82; Feaver, "Touchy Safety Issue for U.S. Railroads," *The Washington Post,* 11/22/81; Feaver, "Louisiana Crash Put Problem in Focus," *The Washington Post,* 3/2/83.

FIFTY-NINE: A RARE VICTORY (pp. 290–291)

Johnson interview, op. cit. California v. Block, op. cit.

SIXTY: MRS. CLEAN (pp. 292–294)

Interview with Shirley Goldsmith, 4/3/91; Gibbs interviews, op. cit.; Shepherd interviews, op. cit.; Fontenot interviews, op. cit.; Tritico interviews, op. cit.; Frankland interviews, op. cit. Testimony of Goldsmith before the congressional Wildlife and Fisheries Subcommittee, 12/7/83. Ann M. McMurray, "BFI, ICG Pass Dumping Buck," *Lake Charles American Press,* 10/23/82; Don Ellzey, "Jurors Urge Action Against Waste Haulers," *Lake Charles American Press,* 10/29/82; Fact sheet submitted by BFI/CECOS International to the Louisiana Department of Environmental Quality, including description of Willow Springs site and status of the company; "EPA Expert Speaks," *Lake Charles American Press,* 11/18/82; "ECC Finds No Hazard at BFI Site," *Lake Charles American Press,* 10/29/82; Ann Kidder, "Hazardous Waste 'Nightmare' Is Possible Locally," *Lake Charles American Press,* 1/25/83; "Parish Gets Grant to Oppose Permit: Report Indicates Waste Is Leaking from BFI Site," *The Southwest Builder News* (Sulphur, La.), 2/6/83; "Everybody Wants Willow Springs Closed," *Lake Charles American Press,* 3/20/83; Mark Ballard, "Groups March on Capital Urging Closing of BFI Site," *State Times* (Baton Rouge), 5/12/83; Ann Kidder, "BFI Ordered to Close," *Lake Charles American Press,* 5/13/83; Ann Kidder, "Court Will Allow More Waste at Willow Springs," *Lake Charles American Press,* 12/31/83; "Citizens Criticize Court for Decision on BFI," *The Southwest Builder News* (Sulphur, La.), 1/4/84.

SIXTY-ONE: THE BATTLE OF BALD MOUNTAIN (pp. 295–300)
Interview with Andy Kerr, 5/19/91; Roselle interview, op. cit.; interview with senior Forest Service soil scientist (the authors agreed not to identify him by name); Forest Service History Series FS-410, op. cit. Scarce, op. cit.; Davis, op. cit.

SIXTY-TWO: GOOD NIGHT, IRENE (pp. 301–305)
Michael Brown, *Laying Waste: The Poisoning of America,* op. cit.; Lois Gibbs interviews, op. cit.; Gibbs, *Love Canal: My Story,* op. cit.; *Citizen's Clearinghouse for Hazardous Waste: Five Years of Progress: 1981–1986* (Arlington, Va.: CCHW, 1986) is full of anecdotes, including story about protest at Lavelle's condo. Mikulski, "...a bake sale": RCRA Reauthorization Hearings, 3/31/82 and 4/21/82. Background on Hugh Kaufman and "...all landfills will leak": congressional hearings 5/15/82; Cass Peterson, "EPA Told to Ease Up on Whistleblower," *The Washington Post,* 12/13/82. See also: "EPA'S Chief Is Cited for Contempt by Panel," *The New York Times,* 12/3/82; Joanne Omang, "Justice Department Backs Gorsuch in Denying Docs to Congress," *The Washington Post,* 12/1/82. Times Beach buyout: Dale Russakoff, "US Offers to Buy Poisoned Homes of Times Beach," *The Washington Post,* 2/23/83; Philip Shabecoff, "House Charges Head of EPA with Contempt," *The New York Times,* 12/17/82.

SIXTY-THREE: A HECK OF A PROBLEM (pp. 306–307)
Interview with Herbert Rigmaiden, 9/20/91; Fontenot interviews, op. cit; Shepherd interviews, op. cit. Testimony of Herbert Rigmaiden, House Subcommittee on Environment, Energy, and Natural Resources, 6/22/83. "...pathology on the farm" further supported by: Gary Tyler, "Willow Springs Animal Deaths to Be Probed," *The Southwest Builder News,* 1/4/81.

SIXTY-FOUR: WILD BY LAW (pp. 308–310)
Roselle interview, op. cit.; Kerr interview, op. cit.; Earth First v. Block, 569 F. Supp. 415. Other background: Robb Fulcher, "Logging Road Confrontation Heats Up," UPI, 5/12/83; Fulcher, "Large Protest Planned for Logging Road Tuesday," UPI, 6/2/83; "More Logging Road Protests," UPI, 6/30/83.

SIXTY-FIVE: WATT'S WRONG (pp. 311–313)
Interview with James Watt, op. cit.; Jonathan Lash, *A Season of Spoils,* op. cit.; Tom Wolf, "The Rise and Fall of the Environmental Movement," *Los Angeles Times,* 3/24/91; *The National Journal,* 11/5/83. Especially helpful was: Bill Gilbert, "Inside Interior: An Abrupt Turn," op. cit. Information about national parks and coal leases in part from: Dyan Zaslowsky and the Wilderness Society, *These American Lands,* op. cit. Some of the material concerning Watt's attempts to scrap RARE II from: Bob Tippee, "Delay of Mineral Leases, Permits Hit," *Oil and Gas Journal,* 11/24/80; "Interior Appeals RARE II Land Handling Ruling," *Oil and Gas Journal,* 12/1/80.

PART NINE: MOTHER NATURE BATS LAST

SIXTY-SIX: THE FLOATING FURNACE (pp. 319–323)
Testimony before House Subcommittee on Fisheries and Wildlife Conservation, 12/7/83; Larry B. Stammer, "Toxic Waste—Are Seas the Answer?" *Los Angeles Times,* 6/20/85; Robert Reinhold, "States Oppose Burning of Toxic Waste in Gulf," *The New York Times,* 6/14/85; Ed Alderman, "EPA: Gulf Won't Be Used for Burns," *Lake Charles American Press,* 9/26/85.

SIXTY-SEVEN: THE SOUTER FILES (pp. 324–325)
Cushing interview, op. cit.; Deposition of Richard J. Campbell, Greater Newburyport Clamshell Alliance v. Public Service Company of New Hampshire, op. cit.

SIXTY-EIGHT: DEBT FOR NATURE (pp. 326–328)
Interviews with Randy Hayes, op. cit.; Thomas E. Lovejoy, "Aid Debtor Nation's Ecology," *The New York Times,* 10/4/84; Rachael Migler, "Tom Lovejoy and the Last Crusade," *Gentlemen's Quarterly,* October 1989; David Quammen, "Brazil's Jungle Blackboard," *Harper's,* March 1988. Further information from Catherine Caufield, *In the Rainforest* (Chicago: University of Chicago Press, 1984); Alan Patterson, "Debt-for-Nature Swaps and the Need for Alternatives," *Environment,* December 1990; Eugene Linden, "Playing with Fire," *Time,* 9/18/89; "The Month Amazonia Burns," *The Economist,* 9/9/89; Otto T. Solbrig, "The Origin and Function of Biodiversity," *Environment,* June 1991; "South American Countries Seek to Save Ravaged Amazon Forest," *Sacramento Bee,* 11/22/79; Spencer Reiss, et al., "Vanishing Forests," *Newsweek,* 11/24/80; Edward O. Wilson, "Threats to Biodiversity," *Scientific American,* September 1989. One of the authors spent three months in Brazil in 1985, and attended COICA conference in Iquitos, Peru, in May 1990.

SIXTY-NINE: THE SKY IS FALLING (pp. 329–330)
Joe Farman, *Nature,* May 1985; Sharon Roan, *The Ozone Crisis,* op. cit.; Robert H. Boyle, "Forecast for Disaster," op. cit.

SEVENTY: A WATERY GRAVE (pp. 331–333)
Brown and May, *The Greenpeace Story,* op. cit.; "A Slow Boat to Safety," *The Economist,* 6/1/85; Hal Quinn, "The Assault on Greenpeace," *Maclean's,* 7/22/85; "A Trail as French as Beaujolais," *The Economist,* 8/17/85; "Blowing Peace Out of the Water," *The Nation,* 8/31/85; Jared Mitchl, "A Storm over the Rainbow," *Maclean's* 8/26/85; David Newell, "Who Killed the Warrior?" *Newsweek,* 8/19/85.

SEVENTY-ONE: THE END OF THE ROAD (pp. 334–337)
Benstock interview, op. cit.; *Congressional Record,* 9/11/85. Opinions of Judge Thomas P. Griesa in Sierra Club, New York v. Army Corps of Engineers, 12 ELR 20533 (4/21/82) and 541 f. supp 1367 (6/30/82); Action for Rational Transit v. West Side Highway Project, 536 f. supp 1225; slip opinion; Sierra Club, New York v. Hennessey, U.S. Court of Appeals, 2d Circuit, 82-6175 (12/6/82). Schanberg firing: see Colman McCarthy, "The Journalistic Double Standard, the Squashing of Sydney Schanberg," *The Washington Post,* 10/8/85. Among Schanberg's numerous op-ed columns on Westway were: "Corruption Ignored," 6/12/84; "Westway's Sleaze Factor," 10/9/84; "Boondoggle by Local Choice," 3/5/85; "The Testimony Doesn't Wash," 7/6/85; "Cajun Flies and Westway," 7/27/85. See also Marcy Benstock, "Divide and Hide Is Westway's Lesson," *City Limits,* Dec. 1987; Sam Roberts, "Westway's Ghost Pays Off, Proving Skeptics Wrong," *The New York Times,* 11/26/90. Wicker's speech to the San Francisco SPJ chapter was heard by one of the authors, who was taking notes.

SEVENTY-TWO: BROWER'S BABY (pp. 338–341)
Brower interview, op. cit; Regional Oral History Project, op. cit; Brower, op. cit.; Turner, op. cit.
See also: Philip B. Shabecoff, "Environmental Group Is Deeply Divided over

Proposed Move," *The New York Times,* 1/3/86; Larry B. Stammer, "Environmentalists' Friends of the Earth Rocked as Founder Fights with Directors," *Los Angeles Times,* 3/2/86 and "Founder Quits Friends of the Earth, Says Situation 'Just Got Hopeless,'" *Los Angeles Times,* 10/11/86; "New Generation of Leaders," *Los Angeles Times,* 1/3/85; Seth Zuckerman, "A Movement Takes Stock," *The Nation,* 10/18/86.

SEVENTY-THREE: THE BANKERS' BURDEN (pp. 342–345)
Interviews with Randy Hayes, op. cit.; interviews with Mike Roselle, op. cit. Information on the World Bank and the IMF: "Efforts to Halt Global Warming by Protecting Tropical Forests," *Congressional Record,* 10/21/88; Andre Carothers, "Defenders of the Forest," *Greenpeace,* July/August 1990; Margo Freistadt, "The Money Trail," *San Francisco Chronicle,* 10/1/89; Thomas A. Sancton, "Hands Across the Sea," *Time* 1/2/89; interviews with Chad Dobson of the Bank Information Center, Raymond Offenheiser of the Ford Foundation, Vawter "Buck" Parker of the Sierra Club Legal Defense Fund in Iquitos, Peru, May 1990. Additional info: Catherine Caufield, "Paradise Lost," *San Francisco Chronicle,* 10/1/89; Catherine Caufield, *In the Rainforest,* op. cit.

SEVENTY-FOUR: BLOOD ON THE SPIKE (pp. 346–349)
Interview with George Alexander, 6/13/91. See also: "Booby-Trapped Tree Was Felled in Area Known for Bizarre Protests," *Los Angeles Times,* 5/16/87; "Environmental Terrorism at the Root of Tree-Spiking Injury," *San Francisco Examiner* 6/26/87; Larry B. Stammer, "Environment Radicals Target of Probe into Lumber Mill Accident," *Los Angeles Times,* 5/15/87; "Louisiana-Pacific Offers $20,000 in Hope of Catching 'Tree-Spiker' Responsible for Injury to Sawmill Worker," Business Wire, Inc., 5/14/87.

SEVENTY-FIVE: DAY OF THE DOLPHIN (pp. 350–352)
Special thanks to the comprehensive article by Kenneth Brower, "The Destruction of Dolphins," *The Atlantic,* July 1989. Interviews with Randy Hayes, op. cit.; Elizabeth Venant, "Making Waves," *Los Angeles Times,* 10/19/89; Todd Steiner, "Death in the Nets," *Earth Island Journal,* Spring 1987.
Info on Dexter Cate: "Japan to Deport Conservationist," *The Washington Post,* 6/5/80; "Japan Holds American," *The Washington Post,* 3/2/80 (and correction on 3/4/80); "Hawaiians Try to Stop Shelling of Sacred Island," *The New York Times,* 4/25/82.

SEVENTY-SIX: HATS AND SUNGLASSES (pp. 352–355)
Congressional Record, 136 Cong Rec S S12583. Information about the Montreal proceedings also came from dozens of newspaper accounts. Among the most helpful: Rochelle L. Stanfield, "Global Guardian," *The National Journal,* 12/12/87; Rochelle L. Stanfield, "Greenhouse Diplomacy," *The National Journal,* 3/4/89; Rorie Sherman, "Motivated by Disaster," *The National Law Journal,* 10/9/89; "Shake or Bake: Environmental Protection," *The New Republic,* 9/12/88; Philip Shabecoff, "Ozone Treaty Nears, but Obstacles Remain," *The New York Times,* 9/15/87; David Lauter, "U.S. Move May Stall Ozone-Layer Treaty," *Los Angeles Times,* 9/9/87; Michael Weisskopf, "EPA Would Make Ratification of Ozone Pact More Difficult," *The Washington Post,* 9/9/87. Testimony found in numerous Senate hearings by the Senate Foreign Relations Committee in 1989, and the Environmental Protection Subcommittee of the Senate Environment and Public Works Committee in 1989.

SEVENTY-SEVEN: WES JACKSON'S LUNCH (pp. 356–357)
Interviews with Wes Jackson, op. cit.

SEVENTY-EIGHT: THE SCAM OF THE CENTURY (pp. 358–360)
Interview with Steward Udall, op. cit.; interview with Phil Hocker, 8/28/91; letter from Interior Secretary Stewart Udall to the chairman and members, Public Land Law Review Commission, dated 1/15/69 (spells out Udall's early and strong objections to the mining law); interviews with Becky Garland, op. cit., Cecil Garland, op. cit.; Mark Gerlach, 8/20/91; Peter Nielsen and Bruce Farling of the Clark Fork Coalition (and its monthly publication, *Currents*); Joe Azure from the Fort Belknap Indian Reservation, 8/20/91; Jim Jensen, Environmental Information Center, Helena, Montana. "Mining Laws of 1872 and 1989," op. cit.; GAO report, "Federal Land Management: The Mining Law of 1872 Needs Revision," March 1989, GAO/RCED-89-72; videos from the Mineral Policy Center library; Mineral Policy Center's informative quarterly publication, *Clementine;* Tom Knudsen, "Golden Land, Shattered Earth," an excellent ten-page special report in the *Sacramento Bee*, 3/21/90; Sherry Devlin, "Superfund Spot-Check," *The Missoulian*, 3/18/90; John Lancaster, "Frontier Legacy: Mining Public Lands," *The Washington Post*, 8/7/90; Elissa Wolfson, "Mine Shaft," *E*, May/June 1990; George Laycock, "Going for the Gold," *Audubon*, July 1989; Dina ElBoghdady, "Clark Fork Basin Illustrates the Environmental Dangers of Mining," States News Service, 7/12/92; Michael Satchell, "The New Gold Rush," *U.S. News & World Report*, 10/28/91; Margaret L. Knox, "Prospecting for Prosperity in Montana," *Chicago Tribune*, 10/14/91; Eric Williams, "Mikulski Hit by 'Complexity' of Butte Cleanups," *The Montana Standard*, 8/10/90; Robin and Phil Tawney, "Building a Citizen's Organization to Last," *The NRAG Papers*, Winter 1977–78; Peter Nielsen, "Jurisdiction," *Northern Lights*, January 1989; Bruce Farling, "At the Water of Surprise," *Northern Lights*, January 1989; "Clark Fork Superfund Sites Master Plan," U.S. Environmental Protection Agency, November 1990.

SEVENTY-NINE: HEAT WAVE (pp. 361–365)
Stephen H. Schneider, *Global Warming* (San Francisco: Sierra Club Books, 1989). Schneider, a climatologist with the National Center for Atmospheric Research, began thinking about global warming before most of his peers. He participated in two early studies: The U.S. Department of Energy "Workshop on the Global Effects of Carbon Dioxide from Fossil Fuels," Miami Beach, March 7–11, 1977 and U.S. Department of Energy "Workshop on Environmental and Societal Consequences of a Possible CO_2-Induced Climate Change," conducted in Annapolis, Maryland, April 2–6, 1979. Both of these studies provided us with detailed background of the evolution of modern scientific thinking about global warming. See also: Bill McKibben, *The End of Nature* (New York: Random House, 1989); The National Research Council, Studies in Geophysics, "Energy and Climate," 1977; Stephen Seidel and Dale Keyes, "Can We Delay a Greenhouse Warming?" Office of Policy, Planning and Evaluation, Washington, D.C., November, 1983; hearing before the Senate Committee on Energy and Natural Resources, "Greenhouse Effect and Global Climate Change," 6/23/88; hearing before the Senate Subcommittee on Science, Technology, and Space of the Committee on Commerce, Science, and Transportation, "Climate Surprises," 5/8/89. Other background: "Changing the Climate," *The Economist*, 6/4/77; "The Weather; Against Nature," *The Economist*, 7/30/77; Thomas O'Toole, "Climate Experts See a Warming Trend,"

The Washington Post, 2/18/78; "The Human Factor in Modifying the Weather," *Business Week,* 2/27/78. OMB forces Hansen to alter testimony: Tim Wirth addressing the Senate, *Congressional Record,* 135 Cong Rec S 13889, 10/24/89. Arthur Ravenel, Jr., "White House Effect," *Congressional Record,* 2/21/90; *Congressional Record* S 14458, 10/31/89; *Congressional Record,* 11/16/89. Jeremy Rifkin, "Fatal Elements," *The Washington Post,* 6/24/88; Philip Shabecoff, "Global Warming Has Begun, Expert Tells Senate," *The New York Times,* 6/24/88; *Congressional Record,* Senate, 3/22/88.

PART TEN: SHOWTIME

EIGHTY: SNUFF FILMS (pp. 370–371)
Kenneth Brower, "The Destruction of the Dolphins," op. cit.; Elizabeth Venant, "Making Waves," op. cit.

EIGHTY-ONE: OF MICE AND MEN (pp. 372–373)
"Products of the Year," *Fortune,* 12/5/88; "What Price Mighty Mouse: Genetic Engineering," *The New Republic,* 5/23/88; "The Genetic Alternative," *The Economist,* 4/30/88; Shawna Vogel, "Patented Animals," *Technology Review,* October 1988; Elizabeth Corcoran, "Patent Medicine; New Patents Challenge Congress and Courts," *Scientific American,* September 1988.

EIGHTY-TWO: THE COLOR RED (pp. 374–375)
Philip Shabecoff, "Senate Panel Urged to Toughen Curbs on Killing of Dolphins," *The New York Times,* 4/14/88; Michael Weisskopf, "Tuna-Fishing Casualties: Dolphins; Thousands Killed, Senators Told," *The Washington Post,* 4/14/88; Scott Armstrong, "Drive to Stop Killing by Tuna Fleets Is Given New Impetus," *The Christian Science Monitor,* 4/14/88.

EIGHTY-THREE: ON THE ROCKS (pp. 376–381)
The chronology of the Valdez oil spill has been documented in great detail in hundreds of official studies and news reports. Among our major sources: Timothy Egan, "Exxon Concedes It Can't Contain Most of Oil Spill," *The New York Times,* 3/30/89; Richard Witkin, Andrew H. Malcolm, and Roberto Suro, "How the Oil Spilled and Spread," *The New York Times,* 4/16/89; William C. Rempel, "Warnings Unheeded," *Los Angeles Times,* 4/2/89; "Spill Concerns Delay Alaska Sale EIS Preparation," *Oil and Gas Journal,* 5/22/89; Bill Dietrich, "A Frontier Spoiled," *Seattle Times,* 3/18/90; William P. Coughlin, "Debate Still Rages over Double Hulls," *The Boston Globe,* 5/21/90; Harry Hurt III, Lynda Wright, and Pamela Abramson, "Alaska After Exxon," *Newsweek,* 9/18/89; Richard Behar, "Joe's Bad Trip," *Time,* 6/24/89.

EIGHTY-FOUR: THE $6 BILLION MISTAKE (pp. 382–384)
Wasserman interview, op. cit.; Cushing interview, op. cit; interview with Robert A. Backus, 7/14/91. New Hampshire Supreme Court decisions and documents: Appeal of Conservation Law Foundation, No. 85-252, 9/18/85; Appeal of Campaign for Ratepayers Rights, No. 89-336, 8/1/90.

EIGHTY-FIVE: THE EMPIRE STRIKES BACK (pp. 385–390
Our best single source of information on Dave Foreman's arrest and trial was the excellent series of articles written by Michael Lacey in the Phoenix *New Times* between May and August 1991, including "Sabotaging the Saboteurs," (5/29/91);

"Spies and Savages," 6/5/91; "What the Evidence Will Show," 6/26/91; "When a Snitch Takes the Stand," 7/10/91; "For Love and Glory," 7/17/91; and "Inside the Deal," 8/21/91. Other major sources include: Susan Reed, "Eco-Warrior Dave Foreman Will Do Whatever It Takes in His Fight to Save Mother Earth," *People,* 4/16/90; Michael A. Lerner, "The FBI vs. The Monkeywrenchers," *Los Angeles Times,* 4/15/90; Sam Negri, "Earth First Founder Targeted," *Arizona Republic,* 4/25/90; David Quammen, "Reckoning," *Outside,* Nov. 1990; Karen Pickett, "FBI Targets Earth First," *Anderson Valley Advertiser,* 7/3/91.

EIGHTY-SIX: THE COLOR OF MONEY (pp. 391–393)

Interview with Joel Makower, 6/30/92; interview with Art Kleiner, 6/28/92. Garbage barge: Victoria Irwin, "Parking the Garbage Barge," *The Christian Science Monitor,* 5/20/87. Gibbs and McDonald's: John Holusha, "Packaging and Public Image: McDonald's Fills a Big Order," *The New York Times,* 11/2/90. Info about garbologists: Melinda Beck et al., "Buried Alive," *Newsweek,* 11/27/89. Allen Gray quote: John Holusha, "Mobil Ends Environmental Claim," *The New York Times,* 3/3/90. *Garbage* magazine was generally very helpful for this chapter, especially: Kleiner, "Despite Corporate Homilies, Real Change," July/August, 1992; Kleiner, "Who Owns Exxon? We Do," May/June 1991. Additional information: Jon R. Luoma, "Trash Can Realities," *Audubon,* March 1990; Leslie Pardue, "Biodegradable Plastics: A Contradiction in Terms?" *E,* January/February 1990; Dick Russell and Owen deLong, "Can Business Save the Environment?" *E,* November/December 1991; Dick Russel, "The Rise of the Grass-Roots Toxics Movement," *The Amicus Journal,* Winter 1990; Tim Redmond, "Wall Street's Environment Scam," *The San Francisco Bay Guardian,* 3/14/90; Christy Fisher and Judith Graham, "Wal-Mart Throws 'Green' Gauntlet," *Advertising Age,* 8/21/89.

See also: Rosalyn Will et al., *Shopping for a Better World,* (New York: Council on Economic Priorities, 1989); Jeremy Rifkin, *The Green Lifestyle Handbook* (New York: Henry Holt, 1990); The EarthWorks Group, *50 Simple Things You Can Do to Save the Earth* (Berkeley, Calif.: EarthWorks Press, 1989); Joel Elkington, Julia Hailes, and Joel Makower, *The Green Consumer* (Great Britain: Victor Gollancz Ltd., 1988).

EIGHTY-SEVEN: SHOWDOWN AT PINEY CORRAL (pp. 394–397)

Interviews with Don Oman, op. cit. Whistleblower Complaint of Don Oman to the Office of the Inspector General, U.S. Forest Service, 1/16/90, and Inspector General's follow-up reports, 3/10/90 and 4/2/90 (PS-899-0021), obtained by the authors under the Freedom of Information Act. See also: Timothy Egan, "Trouble on the Range as Cattlemen Try to Throw Off Forest Boss's Reins," *The New York Times,* 8/19/90; Bill Shaw, "The Lone Ranger Rides Again," *People,* 11/19/90.

EIGHTY-EIGHT: DIRTY JOB (pp. 398–399)

Alexander interview, op. cit.

EIGHTY-NINE: NOT GUILTY (pp. 400–402)

Jay Mathews, "Hazelwood Cleared on Most Counts," *The Washington Post,* 3/22/90; Peter Marks, "Guilty of One Count," *Newsday,* 3/23/90; "Verdict on Exxon Skipper—Not Guilty on 3 Major Charges," *Los Angeles Times,* 3/22/90.

NINETY: BUILDING BRIDGES (pp. 403–408)

Roselle interview, op. cit. Manes, op. cit; Scarce, op. cit. John Balzar, "Northwest Is at War with Itself," *Los Angeles Times,* 8/6/90; Eliot Diringer, "Environmental Group Says It Won't Spike Trees," *San Francisco Chronicle,* 4/11/90; Kevin Ervin,

"The California Forest Fight: Loggers and Activists Look for Middle Ground," *Seattle Times,* 8/27/90; Sam Whiting, "A Crippling Commitment," *San Francisco Chronicle,* 2/25/91.

NINETY-ONE: "DEAR MR. O'REILLY . . ." (pp. 409–411)
Interview with Joel Rubin and Joel Rubin's mother, April 1992. Curriculum vitae of Anthony J. F. O'Reilly as supplied by H. J. Heinz Company's world headquarters in Pittsburgh, Pa. "Maine," *USA Today,* 4/20/90; Trish Hall, "How Youths Rallied to Dolphins' Cause," *The New York Times,* 4/18/90; K. Patrick Conner, "The Conversion of Starkist," *San Francisco Chronicle,* 6/17/90; Elizabeth Venant, "Making Waves," op. cit.; Donnie Radcliffe, "Patti Davis and the Dolphin Victory," *The Washington Post,* 4/17/90; Anthony Ramirez, " 'Epic Debate' Led to Heinz Tuna Plan," *The New York Times,* 4/16/90.

NINETY-TWO: TWENTY YEARS AND COUNTING (pp. 412–416)
Dianne Dumanoski, "Earth Day 1990," *The Boston Globe,* 4/23/90; Ari L. Goldman, "Earth Day 1990," *The New York Times,* 4/23/90; Stevenson Swanson and Casey Bukro, "Earth Day Festivities Remind Millions of Planet's Fragility," *Chicago Tribune,* 4/23/90; James Gerstenzang, "Bush Likely to Allow Drilling Off California," *Los Angeles Times,* 4/23/90; Bottoms interview, op. cit.; *Earth Day: The Beginning,* op. cit.

PART ELEVEN: GIANTS AND THE EARTH

NINETY-THREE: THE LONE RANGER (pp. 421–424)
Whistleblower complaint of Don Oman, and inspector general's reports, op. cit.; Egan, "Trouble on the Range," loc. cit.; Shaw, "The Lone Ranger Rides," loc. cit.; Fred Wortham, Jr., " 'Gestapo' Cattle Count in Idaho," *Western Livestock Journal,* 10/30/84; Ralph Maughan, "Twin Falls Livestock Operators Angry over Changes in Grazing," *Farm Lines,* Nov. 1989.

NINETY-FOUR: THE HUMAN FACTOR (pp. 425–427)
Lacey, ops. cit., especially "For Love and Glory" and "Inside the Deal."

NINETY-FIVE: UNCLE SAP (pp. 428–430)
Udall interview, op. cit.; Hocker interview, op. cit.; Bumpers background from Barone and Ujifusa, *Almanac of American Politics,* 1988, op. cit.; *Congressional Record,* 9/13/91.

NINETY-SIX: ENVIRONMENTAL JUSTICE (pp. 431–437)
Proceedings of the First National People of Color Leadership Summit on the Environment, published by the Commission for Racial Justice of the United Church of Christ (10/24–27/91).
Warren County: See Dale Russakoff, "As in the '60s, Protesters Rally, but This Time Foe Is PCB," *The Washington Post,* 10/11/82; Leon Daniel, "Carolinians Angry over PCB Landfill," *The New York Times,* 8/11/82; United States v. Robert Earl Ward, Jr., 676 F. 2d 94 (2/19/82); 14 ELR 20804 (5/14/84).
See also: Jane Kay, "Minorities: We Won't Be Dumped On," *San Francisco Examiner,* 10/31/91; Bob Dart, "Minorities See Environmental Racism," *Atlanta Journal-Constitution,* 10/27/91; Keith Schneider, "Minorities Join to Fight Polluting Neighborhoods," *The New York Times,* 10/24/91; "Session Set on Racism, Environment," *Atlanta Journal-Constitution,* 10/21/91; Nancy E. Roman, "Envi-

ronmental Racism Rankles," *The Washington Times,* 6/15/92. "NAACP Issued a Policy Paper": Edward Flattau, "Our Environment," Gannett News Service, 11/1/91.

NINETY-SEVEN: THE EYES OF THE WORLD (pp. 438–443)
Hayes interview, op. cit. See also: Alexander Cockburn and Susanna Hecht, "Earth Summit: Rhetoric and Reality in Rio," *The Nation,* 6/22/92; Praful Bidwai, "North vs. South on Pollution," *The Nation,* 6/22/92; Sharon Begley, "And Now, the Road from Rio," *Newsweek,* 6/22/92; Greg Easterbrook, "Why Rio Will Make History," *Newsweek,* 6/15/92; Charles P. Alexander, "On the Defensive," *Time,* 6/15/92; "Earth Conference: Biodivisive," *The Economist,* 6/13/92; Jon Christensen, Jeremy Narby, and Glen Switkes, "Out of Line at the Earth Summit," *Processed World* 30 (Winter/Spring 1992/93).

NINETY-EIGHT: THE PRICE OF JOBS (pp. 444–449)
Interview with Nathalie Walker, March 1993; interview with Wilfred Greene, 3/10/93; interview with Audrey Evans, 3/12/93; Fontenot interviews, op. cit.; interview with Diane Wilson, 3/10/93. Videotape sent to authors by Nathalie Walker at the Sierra Club Legal Defense Fund. See also: Marcia Coyle, "Saying 'No' to Cancer Alley," *The National Law Journal,* 9/21/92; Coyle, "Company Will Not Build Plant; Lawyers Hail Victory," *The National Law Journal,* 10/19/92; "Environmental Policy Tainted by Racism," *The National Law Journal,* 12/28/92; "No Plant, No Jobs, but a Louisiana Victory," *Atlanta Journal-Constitution,* 11/1/92; Christina Cheakalos, "La. Town Defeats Industrial Giant, Rejects Factory," *Atlanta Journal and Constitution,* 10/20/92.

NINETY-NINE: THE OZONE MAN (pp. 450–456)
Albert Gore, Jr., *Earth in the Balance: Ecology and the Human Spirit* (New York: Houghton Mifflin, 1992). Major background sources include: John Eisendrath, "The Longest Shot," *Washington Monthly,* November 1984; Steven A. Holmes, "A Focused Leader on an Uneven Climb," *The New York Times,* 11/4/92; Harold Gilliam, "Will Clinton Put the Earth First," *San Francisco Chronicle,* 1/31/93; Sara Fritz, "Some See Expediency, not Principle as Gore's Guide," *Los Angeles Times,* 7/15/92; "Is Gore's Record Really So Green," *Business Week,* 8/24/92; Philip Shabecoff, "The Green Giant," *The New Republic,* 10/19/92.

EPILOGUE (pp. 457–458)
One of the authors attended Huey Johnson's birthday party and somehow remained sober enough to retain a clear memory of the events.

The quotation on the dedication page is from Tennyson.

INDEX